Praise for Maggie Doherty's

The Equivalents

"*The Equivalents* is written with panache. [Maggie Doherty] adroitly weaves vivid, empathetic portraits of these talented women, focusing on their artistic accomplishments, their impact on the women's movement and its impact on them."

—*The Wall Street Journal*

"This deft history charts the relationships among five of the earliest fellows.... Doherty relates their often fraught intimacies in detail, emphasizing how these dynamics prefigured currents in American feminism and culture. The women's shared story shows both the potential and the limitations of a 'room of one's own' as a liberating force."

—*The New Yorker*

"Brilliant.... Doherty's rigorous history is an empowering reminder that to change ourselves, we must have systemic support outside ourselves—institutional structures that reinforce the belief that all people are created equal, not just equivalent."

—*Los Angeles Times*

"[*The Equivalents*] prompts us to consider the systems of marginalization that continue to reproduce the psychic division that agonized these women.... It is the story of what these women needed from and gave to one another."

—*The Nation*

"*The Equivalents* is an important, illuminating work. Fortunately, it is also a splendidly written page-turner to read for joy."

—*Minneapolis Star Tribune*

"Elegantly composed.... *The Equivalents* also serves as something of a prehistory of second-wave feminism." —*The Boston Globe*

"Opposites attract in Doherty's exuberant account of women artists in the 1960s and '70s that especially probes the fierce connection between poets Anne Sexton and Maxine Kumin, a 'dance of sameness and separateness... something like a song.'"
—*O, The Oprah Magazine*

"*Mona Lisa Smile* meets *Mrs. America*. [*The Equivalents*] tells of the founding students in Radcliffe's Independent Study program, which helped women to receive an education *and* raise a family."
—*Entertainment Weekly*

"[Maggie Doherty] presents the institute as a crucial bridge between first- and second-wave feminism—between, roughly, Virginia Woolf and Betty Friedan. Through examining the five 'Equivalents,' she illustrates the institute's role in midcentury feminism and explores the ways in which both fell short.... A vivid, captivating, and excellently argued work." —*Hyperallergic*

"Rich with insight into the challenges faced by midcentury women as they struggled to pursue their work.... Doherty sheds light on an important story, one that takes place at the fraught intersection of gender, race and class." —WBUR, "The ARTery"

"[An] exciting debut.... A rich tapestry brought to life by Doherty's access to [her subjects'] personal notes, recordings, letters and works, weaving her own strong voice in with the individual women to tell stories of art, radical politics, relationships, and unfettered ambition. Though her eye is on the past, it's most certainly a story to inspire our futures." —*Dazed*

"This phenomenal book captures the tensions, ambitions, activism, friendship and yearning for community found in this incredible place and time." —Observer

"[The Equivalents], and the hundreds of women who followed them over the decades, have in Maggie Doherty a dedicated biographer. *The Equivalents* is a story long overdue. In this age of #MeToo and a president who brags about groping women, it's important to look at the moment when modern, talented women saw in Radcliffe an open door, and walked right in." —*Air Mail*

"A story of neither collective liberation nor midcentury repression.... Doherty is a confident, perceptive critic, and her biographical sketches are expertly interwoven with well-deployed... readings of the poems themselves." —*Bookforum*

"An exciting, engaging, and important book. With great psychological acumen, Maggie Doherty brings these women vividly to life. Being creative while female has never been easy and our best hope for resolution is this variety of historical excavation, one that shows us how people have tried to resolve it before, so we may learn and keep pushing forward, newly enlightened." —Kate Bolick, author of *Spinster*

"Maggie Doherty's revelatory history of female artists and their influential friendships stands as triumphant testament to the powerhouse first known as the Radcliffe Institute for Advanced Study. *The Equivalents* reminds us that generative 'women's work' can literally light up the darkness that discourages women's voices—just when we need them the most." —Jayne Anne Phillips, Bunting Institute Fellow, 1980–81, author of *Black Tickets* and *Lark and Termite*

"An elegant, novelistic history.... Doherty's prose dazzles, and she skillfully integrates her copious research into the narrative while toggling between biographical, creative, and political matters." —*Publishers Weekly* (starred review)

"[A] galvanizing look at a little-explored conjunction of critical feminist voices." —*Library Journal*

"In her thrilling book, Maggie Doherty brings to vivid life the history long hidden of a glorious American experiment that gathered creative women for a year of community in the shelter of a great university. The emotional power *The Equivalents* lies in its revelation of the incremental impact of community on each of these formerly isolated women, prophetic of what would happen two years later with the publication of *The Feminine Mystique* and the arrival of second wave feminism."

—Honor Moore, author of *Our Revolution*

"Doherty's vibrant curiosity and many-faceted expertise infuse this dynamic group biography with light and warmth."

—*Booklist* (starred review)

"Superb.... A welcome spotlight on an overdue 'experiment.'"

—*Kirkus Reviews*

Maggie Doherty

The Equivalents

Maggie Doherty teaches first-year writing at Harvard, where she earned her PhD in English. Her writing has appeared in many publications, including *The New Republic*, *The New York Times*, *n+1*, and *The Nation*. She lives in Cambridge, Massachusetts.

The Equivalents

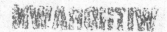

The Equivalents

A Story of Art, Female Friendship,

and Liberation in the 1960s

Maggie Doherty

VINTAGE BOOKS

A Division of Penguin Random House LLC

New York

The Library of Congress has cataloged the Knopf edition as follows:
Name: Doherty, Maggie, author.
Title: The equivalents : a story of art, female friendship, and liberation in the 1960s / Maggie Doherty.
Other titles: Art, female friendship, and liberation in the 1960s
Description: First edition. | New York: Alfred A. Knopf, 2020. | Includes bibliographical references and index.
Identifiers: LCCN 2019036686
Subjects: LCSH: Women intellectuals—United States. | Women poets—United States. | Women artists—United States. | Women authors—United States. | Self-actualization (Psychology) in women. | Female friendship—United States—History—20th century. | Feminism—United States—History—20th century. | Radcliffe Institute for Independent Study.
Classification: LCC HQ1206 .D58 2020 | DDC 700.92/52 B—dc23
LC record available at https://lccn.loc.gov/2019036686

Vintage Books Trade Paperback ISBN: 978-0-525-43460-3
eBook ISBN: 978-1-5247-3306-3

Author photograph © Max Larkin
Book design by Maggie Hinders

www.vintagebooks.com

Printed in the United States of America

For my parents

Contents

Introduction

The poet Anne Sexton spent the summer of 1962 swimming. Months away from publishing her second book and poised on the edge of fame, she soothed her nerves with water. When the weather was warm enough for a dip, she would step out of her house, strip nude, and slide into the pool in her backyard. She delighted in the warmth of the sun, the smooth feel of the water, the quiet of the morning. She could see an old train track from her backyard, while just out of sight, beyond the old, rolling hills of a golf course, the Charles River flowed through Newton Lower Falls, wending its way to the harbor in Boston.

Sexton's young daughters, Joy and Linda, didn't like when their mom skinny-dipped. But the kids were often absent that summer, off with a babysitter or with Sexton's mother-in-law, who frequently helped with child care. Sexton needed the time to work: though she'd only started writing poetry seriously five and a half years earlier, on a whim, her first collection had been a critical success. Fellow poets respected her; some of them expected great things. Sexton was a natural performer: an elegant woman with long legs and slim hips,

Anne Sexton in her swimming pool in the 1960s

she captivated audiences at her readings. But she was also a labile, anxious woman, and she frequently needed time off from mothering simply to relax. On these summer mornings, she would swim calmly from one end of her pool to the other, traversing its twenty-five-foot length.

Poetry usually followed her ritual sun worship. She would experiment with new poems, tinker with old ones, write a letter or two. One of her major projects that summer was reviewing the galleys for her next collection of poetry. The book, her second, was to be published by Houghton Mifflin in October; the esteemed poet Robert Lowell, her friend and former teacher, had already agreed to let her quote some of his words of praise. If she were so inclined, she could drive into Cambridge's Harvard Square and review the galleys in a gabled house where she and twenty-three other women created, studied, and worked, each with her own small office. But most days, Sexton found it more comfortable to work at home—especially now that she could, to her husband's relief, work somewhere other than the dining room table.

Her home study had been built the previous summer. She described it to a friend as a "wooden tower" standing where the porch had once been. It had one long window that faced the backyard. Looking out, Sexton could see the pine trees and the blue hills from her desk, but when she was writing, she faced away from the window—"nature . . . becomes my enemy," she explained. While working, she sat either in her straight desk chair or, more often, in a soft red chair with her feet perched on one of her many bookcases. She could spend hours sitting in this position, drawing inspiration from the great writers on the shelves, many of whom she'd encountered only recently—Kafka, Rilke, Dostoevsky—and many of whom she'd come to love. "I hoard books," she once confessed to a friend. "They are people who do not leave."

There was another advantage to working from home. Sexton lived just a few minutes' drive from her best friend, the poet Maxine Kumin. Tall, lean, and dark-haired, Kumin could seem at first to be Sexton's twin, until one noticed her athletic build, her slightly hooded eyes, the sharp angles of her face. She, too, was a suburban mother and the author of a published book of poetry. She was also Sexton's main source of emotional and creative support.

In the early 1960s, the poets' lives were enmeshed: they spoke on the phone every day, sometimes about writing, sometimes simply about their lives. They watched each other's children. They served cocktails to each other's husbands. After Sexton installed her pool, the friends developed a happy routine that blended work and play. Kumin brought her children over to swim, and she and Sexton sat by the edge of the pool with typewriters in their laps, their legs dangling in the water, and worked together on a children's book, a nice break from their adult compositions. Though Sexton often feared social gatherings, Kumin's dependable, comfortable company was almost always welcome.

But in the mornings Kumin was usually still at her own home, caring for her own children. Sexton was left to appreciate her solitude.

On these summer mornings, no one needed her—not her husband, not her children, not her mother-in-law, not even her friend. The day was beautifully, blissfully hers.

Everything about these summer days—the pool, the study, the solitude, the second book, the second place to write, even the companionship of Kumin—was the product of a novel experiment in women's higher education. In the fall of 1960, the prestigious women's college Radcliffe, the sister school of Harvard, had announced an unprecedented fellowship program, one that targeted a ubiquitous and yet marginalized class of Americans: mothers. In the words of its founder, the Radcliffe president and microbiologist Mary Ingraham Bunting, the Radcliffe Institute for Independent Study was designed to combat the "climate of unexpectation" facing women in mid-century America. As she saw it, too many accomplished female undergraduates were giving up their dreams of becoming scholars or artists because they couldn't see how they could do research or write a book while also managing a family and keeping house. The new program proposed to get these "intellectually displaced women" back on track.

Each woman admitted to the Institute as an "associate scholar" received a stipend of up to $3,000 (nearly $25,000 today) to spend as she pleased. She also received access to Harvard's library resources and a private office—the proverbial "room of her own"—in a little yellow house at 78 Mount Auburn Street, just a few blocks from Harvard Yard. A mother of four children, Bunting believed that most women wanted to find a way to combine professional interests and family life: her own happiest years had been those she spent raising her children on a small farm in Connecticut while commuting twice a week to do research in a lab at Yale. As a university administrator and education reformer, Bunting recognized the role that institutions played in supporting women's professional ambitions. She realized that you couldn't simply tell women to work hard and keep studying if the world didn't give them the tools and resources to do so.

The Institute's founding had been announced on November 19, 1960. A *New York Times* article broadcast the news to the nation: "Radcliffe Pioneers in Plan for Gifted Women's Study." Almost immediately, the phone in Bunting's office rang nonstop. Within ten days, Bunting's secretary had been inundated with over 160 letters of congratulation and inquiry. Once the application process was formalized, the Institute received nearly two hundred applications from women all across the country; other women interested in applying had been turned away because they didn't have the requisite qualifications. And in September 1961, the Institute offered an inaugural group of twenty-four remarkable women—including Sexton and Kumin—the resources they needed to succeed: fellowship money, office space, and, most important, membership in a professional and creative female community, the likes of which had never been seen before in the country's history.

Imagine being a "gifted woman," like the women accepted to the Institute, at the dawn of the 1960s. Perhaps you had graduated from one of the "Seven Sisters" colleges, maybe taken what people called a "little job" in New York after school. Maybe you even worked for the Allied war effort while your husband served overseas. Not long after the bombs fell on Japan, though, your job prospects dried up. The GIs returned Stateside, and they wanted their jobs back, or they wanted spots in graduate school so they could get even better jobs. As the Soviets built their missiles and nuclear destruction loomed, you were told that the best way you could serve your country was to build a happy home.

Now, by all accounts, you have the perfect life: you have the high-earning husband, the rosy-cheeked children, and the Buick in the driveway. But something isn't right. Household tasks don't seem to hold your attention; you snarl at your children instead of blanketing them with smiles. You fret about how little you resemble those glossy women in the magazines, the ones who clean counters and bake cakes and radiate delight. (Looking at those ads, a housewife and freelance writer named Betty Friedan "thought there was something wrong with me because I didn't have an orgasm waxing the kitchen floor.") Everything and everyone confirm that it's just as you suspected: the problem is you. You're oversexed, you're undersexed, you're overeducated, you're unintelligent. You need to have your head shrunk; you need to take more sleeping pills. You ought to become a better cook—all those fancy new kitchen appliances!—and in the meantime be content and grateful with what you have. The cultural pressure of the 1950s was so intense that some women, in order to survive, killed off the parts of themselves that couldn't conform.

Women like Sexton and Kumin didn't want to amputate their passions. Neither did the writer Tillie Olsen, a communist organizer from San Francisco who planned to write the great proletarian novel; nor the painter Barbara Swan, a portraitist who grew up in Newton and studied at Boston's finest art school; nor the sculptor Marianna Pineda, who was born in Evanston, Illinois, and apprenticed at various ateliers in the United States and Europe before settling down in Brookline, Massachusetts. Each of these five women won admission to the Institute during its first or second year. They gathered in Cambridge, where they met historians and psychologists, composers and scientists, poets and painters—all of whom were women.

Many Institute fellows hadn't experienced such female community since their days at Vassar or Sarah Lawrence. Others—including Sexton, who never earned a college degree—were experiencing this kind of camaraderie for the first time. At the Institute, a woman could forget about her housework and her children and simply be a mind among other minds—at least until the dinner hour. The founder of the Institute often called it a laboratory. It was also an incubator where new growth could take place.

The results of what Bunting called her "messy experiment" were not what she, or anyone, anticipated. For the women it supported, the Institute was nothing short of life changing (one called it her "salvation"). It offered each of the writers and artists discussed in this book a crucial mix of solitude and community, ideal conditions for artistic growth. For the first time, these women found themselves in a community of the like-minded. They conversed about everything from their best publishers to their worst marital spats.

They read each other's work and collaborated on different projects. Many a woman discovered that problems she had once felt were hers alone—an absent husband, an excess of housework, a condescending male colleague—were in fact common, even structural. In other words, there was nothing wrong with her, but there might be something wrong with the world.

The Institute became a site for the development of influential feminist art and thought. The writers and artists there encouraged each other to represent female experience in all its difficulty and complexity. They broke taboos about what was a fit subject for lyric poetry; they etched their experience of womanhood into stone. Along with the other associate scholars, they discussed the feminist polemics of the day. (Friedan's *The Feminine Mystique*, a book that Bunting had helped Friedan develop, was published during the Institute's second academic year.) They also advanced some of the first critiques of the ideology behind the nascent women's movement. Was motherhood always a form of oppression? Did all women, regardless of race or class, suffer in the same way? Can a woman ever *really* have it all? At the Institute, with each other, they began to tease out some possible answers to these important questions.

Together, the women of the Institute learned to take themselves seriously; when they left Radcliffe, they insisted that the world do the same. The feminist activist and civil rights organizer Carol Hanisch coined the second-wave slogan "the personal is political" in 1969. Far earlier in the decade, the women of the Institute discovered this truth for themselves.

This book is about a small group of women writers and artists who operated as a hinge between the 1950s and the 1960s, between a decade of women's confinement and a decade of women's liberation. It tells the story of their careers, their friendships, and their art as a way of describing how and why the feminist movement reemerged in 1960s America. But this book is also about their particularities, their inner lives, their conflicts. It attends to the rich, idiosyncratic, loving, competitive relationships that form between women—the kinds of relationships that so often go unexamined and unrecognized.

During their two years at the Institute, from the fall of 1961 through the spring of 1963, Sexton and Kumin met a number of "intellectually displaced" women who thrilled at this chance to jump-start their studies. They befriended historians, learned from psychologists, and listened to educational researchers. They became especially close with three other artists who attended the Institute during its first two years: Olsen, the writer; Swan, the painter; and Pineda, the sculptor. These five women formed a close, collaborative clique. Joking about the Institute's application standards, which required that applicants have either a doctorate or "the equivalent" in creative achievement, they called their friend group "the Equivalents."

The women in this group were unalike in many ways. Vibrant, moody Sexton was a WASP from money who wrote openly about her experiences of mental illness and motherhood while also worrying that her subject matter would prevent her from achieving success. Kumin wrote neat, formal poems about the natural world. A Jewish woman from Philadelphia who never felt that she fit in, Kumin dreamed of escaping the Boston suburbs for the New Hampshire countryside, though she feared that abandoning Sexton would be disastrous. Olsen was charismatic, passionate, an activist who, in the 1930s, had published inventive reportage and fiction. At the Institute, Olsen, at age fifty, hoped to write her long-awaited great proletarian novel, which would underscore the importance of all human lives. Swan, a painter from the Boston suburbs, had studied at the School of the Museum of Fine Arts and received a traveling fellowship to paint in Europe. She painted and sketched portraits, including her own, that exposed the sitter's soul. Pineda, a sculptor since her teenage years, had grown up in privilege and had made a living as a working artist. Her life-sized figurative sculptures portrayed pregnancy, labor, and motherhood in unprecedented ways.

Each woman entered the Institute at a crucial moment in her artistic career. Fresh off the surprise success of her first book, Sexton wanted to become what she called a "lasting" poet. At the Institute, she wrote her strongest collection of poetry and became confident in herself and in her career. Kumin, who was also just starting out as a poet, used her time at the Institute to rekindle her scholarly interests and experiment with different genres; soon after her fellowship, she wrote the first of three novels and became a writer known for her prose as well as her poetry. Olsen, a mother of four, came to the Institute to escape an overwhelming life at work and at home and with the hopes of finishing an ambitious novel. While there, she wrote something far more important: a revolutionary theory of how material oppression had shaped the literary canon. Swan, meanwhile, had long wanted to experiment with media other than pencil and oil paint, but it wasn't until she came to the Institute that she had the time and resources to explore lithography. And Pineda, fascinated by what she thought of as the "mythological" feminine, used her Institute time to create a series of female oracle statues.

The years at the Institute were a tipping point in each of these artists' lives. For the unstable, prolific Sexton, these years were a once-in-a-lifetime blend of productivity and quietude. She began to think she might no longer need therapy. As soon as she left the Institute, however, her mental illness worsened, her writing came in fits and starts, and she once again sought professional help. Kumin's years at the Institute prompted her to think about how to cultivate peace in the rest of her life. During her fellowship years, Kumin began to search for an escape from the demandingly social, creatively stifling Boston suburbs. She bought a farm in New Hampshire—a move that would define the rest of her life and work. Olsen made good on the literary promise she'd shown decades earlier: the research and writing she accomplished at Radcliffe propelled her to literary fame. Her time at the Institute marked her transition from wage laborer to literary celebrity. For Swan and Pineda, two sociable people who usually worked in solitude, collaborating at the Institute drew them into community once again. Swan, who later referred to the Institute years as "a real turning point," started collaborating with the poets (she later illustrated her friends' books and designed their covers), while Pineda, inspired by the women she encountered, began an important sculpture series; one sculpture would end up in Radcliffe Yard. The Institute provided the Equivalents with a refuge, but then it pushed them back into the world, for better and for worse.

Among the group, the relationship that remained strongest and most consistent throughout these years was the one between Sexton and Kumin. It therefore serves as the backbone of this book. Their creative, intimate bond predated their years at the Institute—they agreed to apply at the same time, but they kept their preexisting connection a secret from Institute administrators—and outlasted the end of their fellowships. It persevered through career ups and downs, changes of address, emotional crises, and divorce. This isn't to say it was always easy: Kumin was sometimes overwhelmed by Sexton's needs, while Sexton, in the last years of her life, struggled to grant her reliable companion autonomy. It is because of these ambivalences and complexities that I spend the most time studying the bond between these two women, drawing on their interviews, their letters to each other, and their essays in praise of each other's work. Kumin and Sexton left us a rich archive of their friendship, the love they had for each other, and the words they used to express it.

The Equivalents is the first book to tell the story of the Radcliffe Institute's emergence, a crucial and yet often overlooked event in the history of American feminism. The story of second-wave feminism usually starts with the publication of Betty Friedan's *The Feminine Mystique* in 1963, and with good reason. Friedan's galvanizing polemic—which recast the suburban home, the emblem of American success, as a "comfortable concentration camp"—resonated with thousands of women who wrote to her with praise and gratitude; according to the historian Stephanie Coontz, the book "sold approximately 60,000 copies in hardback, a large number even nowadays, and nearly 1.5 million copies in paperback." Three years after the book's publication, Friedan and a group of like-minded women founded the National Organization for Women (NOW) and began agitating and advocating for women's civil rights. Barriers began to fall: birth control became legal, abortion reform commenced, and women brought sexual discrimination cases before the courts. By the time radical feminist organizing cells sprang up in the late 1960s, "women's liberation" was well under way.

What this story misses, however, is how the groundwork for feminist revolt was laid, sometimes unwittingly, by women reformers, educators, and artists of the 1950s and early 1960s—a decade that can appear to be a dead zone for liberation politics. With a few exceptions, the women at the Radcliffe Institute didn't think of themselves as revolutionaries. Some of them didn't even think of themselves as feminists. They were well-behaved women; they had not yet made history. Their earnest efforts at self-expression enabled those who came after them to make bigger, bolder changes. Sexton's poetry, often called confessional, inspired the angry young women who would later take to the streets. Olsen's talks about the challenges of working-class motherhood riveted audiences; her classes on the literature of poverty radicalized college English departments. Friedan—who had originally invited Bunting to work with her on *The Feminine Mystique,* and who stuck with the project after Bunting dropped out—must have been pleased to see what her former collaborator's project had produced.

The story of the Institute also connects back to a long history of feminist thinking on creative work and intellectual production. In 1929, Virginia Woolf published the essay *A Room of One's Own,* based on two lectures she had delivered in October 1928 at the women's colleges of the University of Cambridge. The title is taken from a declaration she makes early in the essay: "A woman must have money and a room of her own if she is to write fiction." The rest of the essay describes a frustrating day spent by an anonymous woman at "Oxbridge"—a composite of Oxford and Cambridge—who is trying to think about her upcoming lecture but keeps being interrupted. She is shooed from the grass, prevented from entering the library, and forced to eat a bad dinner because she's not allowed to dine in her female friend's room. The essay articulates the importance of material resources for writers and intellectuals—Woolf refers to "the urbanity, the geniality, the dignity which are the offspring of luxury and privacy and space"—and is perhaps best remembered for this. But it expresses too desires for female community and for intergenerational support between women. Sitting with her friend, the narrator imagines an alternate history wherein her friend's mother had made money instead of bearing thirteen children:

> If only Mrs. Seton and her mother and her mother before her had learnt the great art of making money and had left their money, like their fathers and their grandfathers before them, to found fellowships and lectureships and prizes and scholarships appropriated to the use of their own sex, . . . we might have looked forward without undue confidence to a pleasant and honourable lifetime spent in the shelter of one of the liberally endowed professions. We might have been exploring or writing; mooning about the venerable places of the earth; sitting contemplative on the steps of the Parthenon, or going at ten to an office and coming home comfortably at half-past four to write a little poetry.

They might have lived like male writers and scholars who support each other's intellectual growth. The Institute made Woolf's supposition into something real.

I discovered the Equivalents when I was in my late twenties. I was finishing up a doctoral degree in English, and I was contemplating my future. I was dating a man whose career took precedence over my own. A child of the "girl power" 1990s, I was committed to the idea that I could pursue my intellectual interests and devote myself to a career while also having a happy family. I could and would do it all! Still, I couldn't shake the sense that I was going to have to choose between my professional dreams and being a mother. My own mother had struggled to balance career and family even with a supportive spouse. Whenever I thought about raising children, I was filled with dread.

Alone in Radcliffe's library, on the same grounds the Equivalents once walked, I opened manila file folders and sifted through old papers. I read about women who couldn't find adequate child care. I read about women who feared social opprobrium for leaving their children alone while they, selfishly, went off to work and to learn. I read about jealous husbands, condescending male teachers, books sacrificed at the altar of domestic tranquility. I took very good notes.

Later, I unearthed old cassettes, recordings of the seminar talks delivered during the Institute's first years. Across fifty-five years, I could hear the clinking of sherry glasses and the rustling of skirts being rearranged. I felt as if I'd discovered a lost world, one that was oddly familiar. I listened to Kumin charm her audience with tales of a pouty teenage daughter who took revenge by insulting her mother's books. I listened to Sexton read her poetry in a clear, loud voice that belied her intense society anxiety. I listened to Swan joke, in her slight Boston accent, about the "backbreaking labah" required of lithographers. I listened to Pineda speak seriously about the significance of sculpture throughout history. And I listened to Olsen describe the challenges of balancing motherhood, a day job, and writing fiction. She talked about how little time she had alone, how she wrote on city buses and late at night. At that moment, I felt lucky to be the only one in the library—and luckier still to have a boyfriend who lived in a different city.

The years passed. I left my boyfriend; I finished my degree. I visited other libraries: in Austin, Texas; in New Haven, Connecticut; in Palo Alto, California; in Washington, D.C. I kept reading: notebooks, letters, manuscripts, recipe books, bills. I read about child-care challenges, maternal guilt, debts unpaid, dreams unrealized. I read, too, about the ways these five women offered each other understanding, support, and recognition. And I read letters in which the writer, pressed to her limit, responded to a friend with jealousy or with rage.

I knew what it felt like to be hopeful and what it felt like to rage. The gender revolution that began decades ago remains unfinished. So much has changed since the days the Equivalents walked through Radcliffe Yard: Title IX is on the books, female CEOs are on the Fortune 500 list, books by women receive praise in the pages of national magazines. But study after study reports that within heterosexual couples women still do more of the housework. As of 2018, women made just over eighty cents on the dollar compared with men. There is still no widely available state-supported child care.

We're still trying to find, and to fight for, solutions. And as one of the inaugural members of the Institute told me when we spoke in the spring of 2016, women still need institutional support. They need places where they can find community and inspiration, and they need material assistance to pursue their dreams. This is the story of what five women achieved, over fifty years ago. It is, in part, a story of how they changed the world. It is also a story of how much remains to be done.

PART ONE

1957–1961

1951–1961

Little White Picket Fences

T HE SUN WAS ALREADY SETTING one evening late in the winter of 1957 when twenty-nine-year-old Anne Sexton, shaking with nerves and clutching a cardboard folder, walked down Commonwealth Avenue, the main thoroughfare in Boston's Back Bay. She passed Victorian brownstones, statues of local luminaries, and large, stately trees. She soon arrived at her destination, a large stone building on the boulevard's north side.

She passed through the building's imposing gray facade and walked through the opulent ballroom hidden inside. This was one of her first trips out of her home in Newton in recent memory; to accomplish it, she had requested the company of a kind neighbor named Sandy Robart. Sexton had always been a nervous woman, but these days she was something more: anxious, fearful, choked by self-doubt. Public places of any kind produced intense discomfort; most days she didn't leave her house. She had recently attempted suicide; she would make a second attempt in just a few months.

She walked through the building's foyer and wondered what she was doing there. She wasn't cowed by the signs of old money. Wealth was familiar to her. It was what the building concealed that fright-ened her: a small poetry workshop, run by the Boston Center for Adult Education. Sexton, who had been writing poetry seriously for only several months, who had no college degree, who had a bad his-tory in classroom settings, had uncharacteristically decided to enroll in the course. Until that winter evening, only two people had read her poetry: Dr. Martin Orne, her psychoanalyst; and her mother, Mary Gray Harvey. The idea of showing her poems to other people—other poets—was terrifying. And yet here she was, in matching lipstick and heels, with flowers in her dark hair, about to enter a classroom for the first time in a decade.

She stepped into the room; heads turned. The workshop had been in session for some weeks, and newcomers weren't common. The instructor, John Holmes, sat at the head of a long oak table. A man with thinning hair and a long, hangdog face, he was the personifi-cation of dour New England. Holmes was a fixture in the Boston poetry scene: teaching workshops, reviewing books, and working as a professor at Tufts. Many of Holmes's students had published poems, including a thirty-one-year-old mother of three who was also present that evening. Her name was Maxine Kumin.

Sexton and Kumin regarded each other: it was a bit like looking into a mirror. Both women were thin, dark-haired, and attractive. Unlike Sexton, Kumin was not a native New Englander, though by the time the two women met, Boston had become her home. Kumin was an assimilated Jewish woman from Philadelphia whose pawn-broker father had earned enough to send his daughter first to paro-chial school, then to Radcliffe College. For Kumin, education had been a way of becoming an individual, someone who could escape from her mother's expectations. Sexton, by contrast, came from New England wealth. She relied on her parents for financial support and on her husband for emotional caretaking. Sexton was emotionally volatile, plagued by anxiety, depression, and suicidal urges. Kumin kept her temper in check and steered away from instability. She was immediately wary of this nervous, glamorous stranger—a woman who somehow fascinated and repelled. Both were there to do something that felt uncertain, even untoward: to establish themselves as poets. Each had to gather her courage to attempt this, an obviously solitary effort. What did it mean for them to encounter each other in this terrifying space?

Sexton once summed up her life prior to 1957 as follows: "I was trying my damnedest to lead a conventional life, for that was how I was brought up, and it was what my husband wanted of me. But one can't build little white picket fences to keep nightmares out. The surface cracked when I was about twenty-eight. I had a psychotic break and tried to kill myself."

For much of her life, Sexton had believed she was dumb. She believed this because many people in her life told her so. Born in 1928 to a wealthy family in the comfortable Boston suburb of Newton, the youngest of three daughters, Anne Harvey was a skinny and fidgety child in a household that prided itself on grace and decorum. She couldn't sit still. She often refused to eat. She tugged and twisted her hair until it tangled. As an adolescent, she showed up at the dinner table speckled with acne; her father, disgusted, refused to eat in her presence. Unlike her two sisters, who attended elite private schools, Anne attended public school for most of her youth (she was kicked out of a Waldorf school because she failed at naptime). By the time she got to high school, the boarding school Rogers Hall, she had been held back three times by teachers who considered her unintelligent, a "terrible nervous wreck," and "high-strung."

If Anne was dumb, her mother was smart. Mary Gray Harvey, who came from a wealthy family in Maine, was a petite, attractive woman, a true lady. She had been raised like a princess by her doting father, the editor and publisher of a newspaper, and she thrived on being the "brilliant" one in the family. Her husband, Ralph Harvey, a businessman who drank too much, held Mary Gray in high esteem, constantly reminding his daughters, "Oh, your mother is smart; mother is brilliant." "She was the 'writer,' the cultured, brilliant one," Sexton told an interviewer in the early 1960s. "She kind of over-powered us,

I think, at times." (The only thing Mary Gray actually wrote was her husband's business correspondence, but Ralph Harvey lauded each letter as a "masterpiece.") Mary Gray had a cultured air: she read a book a day, and she'd attended the prestigious Wellesley College. Although she never graduated, she let it be known that she had the highest IQ of all the girls on campus. To her, there was something admirable about simply being intelligent, as opposed to deliberately educating oneself. Mary Gray presented knowledge as something you simply picked up, as you would a canapé, when it suited you.

Anne tried and failed to impress her mother. When she was a teenager, she presented Mary Gray with a poem she'd written that had been accepted into the school yearbook. Mary Gray read over her daughter's work, paused, and then launched an investigation. Surely this was not her daughter's original work; surely she had copied it from *somewhere*. She sent this poem and others Anne had written to a family friend, a professor in New York, and asked him to find the source from which her daughter had plagiarized. (The professor wrote back: the poems were original, and they were promising.) Anne, chastened by the experience, didn't show her mother any more poems. Soon, she stopped writing them altogether.

Foiled in her creative pursuits, Anne tried to emulate her mother's stable, high-status domestic life, and she succeeded—but only with lots of help from Mary Gray herself. When she was nineteen, Anne was dating an upper-class boy from the Boston suburbs, Alfred Muller Sexton II, known to friends and family as Kayo, and she feared she was pregnant. On the advice of Mary Gray, the couple drove south, to North Carolina, where the legal age of marriage was eighteen for both men and women. (In Massachusetts, it was eighteen for women and twenty-one for men.) They married, and Anne Harvey became Anne Sexton. The pregnancy was a false alarm—Sexton had started menstruating on the trip south—but the marriage stuck. The young couple bounced back and forth between their respective parents' households before finally finding an apartment in Cochituate, a town just ten minutes from the Harveys in Weston. (The Harveys had moved there in 1941; their house, built from scratch, included seven bathrooms and five garages.) While Kayo served in the Korean War, Mary Gray steered her daughter away from tempting flirtations and encouraged her to recommit to her marriage. When Sexton did eventually become pregnant—she'd flown out to San Francisco to meet her husband during his leave—Mary Gray tended to her, took her shopping for maternity clothes, took her on vacation to Florida, and allowed her to move back into the Weston family home. With Mary Gray's financial help, the young Sextons paid for a house in the comfortable suburb of Newton. They started to carve out something like an independent adult life, though Kayo—who had dropped out of Colgate University, where he had been pursuing medicine—worked in the wool business under his father-in-law.

As long as Mary Gray was alive, Sexton never stopped craving her mother's praise and fearing her criticisms. A harsh word from Mary Gray stung more than any of the insults Ralph had flung at young Anne when he was drunk. Sexton thought that if she could raise a family and run a household as her mother did, she would finally earn approval from this cold, elusive woman who always seemed to know what was best—the best dress, the best drink, the best book to demonstrate that you were cultured. As she later put it, "I had to be just awful or as good as my mother."

By August 1955, with her mother's assistance, Sexton had put together an admirable life: she owned a house in the suburbs, she was tall and beautiful and well-off, and she was mother to two daughters, Linda, age two, and a newborn, Joy.

But she struggled with the responsibilities of motherhood. She found herself reacting with anger and violence to her children's needs. She once threw her older child across a room in frustration. She was eventually diagnosed with postpartum depression. "My heart pounds and it's all I can hear—my feeling for my children does not surpass my desire to be free of their demands on my emotions," she once wrote to a therapist. As the months ticked by and Joy approached her first birthday, Sexton's symptoms lingered and deepened. Worried she would hurt her children, she contemplated using her sleeping pills to end her life. One dark night, she stayed awake for hours, fighting her worst impulses, and then, on a therapist's recommendation, checked herself into Westwood Lodge—the same institution her father had gone to when he needed to dry out. Mary Gray cared for Linda, while Kayo's mother, Billie, took in Joy. Sexton was released from Westwood Lodge after a couple of weeks, but her mental health continued to decline. She took an overdose of barbiturates in November 1956, one day before her twenty-eighth birthday. Her new therapist, Dr. Martin Orne, sent her to Glenside, a grim institution that put her at a safe distance from her family. "Her family was not very sympathetic about her problems," Dr. Orne later recalled. He diagnosed Sexton with hysteria in the Freudian sense.

Sexton was released from Glenside after several weeks. It was a hard winter. Linda returned to her, but Joy stayed with Billie. Sexton was lonely and listless. "I walk from room to room trying to think of something to do," she wrote to Dr. Orne. "I have this almost terrible energy in me," she explained, and "nothing seems to help." All that she'd learned about homemaking eluded her; she found herself incapable of baking a potato. She relied on Kayo as a child depends on a parent, and she feared his absences. He was often quite patient with her, but at times he exploded into rage. He was sometimes physically violent with Sexton (more often in the later years of their marriage). She loved her daughters, but she resented the way they circumscribed her life. "Who would want to live feeling that way?" she wrote to Dr. Orne in February 1957. It was a question that reverberated daily through her mind.

Desperate, Sexton searched for a reason to go on living. She found it somewhere she never expected: lyric poetry.

On Dr. Orne's recommendation, Sexton began watching educational television; her analyst thought it would stimulate her mind and distract her from her emotional troubles. One Thursday evening in late 1956, just a month after her suicide attempt, Sexton tuned in to the local public television station WGBH and watched a program called *Sense of Poetry*. A Harvard English professor appeared on-screen; he looked every bit the academic, with his bald head and spectacles. His name was I. A. Richards, and he was one of the most influential scholars of English literature on either side of the Atlantic. While teaching at Cambridge in the 1920s, he had developed a practice of closely reading poetry without recourse to historical or biographical context. Richards called this "practical criticism"; by the time this practice spread to American universities, in the 1940s and 1950s, it was called New Criticism. This style of literary criticism appealed to university English departments at the mid-century because it made the study of literature seem scientific rather than dilettantish. It was also a very teachable method, perfect for educating undergraduates—or viewers of public television.

In truth, *Sense of Poetry* was a bit boring. Richards wasn't particularly dynamic, though he hosted several different educational programs throughout his career (despite his professed distaste for mass media). He read out famous poems, such as Keats's "Ode on a Grecian Urn," enunciating precisely so viewers could hear the scansion and rhythm of the work. Sometimes, a poem scrolled down the screen, or a helpful chart appeared, but otherwise the camera fixed on this austere man, who seemed better suited for radio than for the screen.

The program was dry and purely educational, and Sexton was rapt. She watched as Richards described the structure of a sonnet— fourteen lines, three quatrains and a couplet, ABABA CDCD EFEF GG—and took careful notes. "I could do that," she thought to herself. The show over, the night dark, she wrote a sonnet of her own. Like an approval-seeking high school student, she showed the sonnet to Mary Gray. This time, Mary Gray believed the poem was original; she even suggested a better image to capture the poem's sentiment. Sexton was grateful: she'd finally earned her mother's approval, and she'd found a new way of managing her distress. She would order her disorder in verse.

Suddenly poetry flowed from Sexton faster than tears. Between January 1957 and December of the same year, she wrote more than sixty poems—a remarkable output. Most of them marched out messages and morals in regular rhythm, like the poems one would find in *The Saturday Evening Post*, the leading middlebrow magazine.

Many referred to therapy or to Freudianism, and some addressed Dr. Orne himself: "Appointment Hour," "The Psychosomatic Stomach," "A Foggy Adjustment." She typed up her poems carefully and presented them to Dr. Orne, who offered her the approval she craved. Untutored in the craft, unburdened by a traditional literary education, Sexton proceeded by instinct, learning "unconsciously," a word she used frequently to describe her method. She set herself little challenges—write a poem in syllabic rhyme, write a double acrostic—just to see if she could succeed. When she made a second suicide attempt in late May 1957, Dr. Orne pointed to her poetry as her reason to live. "You can't kill yourself," he told her. "You have something to give."

Sexton didn't fully understand what she was doing as a poet; for years to come, she would describe poetic technique as "trickery." She was an unpublished amateur. She submitted a few poems to publications, signing them "Mrs. A. M. Sexton," but she heard nothing back. She considered finding a classroom of some sort, somewhere, and trying to learn as she had never done before. Dr. Orne recommended enrolling at Boston University or Newton Junior College. A return to school was a gamble for the girl who had been kept back and kicked out, undermined by teachers and family both. With her mental health still precarious, she weighed the risks against the possible rewards. She would have to leave the house and meet strangers; that would be terrifying. But perhaps some of these strangers would understand her in ways her family never did. Maybe, if she could push through her fear, she would find those she called "my people."

When Sexton appeared in Holmes's workshop, Kumin was at once "taken" with the stranger, as she later recalled, and "terrified." Kumin marveled at the new student's looks: Sexton was "tall, blue-eyed, stunningly slim," a woman who was "all intimidating sophistications in the chalk-and-wet-overshoes atmosphere" of the classroom. Kumin's style was plainer, and her manner was "much more closed up, restrained," as she put it. She wore glasses on occasion and drew her hair back in a bun. Even in her thirties, she could easily slip back into the role of the student. She felt herself to be the "chief frump," while Sexton was "really chic."

But despite appearances, the two women had more in common than they realized. Both were mothers of multiple children—Sexton had two, Kumin had three—and both made their homes in Newton. Though Sexton had plenty of help from her mother-in-law, she still found her home life stifling. "Nothing seems worth while [*sic*]," she wrote to Dr. Orne in February 1957, around the same time the workshop began. "I feel like a caged tiger." Kumin felt similarly. "I chafed against the domesticity in which I found myself," she later wrote. "I had a good marriage and our two little girls were joyous elements in it. But my discontent was palpable." Like Sexton, Kumin had enrolled in the workshop with "great fear and trembling."

Kumin hadn't been raised to be a poet or an intellectual; she had been raised to be a lady. Born Maxine Winokur in Philadelphia in 1925, "Max," as she preferred to be called, bristled against mandatory femininity and her mother's grooming. Doll Winokur was an elegant woman, sophisticated and eager to appear fully assimilated into American society (she discouraged the use of gesture in her children; Kumin thought for years that only Jewish people used their hands during conversation). Kumin once recalled, "My earliest visions of my mother place her in an evening dress, about to depart in a cloud of French perfume for an important social event." Originally from Virginia, Doll was the kind of woman who demanded care and caresses as her birthright.

Pete Winokur, Max's father, owned the largest pawnshop in the city of Philadelphia. Doll, status conscious, encouraged the children to refer to their father simply as a "broker" on school forms. She also tried to mold her only daughter into the perfect lady, and at every turn young Max resisted. Chubby when she was little and athletic in her adolescence, Max preferred running wild at summer camp and swimming competitively to sewing and socializing among her urbane peers.

She rejected an invitation to join her high school sorority (like a college sorority, but for high school girls), mortifying her mother, who had encouraged Max to transfer to this high school from a public school because of its social opportunities as well as its superior education. "The passage through adolescence was a lonely, introverted time," Kumin later wrote. "Forced to attend dancing classes on alternate Saturday nights, where all of the popular girls were indifferent students in my French or history section, I hid in the ladies' room until the ordeal ended." Academic work soothed her anxieties: "I took refuge in scholarship; getting all A's was my only balm."

Her hard work resulted in admission to one of the prestigious Seven Sisters schools, the female equivalent of the Ivy League, which was all male at the time. Max matriculated at Radcliffe in the fall of 1942, where she made her first discouraging foray into poetry. Buoyed by first-year hubris, she skipped an English prerequisite and registered for an advanced creative writing course taught by Wallace Stegner, the man Sinclair Lewis once called "one of the most important novelists in America." At the time, Stegner was writing the semiautobiographical *The Big Rock Candy Mountain,* his fifth novel. He had strong ideas about what constituted good fiction. He believed that a writer must unearth the truth about an experience, handle it carefully, and then include something serious or surprising. "Some element of the unexpected is necessary," he once explained, "or some element, at least, of the—what would you call it?—profound." Such profundity eluded young Max. While her classmates were writing the kind of "good, fat fiction stories" that appealed to Stegner, she was making aborted attempts at both prose and poetry. "I was just floundering," she later remembered. "He [Stegner] let it be known in no uncertain terms that I was totally without talent. And I was making a big mistake if I thought I was going to be a writer. Certainly I shouldn't try to be a poet, because I just didn't have it." Despondent, Max decided to give up on creative writing and focus on literary history; she eventually won a prize for her senior thesis. She didn't write poetry again for eight years.

In the interim, she followed the path laid out for the East Coast, middle-class white women of her generation: marriage, children,

Cape Cod colonial house. Twelve days after she graduated from Radcliffe with honors, she married Victor Kumin, a Jewish engineer she'd met on a blind date in Boston. Vic had spent World War II working on a secret project in Los Alamos—Kumin eventually realized he was working on the atomic bomb—and the couple wrote to each other during their time apart, cementing a relationship before Kumin's parents, back in Philadelphia, even had a chance to meet their future son-in-law. Following Vic's job prospects, the young couple moved first to Woods Hole, then to downtown Boston, then finally to Watertown.

But Kumin wasn't content. She still yearned for intellectual excitement. It was through school that she'd become someone other than "the pawnbroker's daughter." She thought of her high school Latin teachers as inspiring people who had transformed her life. She had always taken solace in study.

And so after the end of the war, and with Vic's encouragement, Kumin used her savings to go back to Radcliffe to study for a master's degree in comparative literature. The couple lived frugally and Kumin worked during the summer, but the sacrifices were worth it: she received her master's in 1948. Soon after, she gave birth to her first child, a girl named Jane. Another daughter, Judith, followed in 1950. As a self-identified housewife, though, she remained discontented. While other women were happy to host bridge games and steer Girl Scout troops, Kumin took adult education classes and picked up freelance work as a researcher. She kept up her freelance work even as Vic's career advanced; his income enabled the family to move to Newton, a step up from Watertown, and buy a house at 40 Bradford Road.

Sitting in her Newton home—a Cape Cod colonial—in 1953, pregnant for the third time, Kumin made a life-changing decision. She subscribed to *The Writer,* a Boston magazine, and purchased Richard Armour's guide *Writing Light Verse.* Even though she'd promised herself that she'd never again write poetry, she wondered if she might have the skills to write poems that weren't serious. She played with the kind of four-line verses that she saw in the pages of *Cosmopolitan* and *The Saturday Evening Post.* "And I made a pact with myself," she later recalled: "If I didn't sell anything by the time this child was born, I would chuck all my creative discontents." She would heed Stegner's cruel prediction.

Eight months into her pregnancy, she sold her first poem to *The Christian Science Monitor* for $5, more than the cost of Armour's instructional book. Her investment had been recouped. The poem paled in comparison to the Renaissance poetry she admired as an undergraduate:

There never grows so red the rose,
So sound the round tomato
As March's catalogues disclose
And yearly I fall prey to.

But as a form of validation—a license to continue her little indulgence—it would do. Kumin exchanged her freelance work for the chance to feed this muse. "I had found a profession that was infinitely portable," she later wrote. "I could try out lines in my head while doing the dishes or hanging the laundry—no dishwasher, no dryer—or conveying a child to a music lesson or the dentist. I grew adept at composing in the car while I waited for the musician or patient to be trained or treated." Within two years, she had been published in *The Wall Street Journal, Ladies' Home Journal,* and *The Saturday Evening Post.* The *Post* was one of the leading magazines at the time, a real coup. There was just one detail that rankled: Vic had had to supply a letter, signed by his employer, certifying that Kumin's poem was original.

By 1957, Kumin was consistently earning money from her poetry. The checks sustained her ambition. She always got a thrill when her name appeared in print. Perhaps somewhere out there in California, Stegner was flipping through the *Post* and stopping, surprised, when he saw her name on a page.

Publication eased her self-doubt, but it didn't cure her loneliness. "I continued to write in isolation," she later remembered, steal-

Kumin family portrait, 1955
Left to right: *Judith, Maxine, Daniel, Vic, Jane*

ing time away from household chores to craft a few lines and then returning to the bustle of family life. As happy as she was with Vic and her three children, a part of her wanted intellectual community, even though she knew it could throw her life into chaos. She was busy enough at home, as a letter to her mother from around this time indicates:

Up sooner than betimes; dryer broken, youngest out of underpants. All underpants soaking wet on line. Pouring. Ten minutes of earnest persuasion . . . Find plastic bag to protect violin case. (Pouring harder.) Write check for violin teacher. Overdrawn? Live dangerously . . . Find cough drops for middle child. Middle child coughs anyhow . . . Husband's sales director coming for dinner. Husband has clean shirt? Whiskey sours? No rye. Can't find noodle pudding recipes. Find it. Make pudding.

The letter continues in this vein, stacking up household tasks like bricks. How could she add another obligation? Decadent as it was to sign up for yet another adult education class, this one with John Holmes, Kumin did just that.

Throughout their first classes together, Kumin studied Sexton. There was something dramatic about her, and Kumin wasn't sure she liked it. Kumin had recently lost a friend to suicide, and she had the sense that this newcomer was unstable in just the same way. Worse, Sexton didn't seem self-conscious about her instability; many of the poems she presented were about her experiences at a mental institution. As the weeks passed, Sexton began to speak openly in class of her suicide attempts. Her behavior horrified Kumin, a woman who prided herself on being presentable—in this way, at least, she embodied her mother's ideals—and who kept shameful secrets hidden away. At Radcliffe, Kumin had learned how to write and talk like a sophisticated intellectual. The idea that one would willingly reveal all the mess that lay underneath one's social persona—it not only confused her; it repulsed her. She decided to keep her distance.

Her plan failed. The following September, as the Holmes workshop kicked off its second term, Kumin and Sexton bumped into each other at the Newton Public Library. As they chatted cordially, they realized that they lived quite near each other: Sexton in Newton Lower Falls, Kumin in Newton Highlands. They decided it was only practical for them to start commuting to Boston together. Sexton usually drove the two of them to class in her old Ford; when the workshop concluded, she'd drive them back to the suburbs. All those hours driving down Route 9 undid whatever suspicions Kumin harbored. Soon, she was offering to drive Sexton to poetry readings around Greater Boston. That year, they went together to listen to the renowned poet Marianne Moore, then seventy, who dressed for the reading in a cape and fantastic hat. They also went together to hear the English poet Robert Graves, who was, in their shared opinion, "ghastly." The readings provided something like a poetic education for Sexton, who had never formally studied poetry the way Kumin had.

And then there was the teaching in workshop. Holmes had an odd teaching method: he refused to distribute copies of student poems. Instead, he read a poem aloud, and the class would listen for the poem's strengths and weaknesses. The method honed the poet's ear. Soon, Sexton and Kumin were running a mini-workshop of their own, using the same method: one of them would call up the other on her rotary telephone, read out a line or two, then wait for feedback.

It wasn't easy keeping the conversation going with children running around. Kumin, writing at home, felt as if she were working in the "eye of the hurricane." Sexton faced a similar storm. Her children climbed all over her, and she hushed them: "Sh! poem! Maxine!" With one finger in her ear, Sexton tried to get a sense of the whole poem and suggested changing a word here, a line break there. Sexton and Kumin were often surprised when, later, they saw what each other's poems looked like on the page. Though each poet sat at her own desk, in her own house, they felt intimately connected. Sometimes they stayed on the phone for hours.

One snowy winter Sunday in 1958, Sexton called Kumin to ask if she might come over and share a piece of writing—something she wasn't even sure could be called a poem. She'd been listening to a 45 on repeat, an old song that reminded her of her time at Glenside, and she'd written down some of her memories of the place. (She'd had to climb over Kayo, who was building a hi-fi set, each time she wanted to replay the record.) Kumin said yes, and Sexton hopped into her Ford.

Just several minutes later, Kumin was welcoming Sexton into her home for the first time. It was a new level of intimacy. They sat awkwardly on a couch—they'd never seen each other outside a classroom, a car, or a lecture hall—and Sexton handed over a draft of the poem "Music Swims Back to Me." "Is this a poem?" she asked.

The poem takes place at what seems to be a mental institution. The speaker, physically restrained in a chair, listens to snatches of a radio song and asks some anonymous "Mister" how she might find her way home. She's lost in a place where "everyone . . . was crazy."

She glimpses older women in diapers and menacing shadows. She hears, or imagines hearing, a song she first heard on her first night in this strange place. The poem circles, repeating its refrain—"Oh, la la la, / this music swims back to me"—again near the end, like a mind caught in its own inescapable cycle. There's no regular meter to anchor the poem. There's no clear path home. With its strange, discordant rhythms, "Music Swims Back to Me" was a break with Sexton's earlier poetry, which was usually in iambic pentameter, a form Kumin found juvenile.

Kumin was floored by "Music Swims Back to Me." This new poem was serious work. As the workshop progressed, Sexton continued to experiment with more complex rhymes. That winter and spring, she composed three poems—"Unknown Girl in a Maternity Ward," "The Double Image," and "You, Doctor Martin"—that were especially strong. "Unknown Girl," a dramatic monologue, contained striking images of mothering: a baby tips over "like a cup"; the mother's arms fit the child "like a sleeve"; the mother, ashamed not to have a partner present, "tighten[s] to refuse" her child's "owling eyes." Sexton was beginning to discover her knack for image making.

Watching and listening to Sexton unspool her soul, Kumin was inspired to write more about her own life—her loud father, her elegant, infantilized mother. She was not inclined to write about any present frustrations, the way Sexton did, but she did mine her past. In a poem called "Halfway," she recalled her house in Philadelphia, which stood halfway up a hill in Germantown, "between a convent and a madhouse." It was a strange place to grow up. Kumin had been educated by nuns, despite her Jewishness, and she was at once fascinated and confused by Catholicism. Her youthful impressions inform the poem: the sounds of Mass and the cries of "the mad ones" mingle in the air, and the speaker can't remember which is which. Was the Mass coming from the convent or the asylum? Were the screams the prayers of nuns or the cries of an impaled Christ? The speaker sees, as only an outsider can, the way pain and pleasure, sadism and asceticism, commingle in the Catholic tradition. "But I have got / The gardens mixed," Kumin wrote.

It must have been
The mad ones who cried out to blot
The frightened sinner from his sin.
The nuns were kind. They gave me cake
And told me lives of saints who died
Aflame and silent at the stake.

The young speaker listens to the legends of Christ; she thinks she sees "their Christ" and begins to cry. The poem ends as it began, in a house on the hill, granting some kind of clarity to memories that remain elusive.

Over the course of the workshop, Kumin composed several more poems about her childhood. Some take seemingly unremarkable events and render them unusually frightening. In "A Hundred Nights," her father is an "avenging ghost" who smacks the bats flying through his house; he aims to "stun," not to "kill." The young speaker cries and wishes her father would stuff the chimney to keep "those flapping rats" outside. The "crepey nights" loom large in her memory, even though her parents claim they were infrequent (there were, in fact, not "a hundred nights" of bat combat, as the title implies). "Once, before my father dies," she resolves, "I mean to ask him why he chose / to loose those furies at my bed." The speaker wants an acknowledgment of the effects of such violence on her vulnerable child-self.

"A Hundred Nights" was Kumin's effort to capture a man with a temper, a father who chased his wife down flights of stairs when they fought until Doll, imperious and composed, locked herself in her music room and played a Steinway piano for hours. Kumin also began to write more about motherhood. The poem "The Journey" is dedicated to "Jane at thirteen"; the speaker bids goodbye to her daughter and remembers how she, too, was once thirteen and was once "stunned, like you, by my reflection." She greets, but also says goodbye to, a younger self.

Marianne Moore, a poet championed by Ezra Pound and T. S. Eliot, wrote difficult poetry about abstract concepts: the natural world, poetry itself. "I, too, dislike it," perhaps her most famous line, might just as well express the reaction of a frustrated reader, befuddled by her line breaks and stumped by her syllabics. Some poets, such as Elizabeth Bishop, followed in Moore's footsteps, though Bishop's poems are more plainspoken. Sexton and Kumin, however, took a different approach. Their poetry was smooth, not discordant, candid, not inscrutable. They believed that the direct expression of difficult, personal experience was as necessary as meditations on the meaning of art.

Though both poets wrote out of personal experience, their work—quite different in tone—reflected their distinct temperaments. Sexton was energetic, a woman who drew admirers to her like bees to an open flower, whereas Kumin was charming but reserved. Kumin was skeptical of emotional intensity, and she disliked too much social time. Once she settled in Newton, she began plotting ways to escape suburbia for the peace and quiet of the country. Sexton, nerves soothed by drink, would be the last guest to leave a party.

And yet they became intimate companions. This was partly a function of proximity—their two homes were mere miles from each other—and partly a sign of their complementarity. Kumin was stable where Sexton was inconstant, responsible where Sexton was flighty. She offered Sexton the knowledge she'd gleaned from college, and Sexton showed Kumin how to write from a place of feeling rather than thought. Their shared inquiry into the use and value of personal experience, and of poetry, drew them together. The bond they hatched by happenstance would endure for as long as both of them were alive.

CHAPTER 2

Who Rivals?

S EXTON AND KUMIN came of age at a strange moment for American women, after a hot war and in the midst of a cold one. During the final years of the 1940s, women were carried aloft by the country's surging optimism. The rationing and austerity of World War II were over. Coffers emptied, flooding the country's cultural institutions with hoarded cash. It was a buoyant time, a time to go to school, to kiss a soldier, to fall in love.

By the 1950s, the culture had shifted from exuberant to wary. Another war seemed to be looming, this one potentially more devastating. In 1950, 61 percent of Americans thought the United States should use the atomic bomb in another war; by 1956, two-thirds had come to fear that the United States itself would be bombed, should another war break out. In an effort to avoid open conflict, now that the stakes of violent conflict were unspeakably high, America aimed to fight on the cultural front. The United States presented and promoted its beliefs, its freedoms, and its inimitable brand of happiness in the hopes of winning foreign nations to its side. The peaceful and prosperous American family became an image of national security.

Though the diplomat George F. Kennan first used the term "containment" to describe American foreign policy with regard to communism in 1947, the word applied equally well to domestic life. Deviance and "softness" could not be tolerated; "red" and "lavender" menaces had to be stopped. Homosexuals, communists, and political dissidents faced public shaming. Meanwhile, women were asked to surrender the freedoms—of movement, of dress, of affiliation—they had guarded closely since V-J Day. They put down their books and wrenches and picked up spatulas. They left college in droves.

Still, in the small circles of Boston artists in which Kumin and Sexton moved, one could find a few women watching and listening. There, a sizable and vibrant poetry scene thrived. The nation's best poets passed through town, teaching classes and giving readings. They took the train from New York and flew overland from Iowa. At well-lubricated parties, one could hear, through the din, the resonant voices of Randall Jarrell, Robert Lowell, W. D. Snodgrass—names that would be known for years to come. And through the smoke and sea of tweed, one could spot the dresses and the pageboy haircuts that belonged to the poetry world's few women: Sexton, Adrienne Cecile Rich, Sylvia Plath. They clasped their drinks like entry passes and shouted over the voices of men.

Like many fledgling writers before them, these women came together to pay homage to the master teacher of their age—the kind of charming, eccentric male genius who earned fame within literary and artistic movements at the mid-century. The handsome Robert Lowell wasn't the first to earn this kind of treatment from novice artists. Pablo Picasso, later memorialized as "terribly famous, not terribly nice," stood at the center of cubism. The cranky, erratic Ezra Pound served as the impresario of transatlantic modernism (his outsized influence on the era led one critic to dub the interwar period the "Pound Era"). Allen Tate, a genteel man of letters, led the charge of the Southern Agrarians and changed the way students and teachers understood poetry. By the postwar era, however, the figure of the master teacher had taken on a new significance. This was the heyday of the American university, a time when higher education was becoming more democratic. Funded by the GI bill, veterans flooded university halls, swelling the undergraduate population and enticing more funding from the state. Schools invested in both the arts and the sciences, founding laboratories and starting fine arts programs. Creative writing programs were also on the rise, producing new artistic circles and offering new points of access to literary genius (by 1975, there were fifty-two programs, a dramatic increase from the several programs that had existed in the 1940s). Though creative writing had been taught at the University of Montana and the University of Iowa since 1920 and 1936, respectively, writers didn't infiltrate the ivory tower until the late 1950s and the 1960s. Now young men and women could formally sign up to study with a superior mind. The classroom became a temple of worship—or, sometimes, a battlefield between one generation and the next.

Wandering through Boston's literary scene in the 1950s, one might stumble upon women, in clusters of twos and threes, learning from magnetic men and clinging to the chances they'd been given. They evaluated the competition; they kept tabs on their rivals; occasionally, they found confidantes; rarely, they made friends.

One February afternoon in 1959, almost two years to the day since Sexton first made her nervous walk down Commonwealth Avenue, the young poet Sylvia Plath stepped into a tiny Boston University seminar room. The windows looked out upon slushy streets; just a few blocks away, the Charles River divided Boston from Cambridge. Her blond hair was longer than usual, and she'd meant to cut it into a pageboy or something similarly fashionable, but she hadn't yet made the time. Still wearing her camel-hair coat, she found a seat directly opposite where an instructor would sit and waited for class to commence. It was not yet 2:00 p.m.

One by one, students shuffled in—mostly graduate students at Boston University, though the course was open to others, and mostly men. As they shrugged off damp overcoats and took their seats, they unfurled the thin, translucent papers on which they had typed up their poems. The room was silent but for the rustling of the onion-skin papers.

Just after 2:00 p.m., Robert "Cal" Lowell entered the room. He was just as Plath remembered him from an awkward recent dinner at her apartment on Willow Street: tall, square-jawed, and, despite his thinning hair and his thick glasses, remarkably good-looking. Rumor had it that Lowell had been unwell recently, either physically or mentally, but today he seemed stable enough. He didn't turn on the overhead light and instead shuffled through the midwinter gloom before taking his seat at the head of the table. The air seemed to grow gradually thicker, as if saturated with student nerves. Because it was early in the spring semester, Lowell began class by asking the students to name their favorite poets. Plath, who was auditing the class, offered Wallace Stevens, to Lowell's approval. Others offered the canonical greats: John Keats, Samuel Coleridge, John Donne. If any student had secretly loved a notable female poet—Edna St. Vincent Millay, for example, or Muriel Rukeyser—she would have been sure to offer a different answer: it was understood that "feminine" poetry had no place in Lowell's classroom. Once all the students had taken their turns, Lowell opened a leather-bound anthology of nineteenth-century poetry, hunched over it, and began to read at such a low volume that students had to lean forward to hear.

He had been speaking for a few minutes when a dark-haired, harried woman burst into the room. She was a bit older than most of the other students; she wore a low-cut blouse and visible makeup. Pretty, certainly, but a bit undone in some imperceptible way. The latecomer sashayed to the back of the classroom, her bangles clanging as she walked. A male student got up to offer her his seat, because the chairs were all taken. Once she settled into it, she removed a high-heeled shoe and a pack of cigarettes and proceeded to smoke, using the heel of the shoe as an ashtray. This woman was Anne Sexton.

For nearly an hour, Lowell muttered in iambs and the students listened in a state of barely contained panic. Their instructor liked to spend the first part of class reading from his favorites: William Wordsworth, William Empson, his good friend Elizabeth Bishop.

He would read a poem and then quiz his students: What does the poem mean? Why is this line good? Sometimes one of the graduate-student types would make a stab at an answer. The women, Plath noticed, always stayed silent. Except for the latecomer.

"I don't think that line is any good at all!" Sexton said, in response to one of Lowell's pressing questions. Lowell, bemused, let her speak. It seemed that these two had an understanding.

In the second hour, Lowell turned to student poems—a move that only heightened the atmosphere of panic. His method was to study a poem, pause, and then offer one or two suggestions, seemingly at random. "This is the best part," he might say, pointing to a single stanza. Or, "put the end at the beginning and the beginning at the end." His remarks were like the pronouncements of an oracle: ominous and ponderable. Few of the students had anything insightful to say to their peers. "Lowell's class yesterday a great disappointment," Plath wrote in her journal that evening, back in her Beacon Hill apartment. She had some teaching experience—she'd taught at Smith College—and she knew what made for a good class. "I said a few mealymouthed things, a few BU students yattered nothings I wouldn't let my Smith freshmen say without challenge. Lowell good in his mildly feminine ineffectual fashion. Felt a regression. The main thing is hearing the other student's poems & his reaction to mine. I need an outsider."

The night she wrote these words, Plath was twenty-six, racked with literary ambition, and keen to be the perfect wife. With her husband, the English poet Ted Hughes, she planned to "publish a bookshelf of books before we perish! And a batch of brilliant healthy children!" But literary success eluded Plath, who had published her first poem in *Harper's* when she was still a student at Smith College. She believed she should have *already* made a name for herself as a writer and that if she had not lost a year recovering from a suicide attempt, she would have established herself already. Instead, she was dragging herself out to Boston University in the middle of winter, trying to make up for lost time.

The following week, she returned to Lowell's dark classroom, suspecting that she was the best female poet in the class. Plath kept track of women rivals, ticking off lists in her journals: "Arrogant, I think I have written lines which qualify me to be The Poetess of America . . . Who rivals? Well, in history—Sappho, Elizabeth Barrett Browning, Christina Rossetti, Amy Lowell, Emily Dickinson, Edna St. Vincent Millay—all dead. Now: Edith Sitwell & Marianne Moore, the ageing giantesses & poetic godmothers. Phyllis McGinley is out—light verse: she's sold herself. Rather: May Swenson, Isabella Gardner, & most close, Adrienne Cecile Rich—who will soon be eclipsed by these eight poems." She stalked her rivals the way a poacher tracks game: diligently, and adequately camouflaged. Her erect posture and neat appearance masked the wild desire within.

To her surprise, she soon realized that Lowell held Sexton, that chaotic classroom presence, above all the rest. He seemed dazzled by her, but not in the way he usually was by pretty women (he'd had more than a few affairs, which his wife, the writer Elizabeth Hardwick, ably handled, along with other aspects of her husband's manic episodes). Instead, he demonstrated real respect for the voice, the confessing voice, that Sexton was honing that winter. Sexton hadn't been writing for very long, and she had only been in Lowell's class since September 1958, but she already had a gift for the construction of images. She expressed difficult feelings quite simply and truly. "She has very good things, and they get better, though there is a lot of loose stuff," Plath observed in her journal.

Once Lowell started reading some of his own work in progress in class, Plath better understood his admiration for Sexton. Here was this educated, celebrated poet writing about his parents, his marriage bed, even his mental illness. For students who had studied T. S. Eliot, the poet who made a pitch for the value of "impersonality" in art, Lowell's new writing was shocking and exhilarating. Perhaps one's own small, domestic life could be a fit subject for lyric poetry.

Lowell's validation meant a lot to his students. In 1959, he was the most respected poet in America. He'd been Consultant in Poetry to the Library of Congress, and he'd received a Pulitzer Prize in 1947 (and would win another in 1974). Dylan Thomas had once laid a hand upon his head. And because his family had come over on the *Mayflower*, to certain snobby Bostonians his genealogy was as impeccable as his sonnets.

The challenge for someone like Plath—a young poet under his tutelage, eager to be anointed—was that Lowell didn't tend to like women writers. He had two categories for writers: "major"— Wordsworth, Thomas, Stevens—and "minor." Almost every female poet was a "minor" writer, with a few exceptions. He praised his friend Bishop—flinty and keenly observant, she'd infiltrated the male canon—as well as Marianne Moore, whom Lowell had once introduced at an event as the greatest "*woman* poet." (Langston Hughes, who was also in attendance, sprang to his feet and suggested that Moore was the greatest "*Negro woman* poet." Perhaps a few grasped the irony.) Female poets who wrote about women's lives, such as Rukeyser and Denise Levertov, were particularly scorned. When Sexton confronted Lowell with a poem by the poet and editor Carolyn Kizer, a poem that indicted men in general—and Lowell in particular—for disrespecting women writers, he simply remarked, "Carolyn Kizer is a beautiful girl."

Such misogyny was ambient in the scene. Kathleen Spivack, a poet who studied at Boston University alongside Plath and Sexton, remembered that the "whole establishment was male!" Women could often be found serving as devoted poets' wives; they typed up manuscripts and managed their husbands' insecurities. Men lounged on couches in the poetry shops of Harvard Square, talking only to each other as women scurried around them. Those women who did write viewed each other as competition. Even the successful, respected poet Adrienne Rich, the winner of the coveted Yale Younger Poets Prize in 1950, worried about being overtaken by some young upstart. "Competing in the literary establishment felt to me very defeminizing," she later recalled.

It wasn't just Boston. Throughout the Northeast—across the nation—educated women were up against walls of self-assured men. This was a time when women without college degrees were employed as typists, and women with college degrees couldn't even get such a job (they were overqualified). But their employment woes didn't penetrate the consciousness of most public officials. As Adlai Stevenson reminded Plath's graduating class at Smith in 1955, a woman's "primary task" was "making homes and whole human beings in whom the rational values of freedom, tolerance, charity and free inquiry can take root." Make babies, not poems.

And so they did. But some women remained curious, and so they learned how to listen. They listened to men try to one-up each other, hoping to glean a bit of knowledge from the words being exchanged. As the writer Anne Roiphe remembered the New York literary scene, women were "at the edges of the conversation." "We girls, not yet called women," she recalled, "were like the Greek chorus, mopping up after the battle was over, emptying ashtrays, carrying the glasses to the sink. The main event was man to man, writer to writer."

Sexton, however, didn't want to be part of the chorus: she wanted to be a writer. But being a woman writer proved difficult, and she worried unceasingly. "Being a 'poet' in Boston is not so difficult except that there are hoards [*sic*] of us living here," she wrote to a friend that February. "The place is jammed with good writers—it's very depressing." Even after she'd won Lowell's admiration, earning his praise both in and out of class—he often called her on the phone to remark on her talents—she still worried that she was simply, irrepressibly feminine. In a letter to the poet W. D. Snodgrass, whom she'd met and befriended at a writers' conference at Antioch College, she worried about "writing as a woman writes," and confessed a "secret fear" that she was "a reincarnation of Edna St. Vincent." Although Lowell hadn't made any such comparison, Sexton still fretted over her femininity. "I wish I were a man—I would rather write the way a man writes," she told Snodgrass. For years, she believed that "she writes like a man" was the highest possible praise.

In March, the same month that Sexton confessed her fears to Snodgrass, Lowell surprised her by asking her to read aloud one of her poems in class. She had written "The Double Image" the prior fall; it had already been accepted for publication by *The Hudson Review*. Sexton had composed the poem during her first semester in

Lowell's class, in the fall of 1958. That fall had been a difficult time for her. Her father had suffered a stroke, and Mary Gray, who had been diagnosed with cancer in February 1957, found that the cancer had metastasized. When she was first diagnosed, Mary Gray had blamed Sexton for the cancer, thinking it was caused by the stress of caring for her mentally ill daughter. Since then, Sexton had harbored difficult, complicated feelings about her mother's illness. "Part of me would be free if she died," she once confessed to Dr. Orne. "It would also be awful—I would dissolve."

By February 1959, Mary Gray's cancer was terminal. Now, with her mother in her last days, Sexton, sitting in a quiet BU classroom, read aloud her poem about intergenerational need. (Mary Gray died the next month.) "The Double Image" is addressed to a young daughter, a child separated from her mother at a young age and for so long that she did not recognize her mother's voice when it called to her. The mother, the speaker of the poem, is reflecting on that period of estrangement—"the three autumns you did not live here"—and remembering her own guilt and distress at her failure to mother in the right way. "Ugly angels spoke to me," she recalls.

> The blame,
> I heard them say, was mine. They tattled
> like green witches in my head, letting doom
> leak like a broken faucet;
> as if doom had flooded my belly and filled your bassinet,
> an old debt I must assume.

Fear and error are passed from mother to child, via blood that simultaneously nourishes and condemns. The speaker knows about maternal curses, for she too is a daughter, a woman who inherited her mother's smile. She recalls recovering in her mother's house from a bout of insanity, "a partly mended thing, an outgrown child," and how her mother couldn't forgive her suicide attempt or her sadness. Instead, the speaker's mother commissions her daughter's portrait and has it hung in the family home next to her own, one of the "double images" of the poem's title. Meanwhile, the speaker's mother grows ill "as if death were catching," an inverse inheritance ("she looked at me / and said I gave her cancer"), while the speaker herself slowly recovers. The poem doubles the "double image"—the mother-daughter portrait—as the speaker, over the course of seven sections of irregular length, alternates between describing her relationship with her mother and her relationship with her daughter. She is the hinge point, the figure that slips between roles, giving care, receiving care, and sometimes doing both at once.

"The Double Image" ends with the speaker's reflections on the selfishness that mothers harbor and the impossible demands they make on their daughters:

I, who was never quite sure
about being a girl, needed another
life, another image to remind me.
And this was my worst guilt; you could not cure
nor soothe it. I made you to find me.

Lowell loved the poem—it fit his idea about the expression of a simple, difficult truth. "I *think* this means that he liked my reading and now likes the poem better," Sexton wrote to Snodgrass, describing the class session. "More better. As a whole it has a good dramatic structure—but many faults when picked apart—He didn't pick it apart tho." Plath, for her part, was intrigued by the poem. Sexton's work was more revealing than anything Plath was writing at the time. Inspired, Plath struck a poem from her book draft: "A leaf from Ann [*sic*] Sexton's book would do here," she reflected. "She has none of my clenches and an ease of phrase, and an honesty." In class, Lowell often grouped the two poets together in the hopes that they would influence each other. "Anne was more herself, and knew less," he said later, about the pair of poets. "I thought they might rub off on each other. Sylvia learned from Anne."

Soon after Sexton read her mother-daughter poem, Plath and Sexton formed their own sort of double image. Along with George

Starbuck, a poet and editor at Houghton Mifflin who had befriended Sexton in Holmes's workshop, they began socializing after class. Each Tuesday evening, the trio piled into Sexton's Ford and headed to the Ritz-Carlton hotel, a place Hardwick once described as "the only public place in Boston that could be called smart." Sexton often parked illegally, in a loading zone. "It's okay," she joked, "because we are only going to get loaded!" With a woman on each arm, Starbuck guided the group into the bar.

The three friends went through three rounds of drinks, sometimes four. The women compared suicide attempts and munched on potato chips. Starbuck, who was, by that point, completely enamored with Sexton, listened to the macabre conversation. (During this time, he and Sexton embarked on a short-lived affair.) Later, the trio headed to the Waldorf Cafeteria, with its checked tile floor and coffee urns, where dinner cost seventy cents. The friends claimed one of the small square tables, with salt and pepper shakers neatly arranged in the center, and they peered out the venetian blinds onto the streets of Boston. Sexton was drawn to "intense, skilled, perceptive, strange, blonde, lovely, Sylvia," but she thought that as a poet Plath was getting in her own way. "I told Mr. Lowell that I felt she dodged the point and did so perhaps because of her preoccupation with form," Sexton later wrote. "Those early poems were all in a cage (and not even her own cage at that)."

Plath planned to be "Poetess of America," as she'd written in her journal, but no matter how she reshuffled her lists of poets, she found that fame eluded her. Meanwhile, everyone else seemed to be meeting with success. That spring, Sexton sold her first book of poems to Houghton Mifflin, where Starbuck worked as an editor (he had encouraged the press to sign up Sexton's book). Plath took Sexton's success as a personal affront. At a celebratory dinner, Starbuck was, in Plath's words, "smug as a cream-fed cat," for, as Plath perceived it, Sexton was "in a sense his answer to me." Not that Starbuck was without his own achievement; in June, he won the Yale Younger Poets Prize. The same day that she heard about Starbuck's prize, Plath resolved to write a story about her suicide attempt (this after toying with the idea of writing a story about Sexton and Starbuck's affair). "There is an increasing market for mental-hospital stuff," she noted. "I am a fool if I don't relive, recreate it." *The Bell Jar*, her story turned novel about a "college girl suicide," was published in 1963. It was the last work of hers to be published while she was alive.

As Plath schemed, Sexton locked herself away in her study and furiously revised her book manuscript. Lowell had suggested replacing fifteen of the poems with new work. She composed at a rapid pace, but she wasn't entirely confident in her teacher's advice. "I am just not sure about Lowell," she wrote to Kizer, author of the accusatory poem, now a friend and regular correspondent. "I think he may like my work because it is all a little crazy or about being crazy and it may be that he relates to me and my 'bedlam poetry.'"

Lowell did share Sexton's interest in writing about one's personal struggles. In May, the same month Sexton sold her manuscript, Lowell's *Life Studies* was published. M. L. Rosenthal, reviewing the book for *The Nation*, argued that Lowell's poetry was "soul's therapy." Titled "Poetry as Confession," the review explained how "Lowell removes the mask. His speaker is unequivocally himself, and it is hard not to think of *Life Studies* as a series of personal confidences, rather shameful, that one is honor-bound not to reveal." The book won the 1960 National Book Award and signaled a revolutionary movement in American poetry, one called "confessional," after Rosenthal's review. The designation was at first meant to be derisive, but after the success of *Life Studies* it was a term a poet might want to claim.

For many years, the writers who once sat in that small, dark classroom on Commonwealth Avenue—Sexton, Plath, and Lowell himself—would all be grouped together as "confessional" writers. The label always annoyed Sexton, who hated to find herself lumped into any category. She particularly resented the idea that she had learned her poetic style from Lowell. At times, she denied his influence entirely and claimed not to have read his work. If anything, she explained, she had learned from him what *not* to write. What he had taught her was a mind-set, a way of thinking about poetry, but her writing was her own. "Jesus, I'm a defensive creature!" she wrote to

Snodgrass in June 1959. "And in manicy moments I say to myself, I'm better than Lowell!—How is *that* for poetic conceit.! ! !"

After the seminar concluded, Sexton spent the summer putting the finishing touches on her manuscript. By the time her book went to the printers in August, she was far from the "reincarnation of Edna St. Vincent" that she had felt herself to be in October. She had sold a book and given a reading at the Poets' Theatre in Cambridge. Kumin—who was herself working on a book manuscript—and Starbuck had been by her side at the event. She had weathered the anxieties and criticisms of Lowell's seminar. In a competitive, treacherous literary climate, Sexton had emerged triumphant.

Others did not thrive. Plath soon left Boston, fearing what a life alone with Hughes would mean for her. "I have no life separate from his, am likely to become a mere accessory," she wrote just a few weeks after leaving, with Hughes, for a residency at Yaddo arts colony in Saratoga Springs, New York. Adrienne Rich, Plath's rival, was meanwhile living "in such despondency"; she couldn't see how she could continue writing while caring for her three children. Her life seemed to be over. Kumin was teaching at Tufts; she was the first woman hired by the English department, in 1958, although she was allowed to teach only physical education majors and dental technicians. Even the formidable Hardwick felt anxious and angry, trapped in a city that she thought of as "spindly-legged . . . slightly mad with neurotic repressions, provincialism, and earnestness without intellectual seriousness." She and Lowell soon left for New York.

Even when women writers managed to find each other in male-dominated, mid-century literary Boston, the friendships they formed were often fragile, subject to competition and jealousy. There were so few seats at the seminar table and so many young writers clamoring to be recognized. The connections they formed were ephemeral: the nights at the bar ended, and the women retreated home to waiting husbands. Come morning, despite its pressures (or perhaps because of them), the married couple was more stable than the female friendship.

This fragmentary collection of female writers—Sexton, Rich,

Plath, Kumin—remarkable for its concentration of talent and future fame, never cohered into a true community. In light of how difficult it was to forge connections between women, Sexton's friendship with her neighbor Kumin—initiated in an adult education classroom and renewed in the Newton library—seems all the more remarkable. But even their friendship sometimes came under threat when a powerful man decided that it was his right, even his responsibility, to intervene in the hopes of helping one woman free herself from the other.

The threat came in 1961, just a few years after Kumin and Sexton had met and bonded. From the summer through the fall of that year, Holmes and several people from his seminar participated in a kind of informal workshop; the poets came together to share works in progress and trade jokes and jibes. The group included Starbuck, Sam Albert, Ted Weiss, and, of course, Holmes. The participants took turns hosting the workshop in the evenings and made sure to provide drinks. Kumin's children hated it when their mother hosted the group. "Oh, the poets!" they complained as the workshop began. "Now we'll never get any sleep." The children fought for the privilege of sleeping in the room over the garage, the part of the house farthest away from the raucous gatherings.

Kumin later described the feeling of this workshop: "During this period, all of us wrote and revised prolifically, competitively, as if all the wolves of the world were at our backs. Our sessions were jagged, intense, often angry, but also loving." The poets spoke passionately, objecting to unwelcome suggestions and arguing for necessary revisions. Sexton was the worst offender. She fought for her poems with the ferocity of a lioness—"it was like they were taking my babies away from me," she later said—only to go home and make the very changes her peers had suggested. She helped herself to whatever alcohol was on offer and then pranced around the room, shouting with delight at her friends' brilliant lines.

Holmes detested Sexton's performances on these evenings. He hated what he called her "insistent me-me-me" way of being, which he thought infected her poetry. He had never liked her: not when she was a novice in 1957, and not now that she was a published poet. Her drinking bothered him—he was a recovering alcoholic—as did her instability. Kumin and Sexton suspected that his first wife had suffered from mental illness and died by suicide and that he disliked Sexton because he saw resemblances between these two women. Everything about Sexton triggered his anger and defensiveness.

The conflict between Holmes and Sexton had been brewing for years. They'd had their first row in 1959, when Sexton, while studying with Lowell, asked Holmes to read her first book manuscript. Holmes had made no secret of the fact that he disliked Sexton's overly personal poetry—the very style that Lowell so admired—and he discouraged her from publishing the book as it stood. Sexton wasn't surprised by her teacher's reaction, but his criticisms stung. She drafted a letter, in which she admitted to being hurt and attempted to flatter Holmes. Despite their differences, she wrote, she was learning so much from him; he'd taught her with "firm patience and a kind smile." How could he turn away from her now? In the end, Sexton didn't send the letter. She couldn't find the courage to challenge such an influential man directly.

In place of the letter, she sent Holmes a poem. She called it "For John, Who Begs Me Not to Enquire Further." She wanted to show Holmes just what value she saw in the experience of madness and why she thought it was a subject fit for poetry. The speaker begins the poem by claiming that she saw "something worth learning" by examining her inner life. She then flies through a string of different metaphors to describe her mind: it's first a diary, then an asylum, then, most intriguing, "glass, an inverted bowl," something that she can study. And it is through this self-inquiry that the speaker comes to understand others. Though her own life once appeared to her as something "private," she sees, by the end of the poem, how sharing her personal experiences can help her forge interpersonal connection. "Then it was more than myself," she muses, imagining how her inner world might be refigured as her reader's house, or her reader's kitchen—private, domestic space. The face she sees in the mirror could just as easily be her reader's: "my face, your face." The poem defends confessional poetry, showing how easily the personal becomes public.

"For John" was an olive branch, and Holmes flung it aside. He believed that poetry should be a form of self-transcendence. Like the John addressed in the poem, he preferred to "turn away" from the cracked, awkward beauty that confessional poetry presented. Sexton was willing to learn from Holmes, but in the end she had no interest in transcending the self; after all, it was her poetic subject. The two never saw eye to eye.

Sexton decided to publish her book without Holmes's approval. *To Bedlam and Part Way Back* was released by Houghton Mifflin in April 1960. She received a positive review in *The New York Times:* "Mrs. Sexton's craft is quick and deft. There are no long-sustained metaphors, no elaborate conceits. She is master of the simple declarative sentence . . . [T]he pauses, accents and rhymes are varied so skillfully that there is no sense of strain." Sexton was pleased by the review and thought it would sway Holmes's impression of her work. She told her therapist that Holmes had indeed "changed his mind about my 'bedlam' poetry . . . he (John Holmes) had been wrong."

But as it turned out, Sexton was wrong about Holmes's conversion. In the summer of 1961, about a year after the glowing *Times* review, Holmes tried to expel Sexton from the informal workshop. To do this, he turned to her best friend.

Holmes had some influence with Kumin. Responding to her work, he was encouraging. He also helped her secure her first teaching job. Perhaps he thought that Kumin would have influence over Sexton where he did not, or perhaps he wanted to drive a wedge between the two women, such that Sexton, the more vulnerable one, would begin to feel herself unwelcome. He wrote a letter to Kumin, confessing his frustration. Sexton was "on my mind unpleasantly too much of the time between our workshops," he wrote. "I can't stand another meeting and her there," he continued. "She is utterly selfish, blood-sucking, destructive, and I'm not sorry for her, not one bit, but instead getting pretty damned bored with her." (One wonders if "bored" is the best adjective to describe Holmes's feelings here.) "I not only think she is poison for you," he continued, "but no good for anyone else." He knew the two women were close, and he claimed to feel bad about sharing these thoughts with Kumin—though he had lodged versions of this complaint with her several times before. But he was adamant that Sexton was a bad influence; others, he claimed, shared his opinion. He also "resented her dependence" on Kumin. He explained, "I think she has been very bad for you. If I were Vic, honest to God I'd make every effort to get you to break up with her. I wish I knew what he thinks."

The paternalistic letter tested Kumin's loyalties. Kumin confronted a decision that could alter the course of her budding poetic career. Would she obey her respected instructor, the man who had arranged her first teaching job, who placed her poems on his undergraduate exams, who called her "darling" in his letters, who wrote that he thought that she and he were much alike? Or would she support her friend—a woman who had once scared her, who demanded much of her, but who also gave her much in return?

"Here was my Christian academic daddy, saying stay away from her, she's bad for you," Kumin recalled years later. "He was my patron; he got me my job at Tufts." Denying Holmes could have disastrous consequences. Kumin pondered his request for several days; when Holmes hadn't heard back by the weekend, he wrote another letter, half apologizing, half reiterating his request that Kumin sever ties with Sexton.

Finally, Kumin wrote back. She told Holmes she felt he had put her in the middle and that she had somehow been included in his "disapproval and anger." Holmes reassured her that this was not the case, and he allowed that the workshop wouldn't break up; Sexton would not be expelled. But he insisted again that Sexton be steered in a new creative direction, and he saddled Kumin with this responsibility. "You can't let her alone to go on doing this," he warned. "It could be on your conscience, that fierce and famous conscience, that you didn't do what is to be done."

Kumin had a choice to make, a choice that could affect her budding career and her friend's life. She chose her friend.

For the next thirteen years—that is, for the rest of Sexton's life—

she helped Sexton write the confessional verses that so chafed Holmes. She stayed on the other end of the telephone as Sexton composed poems one line at a time. She watched Sexton's daughters. She dropped in on Sexton's husband when Sexton traveled to Europe, and she helped her friend come home when the travel proved to be too much. She was Sexton's friend and confidante, collaborator and colleague. She offered support and love that Sexton valued deeply and did her best to reciprocate. No matter what Kumin had on her conscience, it is hard to imagine any friend doing more.

CHAPTER 3

Writer-Human-Woman

IN SOME WAYS, the women of Boston were lucky.

Provincial in comparison to New York or Paris, Boston in the 1950s could still claim to be a cultural center. It boasted excellent art schools and universities, as well as a robust population of educated elites, people who would purchase books and attend poetry readings hosted in cavernous halls. Like-minded women passed through town, and small circles of friends formed for a few months or for half a year. To be sure, Boston was cold and intimidating; women like Plath, Sexton, and Kumin often found themselves in classrooms filled with men, where, nervous and eager, they were reminded that greatness could never be theirs. Still, the city provided these young poets with plenty of examples of those who did become great, and it facilitated their ephemeral, complicated friendships.

It was harder elsewhere. Away from the East Coast, writers, particularly women writers, were even more lonely and isolated, desperate to succeed and yet flummoxed about how to do so. They didn't have access to the institutions and networks available to a writer like Sexton. Instead, they had to work to live, then find time to do the work that made them want to live. They wrote in quiet houses with sleeping children; their drafts languished in drawers. Instead of reading to others in workshop, they reread their own words in silence.

The only way to meet like-minded women was, appropriately enough, through the written word. Women writers read each other, and when they were brave, they wrote to those whom they admired. In this way, isolated women made seemingly impossible connections and began to imagine possible lives.

In November 1960, roughly a year after she'd finished drafting "The Double Image," Sexton received an exciting mail delivery. *New World Writing*, a literary anthology edited by Stewart Richardson and Corlies M. Smith, contained her first published work of fiction: a mother-daughter story, another attempt to wrestle with the shadow of Mary Gray. "Dancing the Jig" is narrated by a woman at a suburban party who is battling frenetic impulses: she wants to leap up and dance; she wants to speed up time rather than wait for conflict to arrive or for chaos to descend. Like a patient on an analyst's couch, she thinks back to a dinner table scene from childhood that, she suspects, gave rise to her condition. In this memory, the narrator, a preteen, faces a drunk father, hostile sisters, and a difficult aunt—clear avatars for Sexton's own family members. The figure that looms largest, though, is the mother, who holds her daughter's attention by criticizing her steadily and without interruption. The narrator, experienced in the art of self-examination, connects her childhood anxiety with her present restlessness; she realizes that she anticipates disaster and so, through her own behavior, invites it. "Dancing the Jig," one of Sexton's favorite phrases for describing her vulnerability to Mary Gray, is an analysis session rendered in prose.

Sexton had been pleased with the story when she'd first written it—she thought it demonstrated good psychological insight—but seeing it now among work by more experienced writers, she felt deflated. Other writers demonstrated more judiciousness, more critical instincts. "There are no guards in prose," she once mused, alluding to how poetic form restrains overwhelming feeling. In prose, as in life, Sexton was unguarded and less graceful than she would have liked to be.

There was one long story in the anthology that struck Sexton as the ideal representation of a difficult mother. "Tell Me a Riddle," by Tillie Olsen, narrated the last months of an old woman's life. Eva, married for forty-seven years, is committed to finding solitude, even within her marriage. Her husband, David, wants to move to a retirement community, but Eva refuses; she is enjoying the privileged privacy of the old. "Tranquility from having the empty house no longer an enemy, for it stayed clean," she reflects. "Not as in the days when it was her family, the life in it, that had seemed the enemy: tracking, smudging, littering, dirtying, engaging her in endless defeating battle—and on whom her endless defeat had been spewed." She swears that she will never again "be forced to move to the rhythms of others." When Eva is diagnosed with terminal cancer, she and her husband make a pilgrimage to see their children and grandchildren. David having sold their home, they end up in Los Angeles, where David and a granddaughter, Jeannie, care for the dying Eva, who sings songs from her Russian girlhood and shares memories. As observers perceive it, her spirit leaves at the story's end, and Jeannie implores David, who is racked with grief, to return to his wife's deathbed and "help her poor body to die." The story is a masterful blend of vernacular speech—"Because I'm use't," says Eva, explaining why she won't leave her home—and modernist style. Olsen wove together allusion, stream of consciousness, and lively dialogue to create a moving portrait of an elderly couple. It was based on her own parents and on her mother, Ida, who had died from cancer in 1956.

"Tell Me a Riddle" struck a chord. As a writer, Sexton admired Olsen's facility with images: in her weakness, Eva is "light, like a bird, the fluttering body, the little claw hands, the beaked shadow on her face." As a woman, and as a daughter, Sexton was moved by the exquisite rendering of the complicated love that family members feel for difficult women. Admiring and a bit jealous of Olsen's skill, she later wrote to Nolan Miller, "I read Tillie Olsen's story and I cried and I was ashamed to have my story appear . . . She is a genius." She decided she wouldn't write any more prose until she could find another writer who could teach her.

Remarkably, Sexton's insecurities didn't prevent her from heaping praise on those she envied. She decided to write to the story's author; she didn't know Olsen at all, but she felt as though she'd come to know her through her fiction. Writing fan mail was nothing new: Sexton was an avid letter writer, and she didn't hesitate before writing to writers she admired. These writers were often men: Sexton wrote consistently to Snodgrass, Lowell, and the poet Anthony Hecht. With these correspondents, she wheedled and charmed as she might have done at a party, making herself seem attractive and vulnerable at once.

With Olsen, a woman whom she didn't know, a woman with whom she shared no mutual acquaintances, Sexton struck a different note. "My eyes are still crying and I cannot possibly tell you how much your story has moved me," she began. She praised Olsen's perfect story, written in a "human key," then confessed that she too had a story in the anthology. She was embarrassed by her work, though, when she compared it to Olsen's. She was a novice at fiction writing, she explained; she'd never published prose, but she did have some better poems. With typical self-justification, she explained that she was talking about her own talent only to show that her evaluation was worth something. And she evaluated the story quite highly: she believed it would be read for years to come. (Sexton's admiration for this particular story never ceased; years later, she sat alone in a red chair, rereading "Tell Me a Riddle" and crying.)

The letter reached Olsen on Laidley Street in San Francisco's Mission District, a place far from Boston in both geographic and spiritual senses. The Mission was a working-class neighborhood, populated, as Olsen once wrote, with "many Latin American, Negro, Samoan, firstgeneration [*sic*] Irish & Italian, families." Olsen loved it. A beautiful adobe church, the oldest building in the city, stood at its center, and Dolores Park extended from its western border. Riding the bus, or watching her children play, Olsen could hear snatches of different dialects. She recorded interesting phrases on scraps of papers, then balled them up and stuffed them in the pockets of her slacks as she carried about her day.

Olsen herself was as different from Sexton as bohemian San Francisco was from a stuffy Boston suburb. Sexton was a glamorous woman who wore makeup and matching jewelry. Olsen dressed in wash-and-wear slacks and had worked since she was eighteen. Sexton's only work experience had been the small jobs she held during the early years of her marriage; then, if she and Kayo were ever a little short on funds, her mother helped out. Sexton was born into money, a homebody who stayed in the Boston area all her life, while Olsen was a first-generation, working-class American, an itinerant, and an agitator.

But she was also, like Sexton, a writer, although writing had frustrated her for much of her life. At the time she received Sexton's letter, Olsen had just gotten back into writing after twenty years. She had been something of a literary celebrity in the 1930s. Back then, she was a good-looking and energetic activist, a woman who prompted comparisons to the Marxist theorist and activist Rosa Luxemburg. Two men had fought for her affections: Abe Goldfarb, with whom she had her first daughter (Karla, after Karl Marx), and Jack Olsen, her eventual husband, with whom she had three more girls. Two different publishing houses, Random House and Macmillan, sparred over the right to publish her first novel. She befriended leftist literary figures like Jack Conroy, Nelson Algren, William Saroyan, and Sanora Babb. For a few years, she was, according to a local San Francisco paper, the "most sought-after writer in the United States."

By 1960, those years felt like another life. Olsen had spent the 1940s and 1950s raising four children, doing community organizing, and working a bunch of day jobs to support her family. She wrote when she could—on the bus home from work, at night after her children were asleep—but she struggled to complete any works of fiction. It was only within the last five years that she'd managed to write and publish a few short stories. At the time she published "Tell Me a

Riddle," she was overworked, underpaid, and nearly fifty years old. She was afraid that she'd missed her chance at becoming the great proletarian writer she had long hoped to be.

As far as she could remember, Olsen had always wanted to write. Born in 1912 in Omaha, Nebraska, Tybile "Tillie" Lerner was something of an organic intellectual. She placed a portrait of Virginia Woolf on a desk in her childhood home; she modeled her adolescent writing on Woolf and Gertrude Stein. She read John Dos Passos and Willa Cather. When she was in high school, she wrote a column for the student newspaper called "Squeaks" that satirized schoolteachers and the mandatory Shakespeare requirement.

Tillie was as passionate about politics as she was about literature. Her parents were Yiddish-speaking Russian Jews and avowed socialists—Sam Lerner, her father, was a fan of Eugene Debs—and they were suspicious of communists. In 1930, however, the Communist Party had enormous appeal for young, idealistic Americans who believed that the social order could be radically transformed. Across the nation, Communist Party organizers gathered. John Reed Clubs—organizations of Marxist artists and intellectuals—launched in major cities. Towns big and small crawled with members of the Young Communist League, who cast off bourgeois notions of sexual propriety and thrived on a mix of romance and revolution. Tillie joined the class struggle, dropping out of high school and hopping from boxcar to boxcar as many underemployed people did in the second and third decades of the twentieth century, organizing labor power.

She and Abe, whom she'd met at eighteen, eventually made their way west and settled in Stockton, California, in the Central Valley. Tillie merged her literary and political interests and began writing for the Communist Party publication *The Daily Worker* and a new magazine called *Partisan Review,* published out of New York's John Reed Club. In 1934, *Partisan Review* accepted half of the first chapter of her prospective novel about life in the Wyoming coal

Tillie Olsen as a young woman

mines. The editor, Philip Rahv, was eager to publish the voices of the proletariat; he accepted Tillie's excerpt immediately and gave it the title "The Iron Throat." The piece, published later that year, was remarkable. Tillie married the kind of stream of consciousness used by Woolf and James Joyce to the socialist realism demanded by the 1930s political Left.

Tillie aimed to live the same political ideals she advanced in her fiction. In 1934, Tillie and Abe moved to San Francisco to support a strike by the city's longshoremen. During the strike, Tillie met a union leader named Jack Olsen. He was strong, handsome, and energetic, the kind of man who spoke easily at rallies. Together, they took on a slew of projects—leafleting, organizing, and registering voters. (In his later years, Jack befriended all the sex workers who walked his neighborhood streets in San Francisco; he registered each of them to vote and talked over every ballot issue.) Tillie took to sleeping at Communist Party headquarters in downtown San Francisco. She wanted to stay close to the action—and to Jack. Her interest was reciprocated, though the two did not marry until they reconnected in 1936, by which point she had left Abe. They had three daughters together: Julie, born in 1938; Kathie, born in 1943; and Laurie, born in 1947. According to Olsen's biographer, Panthea Reid, Jack's co-workers teased him about having "nothing but girls."

While she was organizing in the 1930s, Olsen found, to her delight, that her literary reputation was growing. "The Iron Throat" was praised in *The New Republic* as an example of "early genius." Publishers, looking to showcase a woman's angle on Depression-era America, besieged Rahv for Olsen's contact information. Both Bennett Cerf of Random House and the renowned writer and editor Malcolm Cowley, then at *The New Republic,* reached Olsen and requested to see more writing; other editors expressed interest as well. Olsen thrilled to these overtures, but at the time she received them, her hands were tied; she had been arrested for her involvement in the strike and imprisoned. A lawyer facilitated her correspondence with editors and publishers. After the investigative journalist Lincoln Steffens helped pay her $1,000 bail and got her released from jail, her first priority was the completion of her report on the summer's many strike activities. Her piece, titled "The Strike," which ended up the cover story of *Partisan Review*'s 1934 summer issue, began,

> Do not ask me to write of the strike and the terror. I am on a battlefield, and the increasing stench and smoke sting the eyes so it is impossible to turn them back into the past. You leave me only this night to drop the bloody garment of Todays, to cleave through the gigantic events that have crashed one upon the other, to the first beginning. If I could go away for a while, if there were time and quiet, perhaps I could do it . . . I could stumble back into the past and slowly, painfully rear the structure in all its towering magnificence, so that the beauty and heroism, the terror and significance of those days, would enter your heart and sear it forever with the vision.

Olsen told of the "heroism, the terror and significance" of the longshoremen, but she also told of her own terror and her own literary role. The piece was as much about her own struggle as a writer as it was about workers' rights. It described the value of time and quiet for the working writer; attaining both would prove to be elusive for her for years to come.

By 1961, these heady days of bidding wars and literary parties were long in the past for Olsen. The optimism of the Popular Front, the coalition of leftists and liberals that had come together to fight fascism, had given way to the paranoia of the McCarthy era. Throughout the 1950s, the Olsens were often near broke or on the edge of poverty. (Jack was apprenticing as a printer, and Olsen picked up odd jobs and occasionally borrowed money.) Instead of writing, Olsen worked as a community organizer, a typist, a secretary. "She worked, she had a job, just like my father had a job," her second daughter, Julie, recalled. "They weren't careers." Most of the time, Olsen worked not for her own fulfillment but simply to earn a living. While some of her work, such as her political organizing, accorded with her values, much of it did not. She sheltered her daughters from the worst of anticommunism and conformity; she saved up for their birthdays and showered them with as many books as she could afford. She even handled surprise visits from FBI agents—who kept a file on Olsen until 1970—with humor and grace.

Still, Olsen churned with discontentment. She had a bunch of ideas for stories, including one about her eldest, Karla, but she had so little time to write. Jack was still making apprentice wages, which forced Olsen to pick up modeling jobs for print advertisers and to get creative about maintaining a household of six on a strict budget. She loved her daughters—in 1954, they were twenty-two, sixteen, eleven, and seven—but she had been mothering for many years now, and she was far from done.

She described her frustration consistently in journal entries from these years. Olsen rarely had a notebook; instead, she typed out her thoughts in incomplete sentences on scrap paper, and she usually forgot to write the date. "Not a moment to sit down and think," reads one such entry. "That death of the creative process . . . I am being destroyed." In another: "I don't even know if I could still write . . . Life (the job that takes so much of me, the family that takes somuch [*sic*] of me) has its own anaesthesia. I am so weary physically at night I sleep well and dreamlessly." Elsewhere, she powerfully described her craving for time and space:

Pushed by the most elementary force—money—further more
impossibly away from writing . . . Compulsion so fierce at
night
    brutal impulse to shove Julie away from typewriter
    voices of kids calling—to be able to chop chop chop like
hands from the liveboat to leave me free . . . My conflict—to
reconcile work with life . . . Time it festered and congested
postponed deferred and once started up again the insane
desire, like an aroused woman . . . conscious of the creative
abilities within me, more than I can encompass . . . 1953–
1954: I keep on dividing myself and flow apart, I who want to
run in one river and become great.

This was Olsen's rendition of the acrobatics Kumin had described
to her mother. It was her way of pacing like a caged tiger, as Sexton had put it. But unlike Kumin or Sexton, at the time she wrote
these words, Olsen had the additional burden of wage earning.
(Kumin worked, too, but she didn't face the same economic pressure
as Olsen.) She was split in more directions than either of the poets
could have imagined.

Olsen could never clear enough time and space to work in the
way she liked: slowly, meticulously, and with numerous revisions.
In 1954, thanks to a strange twist of fate, she found the time she
needed: ulcerative colitis landed her in the hospital, and she received
six weeks of disability granted by government-funded insurance,
weeks she used to write. (She called the disability leave her "Dr. Raimundi fellowship.") She finished a story she had been working on
for nearly a year, a dramatic monologue delivered by a working-class
woman, "a young mother . . . a distracted mother," struggling to care
for her children while holding down multiple jobs. The unnamed
narrator feels guilty that she cannot afford for her children "the soil
of easy growth." Her remembrances of earlier years are interrupted
by the demands of the day: ironing that needs to be finished, a baby
crying who needs to be changed. The story ends with a kind of secu-
lar prayer, a plea to someone—perhaps to the teacher, to whom the

monologue is addressed, or perhaps to the reader, who is witness to this private suffering—to help her eldest daughter believe that she is "more than this dress on the ironing board, helpless before the iron."

When she finished the story, then titled "Help Her to Believe," she sent a copy to Arthur Foff, her eldest daughter Karla's creative writing instructor at San Francisco State. She also described to him some of her challenges in balancing writing with motherhood. For instance, she had just taken Kathie, now in junior high, to a clinic for a serious ear and throat infection and then spent weeks caring for her as she recovered. Foff, who had seen an early version of the story and had at that point agreed to let Olsen sit in on his class, encouraged her to apply for a real fellowship, one that would give her time away from work and from family obligations. Olsen mailed "Help Her to Believe," along with a recommendation from Foff, to Stanford's Creative Writing Program. A few weeks later, in April 1955, she answered the phone to hear a strange man's voice. He claimed to be the eminent novelist Wallace Stegner, Kumin's former teacher, who had left Harvard to found the Creative Writing Program at Stanford. Stegner offered her one of three Jones fellowships (later renamed for Stegner) for the coming academic year. Olsen was speechless.

From the fall of 1955 through the spring of 1956, Olsen rode the bus south twice a week to Palo Alto to study. The sprawling, luxurious Stanford campus, with its Spanish ranch-style architecture and palm trees, seemed a world away from the crowded, chaotic Mission District where the Olsen family lived. Bougainvillea and cacti lined the paths that took her to a red-roofed building where her workshop was held. The social novelist Richard Scowcroft taught the fall section of the course, and her old correspondent Malcolm Cowley, now an editor at Viking, taught in the spring. At Stanford, Olsen offered encouragement to her classmates and worked on a story about a sailor who was down on his luck. She was nervous that she would be the oldest student, or that she wouldn't be good enough, but she fit in better than expected. The other students had heard of her success during the 1930s, and they admired the writing she presented. By the end of the spring semester, she had three new stories.

Olsen hadn't published anything since before World War II; within a year, she placed three stories in different magazines. "Help Her to Believe," the piece that had restarted her writing career, appeared first in *Stanford Short Stories* and then in *The Pacific Spectator*. A story about race relations called "Baptism" was published in *Prairie Schooner*. "Hey Sailor" appeared in Nolan Miller's *New Campus Writing No. 2*. These were little campus magazines, not the prestigious magazines that had published her during the 1930s, but this was still progress. What's more, the Olsens finally had the money for a washing machine (up to this point, Olsen had used a device with a hand crank that could be turned to squeeze out soap rinse—a very labor-intensive process). Olsen was exuberant.

Still, she craved more time to write. Family and work obligations reduced her writing time to a sliver. In the years leading up to and during her Stanford fellowship, she had taken on additional responsibilities: she had supported her mother-in-law when the latter's husband died; she had hosted for a period of months T. Mike Walker, a young man from a troubled family who had befriended Julie, now a student at Mission High. Olsen had managed to use many of these familial obligations as inspiration for her work. She took notes on the friendship between the adolescent Kathie and an African American classmate and used them to write the story "Baptism." Another visitor, Whitey Gleason, served as the inspiration for "Hey Sailor." But she struggled to find the time to transform her notes and scraps into stories. It seemed that there would never be a time of ease for her, a time when she could write freely and without worrying about neglecting her household tasks. "Last night—be honest—wanting—needing a different life," she wrote in her journal. She made a list of the features of this "different life." The first thing on her list was "solitude."

And then there was the matter of money. Unlike the stereotypical (though far from universal) mid-century nuclear family, the Olsens couldn't rely on a single male breadwinner. Thus, when her fellowship at Stanford finished, Olsen returned to secretarial work. Some days, there was no one in the office, and Olsen could use the time to write. Other days, she resented the ways that what she called "business-ese" and "legalese" adulterated her prose. If work was stifling, home could be chaotic. She won another writing grant, from the Ford Foundation, but like the Stanford fellowship, it too had an expiration date. Wage labor always loomed.

And so, when Olsen and Sexton connected in the spring of 1961, they were moving in opposite directions. Sexton was surging. She'd published her first book, *Bedlam,* and was beginning work on a second project. Her daughters, now eight and six, were often in the care of others. Olsen, though, was like a rock climber clutching a precipice; she needed to use all her strength and concentration to keep from falling. Though she was about to publish a book with the small press Lippincott—a collection of four short stories called *Tell Me a Riddle*—she was far less optimistic than Sexton. She was further along in life: she was now forty-nine, silver-haired, striking but no longer young, in her own words "substantial . . . sze. 14 clothes; 9-C width clodhoppers; stubby, clumsy hands." She'd been living with her writing ambitions for decades—Sexton had harbored them for only a few years—and she knew all too well how easy it was to get caught up in work and family and to let go of writing time.

While both women were passionate about writing, they approached the craft differently. Sexton had a tremendous work ethic and a knack for getting her poetry in print. ("Jesus God! You're publishing everywhere!" her mentor Snodgrass once remarked.) Sexton might revise a poem six or seven times, but eventually she would send it out, even if she weren't fully satisfied. Olsen worked more slowly. She was a perfectionist who rarely let anyone see her work prematurely—not teachers, not editors, not even prospective agents. When she saw proofs of a story prepublication, she'd insert a number of changes. She even revised material that was already in print, making notes on her own copies and sometimes even requesting changes post-printing. Some, including Cowley, saw her perfectionism as a bad habit to be defeated; others, like Miller, defended Olsen's process. "I suppose some would say she has the fault of being too slow a producer," Miller once wrote. "These must be impatient people . . . who are as well satisfied with synthetic diamonds as real ones." But it was nonetheless true that Olsen had lost many opportunities because she'd lingered over stories or refused requests to show someone her writing. Her perfectionism hampered her as much as her jobs and mothering duties did; it wasn't clear that doing away with the latter would improve the former. Scowcroft once accused Olsen of being most productive when her conditions were hardest.

Despite all these differences, Olsen saw what she and this faraway poet had in common. In her response, she called Sexton "dear related to me" and expressed her desire to talk more. She also informed Sexton she'd cut out the latter's author photo from a copy of *Bedlam* and hung it above her crowded writing desk, among portraits of Leo Tolstoy, Thomas Hardy, and Walt Whitman—"writers who help," Olsen called them. In a subsequent letter, she chided Sexton for being overly self-critical: "That was your *first* one, remarkable and asks pride, not harshness." Olsen was generous and humble in ways that belied her own insecurities. She invited Sexton to write to her again sometime. Sexton did so almost immediately, and a vibrant correspondence took shape.

Their exchanges were remarkable for their generosity and their candor. Each writer was willing to confess to fears and errors. Each noticed the specific talents that the other possessed. In 1961, Sexton might have been the more famous of the two writers, but she didn't have Olsen's quiet confidence. "As a writer, I am jealous of your talent," Sexton wrote once to Olsen, "but then, as a writer-human-woman, I am so glad of it and for it." She managed to push aside any competitive feelings to participate in what would become a symbiotic relationship. Each had something the other wanted. Olsen had hard-earned wisdom, accrued through years of experience as a writer and as a worker. In her letters, she would reassure Sexton, offer book suggestions, and, simply by writing about her own struggles, give her a dose of perspective. Sexton, meanwhile, offered Olsen something the older writer desperately needed: access to the literary networks of the East Coast.

Olsen occasionally described how hard it was to find time to write, given all her obligations, including her need to work outside the home. In a letter written in May 1961, just before the publication of *Tell Me a Riddle*, she described how she must "leave writing (for a job, to earn money)." Sexton, self-conscious about her own economic privilege, wrote a sympathetic letter in response. She tried to imagine a way that Olsen's loss could become a gain and suggested that maybe hardship and work experience could be inspiring. But she realized she was being naive: "It takes such time to build your stories and without the time . . . how can you write?"

Unknowingly, Sexton had tapped into one of Olsen's major social justice issues. To Olsen, one of the great tragedies of social and economic inequality was that art became inaccessible to many people. Working people couldn't afford to buy books or see plays, nor could they scrape together the time to make art of their own (and certainly the wages they'd receive for any artistic labor wouldn't be enough to support a family). So many stories remained untold. She knew that it didn't have to be this way. During the 1930s, Olsen had glimpsed another world, one in which the federal government provided financial support with the Works Progress Administration (WPA), propping up the art world—theater, music, drama, writing, photography—in a time of economic crisis. Olsen imagined a time when everyone would have access to art and culture and everyone would have a chance at producing the same. Sexton knew nothing about this dream; she struggled when she had *too much* free time, with only her thoughts to fill it. She had never had to balance writing and wage earning. Through their correspondence, each learned that there were other hells quite different from her own.

Rarely did a friendship from mid-century America cut across class and political divisions, as Sexton and Olsen's did. During the 1950s, the height of anticommunism in America, working-class activists like Olsen lived in states of acute paranoia, and rightly so. Senator Joseph McCarthy conducted a witch hunt, and J. Edgar Hoover kept files on anyone who expressed a hint of leftist thinking. The Hollywood Ten—prominent screenwriters and directors persecuted by the House Un-American Activities Committee—made national news. After World War II, one-third of Americans believed that Communist Party members should be killed or imprisoned; by 1950, only 1 percent of Americans thought that communists were entitled to freedom of thought. Twenty percent of American workers faced some kind of loyalty test from their employers. And yet Sexton was open to Olsen, to her different and unusual life. Likewise, Olsen, who grappled with her own fears of inquisition and arrest, opened up to a woman from the other side of the country, even though she could not be sure of her correspondent's allegiances.

This was more than an act of sympathy; it was an act of trust.

Slowly, letter by letter and poem by poem, a network of women writers was starting to form. It stretched from the Bay Area to the suburbs of Boston. It extended over the Atlantic, to London, where Plath waited for news from Sexton and others in the States. They'd approached each other tentatively, these women, with a mix of formality and fear; they'd waited for signs before revealing too much of themselves. They were deploying a timeworn strategy: seek out the other woman in the room and assess whether she is a foe or a friend.

A woman can be an ally—a shoulder to cry on, a sympathetic ear—or she can be a turncoat, a double agent, someone who will smile at you and then exploit your insecurities. In a literary world where women competed viciously—with men and with other women—relationships formed slowly, over the course of years. It took months before these friendships held firmly. Sexton and Kumin, alike in status and age, cemented a friendship in person, while Sexton and Olsen had to transcend distance and differences in order to become friends. They eventually learned a lot from each other—what books to read, what kind of literature to write—but first they had to learn to trust. This was no easy task in the late 1950s, a time when suspicions ran high. The writer Janet Malcolm remembers this as an era of "duplicity," a time when women in particular became so used to lying—about their desires and about their actions—that deception became integral to their identities. "We were an uneasy, shifty-eyed generation," Malcolm recalled. "We lied to our parents and we lied to each other and we lied to ourselves, so addicted to deception had we become." To bare one's true struggles—one's true self—was to run counter to all the edicts and habits of the time.

Sexton and Olsen spoke their truths to each other, becoming confidantes and friends. But they remained separated by an insurmountable geographic distance—at least, for the time being. As the 1960s dawned, another woman was moving forward with a plan to bring together a group of women she suspected were out in the world, hiding away in suburban homes: highly educated, creative, intellectual women who had paused their careers while they raised their children. She wouldn't offer them friendship, exactly: she would grant them something more—a place where they could come together and could speak aloud, to each other, the thoughts currently trapped in their minds. It would be a great experiment, she decided. An intellectual community of advanced scholars and writers and artists, made up entirely of female minds. One could only imagine the conversations that it would start.

CHAPTER 4

A Messy Experiment

O N NOVEMBER 20, 1960, Sexton opened the Sunday papers to read of a revolutionary program, the Radcliffe Institute for Independent Study, a place for "intellectually displaced women." Such women, she came to understand, were highly educated, women who had begun careers as scholars and artists but who had gotten off track. Like so many brilliant women of the age, they had let their research projects lie fallow while they birthed and reared the next generation of Americans.

The article described a prototypical displaced woman as someone in her mid-thirties who had gone to graduate school and done some promising scholarship but had been unable to follow up on her initial discovery. Another version: the displaced woman was a painter who had trained with the best but who had borne children before she could secure her first one-woman show. Women like these, the *New York Times* education reporter explained, find it "difficult, if not impossible, without incentive to return to sustained intellectual creativity." Sexton read with a mix of recognition and awe. She was a woman in her thirties, and she had creative promise, but she did not have a doctorate or any academic publications to her name. It wasn't clear whether she was qualified for such a program, nor that it would be a good fit for a socially anxious person like herself. She read on.

The Radcliffe Institute, she learned, would give "a group of gifted but not necessarily widely recognized women" just the incentive they needed. Starting in September 1961, twenty women, with doctorates or "the equivalent" of success in an artistic field, would be named associate scholars. They would receive work space, access to Harvard's vast resources, and an annual stipend of $3,000—not enough money to strike out on their own, but just enough to make a practical difference in their lives and to be taken seriously. The program was open to any college graduate living in the Greater Boston area, not just those with degrees from Radcliffe. If you wanted to win one of the twenty spots, you had to show evidence of past achievement and a plan for future work.

Within twenty-four hours of reading the announcement, Sexton was on the phone to Radcliffe. She wanted to know more information about this curious institute and to express her keen interest in applying. She wasn't alone. The phone in the office of the Radcliffe president had been ringing incessantly since the start of the workday, forcing the staff to hire an extra person just to handle the calls. Many callers were women like Sexton, requesting information and applications. Others were simply calling to express their gratitude for the idea and their good luck wishes. Half of the callers had a baby crying in the background.

Sexton's children were no longer at the tears-and-diapers stage—Linda was seven, and Joy was five. Her mother-in-law, Billie, was a great help with the children: she took them to their extracurricular activities, cooked dinner, and generally mothered during the times that Sexton was incapable of mothering herself. As Linda later wrote in her 1994 memoir, *Searching for Mercy Street*, "it was she [Billie] who provided the freedom that enabled the poet to do what she did so well." But the Institute nonetheless held a particular allure. Though she had published a book of poems, and had wedged her way into Boston's poetry circles, Sexton still felt like an outsider in a city that prized academic prestige. She didn't have Kumin's scholarly pedigree (the latter had both a BA and an MA from Radcliffe); she didn't have a college diploma at all. To be sure, the Institute wasn't a degree-granting program, but it still offered association with one of the best universities in the country. Acceptance by the Radcliffe Institute would mean, in some sense, acceptance by Boston's intellectual elite.

On January 13, not even two weeks after applications to the Institute officially opened, Sexton drafted a tentative letter requesting a formal application. Sitting at her dining room table, she typed out a letter that expressed her excitement about the Institute and her intention to apply. "My qualifications are unique—uniquely wrong," she typed. Such self-deprecation wouldn't do; she tried again, with more neutral language. "I think my application will be one of the most unorthodox you will receive because I have only a high school diploma but have achieved status in the field of creative writing," she explained, hedging and qualifying in her typical way. She promised to make a better request in her formal application.

In the meantime, she wanted to offer her opinion on the Institute's role in restarting the gifted woman's intellectual or creative career. In the press release, the Institute had been careful not to make any firm promises; the document implied that lucky associate scholars might only restart their work "temporarily." Sexton didn't agree. To Sexton at age thirty-two, the Institute represented something powerful, lasting. It seemed like a program that might quell her insecurity and give her permanent status in the competitive poetry scene. It might show Kayo, who still resented his wife's absorption in her wordplay, that this was a career that deserved respect. It might give her a community, a way of getting through the bouts of loneliness without leaning too much on Kumin. It might save her marriage; it might even save her life.

The plan to build this lifesaving institute originated in the unlikeliest of places: a national war room populated almost entirely by men.

On December 6, 1957—the same day as a failed satellite launch from Cape Canaveral in Florida—the National Science Foundation (NSF) assembled a committee to study the nation's schools. Committee members began looking at studies on American education, seeking ways to bolster resources and to encourage more students to take up science and engineering. It convened for the first time in January 1958. The mood was anxious; as one committee member later recalled, "We were scared stiff."

The Soviet Union had successfully launched the satellite Sputnik the prior October, and the United States and the rest of the Western world were afraid of falling behind. Within months of Sputnik's launch—a watershed event likened to Pearl Harbor—the National Aeronautics and Space Administration was formed. Federal money poured into research and development coffers. (From 1957 to 1967, federal R&D spending increased by more than 100 percent.) In 1958, Congress passed the National Defense Education Act, which aimed to strengthen education in fields that would prove useful to national defense. The act claimed that "the security of the Nation requires the fullest development of the mental resources and technical skills of its young men and women." America needed to develop more scientists, and it needed to develop them quickly. The task of the NSF committee was to figure out how.

The lone woman in the room was Mary Ingraham Bunting, known to her friends and family as Polly. A stoical, bespectacled woman of forty-seven, with cropped gray hair and a penchant for sweaters, Bunting was the dean of Douglass College, the women's college of Rutgers University. A microbiologist by training and the widowed mother of four children, she had ended up in university administration by accident, following the sudden death of her husband, Henry, from a brain tumor in 1954. As dean, Bunting had made important changes to Douglass. She abolished formal lunches and "hats required" affairs, both of which smacked of finishing school etiquette. She invited famous speakers—including Allen Ginsberg, John Cage, and Martha Graham—in the hopes that they would inspire her students to dream big. But her undergraduates remained completely preoccupied with the search for husbands, so much so that they barely seemed to notice the intellectual opportunities around them. The student newspaper announced recent "pinnings" (when a woman received her boyfriend's varsity pin as a sign of commitment) and engagements, as if the college were a marketplace and its women commodities waiting to be claimed.

Bunting suggested that the NSF committee begin their research by identifying the smartest kids who weren't going on to college, those who were, somehow, being dissuaded from fulfilling their potential. To answer her own question, she looked up a study done by Donald Bridgman, an education researcher who had broken down his data by gender. Bridgman was studying extremely bright students whose IQs put them in the top 10 percent, and he identified the students in this percentile who had not pursued a college education. Of these bright students who didn't go on to college, at least 90 percent were women.

As Bunting later explained to her biographer Elaine Yaffe, the study showed that nearly "all of the males with that kind of identified ability were continuing their education; practically none of the females were." She was stunned.

It wasn't just that America was losing so many brilliant female high school students—women who might have gone on to study the atom or to crack a new code. It was also that her fellow committee members were largely unmoved by the data. She knew that these were "nice men—not sexist people," and yet they demonstrated little interest in stanching the female brain drain. They seemed a bit embarrassed by the data, and they were willing to set it aside, even to conceal it.

"I was deeply puzzled," she recalled later. "I felt that I was looking into a great dark cave that had been right beneath my feet all of my life without my knowing it. Beneath their feet too."

Years later, she would describe her experience on the NSF committee as "her awakening." Bunting had "never been interested in women as such," as she confessed in a 1957 speech, in part because she had felt her own life had been relatively free from sexism. She was the unusual woman who had seamlessly melded personal and professional fulfillment at a historical moment when women were told, time and again, that they had to choose.

Passionately interested in science since her high school days, Mary Ingraham studied bacteriology at Vassar College, one of the elite Seven Sisters schools. After graduating in 1932, she pursued a PhD at the University of Wisconsin, where she met Henry, a second-year medical student. The couple married and spent twenty happy years living all over the Eastern Seaboard—from Baltimore, Maryland, to Bethany, Connecticut—pursuing their respective careers and raising their growing family. Bunting taught at Bennington College and Goucher College. When Henry went to Yale for a medical residency, she took a part-time job in a laboratory at the university. They fixed up houses together and raised goats and chickens and bees. On warm days, Bunting gardened topless, with bandages covering her nipples. She took evident pride in her cooking and housekeeping—"Well this housekeeping game is a push-over," she wrote to her mother, a woman who used to send her unwanted evening gowns in the mail—but she never felt that homemaking defined her more than, say, her research on *Serratia marcescens* bacteria.

For the Buntings, homemaking was a shared process, one that required the efforts and patience of both parties. The same could be said of their careers: Bunting looked over Henry's X-rays, and Henry performed a cat dissection for Bunting's class. Their marriage was still traditional in many ways—Henry was the breadwinner, and Bunting was relieved that she could pursue science without the pressure of supporting the family—but it was far more equal than what most women experienced in the 1930s and 1940s.

Presented with Bridgman's data, Bunting saw her happy life differently, like a photograph drained of its color. Her rapid graduate training, her part-time job at Yale, her grants signed by male colleagues, her small salary: all of these were symptoms of a broader problem. She had been waved through lazily by authorities paying her little mind. The nation expected so little from its women, even its most brilliant ones. And she had been lucky: most of her peers had endured much worse. She recalled the neighbor in Connecticut who thought she should be grateful that her husband allowed her to drive the family car, and the women who, in her eyes, lacked all sense of purpose. "I didn't have to worry about whether to get married or not," she reflected years later. "I had to decide when and to whom. Actually I think my family always expected me to get married and have a family *and* do other things. I took that for granted."

Looking at the statistics about brilliant young women who never even got on the college track, Bunting realized how many factors conspired to keep American women away from intellectual pursuits. There were the parents who never encouraged their daughters to do "other things," the guidance counselors who failed to recommend college, the student newspapers that highlighted engagements but not honor roll grades, and the many professional men—like her colleagues on the committee—who were entirely unbothered by the thought of thousands of women dropping out and fading away from sight. Everyone and everything told American women—both those in Bunting's generation and those who followed her—that their "real lives" were in the home, away from the public sphere. The nation was going to lose the Cold War to a country that relied on both men and women for research and innovation. The women of the Soviet Union demonstrated their scientific acumen: they made up 30 percent of Soviet engineers and 75 percent of the nation's doctors. Meanwhile, American women made up only 1 percent of the nation's engineers and 6 percent of its doctors. The United States was wasting a precious resource, what Bunting would later call "educated womanpower."

Bunting wasn't alone in thinking about this problem. Many administrators and education scholars agreed that something was wrong with the way the nation educated women, but they couldn't agree on what the problem was or on how it should be solved. Between 1948 and 1963, the number of women enrolled in college dramatically increased, from 700,000 students to almost 1.7 million. Still, female undergraduates looked like "incidental students" to university administrators, according to the historian Linda Eisenmann. Women didn't really belong at research institutions (which were rising in prominence thanks to an influx of federal dollars), and they didn't merit professional training, because it was assumed that they would leave the workforce at the first signs of pregnancy. Some education reformers thought that women needed more classes in marriage counseling or the domestic arts, to better prepare them for their lives as housewives. Others reinforced the value of a liberal arts education, even for the stay-at-home mother. An educated woman could recite sonnets while changing diapers, they suggested, thus keeping herself entertained.

Bunting disagreed with both camps. She thought women needed to be educated so they could contribute to research and innovation. Furthermore, she believed that most women, if they found willing husbands and stuck to strict schedules, could have both family and career. At Douglass, she was dismayed by how many parents, teachers, administrators, and alumni believed that women either couldn't pursue intellectual goals or could do so only at the expense of their personal lives.

American women lived in what Bunting started to call a "climate of unexpectation." She set out to change the climate.

Bunting returned to Douglass energized. She persuaded the school's board to green-light an educational initiative for a small group of older, part-time students, women who were married with children and who could only come to campus for an hour or two a day. Part-time study was generally derided at the time—some thought part-time students were dilettantes—but Bunting was convinced that these part-time students would succeed. A group of ten women were admitted, and succeed they did: the group was over-represented on the honor roll. One faculty member called them the "GIs of Douglass."

The program helped validate Bunting's emerging understanding of the trajectory of a woman's education: it was full of starts and stops, and it took place over the course of a lifetime. Women were living longer compared with the women of previous generations, and the majority of them were done with the most demanding stages of motherhood by their early thirties. They had decades of empty time to fill. As Bunting described it, these women entered and exited the workforce much like drivers merging onto, and then exiting, the interstate highway system. Education needed to operate more like the nation's highway system, Bunting decided; it needed to provide women with on-ramps and off-ramps that they could use at will.

Despite all her activism on behalf of women, Bunting didn't identify as a feminist. For her, as for many women in the 1950s, feminism seemed radical, even sinister; it smacked of communism, bohemianism, and radicalism. What's more, women like Bunting had a different idea of social change from self-identified feminists. Whereas feminists wanted to change the rules that governed the social world, Bunting and reformers like her wanted to help individual women learn the rules more quickly and be more at ease within them. As Esther Raushenbush, the former president of the women's college Sarah Lawrence, recalled, "The research of those years was directed toward helping women make adjustments; little concern was ever expressed about the responsibility of society to change those social patterns." The idea that society itself must change was a revolutionary idea—an idea whose time had not yet come.

Nothing made these differences clearer than a chance encounter between a reformer and a revolutionary. Just as she was reforming Douglass College, making it into an on-ramp for married women, Bunting met another woman who was thinking about similar problems. Betty Friedan was a freelance journalist and a fellow alumna of a Seven Sisters school (she had graduated from Smith) and, as Bunting remembered later, a woman who was "boiling very fiercely."

At the time they met, Friedan was researching the "return of mature women to the labor force" and was preoccupied with the predominant myth of the "happy housewife"—the woman who needed nothing more than sturdy oven mitts and a good vacuum to be content. She wanted to write something about it—something longer than a magazine article, a book, perhaps. Friedan asked Bunting to collaborate on the book project: Bunting would offer her ideas about education, and Friedan would write forcefully about the "ways in which women were prevented from living their own lives."

Four or five times, Friedan boarded the commuter train from Rockland County, New York, and traveled to New Brunswick, New Jersey, where she and Bunting discussed plans for what Bunting called their "small book" (she was never grandiose about her projects). They met in Bunting's office, where they would spend an hour or two reading over drafts of possible chapters. As they got to know each other better, as women and as thinkers, Bunting grew wary. Friedan was outspoken. She was angry. She saw women's problems as a result of male interference in women's lives; to Bunting, it seemed that Friedan was thinking "in terms of men against women, and was feeling very bitter about men and what men did to women." Bunting—a humanist, a happy wife, and the descendant of a Quaker—found Friedan's polemical style and vitriolic tone unappealing. (It was not atypical for a WASP to find a Jewish woman overly emotional.)

"I was thinking much more in terms of the climate of unexpectation," Bunting later explained, "in which men and women were both trapped. The book was going to have a lot in it that was quite dramatic that I couldn't really support." Her social vision didn't include villains and victims; she refused to blame men for women's problems, or even to think about how they might benefit from women's suffering. She thus encouraged Friedan to take a different approach, to admit that there was more than one way of looking at some of these problems, but Friedan refused. They eventually parted ways. Bunting returned to the work of running an institution, while Friedan raced to finish *The Feminine Mystique*.

In March 1960, Bunting finally got her chance to test some of her more innovative ideas about how to generate educated womanpower. She had just been appointed president of Radcliffe College, though her term as president hadn't officially started (she had been offered the job after a Radcliffe trustee heard her give a talk at Smith). She proposed, to a skeptical board of trustees, the creation of the Radcliffe Institute for Independent Study. Bunting explained how funding a small community of female scholars would help not just the women appointed to the Institute but also the Radcliffe undergrads, who, like the students at Douglass, would be inspired by the older women's example. If the experiment was successful, colleges around the country might imitate its approach.

When Bunting proposed this plan, there was nothing like the Institute in the country. The closest thing might have been her own "female GI" program at Douglass. (A couple years later, the University of Minnesota would start a similar continuing education program.) But Bunting didn't need a model; since her days in the bacteriology lab at Vassar, she had always loved researching questions to which no one knew the answer. The idea for the Institute had been taking shape in the back of her mind since her days at Douglass—truly, since her happy days in Bethany, Connecticut, when she farmed on some days and researched on others.

For several years, she had nurtured what she thought of as a hypothesis (she had many hypotheses, scribbled down in her notebooks, alongside her hour-by-hour daily schedules): educated women could restart their intellectual careers if they were given time, money, and university resources. She pictured a woman much like her younger self: mother of four, PhD in hand, energized equally by her young children and recent research in her chosen field. This woman needed the equivalent of the Yale laboratory: a place within commuting distance where she could explore her research at her leisure, without the burden of breadwinning. She recalled her neighbors in Bethany. "Every one of these neat little brick houses has at least one woman who doesn't seem to have enough to do," she had written to her mother when she was living there. "If they did all of their own wash etc. they could keep busy, but they dont [sic]. Most of the time they spend visiting with each other or yelling at their kids, just out of boredom . . . They all talk, I hear them out the back window, about how hard they have to work, but in reality they wander aimlessly about looking for amusement." Though a bit unfair to those women who lacked her unflagging energy, Bunting nonetheless identified one of the key problems with the suburban American ideal: keeping house simply didn't keep most educated women fully occupied.

What would happen if a brilliant, bored woman were given all of the advantages that she, Polly Bunting, had enjoyed as a young wife? What if women around the country saw that they, too, could continue with their educations and leaped, en masse, into the workforce? What upsurge in female intelligence—in national brainpower—might result? Radcliffe, she argued on that day in early March, was in just the position to run this "messy experiment."

This was a bold suggestion for a woman who hadn't even been officially inaugurated as Radcliffe's president. But Bunting was a bold woman: an anonymous Harvard professor once said of her, "I wish Harvard had a president who was as much of a man as Mrs. Bunting." The board listened with concern. If this was an experiment, then there was no guarantee of its success. Radcliffe could spend hundreds of thousands of dollars on women with no connection to the institution—and for what? Was there any way to know that this project would influence the Radcliffe undergrads? Moreover, so many Radcliffe alumnae were seemingly happy homemakers; they might take offense at the idea that they had been displaced or that their lives had stalled. The board told Bunting that she would have to do the

Constance Smith, left, and Polly Bunting, center, at Radcliffe College

fund-raising for this project alone and that she wasn't to approach the usual Radcliffe donors. Bunting welcomed the challenge.

Bunting never let anything slow her down—not money problems, not travel fatigue, not even her husband's death. She gathered a brain trust of women to help her develop a budget and make a plan. She secured a five-year, $150,000 grant from the Carnegie Corporation, then a five-year grant from the Rockefeller Brothers Fund, totaling $250,000. She won the support of Harvard faculty, of public figures including Harvard government professor (and future national security adviser) McGeorge Bundy, and of prominent women writers, including Adrienne Rich, the political theorist Hannah Arendt, and the playwright Lillian Hellman, the last of whom joined the Institute's advisory committee. She found a director, Constance Smith, known as Connie to her friends, an associate professor of political science at Douglass. Smith had dark hair, bright green eyes, and a broad smile. Eager to take the position, she was officially appointed on January 9, 1961, for a salary of $12,000.

By all accounts, Smith was a natural at the director job. She was warm and attentive, someone who could intuit the needs of others, "a sweet kind of whirling dervish." One Institute fellow remembered her as "terrific" and "the best person that they could have there." She charmed Bunting's assistant, Rene Bryant, and wrote to Bunting that she expected that all three would have a fine working relationship.

Everything was falling into place. A press release went out in November 1960; it "deplore[d] the lack of incentive and opportunity in this country for the talented citizen" and lambasted the nation's "anti-intellectual climate," which was "particularly limiting to those women whose major responsibilities during at least a decade are in the home." A glossy brochure, also published in November, went further, showing how female intellectual frustration put families—and thus nations—at risk. "This sense of stagnation can become a malignant factor in even the best of marriages," the brochure warned, "when the gifted woman must spend her time inventing ways to employ herself mentally and failing, or only half-succeeding, may turn against the marriage itself in sheer frustration." Educated women need not be unruly activists. While the pioneers of women's education had been "crusaders and reformers, passionate, fearless, articulate, but also, at times, loud," today's women didn't have to conform to this stereotype. After all, the brochure announced, "the bitter battles for women's rights are history." The Institute, like so many other women's education reforms of the era, was framed as a gentle corrective to a life course that was already moving in the right direction.

It was in large part because the Institute was supposed to be norm reinforcing and nonthreatening that it failed to address the particular concerns of working-class women and women of color, whose lives took a very different course. To start with, a program that pitched itself as part-time employment would do nothing for women wage earners who needed a full-time salary. The problem for these women was not that they didn't have an opportunity to work but that they didn't get paid enough for the work they did. In an era when it was still legal to advertise jobs according to sex, women usually accepted lower-paid positions. (Though sex discrimination in job hiring is now illegal, this trend persists today.) In 1960, the median full-time female worker earned $24,590 a year, compared with $40,586 for men (these earnings have been adjusted for inflation according to the year 2019).

Educated black women, meanwhile, were dramatically different from their white counterparts. According to the historian Paula Giddings, in the 1950s, when white women were dropping out of college, the rate of black women graduates was actually rising. By the academic year 1952–1953, black women earned 62.4 percent of all degrees from historically black colleges; their college graduation rates rivaled male graduation rates from all colleges across the nation. As a result, the number of black professional women rose as well; they soon outpaced black men, percentage-wise, in professional and semiprofessional positions. This didn't free them from domestic responsibilities, however: in fact, in the 1950s, upwardly mobile black women, many of whom continued to work outside the home, largely felt confused about how to perform middle-class domesticity, because their own mothers often had not had the means to do so.

Middle-class black women faced many of the same pressures and expectations that their white peers faced, but their conflicts manifested themselves in different ways, and they required different kinds of solutions. In short, exhortations to avoid "stagnation" and to take "initiative" would have sounded strange and uncompelling to many black women who had been striving to improve their economic positions all their lives.

But the American media, with its default white perspective, lauded the formation of the Institute. The announcement of the Institute made headlines from Toronto to Tulsa. "Radcliffe Launching Plan to Get Brainy Women out of Kitchen," broadcast *Newsday*, out of Garden City, New York. The *World-Herald*, in Omaha, reported, "Female Brain Outlet Sought." Bunting was fluent in Cold War rhetoric, and she wrote a long piece for *The New York Times Magazine* about the "waste of highly talented, educated womanpower" that connected her experiment to the nation's foreign policy goals. In "A Huge Waste: Educated Womanpower," she argued that "educational institutions must provide for, encourage and assist the able, part-time student—the married woman—by creating more flexible schedules." She reassured her readers that "studying, in appropriate doses, mixes wonderfully well with homemaking" and acknowledged that there may be "innate differences" between men and women, though this could not be determined with any certainty without standardizing their conditions of growth. (Bunting was ever the scientist.)

She then described the Institute, a solution to the problem her article outlined. The Institute would offer "a place to work free from the unpredictable distractions of family life, the compulsion to pursue the daily routine at the expense of a half-finished conception or dream, and the guilt over children rebuffed, or questions unanswered." She ended with a clarion call to women to contribute to society, appealing to their typically feminine altruism. "It is not so much for women," she wrote, "as for our heritage and our aspirations that America must assess again, thoughtfully and purposefully, their places in our society." Don't apply to the Institute for yourselves, she implied; do it for your country. It was only a happy accident that personal achievement and patriotic duty overlapped.

In the months after the announcement, letters arrived at the Radcliffe offices from all over the country: from Staten Island, from San Francisco, from Pierrepont Street in Brooklyn, and from Gray Goose Farm in Jaffrey, New Hampshire. Mail came from around the corner in Cambridge and from overseas. Most letters were written by married women, the kinds of women who were inclined to include their formal, married names under their signatures or on their stationery. Some included a small check for $5, for $10, or for as much as $300 (nearly $2,500 today). Jane M. Chamberlain (Mrs. David B.), a Radcliffe alumna from the class of 1950, sent along a $5 check and a brief note, inked in bright red: "Dear Radcliffe, I love you!"

Usually, though, the letters were more extensive. The women who wrote to the Radcliffe president's office ranged in age, but they were almost all mothers. In their letters, they described the familiar challenges of domestic life ("children are sick, appliances break down"). In the same paragraph, they presented plans of study, both future and past. Their letters must have kindled Bunting's memory: as she read their descriptions of busy households where children scurried underfoot, she must have thought of her home in Bethany, where she gardened in the warm sun while her children played in the yard. These years had been her happiest in fact; her second life, as a widow and as a university administrator, never quite matched the joy of her first. Pastoral Connecticut, however, had been only one part of Bunting's life; there had always been the lab, and there had been Henry, her intellectual companion. The Bethany years were fixed in Bunting's memory because they had not lasted. For the women writing to Bunting, though, domestic life was not a lost Eden but an inescapable quagmire. And the Institute, to them, signaled one possible way out.

Bunting had envisioned her small society of scholars as a test case, a stepping-stone on a path toward reforming women's higher education. Whatever effect it might have on the scholars who attended would surely be temporary. But Sexton, hearing the news of the Institute, could see from her dining room table in Newton what Bunting, in the President's House on Brattle Street, could not. In Sexton's letter of interest, a letter she never sent, she proved prescient. The impact of the Institute would not be fleeting, she suspected; it would change some things—some people—for life. Excited, encouraged, Sexton did what she did every day: she picked up the phone, and she called her best friend.

CHAPTER 5

I Got It!

As 1960 DREW TO A CLOSE, Connie Smith and Rene Bryant, Bunting's assistant, sorted through their growing mail pile—manila envelopes, multicolored stationery—and unearthed the serious applicants. It was barely a month after the Institute's announcement, but already 120 women had been classified as "preliminary applicants." These were women who had the necessary qualifications to apply; they would receive the application blanks once those were ready. Some of them Bunting had recruited personally; she wrote to outstanding female scholars encouraging them to apply. According to Bryant, the "caliber of applicant has been astonishingly high." Within the preliminary pool, forty-one held PhD degrees, three had MDs, and nineteen had some form of master's degree. (This was at a time when women made up 33 percent of master's degree holders and only 10.4 percent of those who earned PhDs.) The youngest of the potential applicants was twenty-eight, and the oldest was fifty-six; the average applicant was in her late thirties, just as Bunting had anticipated and highlighted in the press release. Just over half of these women were married, with anywhere between one and five children. (Nine were widowed or divorced; sixteen had never been married.) They were exactly the kinds of women that Bunting had imagined assisting: highly educated, ambitious, maternal, and ready for a second life. They were, in other words, women much like her younger self.

Sexton was one of these eager women. She received application blanks in February. Her application, submitted in early March, toggled between charming self-effacement and almost galling hubris. She listed the required personal information: in addition to their ages and addresses, the applicants were asked to list their husbands' names, occupations, and the names and ages of their children and other dependents. The fellowship was not need-based, so a high-earning husband wouldn't eliminate an applicant; neither would grown children who no longer required maternal care. Presumably, the Institute asked for this information as a way of identifying women who could serve as test cases for—or who best exemplified—Bunting's theories about the life course of the American woman.

One of only a few applicants without a college degree, Sexton left bare the sections that requested education and languages. The only talent she listed was an ability to give poetry readings. She described her academic credentials as "anemic," but she emphasized that she was a self-taught writer who had made a successful career for herself. To demonstrate her success, she alluded to ten good book reviews that she could send to the selection committee. (She also mentioned rather coyly "two poor reviews which I would rather not show you.") But Sexton wanted to write for posterity. She claimed not to care much for sales or for the fleeting approval of contemporary audiences. She yearned to be more than a lady poet; she wanted to transcend what she called her "female role." (She was also careful to praise the Institute for supporting the careers of women.) Like an awkward guest at her first literary party who laughs too loudly and talks too much about work, Sexton stressed her desire to secure a position among the nation's literary greats. "I feel that I am already an accomplished poet," she wrote. "What I ask now is for the opportunity to be a lasting one." Here was a woman who wanted to be nothing less than extraordinary.

Prompted by Sexton, Kumin also applied to the Institute. In her application, she emphasized her scholarly credentials: her BA and MA from Radcliffe, her undergraduate prizes, her command of four languages. Where the application requested the name of a doctoral thesis, Kumin listed instead the title of her undergraduate honors thesis, "Amorality and the Protagonist in the Novels of Stendhal and Dostoievski." Though she was at this point an accomplished poet— she'd published nearly forty poems in *Harper's*, *The Atlantic*, and *The New Yorker*—she downplayed her creative achievements, as if she were afraid of seeming self-aggrandizing. Instead, she emphasized her role as a teacher: she was dedicated to her students at Tufts, where she taught part-time, and she believed that a year of reading and study at the Institute would make her a better instructor. "I am interested in contrasting Conrad's journey into the pre-conscious with that of Saul Bellow," she wrote in her research proposal. "I would like to read Sartre and Camus fully and to examine the impact of existentialist philosophy on the existing Freudian concepts in American literary criticism." She wanted to translate French and Russian poets, to read essays on the creative process, and, possibly, to develop her own theories about how the creative mind works. Her one-page proposal could barely contain all the different intellectual avenues she wanted to pursue. She seemed eager to pick up her studies.

When Bunting had first conceived of the Institute, she imagined it as a place for female scholars. In her initial discussions with fundraisers and trustees, she suggested that only women with doctorates would be admitted. The other prerequisite was geographic location: only those who could easily get themselves to Radcliffe Yard, or who could commit to living in Cambridge for the year, would be considered for a fellowship. It was a harsh but necessary barrier to entry: otherwise the Institute would be inundated with applications. But by the time of the November 1960 press release, the Institute administrators had decided artists with the "equivalent" of doctoral training would also be eligible for the Institute. As a result, they accepted applications from writers, composers, and visual artists—including one from a local painter named Barbara Swan Fink.

News of the Institute had reached Barbara Swan (her professional

Barbara Swan at work, 1960s

name) at 32 Webster Place in Brookline, a busy suburb just west of Boston. Like Sexton, Swan was a New England native: she'd been born in Newton, the same city where Sexton now made her home, in 1922. She had begun sketching as a small child and went on to take classes at the Massachusetts College of Art. With just a few strokes of a pencil, she could capture a person's likeness: her Yankee mother, her Swedish father, and, later, the faces of fellow artists and friends. Years later, when asked to describe her introduction to art, she cited neither mentors nor books. Drawing was a skill she considered innate: becoming an artist, she claimed, was her inevitable fate.

But at the mid-century, it wasn't easy for a young woman to become a working artist (not that it is ever easy). Though she yearned to go to art school immediately after high school, her strict father insisted she pursue a liberal arts degree instead. He pestered her with worries about making a living and having a career and "also were you going to become bohemian and have some lifestyle that would be appalling." To appease him, she attended Wellesley College and commuted from home in order to cut costs. The studio offerings at Wellesley disappointed her—she thought they were "for dilettantes"—so Swan changed her major to art history. She experienced everything a Seven Sisters school had to offer, and she was underwhelmed.

In between memorizing slides, she sketched portraits of her fellow female students. "I was running like a business where I had appointments for sitting in my dormitory room," she later recalled, "and I was knocking off these pastels and there was a framer in Newton Corner who . . . would frame them for $3.98 . . . and then they would be shipped and . . . some of mine went to California." She charged $15 per portrait—"maybe that was a little expensive," she later reflected—and she had a steady stream of customers. By this time, she'd gathered the funds and the courage to move out of her father's house.

Swan wanted to be a serious artist, and at that time being serious meant studying among men. After graduating from Wellesley in 1943, she enrolled at the School of the Museum of Fine Arts, known as the Museum School: the best art school in the city. Swan trained with Karl Zerbe, a portraitist and German exile; Zerbe had fled to Boston from Berlin in 1934 after the National Socialists labeled him one of the country's "degenerate" artists. He headed up the painting department at the Museum School from 1937 until 1955. He demanded his students train rigorously, and he encouraged them to go beyond classicism, to communicate feeling, and to see paint as a fundamentally expressive medium. His students were "figurative expressionists," painters interested in breaking with tradition—in following the modernist dictate to "make it new"—but sticking with the study of the human form. This made them paradoxical renegades. The 1940s and 1950s were an age of abstraction, a time when avant-garde painters in New York City—Jackson Pollock, Willem de Kooning, Jasper Johns—experimented with color and texture and shape. Their art wasn't representational or figurative. In the words of the art critic Clement Greenberg—who theorized the avant-garde—content, in the hands of these artists, was "to be dissolved so completely into form that the work of art [could not] be reduced in whole or in part to anything not itself." While all this was happening just a four-hour drive south, the artists in Boston continued to paint recognizable people and places.

Swan, called "one of the more gifted students" at the Museum School by *The Christian Science Monitor* in 1947, found her way into Zerbe's inner circle. This was no small feat. Women were few and far between at the Museum School. The hallways were crowded with ex-GIs who stomped around in their fatigues and gave off an air of seriousness. (The year after the war ended, ninety-six veterans enrolled in the Museum School.) Women rarely won teaching assistantships, and even more rarely won traveling fellowships, a key resource for up-and-coming artists who wanted to study abroad. "They didn't trust a woman to go to Paris and not have a love affair with a Frenchman," Swan later explained. A fellow female student, Lois Tarlow, believed that Zerbe "absolutely categorized all women as not worthy of serious interest . . . Zerbe did have his favorites and they weren't women." But somehow, as Sexton did with Lowell, Swan won the master's approval. Perhaps it was her excellent draftsmanship, something Zerbe emphasized to his students, that appealed to him; perhaps it was her quiet tenacity, her determination to become an artist by any means. "I was so determined to be an artist," she later explained. "It was against my parents' wishes." In any event, during her later years at the school, she helped Zerbe teach his class. When he held court in the school's basement cafeteria, she was the only woman seated at the big round table.

Improbably, Swan won a fellowship to Paris, where she rented a cheap hotel room with a friend and, in the winter, painted in the cold, poorly heated room until her hands turned blue. She met her future husband, Alan Fink, a former accountant who was now spending his savings traveling Europe, at a restaurant on the Left Bank. Swan—who was now the bohemian child her father had feared she would become—traveled with Fink and his friends to Provence, where she banished what she called the "somber tonalities" of Boston and painted with the bright blues and reds of Cézanne.

Swan and Fink returned to Boston in 1952, where they married (against her parents' wishes—they worried about Fink's "economic prospects"). Swan had her first solo show a year later, an event that announced her arrival on the arts scene. The show took place at the Boris Mirski Gallery on Newbury Street (later, Alan would become the gallery's director). Mirski was the linchpin of the Boston art world—he represented Swan's fellow Museum School graduates and other rising stars—and the show was a critical success. Dorothy Adlow, one of the city's most respected critics, praised Swan in *The Christian Science Monitor:* "There is a quivering vitality in these drawings, an inner force, a discriminative distinction. In her portraits it is remarkable how searching a characterization can result from so few lineal indications." Adlow concluded, "She has an uncommon gift for personal representation."

But children soon paused Swan's career. She had two children—Aaron, born in 1955, and Joanna, born in 1958—and though she was a happy and relaxed mother, she found it nearly impossible to paint with her children underfoot. Instead, she drew; mostly, she drew her children. It would be four years until she exhibited another solo show.

By the time the Institute was announced in the fall of 1960, Swan had found a rare and happy balance between raising children and making art. She had set up a home studio on the second floor of her Brookline house, and she had shifted her subject matter to her children. This change was more a matter of convenience than anything: her children were usually only steps away from her easel. "I was involved in the mother-child relationship simply because it was autobiographical," she later reflected. She sketched her children lying on the floor together: Joanna prone and inquisitive, Aaron supine and small. She managed to do a few paintings of her children (when they would sit still, before they were at the crawling stage). In rich oils, she painted Aaron sitting in her husband's outstretched hand, gazing down at the world below with fascinated, clouded eyes. These portraits demonstrated her technical skill, as all of her paintings and drawings did, but the slight distortions seen in earlier portraits—

Baby (Aaron at Four Months), *by Barbara Swan, 1955*

the too-loose limbs, the large eyes—had been banished. The family portraits were warm, careful, and caring, though the bold color and composition kept them from being sentimental. When she exhibited some of this work in 1957, *The Boston Globe* called it a "humanistic shot in the arm"—a much-needed vaccine against Cold War despair.

This was the work she placed in a portfolio and mailed off to Radcliffe. She had applied at the behest of a friend who knew she was feeling "bogged down" with household responsibilities. Her children were five and two; though Swan was finding ways to "be all"—mother, artist, and occasional art teacher—she still thought "it *would* be satisfying to have a little help along the way." She applied to the Institute in late February 1961. A few months later, in April, she sent along a supplemental portfolio, which included two framed paintings, one framed and glazed drawing called *Mother and Child*, a portfolio of drawings, and an envelope with photographs of and information about her other work.

The Nest, one of the two framed paintings, exemplified how Swan combined motherhood and art. In the painting, a woman, supine, reclines in a reddish armchair; her head lies at the bottom-left corner of the frame, and her legs extend upward, into darkness. The red robe wrapped around her body seems to blend into the red of the armchair so that one can't quite tell where her body ends and the furniture begins. An infant, swaddled in blue cloth, suckles at the woman's bare breast, eyes wide and unseeing. It could be a sweet scene, but the painting is no Madonna with child. The work is bold, even a bit off-putting: the strong contrast between red and blue, the intense chiaroscuro, the bare breast, the bright child, unnaturally lit against the dark backdrop. The painting denaturalized maternity, rendering it almost unearthly.

What Swan demonstrated in *The Nest*, and what she expounded on in her application to the Institute, is the strangeness—the surreality—of motherhood. Her representation of motherhood was not quotidian or banal or uninspired; it was groundbreaking, spiritual, unnerving. "I feel that a woman artist can derive enormous inspiration from her role as a wife and a mother," Swan wrote in her application. "It is a profound, mystical experience and in every sense life-enhancing." This line of thinking dovetailed perfectly with the animating spirit of the Institute: that motherhood and creative work can be mutually sustaining.

Soon after submitting her full application, Swan learned that she had made the cut and that she would interview for a place in the Institute's inaugural class. To win one of these spots, she would have to distinguish herself from the scores of other qualified women—lapsed medievalists, amateur philosophers, erstwhile chemists eager to serve their country—who hoped for nothing more than "a little help along the way."

Meanwhile, at 10:00 a.m. on Saturday, April 29, 1961, Sexton arrived for her interview at Fay House on Radcliffe's campus. She was one of roughly a hundred women invited to interview; approximately twice as many had sent in formal applications. Hundreds more had sent in letters of inquiry, notes of congratulations, and gentle criticisms of a program that catered only to "extraordinary women" and ignored the rest: the stay-at-home mother with a college degree but with no hard proof of her intellectual potential; the working-class mother desperate for financial assistance or child care; the woman who had been discouraged from ever pursuing an education. Although Bunting's Institute appealed to many of the twenty-two million women working outside the home, the program wasn't for the average working woman. It was for a "special" woman, a woman who was educated, who had accomplished much despite the obstacles in front of her. Such women tended to have many things already working in their favor: money, racial privilege, some degree of social support. Sexton was thrilled to be seen as special. Part of her couldn't believe she'd made the first cut; another part believed it was her due.

She approached the building where she would interview. Fay House, at 10 Garden Street, looks more like a mansion than an administrative building. This is because it was once a family home: the Fay Mansion was purchased in 1885 to offer "permanent quarters" for Radcliffe College. In old photographs from the early twentieth century, women with ruffled bodices, trained skirts, and large, cantilevered hats gather just outside the building's front door. A small widow's walk sits above them; one can imagine a Bostonian matriarch pacing across its narrow expanse, looking out toward the Charles River. In the years since these photographs were taken, the house had been renovated and converted to administrative use. Through it all, the women of Radcliffe continued to pass through its doorway, some of them on their way to new lives.

Sexton made an entrance everywhere she went; this interview was no exception. Sexton always dressed carefully, applying the right lipstick and picking out the perfect jewelry. In the morning sunlight, she must have gleamed. Smith, the director, who had made an exception to the Institute's policy by considering an application from someone without a college degree, opened the interview. Like a well-trained actress hearing her cue, Sexton began to perform.

Sexton knew how to handle direct attention, even though she sometimes feared it. Her energy was up; she was lively and talkative. As confessional in person as she was on the page, Sexton spoke readily about how she had discovered poetry (that is, through her suicide attempts) and about her struggle to learn to write. She left out nothing: not her death wish, not her days at Glenside. In her application, she had sounded touchy about her academic background, but in the interview she expressed enthusiasm about the Institute's educational opportunities. She wanted to audit classes and to read widely. Aware that her temperament, and her history, could make her seem an unreliable investment, Sexton assured Smith that she had her life in balance now and that she was committed to being a good mother no matter her professional obligations. In fact, she'd recently canceled a meeting with a very important publisher because she'd promised her daughters that they would go visit the pussy willows. "WOW! We'll know she's around," Smith wrote in her notes afterward. "She has enormous vitality and zest!" She recommended acceptance.

Kumin arrived at Fay House a few hours later, just before 2:00 p.m. She was on familiar ground. When she had first seen Radcliffe, in the fall of 1941, she had marveled at its beauty. The campus comprised Radcliffe Yard, where the administrative buildings were and where Fay House is located, and the Radcliffe Quadrangle, where the dormitories were located. Radcliffe Yard was just a few minutes' walk from the center of Harvard Square, where the Harvard College campus was, and the Quad was a seven-minute walk up Garden Street. The Quad was isolated from the noise and bustle of the square; the tree-lined streets that bordered it were some of the most beautiful in the city.

Kumin later described the transformation she experienced upon arriving at Radcliffe: "Epithets with which I had been branded— bookworm, greasy grind, brain trust—now became a badge of honor . . . At Radcliffe my life began anew. My parochial Jewishness fell away." Her Radcliffe years had been happy ones: she had felt at ease around her fellow "Cliffies," who had been quick, smart, and passionate about art and politics—nothing like the sorority sisters at her high school. She had had no idea there were other women like her in the world, women with the same "interests and attitudes and values." She had thrown herself into undergraduate life. With like-minded classmates, Kumin had joined the Labor League (and had scandalized her father with her far-left politics). She had captained the swim team her senior year, written a satirical comic strip, and attended football games and dances. Swimming had long been a passion of Kumin's, and at first she was disappointed by Radcliffe's basement pool (as a high school senior visiting colleges, she had preferred the pool at Wellesley), but she ended up enjoying her first years swimming and even taught swim lessons to her fellow Cliffies who needed to pass a swim test to graduate. "I would say that the unhappiness of the years between 8th and 12th grades were totally dissipated," she later said. "I was starting fresh and in a new country." For the first time in her life, Kumin had felt "supremely and sublimely happy."

Kumin, whose own children were now in their preteen and teenage years, applied to the Institute for many reasons—she wanted time off from teaching at Tufts, the prestige associated with the "associate scholars" program, and to stay on the same path as her best friend—but surely one of them was a desire to recapitulate her happy college years.

In some ways, it was more surprising that Kumin made it to the interview stage than that Sexton did. Neither a true scholar nor yet a dazzling artist (her first book had only just been published in March), Kumin closely resembled many of the Radcliffe alumnae whose letters of inquiry had gone into the Institute's office wastebasket. Kumin was a woman who, in her words, had been "playing the triple role of part-time writer, part-time teacher and part-time homemaker." Her supervisor at Tufts described her as a "fine teacher" as well as a "first-rate" scholar and noted how rare it was that someone could master both those tasks and also "do creative work of excellence." She was clearly reliable, sensible, and, if not a case of female genius, then at least a compelling example of the Institute's underlying theory: that motherhood and intellectual work might be seamlessly intertwined.

As soon as Kumin began to speak, she revealed herself to be quite different from her fellow Newton poet. Whereas Sexton was vivacious and intense, passionate about her work and frank about her personal struggles, Kumin was at once breezier and more self-serious. She spoke enthusiastically about her teaching at Tufts and described how she would return armed with new knowledge, after a year of study at the Institute. She ran through her many interests—poetry, the creative process, Freudian psychology, existentialist philosophy—in a way that Smith found both impressive and a bit dizzying. Attractive, intelligent, and the author of a published collection of poetry, Kumin promised to make good use of an Institute year. To Smith, Kumin seemed a bit like an overeager first-year student, restlessly moving from one area of study to the next. "Has many interests and this may be a problem—she may not concentrate on any *one*," Smith wrote in her notes. "Suspect she has more drive than real creative talent but that's just a guess." Still, Kumin was compelling, companionable, and overall a pleasing presence. More than that, she was a teacher, someone who might offer a community course or compel female undergraduates. Ultimately, Smith decided to recommend acceptance.

She passed on her recommendations to Harvard faculty members—accomplished scholars in their fields of study—who would evaluate the applicants and decide whether they had potential. These experts—most of them male, in keeping with the typical gender breakdown of university faculty—would determine which women got the chance to pursue a dream.

Many eager applicants never made it to Fay House. Many didn't even merit an application packet. Bunting had designed the Institute with what she thought of as the exceptional woman in mind: the brainy types, the ones who, as adolescents, had tested among the top 10 percent of high school students, the types of women who had caught her eye when she was on the NSF committee. But her project resonated with the most ordinary women in America: the clerical workers, the store owners, those with or without college degrees. These were women who had been discouraged from further study. They had dropped out of college; they had married young. They had failed to win this fellowship or had been fired from that lab. Gender discrimination was still legal, and in 1960 Title VII and the workplace protections it installed were still several years away. Unlike the impressive tenure-track professors whom Bunting had herself contacted to encourage them to apply, these women hadn't had the luck to beat the odds and attain an impressive career. Now, as they made inquiries about their eligibility, they feared that no matter what kind of promise they had once shown in a college classroom, they would look, to a selection committee, as unremarkable as a Formica countertop.

In the first few weeks after the Institute was announced, underqualified women wrote directly to Bunting, unaware that they were not the "talented" applicants that the Institute was looking for. Barbara L. Rozen (Mrs. Jerome G.), a woman from New Jersey who had received her college degree ten years earlier, wanted to undertake a study "of a little known family of spiders." She was disappointed to learn from Bunting that her undergraduate achievements were insufficient for Institute membership. (She had hoped to use her stipend to hire a housekeeper.) Rose Pavone, a New York–based mother of two without any formal education, wrote to ask to be considered for the Institute; she wanted to "at long last somehow be able to continue my search for knowledge." Pavone had filled four pages with cramped handwriting, describing her many and varied interests, broadly humanistic in nature. She must have written the letter in between watching her two preadolescent boys and working at the family general store, which she owned with her husband. Her excitement at the idea of study—real, formal study—animated each word. Bunting, seemingly unmoved by Pavone's plight, wrote a crisp letter back explaining the Institute was not for undergraduate study. She encouraged her to find a college closer to home.

Other women knew better than to even apply. Mary T. Blanchard (Mrs. John A.) of Dedham, Massachusetts, had a bachelor's degree from Radcliffe. She had long wanted to return to school for further study, she explained in her letter, but she had never found the time or the money. The family had five children and tons of bills. Even though she was cheered by the prospect of the Institute, she recognized that she, an educated woman but, ultimately, a housewife, would not benefit from the support it offered. "I hope that the present program will someday be expanded to include women in my position," she wrote.

Even highly accomplished women found themselves unable to meet the Institute's specifications. Denise Levertov, a thirty-seven-year-old British poet, was desperate to find a source of income that wouldn't force her to abandon her family. Levertov was distinguished in her field—she had published five books and won praise as a member of the American literary avant-garde—but literary fame didn't translate into material comfort. Between her poetry and her husband's magazine writing, the couple made just enough money to live in what she called "a simple style" in downtown Manhattan and to send their son to private school. (At the time she inquired about the Institute, Levertov and her family had just moved into a loft above a ham-canning factory at 277 Greenwich Street.) But when she learned that even the most accomplished grantees, called resident fellows, would need to be in residence in Cambridge, Levertov decided not to apply. She couldn't move her young son for such a short period of time and force him to switch schools. She would wait another two years before deciding that the lure of the Institute was such that she was willing to leave New York.

The influx of letters and applications demonstrated, as Bunting's assistant put it, that the time "was ripe for such a conception as the Institute." Women's enrollment in college had rebounded from its low point in 1950; in 1957, 20 percent of women went to college. By 1960, 37 percent of all college students were women. Upon graduation, these women, degrees in hand, entered a world on the precipice of change. The 1950s might have been the decade of home and hearth, but throughout the decade more and more women were entering the workforce (women of the working class, of course, had never left it). It was not only accepted but expected that a woman would work outside the home for a portion of her life—either before she had children or, more likely, after her children were of school age. "Women are going back to work—a vast new army of them," wrote *Woman's Home Companion* in 1956. Nearly three-quarters of working women were married, and half of these married women had children in school. Some were armed with bachelor degrees and liberal arts educations, others with nothing but the desperation of the broke. They were typists and salespeople; they worked in factories and in retail. By the time the Institute was announced, nearly 40 percent of American women—twenty-two million total—were working outside the home.

The promise of the Institute was the promise that the scholars' lives could be, at once, more stimulating and less demanding. Bunting deliberately designed the program to be part-time so that women could enjoy time with their children. She offered a stipend so that women could get help with those troublesome chores. She promised community so that women could share their challenges and their ideas. The Institute opened doors to seminars and lecture halls so that the intellectually curious could put their bachelor degrees to use. To many working women, this novel Institute—with its prestige, its financial support, and its recognition of the challenges facing thirtysomething housewives—must have seemed tailor-made for them.

What the average working woman didn't recognize, however, as she wrote her letters of congratulations and appeal, was that the Institute was made for the unusual woman who had somehow managed to find many of these things already.

Some were disappointed to realize this; others believed that the benefits awarded to the select few would trickle down to them. "It's liberating to read about what you're doing and I feel sure it will have an immensely positive effect on the country and on all college women," wrote one Radcliffe alumna. "Whatever benefits the gifted few will have beneficial effect for the rest of us," relayed another. One woman called the Institute "a gift from the gods"; another characterized her feelings about the announcement as "the most intense pride I have experienced since the birth of my first child."

Not everyone was so pleased. More than a few Radcliffe alumnae wrote nasty letters, accusing the Radcliffe president of "pulling woman-the-homemaker down from her pedestal." One letter writer reminded Bunting of all the things a working mother misses: "seeing her child take its first steps or hearing it speak its first words." Another, a mother of four, wrote a scathing critique: rather than support women who abandoned their children, this woman said, a university should consider conferring "on those who have done an outstanding job a doctor of Domesticity degree which has never been done before." (The letter closed with a twenty-three-line lyric poem, a paean to the ephemeral joys of motherhood.) These alums thought Bunting was asking women to give up or minimize their most important work.

The critics wouldn't apply. Neither would some of the aspirational applicants who realized they didn't qualify. As the application cycle continued without them, both camps watched, either with envy or with contempt, curious to see who would be awarded the Institute's inaugural fellowships.

On a Friday afternoon in late May, Kumin was looking through the mail when she discovered, amid the bills and personal correspondence, a letter from Radcliffe College. "Dear Mrs. Kumin," she read. "I am pleased to notify you of your appointment as an Associate Scholar of the Radcliffe Institute for Independent Study." Smith, the author of the letter, would be in touch soon with further news; for now, she offered her congratulations and good wishes. This was not Kumin's first high-stakes admission gauntlet, nor even her first time being admitted to this particular institution. Still, she had always found study soothing, and it would be nice to exchange her position at the front of the classroom for one behind a desk. She was ready to be a student again.

Pleased and satisfied, Kumin did what she always did when she had career news to share: she called Sexton, who lived just a few miles away. She must have gotten the day's mail by now, and her acceptance letter would also be waiting. It was strange that Sexton hadn't called yet; perhaps she was busy with a poem or tied up with one of her children. Sexton answered and celebrated Kumin's good news. Then, anxious and wary, she went to check the mail. There was no letter.

Assuming the worst, Sexton was crushed. As she later recounted, she had wanted this desperately, more than she had wanted anything else in her life. She had been denied many things in the past—publication, the attentions of an editor, her mother's affection—but this seeming rejection stung acutely. She had longed for the validation that the title of "scholar" would have provided. A Radcliffe grant would have disproven all the teachers and family members who had discouraged her and doubted her intelligence. But it seemed that the scholarship had gone to the real scholar: bookish, credentialed Kumin, the woman with multiple languages and a master's degree. To Sexton, this was a predictable outcome, and all the more disappointing for being so. If Sexton felt a twinge of jealousy, if she felt even momentarily resentful of her closest friend, she would have been quick to recall all the times Kumin had helped her over the course of the last few years: the times she'd listened to a line of poetry, the afternoons she'd told Sexton that yes, this was a promising poem, and yes, Sexton did have talent. Kumin was her creative partner and her true intimate. A rivalry with her must have been too dangerous to contemplate.

Sexton resolved to be pleased for her friend, but she allowed herself a period of mourning. She called her husband and told him to pick up the girls (they were at a neighbor's house); she was going straight to bed. Lying in her upstairs bedroom, Sexton turned over the failure in her mind. To be sure, she had learned much since her boarding school days at Rogers Hall, and she had worked hard, but perhaps she simply did not have the talent to become a lasting poet. (Had those two negative reviewers been right, after all?) She would never be the student that Kumin was; she had studied at Brandeis University during the summer of 1960, but she feared that these few months couldn't compensate for all those missed years in her youth. She felt ordinary.

But surely to Sexton, an ordinary life was no tragedy. It would certainly have felt better than the haunted days and nights at the mental institution. Her life now might be conventional and unexciting, but it had its benefits. She had both her daughters back. She had a firm routine with Dr. Orne. She had the practice of her poetry. Life was much better in 1961 than it had been in 1956. Calmer, if not entirely pacified, Sexton went downstairs to face Joy and Linda. Eager to put the day's disappointment behind them, the Sexton family went out for dinner.

The following Monday, at home at 40 Clearwater Road, Sexton collected the day's mail. To her shock, she saw that she'd received a letter from Radcliffe. Perhaps they'd sent out rejection notices? Her heartbeat quickened; she slit the envelope. Stunned, she read over the same words of congratulations that had greeted Kumin three days earlier. College degree or no college degree, she had done it: she had gotten the fellowship.

Ecstatic, Sexton rushed out of her house and ran through her quiet Newton neighborhood, knocking on her neighbors' doors and demanding immediate entry. "I got it!" she yelled to anyone who would listen. "I got it!" ("I think everyone must have thought I had gotten my period," she later joked.) That evening, exuberant, she penned a letter to her therapist Dr. Orne; she included some lines of verse, written just for this occasion: "Hark Hark the lark / Gadzooks Hear Hear / My I.Q.'s OK this year." The announcement of the selection went out with the Friday papers on June 2. Her family celebrated her achievements: Kayo's parents bought copies of the local papers and cut out the announcement of her award. Kayo himself was proud of her (and grateful that she would soon have a work space that wasn't the dining room table). Her neighbors enjoyed the publicity her achievement brought to Newton. She had earned admittance to the nation's most august educational institution—not even her mother, with her impressive IQ, had won Radcliffe's approval.

And, to Sexton's comfort and delight, her best friend would be with her. The two poets would not be parted; they would embark on this new adventure together. That December, feeling "flush and important," as Kumin later put it, the women finally installed a second phone line. Their husbands would no longer complain about their tying up the line or about the bills. After all, with their stipends, the women were now, as Sexton saw it, "contributing." The Institute granted up to $3,000 for each fellow, nearly $25,000 in today's currency. Sexton and Kumin received $2,000 each; the money was theirs, to use as they wished.

For the rest of the month of May, the offices at Fay House were comparatively quiet. The phone rang a handful of times—far less frequently than it had during those exciting weeks in the winter of 1960—as the future Institute scholars called to accept their awards. Swan, the portrait painter, called on May 31 to say she'd be happy to attend. She was delighted at the prospect of a year's support. Perhaps she could now experiment with lithography, a medium she longed to explore. Sexton and Kumin each wrote brief notes of acceptance. They too looked forward to the year to come. It doesn't appear that anyone admitted turned down her chance at an intellectual adventure.

Sexton, Kumin, and Swan were among the first twenty-four women chosen as Radcliffe Institute fellows. It was a huge achievement: the admission rate was under 10 percent. The fellows' backgrounds were remarkably similar—they were white, well-off, and, except Sexton, highly educated—but their disciplines were diverse: the women specialized in everything from children's poetry to endocrinology. The vast majority of the women had children, ranging in age from ten months to twenty-six years. Nine of them were married to other academics, including members of the Harvard faculty. Nearly all were admitted as associate scholars. Ursula Niebuhr, wife of the theologian Reinhold Niebuhr and a theologian herself, was appointed a more senior research fellow, a distinction that reflected her academic standing. The fellows included a lawyer from Greenwich, Connecticut; a musician from Arlington, Massachusetts; three historians from the Greater Boston area; and three scholars—in political science, Spanish literature, and theology—all from Cambridge. In addition to Swan, there was another painter, Lois Swirnoff, who held a

BFA and an MFA from Yale and who taught at Wellesley, Swan's alma mater. In the first class of fellows, there were five artists whom the selection committee had deemed the scholars' "equivalents."

The married women looked forward to mingling and to introducing their husbands to women who would be their new friends. There was one woman, however, who throughout the next academic year would be attending the Institute's special events alone. Alma Wittlin, an educational psychologist from Albuquerque, was the only single woman in the first class of fellows. It was a rare thing to be a single woman in 1960—only 8 percent of women over twenty-five had never been married—and it was not easy. Birth control for unmarried women was elusive, if not illegal. Banks could reject a single woman's application for a credit card (some banks required a husband's signature). And then there were the social slights: the "missing" invitations, the invasive questions, the pitying whispers that started up, like radio static, when you passed from one room into the next. Beryl Pfizer, writing in *McCall's*, encouraged single women to arm themselves with "six rude answers to one rude question"—that is, "Why aren't you married?" The next time a married woman asks you why you're single, Pfizer suggested, say sotto voce that you prefer affairs, then cast your gaze hungrily over her husband. (Other strategies included dragging out the story for hours or spilling your coffee on your interrogator.) To be a "spinster" in 1960 was to do battle with social convention each time you stepped out into the world.

And yet Wittlin had persevered, building a career for herself in the field of educational psychology. In consultation with Connie Smith, Bunting awarded a special grant to bring her east, where she would live in graduate student housing at 6 Ash Street. Whereas many of her fellow scholars would have to rush back to the suburbs in time for dinner, Wittlin could simply stroll from the library to the dining hall, then retire to her separate room. She would lead a contained but convenient life, perfectly sized for the solitary woman.

By July, plans for the following academic year were mostly in place. The names of the Institute fellows were sent to the Harvard Corporation, one of Harvard University's two governing boards, and office space was secured. Bunting had hoped to use Byerly Hall, where science labs met, for the Institute, but science faculty had objected; instead, she worked out a temporary arrangement with a space in Harvard Square that had once held the Harvard Health Center. All told, the first year of the Institute would cost about $150,000 (roughly $1.2 million today). To Bunting's mind, it was a worthwhile investment; what the deans and teachers would learn from her experiment was beyond financial calculation.

As for what the fellows themselves would learn, that could not be predicted. Would they produce great work? Make good friends? Would a year or two at the Institute allow a woman to shift course, or would it amount to nothing more than an interlude, a brief moment of freedom in an otherwise bounded life?

These questions weren't always at the forefront of Bunting's mind—she was more concerned with producing a scalable model for those who wished to enact similar education reforms—but they did capture the imaginations of the fellows themselves.

That summer, twenty-four women from Greater Boston and beyond prepared to undertake a shared social and intellectual journey. Come September, they would pack up their books, kiss their kids, and commute to Cambridge. For many, it was a short distance to travel, but really they would be entering an entirely new world.

1961–1963

CHAPTER 6

The Premier Cru

IT WAS JUST BEFORE 6:00 P.M. on September 13, 1961, and Barbara Swan, finished with painting for the day, was walking down a narrow, tree-lined street in Cambridge's Harvard Square. The summer heat had dissipated, and the air was cool and pleasant. As she walked, young men weaved in and out of the Harvard College dormitories along the Charles River; they were heading to the boathouse, the dining hall, the undergraduate library a few blocks north of the river. It was the beginning of a new academic year, a time of first encounters and fresh starts.

Swan and her husband, Alan, were on their way to 6 Ash Street, the Graduate Center of Radcliffe College, a recently constructed building designed to resemble the old brick ones found elsewhere on campus. The building was located a block from Radcliffe Yard just a few blocks down Brattle Street from the center of Harvard Square. Connie Smith, their host for the evening, was waiting for them inside. Smith had planned an informal dinner for the inaugural class of Institute scholars and their husbands. She wanted the fellows to get a chance to meet each other in a social setting before settling down to business the following week. There were twenty-three other women on the guest list, and Swan knew none of them.

The couples approached the front entrance. The dress code for the dinner was informal, but the guests still looked sharp. Women in heels, wearing dresses with nipped waists, walked carefully over the uneven sidewalks. The men sported casual suits. There was at least one strand of pearls.

Swan had made this kind of pilgrimage once before. She had been just a teenager then, a doggedly determined young artist, biding her time until she could go to the art school of her dreams. At her father's insistence, she had driven daily to Wellesley College. She had introduced herself to other women—many in heels, a few in pearls—and had prepared for nine months of learning alongside them. On the whole, she had found her time among the women of Wellesley uninspiring. The Museum School had been a better learning environment, and her time with vagabond boys in France had inspired her art.

More than twenty years later, in the fall of 1961, Swan was not sure what an all-female community had to offer her, but seeker that she was, she was willing to find out.

She stepped inside. Though a sociable, charming woman, Swan didn't love a large party; she preferred to host intimate dinners of six to eight people so everyone could really talk. She made the best of it, winding her way among the scholars as sunlight streamed in through the building's many windows. At the end of the evening, she still wasn't sure who was who: Which poet lived in Newton? How many historians were there? Was she going to like anyone? She longed for a more leisurely gathering so that she could match faces with names.

Several weeks later, she found herself back at the Graduate Center for just such an event. Smith had called the first official meeting of the Institute for Tuesday, October 3, at 3:00 p.m. She had already distributed the first installment of each fellow's stipend in the mail ($1,000, worth $8,165 today). That Tuesday afternoon, the women of the Institute came together without their male chaperones. Smith introduced them to the Institute's policies and went over logistics.

The situation was simple: each fellow was granted office space and access to Widener Library, the university's main library, located in Harvard Yard and home to a staggering number of books (today, the library holds 3.5 million volumes). They also had access to other Harvard University resources—although not to Harvard College's Lamont Library, primarily for undergraduates, which barred women from entry. Each woman also received a stipend to use as she pleased.

The Institute was headquartered at an old yellow house at 78 Mount Auburn Street, which contained a veritable labyrinth of offices and a big, open downstairs living room. There was a small garden out back, perfect for a cigarette break. Fellows could tuck themselves away in the gabled attic, far out of reach of their families. All this was familiar to the fellows—the Institute had advertised these features from the beginning—but there was one new element to be discussed: Smith wanted to arrange seminars at which fellows would share their works in progress. Starting in February, seminars would be held every other Tuesday, from 1:00 to 3:00 p.m., in the living room at 78 Mount Auburn. The fellows would have to bring their own lunches, but there would be tea and coffee and, if Smith had the time and energy, some homemade baked goods. The seminars should be warm and friendly; the point was to learn from each other, rather than to pass judgment on the work being displayed.

Swan left this first meeting with better face recognition—the older woman with the narrow eyes was the Austrian educational researcher Alma Wittlin; and the striking, sophisticated Greek woman, with the deep-set eyes and full lips, was the historian Lily Macrakis—but there had been too little time to talk. Swan was eager to engage these women: they would be her audience, and maybe even her collaborators, in the months to come. The other fellows felt similarly: at a tea held later in the week, the women "pounced on each other," as Swan later put it. They exchanged essential information—phone numbers, fields of study, names and ages of children—as they searched for kindred spirits.

Swan spent part of the tea chatting with Lilian Randall, an art historian from Brookline. Like Swan, Randall had a bachelor's degree from a Seven Sisters school (Mount Holyoke). And like Swan, she had two children. The women chatted about early manuscripts—Randall had been working for many years on an index of Gothic marginal decoration from the thirteenth and fourteenth centuries—and Swan, with her art history background, knew enough to keep up. Almost twenty years after her undergraduate study ended, Swan now participated readily in the kinds of academic discussions that had bored her when she was young.

At some point during the gathering, Swan looked up to see two dark-haired women approaching her: Sexton and Kumin. They were a striking pair; one Institute fellow later remembered them as "exotic birds . . . both dressed in red, with black hair and shining eyes." The two frequently traded clothing; they fought over a red-and-white polyester dress that looked great on both of them, though they were built slightly differently. Swan, with her straight, cropped hair and plain style, might have felt intimidated by their elegance. But it soon became clear that these glamorous women had sought her out deliberately and that they were excited to meet her. They were both poets, they told her, but they also painted and sketched. They found drawing helped loosen them up. Kumin had taken watercolor classes when she was first married, and now that she had the grant, she resolved to draw more. She planned to reserve every Tuesday morning for art.

Rather than feeling slighted, as professionals often do when faced with amateur enthusiasm, Swan welcomed the poets' interest. She looked forward to reading their work, and they looked forward to seeing hers. They promised to visit her in her home studio, and she asked to hear their poetry sometime. All three artists had decided to work most of the time at home, rather than tuck themselves away in the "rabbit warren" that was 78 Mount Auburn.

A few days after the tea, Swan related the encounter to Smith, who must have been pleased to see that relationships were already being formed. Swan, for her part, was relieved: it looked as if her second pass at women's education might go better than the first.

·   ·   ·

When Swan was ten years old, she drew a picture of her grandmother. "It looked just like her and everyone was astounded by that," she later recalled. This child, who could barely sit still for piano lessons, had the patience to get a portrait perfectly right. Her father, who taught mechanical drawing at Newton High, was impressed: he knew how hard it was to capture a likeness.

For years, Swan was primarily a portraitist; this is how she'd put herself through college. Now she again turned to portraiture as she attempted to navigate her new academic environment. She commenced sketching her fellow Institute scholars, varying her pencil strokes in an effort to capture the unique vibrations of each woman's mind, the exact shade of her soul. (She always spoke in mystic terms about her work.) With her portraits, Swan showed that each woman was distinctive, despite any surface similarities.

Elizabeth Barker sat for a portrait. Barker, then a fifty-year-old PhD student in English at Boston University, was a high-energy, intensely verbal woman. She smoked as much as she spoke; her cigarette seemed like a sixth finger. In the portrait, a headband draws Barker's hair back in a severe manner; her hand, curled into a loose fist, grasps at the air in front of her. She seems caught mid-gesture, and probably mid-speech. Using nervous pencil lines, Swan captured Barker's intellectual dynamism. A fellow artist, the painter Lois Swirnoff, also sat before Swan. Swirnoff was from Wellesley, and her paintings were elegant and clean (later, she would be internationally recognized for her work on color). Swan feared producing a portrait that was fussy and overworked (what would her subject, a fellow painter, think?) and stuck to pure, simple lines. Ursula Niebuhr, an intimidating presence at the Institute, sat for her portrait well. Swan was in awe of Niebuhr, in part because of the theologian's intelligence and in part because she was attached to such a famous man. The portrait she produced of Niebuhr's lovely English face, with its strong bone structure, has a great deal of cross-hatching, reflecting Swan's intimidation and uncertainty. Try as she might, she couldn't quite figure out what this esteemed woman was all about.

But Swan took special delight in her drawings of the poets Kumin and Sexton.

Portrait of Anne Sexton by Barbara Swan, 1961

They looked so similar at first, these two attractive, dark-haired women: it would take an astute eye to tell them apart. Swan looked beyond their coiffed hair and their collared dresses and sought out their temperaments. Kumin was tranquil, she decided, while Sexton was riddled with tension. There was a nervous air about Sexton; she was charged, electrified. When Swan drew Sexton, she used sharp pencil strokes. She pressed down firmly, making the folds of Sexton's dress stand out. She crosshatched quickly, such that Sexton's skin took on a darker shade and provided a sharp contrast to the white dress. Though Sexton sat for her portrait in a position of repose—her left hand propping up her head, her bright eyes gazing out into the distance—in the drawing she is all taut energy. She looks as if she could spring into motion in an instant. Kumin's portrait, by contrast, makes the poet appear gentle. Swan softened her lines; her pencil seems to have brushed the page more than imprinted it. Kumin's face, in three-quarter profile, emerges from what looks like a cloud of smoke. A cigarette between her fingers, she seems lost in thought, and content to be so. The portrait is a bit too relaxed; Swan seems to have missed Kumin's self-discipline, mistaking the poet's calm for a natural state, rather than a deliberate achievement. But what Swan recognized was how the two poets complemented each other.

One woman at the Institute deserved a special portrait. Swan decided that Smith, the miracle worker who always found a way to get her fellows the help they needed, should have a professional portrait, something she could hang on her office wall. Though Swan planned to execute it on her own, she wanted it to be a gift from the "Premier Cru," her nickname for this first group of Institute fellows.

One evening, Swan invited Smith over to dinner at 32 Webster Place—a one-on-one dinner was far closer to her ideal evening than a group cocktail party—and planned to sketch her portrait that same night. But Smith was so convivial, such wonderful company, that the two women got distracted during cocktail hour: it turns out that Irish whiskey does not produce portraits for posterity. They tried again, not long after, and this time banned alcohol from what was to be a serious portrait sitting. Swan took care to pose Smith appropriately and paid special attention to the folds of her dress. Her aim, as always, was to render the eyes perfectly; she wanted to put a certain glint in them, the sense of humor for which Smith was known and loved. She couldn't quite get it, in the end; one eye was good, the other not so much. The mouth was flawed, too. Swan hung on to the portrait, thinking she would improve it in years to come—a new line here, a bit of shading there. She couldn't have known then, in the exuberant fall of 1961, how few years Smith had left.

Swan was not the only one closely studying the Institute scholars. When the women began their year at the Institute, they knew they were being watched. The media couldn't take its collective eyes off this groundbreaking program, which one paper called "Radcliffe's new baby." Throughout the summer of 1961 and into the academic year, newspapers and magazines reported on the Institute, its founder, and the women who were taking advantage of this incredible opportunity. National magazines used the Radcliffe Institute as a case study to report on new trends in women's education. Local papers profiled some of the more photogenic fellows, asking them to re-create sweet domestic scenes. In one photo, Sexton, wearing a sleeveless top and striped skirt, appears with her daughters, Joy and Linda. In another, Kumin sits with her arm around Daniel, her youngest child, and a book open in her lap; she looks a bit stunned, as if the click of the camera had frozen her in place. (Swan's chance in the local media spotlight came later: her profile appeared in 1963, under the headline "Do Dishes? No, Rather Paint.") "We were pioneers and guinea pigs," Kumin reflected later. "We were questioned and photographed in our natural habitats until my kids got so they said cheese! if you merely glanced their way." In November, in the biggest media coup for the Institute thus far, *Time* magazine placed Polly Bunting on its cover. In an accompanying profile—"One Woman, Two Lives"—Bunting was praised for her "reasonable, constructive, moderate, and just slightly outraged stand" on women's issues. Mild, humble Bunting, just a few years out from her low-profile life at Douglass, had become a national symbol of a bright future for American women.

The popularity of Bunting's ideas reflected a major change in the way Americans thought about women, and in particular about women's roles in the family home. In the early 1960s, the gendered division of labor remained largely intact—men were the breadwinners, while women took care of home and hearth—but the expectations for women had shifted. (Only 11 percent of families included a woman who was the primary or sole breadwinner, compared with 42 percent in 2015.) In the aftermath of World War II, experts and advertisers placed new emphasis on mothering. They encouraged white middle-class women to spend more time nurturing children and less time doing laundry (there were now machines for that!) and mopping the floors. (Credit the influential Dr. Benjamin Spock, whose *Common Sense Book of Baby and Child Care*, published in 1946, had become a staple in middle-class homes.) Even middle-class women who didn't work outside the home hired part-time household help; untroubled by empty pantries or dirty bedsheets, they could be more present for their children. By the time the Institute scholars received their first checks from Smith, household help was no longer seen as a luxury or taken to be a sign of one's superior class status. Instead, it was framed as a necessity: something middle-class women deserved, something they should demand.

Bolstered by this broad cultural change, almost all of the Institute women spent their stipends on help with housework. Some bought time-saving household devices. Swan bought a dishwasher; she'd calculated the number of labor hours it would save her and decided it was a worthy investment. Kumin went in a slightly different direction, spending hers on a file cabinet, a tape recorder, and a typewriter with an international key—"which is more of a status symbol to me than a Mercedes Benz," she said. Two fellows used the money to pay for their children's extracurricular activities, thus arranging a few more hours of child-free time. Others hired housekeepers or babysitters, usually women of color. At the time, black women provided the bulk of domestic labor in America. In 1960, one-third of all employed black women were domestic workers. (Although the economy and labor force have changed greatly since this date, black women remain overrepresented in low-paying and low-prestige jobs. According to the Institute for Women's Policy Research, "Black and Hispanic women are more than twice as likely to work in 'service' occupations as White women"; these jobs tend to be low paying, irregular, and precarious.)

The fact that the women of the Institute used their stipends to hire domestic workers tells us something about how Radcliffe imagined what one article called "women of talent," both who such women were and what they deserved. A woman of talent would have a college degree; a woman of talent could hire another woman to sweep her floors and care for her children. Radcliffe had yet to reckon with the idea that a domestic worker could also be a "woman of talent," a creative mind. The Institute didn't consider the lives of talented, working-class women until later, when Olsen used her seminar talk to lament the loss of so many brilliant careers to hard labor. It didn't begin to address long-standing racial inequality, inside and outside academia, until Radcliffe undergrads began agitating for improvements to admissions. In this first year, laboring women were forgotten, and white women, both middle-class and wealthy, benefited from the work done by those less privileged.

Sexton, white and relatively wealthy, found her life vastly improved by her stipend. Like the other fellows, she hired extra household help. Her mother-in-law was already paying for someone to come in once a week, but Sexton increased it to twice and hired a monthly cleaning service, for Kayo's sake. ("He doesn't like a messy house," she explained. "He's kind of a perfectionist.") But the bulk of the money went to home renovations. She turned their porch into a study, and she installed a swimming pool in her backyard. The pool became something of a local scandal: for decades, literary Boston gossiped about the Newton poet who had used Radcliffe's money to build a private pool. When Bunting heard that one of her scholars had used funds in this fashion, she was dismayed. This was frivolousness; this was not how someone lived a serious, moderate life.

To Sexton, though, the pool was an invaluable, therapeutic addition to her daily routine. It became a daily ritual. She swam her laps languidly, her long body slicing through the water. With her eyes closed, listening to birdsong, she could reimagine the stultifying suburbs as a kind of pastoral idyll.

Thanks to the Radcliffe stipend, the house at 40 Clearwater Road became a kind of sanctuary. Sexton hated going out into what she called "the frightening world"; she could overcome any number of creative obstacles, but her anxiety made even the brief trips into Cambridge seem daunting. Now she had a proper, pleasing workplace. No longer would she have to work at the dining room table, her papers and books strewn about, her husband chastising her for the mess. Never again would she have to climb over Kayo to adjust the record player as she tried to pull a poem from the depths of her

Photograph of Anne Sexton in her home office, October 1961

mind. She could shut out Linda and Joy if she needed a moment alone at the typewriter or on the phone with Kumin. Counting the office on Mount Auburn Street, she now had not one but two rooms of her own.

There is a photo of Sexton from this first fall, sitting in the new home office. She rocks back in her chair, with her long legs propped up against one of the office's bookshelves, her feet shod in dark flats, her slim ankles crossed. A book sits open on her lap, and a cigarette dangles from her hand. She has turned away from her typewriter to look in the direction of the photographer. She is smiling broadly, her mouth open, her entire being relaxed and radiant. She looks as if she has been caught in a moment of learning. She looks delighted.

The camera didn't lie: Sexton was unusually happy that fall, as well as newly confident. She was hard at work on her new book of poems and had been very productive: by November, she had written twenty pages of a new book. She had also taken up a teaching position, teaching creative writing to Harvard and Radcliffe students. "It is more work than I had planned," she wrote to a friend, "but enjoyable in a way." Things were also going well at home: Kayo, who had been prone to fits of anger and physical violence, had entered therapy. A couple infatuations on Sexton's end had attenuated. The couple fought less, and they enjoyed more outings with their daughters.

For Sexton, admission to the Institute had eased the conflict she felt between her family and her work. The Institute was a "status symbol," she told Alice Ryerson, an education researcher who conducted extensive interviews with every member of the "Premier Cru." "It's like I just graduated." She felt that the Institute proved her worth to the poetry world—as well as to her family. "Since I started to make money and get status . . . I don't feel so guilty because I'm contributing . . . And I have people approving of me and thinking it's good when I'm doing this." She upped her speaking fees to $250—at the time, very few poets commanded more—and she signed a "first reading" agreement with *The New Yorker* (in other words, the magazine had right of first refusal), which gave her a ready market for new work. She was soaring to the next stage of her career.

One day that fall, Sexton lay down indoors to take a nap with Linda, then eight, the child who often prompted her to reflect on her own life. Outside, the leaves were turning. Mother and daughter dozed and reminisced. (It was still early evening, but there had been wine with dinner.) Sexton gently corrected Linda's memories, as mothers often do: no, that event you remember wasn't yesterday; that was a long time ago. Outside, the trees swayed in the fall wind, and birds moved across the grass. There was something about this moment of reflection and repose that inspired Sexton. She asked Linda to get a pencil and paper and started writing a poem right there in bed, writing down what Linda said and then recording her own responses. Within two days, she had assembled these notes and fragments into a poem, one that she eventually called "The Fortress."

In many ways, "The Fortress" resembles "The Double Image," the poem featuring twinned, mother-daughter portraits that Sexton composed while in Lowell's seminar. Like its predecessor, "The Fortress" is a poem about generational continuity and about what mothers pass down to their daughters. In the poem, a mother and daughter are lying on a square bed under a pink quilt; outside, the woods display leaves left over from summer. The mother, the speaker of the poem, explains seasonal change and natural phenomena. Her lines are half-serious but entirely elegant: "the leaves have been fed / secretly from a pool of beet-red dye," she says. The speaker, "half in jest, half in dread," presses her finger on the brown mole on her daughter's face. It is a mark "inherited / from my right cheek: a spot of danger." Will the daughter inherit her mother's instability, along with her beauty? Were the two bound up in each other? Will the daughter become a writer, too, and suffer for it? The mother, who so confidently corrects her daughter's impressions of the external world, finds herself incapable of explaining the future, let alone protecting her daughter from it.

Soon enough, the speaker suggests, the daughter will find herself providing comfort and care—"your own child / at your breast"—and her struggles—inherited though they may be—will be her own. "The Fortress" ends with the speaker's assurance of timeless and constant love, whatever the season. The poem is at once a promise and a prophecy, a way of reckoning with one's inescapable womanhood.

Sexton had never shied away from addressing her female identity. After all, her first collection had included poems about mothers and maternity wards. But the poems in her second collection, which she was in the process of arranging that fall, were even more open about female experience. "With Mercy for the Greedy" proposes poetry as a way to heal after an abortion. (In 1960, Sexton had opted for an illegal abortion rather than bear a third child, in part because she was not sure her husband was the father.) "Woman with Girdle" is a kind of blazon; it describes a woman with a sagging midriff and thick thighs removing her undergarments, revealing herself to be at once soft and strong, imperfect and beautiful. "The Operation," a poem in three parts, combines images of Mary Gray's cancer with images of Sexton's own medical trial, the removal of an ovarian cyst; "woman's dying / must come in seasons," the speaker muses. "The Fortress" thus represented a concentration and intensification of her great poetic subjects: motherhood, the female body, and love, romantic and otherwise. Like Swan, who painted her babies, and Kumin, who wanted to write the kind of children's verse that she could read to her young son, Sexton was attempting to ease the conflict between her life as an artist and her life as a mother by letting the second inspire the first.

More than that, Sexton was beginning to think more carefully about what it meant to write as a woman. In Lowell's seminar, she had fretted about her female identity, worrying that she would always seem inferior to serious male poets. At Radcliffe, though, her views about women and art started to shift. Perhaps it was the explicitly political mission of the Institute, a mission reiterated in promotional pamphlets and press releases. Perhaps it was the media frenzy, the profiles in the press, the approving attitude shown by the American public. Perhaps it was simply being surrounded by women: even though Sexton worked most days from home, when she did drive into Cambridge, she found herself enmeshed within an all-female society of fellows. At 78 Mount Auburn Street, there was no condescending John Holmes, no enigmatic Robert Lowell. There were only women like her. Sexton had replaced the sexually tense workshop setting with a supportive female community.

Whatever the reason, Sexton started to take a firmer stance on sexism in the literary scene. In her interview with Ryerson, she stated that she had been at a disadvantage in her profession, not because of her lack of education or any other deficiencies, but simply because she was a woman. She thought that her male peers scorned "lady poets," and she felt pressure to be especially firm and controlled in her writing—to be twice as good, in other words. "You've got to be hard," she explained. "You've got to be kind of cruel with the language." She said that her husband and her mother-in-law hadn't taken her poetry seriously; they had wanted her to dabble in it, as if it were a hobby. It wasn't until she received the Institute grant that she felt that she commanded their respect. She felt that the worst problem of her life was "being a woman who does something like write poetry."

At the same time, though, Sexton was starting to see how fulfilling her creative desires could improve her life and the lives of her children. When asked if she thought she was a better mother since she started writing poetry, she responded, "Yes. Much better. Because I'm not asking them to create a life for me and a reason." Though she still longed to hear the praise "she writes like a man," she was also beginning to see the advantages of "being a woman who does something like write poetry." Maybe writing was the only way she could be a good mother and sustain her marriage. Maybe, as Bunting kept insisting, a woman needed to combine the domestic and the professional, or at least find a way of alternating between the two.

By late 1961, Sexton, like the other Institute fellows, had become convinced of the merits of this approach. The next step was to convince the rest of the world.

"I don't think that many of us . . . at the Institute were revolutionaries," Lily Macrakis, the Greek historian in the Institute's first class, remembered decades later. The Institute had been founded on a political premise: that American women were at a disadvantage intellectually and professionally, and that educational and social institutions needed to be reformed. And yet, the atmosphere at the Institute was neither combative nor politically charged. If anything, Macrakis recalled, the women simply felt lucky to be there. They walked around affirming their gratitude; "what a nice thing," they said to each other, "what an exceptional thing." It was only later that Macrakis and her peers began to question why places like the Institute weren't more common. But even during the Institute years, they began raising other questions with each other. Why was it so hard for women to do intellectual work? Why did female academics have so much trouble finding institutional positions? Why had it taken until now for something like the Institute to form? "And slowly we started thinking . . . 'Why don't we push it more?'"

The women Macrakis met during her year at Radcliffe were neither political agitators nor cultural rebels. They were not part of the 1950s counterculture, the precursor to the hippies of the 1960s. They did not line their eyes in kohl; they did not wear blue jeans. They avoided Sarah Lawrence, the school for rebel women. They did not declare, along with the writer Anne Roiphe, that they were "opposed to country clubs everywhere."

The women who gathered at Radcliffe in September 1961 had, for the most part, embraced everything that a woman like Roiphe had rejected. Roiphe, who considered herself the "anti-Smith girl," the "enemy of suburban lawns and gold bracelets, fraternities, Fascists, and stockbrokers," was a perfect foil. The average Institute scholar had married the stockbroker (or the salesman, or the engineer, or the banker). She had purchased the nice house in the suburbs. She had applied for and been granted membership in the country club. Many Institute fellows had spent their early adult lives following the path that had been laid out before them by the culture at large. Before they came to Radcliffe, they spent their days caring for their children and their nights waiting for their husbands to finish their work. They often wondered, as one of them put it, "Is that going to be my life?"

Macrakis was one woman preoccupied with just this question. In the fall of 1960, she was living in the town of Belmont, a pleasant suburb just west of Cambridge, with her husband, Michael, and their three young children, and fretting about her future as a "Belmont matron." This would have been a sad fate for an unconventional woman who had demonstrated such brilliance all her life. Born in Athens in 1928, Macrakis was an intelligent, independent young woman who went to college to study history and archaeology at a time when most Athenian girls married right after high school. She bucked convention again when she followed her husband-to-be to America before they were even married, arriving in New York in the fall of 1953. In America, the couple pursued their academic interests. Michael Macrakis began a PhD program in mathematics at MIT and eventually transferred to and graduated from Harvard. Lily, meanwhile, had been accepted into a master's program at Radcliffe. A timid young woman, she nonetheless impressed her professors with her multiple languages—French, German, Italian, and modern and ancient Greek—and her elegant bearing. During the first week of classes, she found herself confessing to a particularly intimidating

Byzantine history professor that she would miss the first session of his seminar. She had a prior engagement: she was getting married.

Macrakis received her master's degree in history in 1955. She was pregnant with her first child, a son, while studying for her degree. She had her twin daughters a few years later. The family was doing well financially, and she had domestic help. What she didn't have was any kind of outlet for her intelligent mind. She played tennis; she read mystery novels. She watched her husband work on his scholarship late into the night; she accepted that he would take his work seriously, because he was a man. Bored and listless, she thought of her Athenian mother, with her beautiful dresses and her styled hair, and she tried to become the same kind of woman. "There were certain things you were doing that you had accepted," she said later, looking back on her housebound years. "I mean, that was life."

Her life changed in November 1960. "You know, I read a very interesting thing today," Michael said to her one day. He was an avid *New York Times* reader, and he'd seen the announcement of the new program for female scholars. He explained the program to his wife: money, an office, time and space to think. "So what?" Macrakis replied. "I don't have a PhD. I have three children that are under five." But Michael was adamant that she apply. He always pushed her; while she was finishing her master's thesis, he would send her upstairs to work while he finished the dinner dishes. ("My husband was the most pro-female person I have ever met," she later said.) Macrakis relented, though she was sure they wouldn't accept her. When she got a phone call from Connie Smith, informing her that she'd made it to the round of a hundred interviewees, she relaxed, because she was even more convinced: How could she win one of twenty spots? She didn't even have a scholarly publication to her name. What she did have, as Smith later told her, were the best recommendation letters the selection committee had ever seen. She was accepted into the inaugural class of twenty-four Institute scholars (more women had been admitted than planned), along with Sexton, Kumin, and Swan. Years later, she called the Institute "my salvation."

Unlike some of the Institute scholars—unlike hundreds of thousands of women all over America—Macrakis already had domestic help when she applied for the Institute. What the Institute offered her was a sense of direction, a way back into her scholarly work. Each morning, her children bade her goodbye—"you're going to the big school; we're going to the small school," they said—and she drove into Cambridge, where she sequestered herself in the stacks of Widener Library. The stacks were dim and labyrinthine, with innumerable rows of books. The space was dusty and a bit foreboding, but Macrakis loved working there. She would sit in one of the carrels that lined the perimeter of the floor and work for four uninterrupted hours on her study of the Greek politician Eleftherios Venizelos. She was loath to leave her hard-won work space, even for the few minutes it would take to put another nickel in the parking meter. In what seemed to some like a wanton display of wealth, she used part of her Institute stipend to pay the parking tickets she accrued while her car languished on the streets of Cambridge.

That first semester, Macrakis fell into a friendship with Sexton and Kumin, whom she referred to as "the poets." An excellent cook, Macrakis regularly hosted Kumin and Sexton at her house in Belmont. They'd enjoy her Greek cooking and chat about their work. As the evening drew on, and the wine continued to flow, the three women would begin to talk about their private frustrations and fears. All three had tried to live the lives expected of them. Macrakis had been proud of herself for what she thought of as "doing my duty": cooking, loving her husband and children. Kumin had willed herself to participate in all the rituals and practices of suburban life: the carpools, the dinner parties. It was as if, at long last, she had caved to those sorority girls who pestered her throughout her senior year of high school. Sexton had pursued the dream of domestic bliss fervently. "I thought that before I had children the answer was to have a home and children," she once said. "I was always all my life striving for something I wanted. It was just that I never knew what it was I wanted." Since thirteen, she had known she wanted to be married. She was so grateful to meet a suitable man, and she believed that having children would cure all her problems: "This feeling or frustration or whatever it is then would be gone."

Now, among each other, each confessed to her irritation with her children, her occasional disinterest in her husband. The friends admitted to their boredom with bridge parties and similar social offerings. "So you felt the same as me?" they would ask each other, reflecting on their lives before Radcliffe. "Because I felt like a prisoner."

The three friends swore that things would be different for their daughters. Just as the speaker of "The Fortress" worries that her daughter's life will recapitulate her own, these women feared that their daughters would face the same oppressive expectations, the same pressure to conform. Would their daughters end up like caged creatures, stalking back and forth across the small plots allotted to them? Kumin worried about her middle daughter, Judith, then nine, who seemed like an "exact carbon copy of myself." Unlike her own mother, Kumin wanted Judith to be different, to escape the pressure of social convention. She began to contemplate fleeing from the suburbs, perhaps to a farm somewhere. Sexton expressed similar fears. "I would just as soon they didn't become writers," she said once of her daughters. "I don't want them to just try to become me."

The Institute hadn't eliminated the conflict each woman occasionally felt between caring for her children and honing her craft. Sexton experienced this conflict most acutely. On Tuesday and Thursday afternoons, she watched her daughters at home, and they pestered her with requests typical of children under ten: "Can we play?" "Mommy, can I have 5 more kids in?" "Can you give them something to eat?" "Can I go here?" With lingering guilt about having been absent during their early years, Sexton did her best to meet her daughters' needs. Sometimes, she stopped her work to play with them, or she read a story, or she talked with them about the progress they were making with the violin. She let them invite over friends, if only to stop the incessant ringing of the telephone. The Sexton backyard, improved by the pool, became a gathering place for the neighborhood kids.

On other days, though, her frustration boiled over. "There are times when I shriek at them," she confessed. "Get out of here. I'm working. No, I won't talk to you. No. Mommy's busy." She could run into her study, but the odds were good that they would tap their small fists on the closed door. By November, a malaise had set in, and she again contemplated ending her life. One evening, she took an overdose of sleeping pills—more a gesture toward suicide than a deliberate act—and made notes on her forthcoming poetry manuscript for those who would publish it posthumously. She survived, though unhappily. "My writing, Bah, is terrible now," she wrote to Olsen around this time. "Bah, I am a commonplace, or if not then why are the objects of my life not worth noting."

Sexton might have carved out a space for herself, but she was still surrounded by the objects of her prior life: her husband's briefcase, glassware, her children's dirty socks and shoes. Even her book-lined fortress was not impregnable.

Well-to-do women weren't supposed to complain. Prior to the Institute, the fellows, many of them reserved New Englanders, would never have spoken against the limitations the culture had placed on their lives; they might not have even acknowledged such restrictions to themselves. American women were supposedly the luckiest on the planet, content in their conformity. A 1962 issue of *Harper's* described the American woman, approvingly, as "not very different from her mother or grandmother. She is equally attached to the classic feminine values—sexual attractiveness, motherly devotion, and the nurturing role in home and community affairs. She is no great figure in public life or the professions. And like most men, she is repelled by the slogans of old-fashioned feminism."

But soon enough, as they experienced what Kumin called the "instant sympathy" of the Institute, they began to speak more boldly about all they didn't yet have.

Not everyone wanted to hear their complaints. Educated women, and especially Radcliffe alumnae, proved to be a surprisingly hostile audience. One day during her first year at the Institute, Smith asked Macrakis to accompany her to a lunch at a local Junior League; she was hoping to do some fund-raising, and she needed a representative from the Institute, someone who could give the program a face. The two women were in a taxi on their way to the event when Smith, usually so sensitive to the fellows' fears and needs, sprang on Macrakis that she, Macrakis, would need to give some remarks about her Institute experience. The young historian panicked. She hated public speaking—she was already dreading giving her seminar talk in the spring—but her companion soothed her. All you have to do, Smith said, is tell your story: say who you are, and how you got here. Macrakis nervously agreed.

Just a few minutes later, Macrakis was standing in front of a crowd of fifty or so well-heeled women, trembling. She didn't know any of them, but she knew that you had to have a "good name" to get into the Junior League. Their families must have been among the most powerful in Boston. Haltingly, she started to talk about the Institute, about her work and her household help and her husband's support. She had barely finished when the attacks began. "You leave your children?" they asked incredulously. "Don't you think that you are sacrificing the well-being of your children to your own ambition?" Never mind that Michael was supportive, or that the Macrakis children were perfectly happy to see their mother off in the mornings and come home to her in the afternoons. The women of the Junior League expressed skepticism that there was anything more important than a woman's domestic responsibilities, or that the part-time program at the Institute offered a workable solution for all parties involved. They continued with their critical, cruel questions. Macrakis found herself largely caving to their objections, though she snuck in a few moments of self-defense. "This is war here," she thought to herself. She was relieved when she was finally able to step out of view. She never forgot the event, nor did she forgive the women who so rudely questioned her commitment to her family and her children. Looking back on that lunch decades later, she expressed an antipathy untempered by time: "They were horrid . . . I hate them. I hate them."

The complaints of the Junior League women echoed earlier criticisms of the Institute, the kind that alumnae and others had written to Bunting upon the Institute's announcement. These women felt personally slighted by Bunting's project. They had thought they were doing everything right: they had fulfilled the homemaking mission that the culture had set out for them. And now here was this woman—odd, overeducated, and, in their eyes, unfeminine— suggesting that if they dedicated their lives to their children, they were somehow *worse* mothers than if they'd pursued a career. The equation was absurd, and their anger was real. Despite Bunting's repeated insistence that homemaking was important—she herself had loved her years at home—some women never softened their stance toward the Institute. Like communism and homosexuality, the Institute was yet another threat to the American family.

During that first year, the fellows found themselves surveilled. As they strutted out their doors, books under their arms, lunches packed, they felt their neighbors' eyes upon them. Kumin had dealt with this kind of opprobrium before; some of the women in her neighborhood had openly criticized her for working during the early years of her marriage. (It was not a choice, Kumin reflected later. They'd needed the money.) Now she felt guilty about her admission to the Institute, and she worried that she wouldn't be able to write enough to justify receiving the grant. "There were friends and neighbors who acted sincerely pleased," Kumin recalled, years later. "And there were acquaintances who spoke quite venomously about how lucky I was to have such a patient, longsuffering [*sic*] martyred husband and how nice it would be for the children who might not see more of their already parttime [*sic*] mother since it meant a year off from teaching." Her neighbors were far more concerned about Kumin's absences than her children were: now older, her kids were often out of the house. Like Macrakis, she was being charged with crimes against the American home.

Macrakis knew how lucky she was to have an encouraging husband and how different her life would have been if she'd married badly, or too soon. A year after the Institute, while at her first teaching job, Macrakis would shock her students by refusing to admire their engagement rings. "Too early," she would tell them. "You're twenty-two!" She told graduating seniors they needed to see the world first, before they settled down and had children. "You never know if your husband will allow you to do certain things you want to do," she warned them, "so you better be free." For the rest of her life, Macrakis received letters from her former students in which they thanked her for steering them away from early marriage and showing them how a fulfilling life could be lived. "You saved me," they wrote. Just as Radcliffe had been her salvation, she had been theirs.

Years later, looking back on those evenings in 1961, Macrakis struggled to define what she and the poets had been doing when they vented and empathized and imagined alternative lives. She didn't want to attribute too much political consciousness to her former self. After all, when she was at the Institute, women's liberation was still a few years away. Kennedy had only just commissioned an investigation into the status of women, in December 1961; the commission was "charged with evaluating and making recommendations to improve the legal, social, civic, and economic status of American women." (Eleanor Roosevelt chaired the committee until her death in 1962, at which point Esther Peterson, the assistant secretary of labor, took over.) Its report, which criticized inequalities facing women in this supposedly "free" society, would not be released until October 1963, after Macrakis had moved on to her teaching job. That was the year things really changed: Betty Friedan named the problems facing Macrakis and her friends and sparked conversations between women across the nation. They began to organize; within a few years, feminist organizations stated their goals and started to lobby Congress.

This highly visible women's movement raised new questions about who counted in the movement and whom the movement served. Was women's liberation only for suburban housewives? Or could the women's movement also liberate housekeepers and other domestic workers? Could it be for black women as well as white? At the Institute in 1961, such questions had yet to arise. As the "Premier Cru" member Brita Stendahl put it, "How little we knew then that we were on the edge of women's liberation and that feminism was about to emerge as a conscious analytical tool."

Still, Macrakis admitted, they were onto something during those casual dinners, something that this particular group of women didn't yet have the language to express. "Well, it was feminism without, you know, without the word," she said. The word would come later, after Macrakis had left the Institute for a teaching gig and a new crop of associate scholars took up residence in the yellow house. In the meantime, the women of the Institute kept up their conversations, gifting each other, in Kumin's words, "a readiness to listen and give and hear and take."

CHAPTER 7

We're Just Talking

O N THE AFTERNOON OF FEBRUARY 13, 1962—one day before Jackie Kennedy, the impeccable hostess, took the press on a tour of the White House—the female scholars and artists of the Institute crowded into the first floor of 78 Mount Auburn Street for the very first seminar of the spring semester. They pulled hard-backed chairs close together or grabbed seats on a bench. Bagged lunches emerged from purses; coffee cups were passed from hand to hand.

The seminars were not mandatory—Bunting and Smith didn't want to impose on the scholars' work—but most everyone was in attendance. They sensed that this gathering would help them get over their insecurities and motivate them to take their own research more seriously. There was Shirley Letwin, a political scientist with a PhD from the University of Chicago; she was an elegant, cosmopolitan woman who favored blue suits and owned a gray Persian lamb toque. There was Vilma Hunt, a dentist originally from Australia (she had moved to Boston in 1952), who could be spotted most days in a white lab coat scurrying around campus on her way from lecture to lab. And there was Smith, looking, to one scholar, just like a "mother hen" watching proudly over her brood.

The scholars were gathered to hear Kumin and Sexton give a joint seminar on poetry. It was the first seminar of the semester, indeed the first seminar that the Institute had ever held. The two poets promised to discuss their methods of composition and read from their work.

Kumin was calm; she was well prepared. She had written out her remarks in full, then gone back over them with a blue pen to make changes. She had also annotated the poems she'd planned to read, noting in the margins various poetic devices—fulcrums, trochees, and the like—that she wanted to explain to the audience. She had mimeographed the poems she would read that day: "Morning Swim," "The Practice of Shame," "Sunset Blues," among others. Each had been chosen for the lesson it could illustrate about how poetry works.

Sexton, by contrast, was an anxious mess. A poetry reading was both her natural habitat—she was always performing, in person and on the page—and a kind of gauntlet, a setting that tested her nerves. When she gave formal readings, she showed up late deliberately, to give the crowd time to anticipate her arrival and to postpone the inevitable moment of appearing onstage. She usually downed a drink or two beforehand. On this winter Tuesday, she met Max before the seminar to calm her nerves. She had no prepared remarks; she would give no lessons. All she could do was read her poetry and try to explain the strange alchemy by which she transformed her personal life into art.

"I think we might as well get started," Smith said around 1:00 p.m., and the room quieted. She indicated a tape recorder and explained that the seminar would be recorded because "we're certain that we're recording history." For centuries, scholars had gathered in rooms around Cambridge, to present, to debate, and to assert their investment in each other's work. But this was a relatively rare occurrence: a scholarly symposium that featured women exclusively.

·   ·   ·   ·

Kumin and Sexton gave a seminar together because they did everything together, though this was something few people knew. For years, they kept their long-standing collaboration a secret, even though it was clear to anyone who knew them that the two women were close. There were several reasons to be cagey. First, their intimacy could seem unnatural to the wrong audience. Sexton and Kumin worried that their friendship would be insulting to their husbands. Women were supposed to prioritize their husbands and children, not female friends who had families of their own.

Second, early in their careers, each woman was struggling to establish herself as a legitimate poet. They worried that if critics knew about their collaboration, they would fail to distinguish between their bodies of work, or they would place them in head-to-head competition.

Of course, they were far from the only poets to support each other's work. Ezra Pound reshaped T. S. Eliot's *Waste Land;* Elizabeth Bishop and Robert Lowell exchanged poems over airmail. Their shame, they confessed later, had everything to do with being women: there was no room in mid-century Boston for intellectual female friendships. Men dominated the poetry scene; they grabbed most of the spots in literary magazines and snapped up many of the prizes. A representative issue of *Poetry* magazine from 1960 featured work by nine men and only two women. (This gender ratio was only slightly better than that of other industries: at the time, women made up only 6 percent of American doctors, 3 percent of lawyers, and less than 1 percent of engineers.) That same year, male poets won the Pulitzer, the Lamont Poetry Prize, and the National Book Award for Poetry; a man also served as the national consultant in poetry. The poetry world was a man's world, and women had to fight—with men, and with each other—just to get a foothold in it. Both poets later claimed that if their relationship had bloomed during the height of women's liberation, they would have felt much less ashamed of their intimacy.

The poets also had personal reasons for hiding their creative relationship. Keeping quiet about their collaboration allowed them to pass over in silence some of the trickier aspects of their friendship.

By the time of the Institute, Sexton—a novice poet until the end of the 1950s—had surpassed Kumin, the more practiced and educated writer. When she first started in Holmes's workshop, in 1957, Sexton had seen herself as something like Kumin's student; she learned from the more experienced poet, which meant that she also copied Kumin's flaws. Now that she had developed her own poetic style and subjects, she wanted to maintain her independence—and, perhaps, her superiority. Kumin, meanwhile, grew frustrated with those like Holmes who saw her as responsible for her friend. She wanted to be seen as a separate artist, someone other than Sexton's keeper. Even later in their careers, Kumin hated when she and Sexton published collections at the same time.

And so for years they worked together in secret. They typed poems while on the telephone with each other, often leaving the phone line open for hours. Theirs was a workshop for mothers: they could be at home tending to children and simultaneously receiving edits. This composition strategy required incredible empathy on the part of the listener: she needed to imagine herself as someone else—a different poet who wrote in a different register. Sexton once compared it to entering someone else's consciousness. "You enter into the voice of the poet," she explained, "and you think, how to make better, but not, how to make like me."

That first fall at the Institute, Kumin and Sexton fell into a reliable routine. Each woke and breakfasted with her children, all of whom were now of school age, then retired to her home office. Both preferred to write at home: Kumin working, in her own words, "in the eye of the hurricane," insulated by her books and papers. Sexton felt similarly about her book-lined study. "My books make me happy," she once explained. "They sit there and say, 'Well, we got written and you can too.'" One poet would phone the other. They'd begin by updating each other on their lives, on anything that had happened since the last time they had talked. Eventually, one of them would say, "We're just talking. Why the hell aren't we writing!" One poet would suggest a line or a concept. Either she would ring off, promising to call back in twenty minutes, or she might stay on the line, whistling into the phone when she was ready to share a verse or two.

Sexton loved the pressure of the twenty-minute interlude. "It is the most stimulating thing. It's a challenge," she once said. "We've got this much time, and goddam it, I'm going to have something there." Inevitably, when they reconnected, both poets had put words on the page. They would work until their children came home for lunch, and then, if the younger children had half days and the weather was nice, they would gather at the Sexton pool. The kids, ranging in age from six to thirteen, would run around the yard, while Kumin and Sexton sat with their legs in the water, swapping Sexton's typewriter back and forth as they worked on their children's book. Around 5:00 or 6:00, when their husbands returned from work, they would go their separate ways to make cocktails and, eventually, dinner. As Bunting had suggested, studying and homemaking mixed wonderfully.

Kumin loved the rhythms of her life that fall. She had no courses to teach, no commute to endure. She could start making notes toward a novel; she wanted to try her hand at fiction again (she hadn't written any adult fiction since her days in Stegner's classroom). She could also return to her first love: poetry. Her first collection, *Halfway*, had been published by Holt, Rinehart and Winston in 1961. In it, her powers of observation were on display. She built poems around specific, sensory details: the way lightning bugs sealed in a milk jar "winked and sulked," the seductive face of Humphrey Bogart on the silver screen, the way a swimmer scoops water behind him, the feel of the first spring rain. If Sexton called her poetic process "image making"—imagining the right image that could communicate an emotional state—Kumin could have called hers "image mining": locating a poem's perfect images in the already-existing world.

Though *Halfway* sold only three hundred copies out of a print run of a thousand, reviewers praised Kumin's facility with different lyric modes, as well as her ability to fuse the vanguard and the traditional. In a roundup of new poetry in *Commentary*, the esteemed critic Harold Rosenberg said that of all the poets being reviewed, a group that included Allen Ginsberg, Kumin "had unquestionably the most talent." She had put poetry for adults aside while she taught and worked on her children's books; she published four of them in 1961, all seasonally themed, and another in 1962. (She would write twenty-five children's books total, including four that she co-wrote with Sexton.)

Now, with more free time in front of her, Kumin could once again write her detailed, loving descriptions of the physical world.

This was the world—sensual, mysterious—that Kumin introduced her listeners to during her Radcliffe seminar. In "Morning Swim," she described what it was like to "set out, oily and nude / through mist, in chilly solitude" for a swim in a green lake. In the poem, Kumin blended domestic and natural imagery: there is "a cotton beach" covered in "night fog thick as terry cloth," through which the early morning swimmer cuts her path. The communion between swimmer and lake is erotic: the swimmer takes the lake "between my legs" and thrashes her way through the water. Listening, one might mistake the swim for a sexual encounter, the lake for a bed. She infused natural landscapes with human desire.

She turned to another water poem to make an explicit connection between love and the natural landscape. ("Water and I have an old understanding," Kumin noted cryptically; her audience wouldn't have necessarily known about her swimming in high school and college.) Inspired by a beach vacation, "In That Land" is all appetite and abundance. "Hungry for oysters to suck down with gin / we go at sunset and low water," it begins. The speaker and her companion step over stones in the shallow sea, there discovering oysters, "grown in on each other / lip over lip, greasy with algae, to cover / the eyeball we eat." There is something violent about the couple's desire for oysters, dead or alive. "We are the oyster killers," she declares at one point. Later that night, she looks at her lover from bed, admiring his body, waiting for him to come back to the salt-smelling bed, where she winds her body into his like a creature securing itself in its shell. "We hold ourselves in one world at a time," the poem concludes: a world of sea salt and summer oysters, a season of life that will surely pass.

Kumin said little about the life that inspired the poetry, though she did acknowledge that she and her husband were the gin drinkers that "In That Land" made them out to be. For her, the seminar was an occasion to teach, not to confess. When she began her presentation, Kumin had claimed to be offering "an apologia for . . . the schizoid worlds of Maxine Kumin," but what she really provided was a thorough lesson in the components of poetry. She read one poem and explained what constitutes an iamb; she read another and talked about off rhyme; a third became the occasion for a discussion of alliteration and assonance. Her manner was teacherly, even a bit pedantic; as she read, her confident voice enunciating clearly, she emphasized the specific words to which she wanted her audience to attend. "Form is terribly important to me as a poet," she explained, as if to justify the fine-grained detail of her presentation. Though she had been experimenting with more free verse while on the Radcliffe fellowship, she found herself slipping back into intricate, complex formal poetry whenever she had "something really difficult or really painful to say." Form was what granted Kumin control over her feelings.

After forty-five minutes, Sexton took her friend's place. Even at this early stage of her career, Sexton was already a talented performer. She had a deep, dramatic reading voice that held the audience rapt.

But her skill as a performer belied her intense anxiety, which was even worse on this afternoon. She knew that she couldn't approach the Institute seminar as she did a formal reading, when the audience was at a distance and her job was, alternately, to alienate and to awe. This was a more intimate gathering, comprising women who would recognize her major themes and who might be appalled by her dramatic style. She felt anxious about baring her soul to these women, but she wasn't a scholar, and she couldn't hide behind discussions of the lyric tradition. She would have to do as she always did: construct a persona, a woman who was at once her and not her.

"I'm not awfully well-prepared today," Sexton began, self-deprecating as always. She wasn't going to give instruction as Kumin had, she explained, because she didn't really understand what she called the "technical stuff"; to her, poetic devices were just so much "trickery" to be snuck into a poem. Instead of a lesson, she promised her audience entertainment. She would tell them stories, and she would try to immerse them in the world of the poem. If nothing else, her talk would be engaging. "One of my secret instructions to myself as a poet is: whatever you do don't be boring," she said.

Sexton opened her reading with a poem called "Young," a poem set "a thousand doors ago," in her childhood home. She then flashed ahead, taking the audience from her parents' house to her father's funeral. "The Truth the Dead Know" was an elegy to her parents. It reflected the preoccupations of her second collection, what she referred to as her "morbid sensibilities." She had submitted the manuscript in November; the book would be published in May. The collection would be called *All My Pretty Ones*, after a lamentation from Shakespeare's *Macbeth*. Death preoccupied her.

In the silent seminar room, she began to read her poem for her parents. The poem begins with a "stiff procession" to the grave site. The speaker, "tired of being brave," skips the burial and decides to drive to Cape Cod, when she begins to "cultivate" herself. This form of self-cultivation is sensory—visual and tactile—in nature: the speaker observes the light of the sun, the cold ocean before her, the feeling of another person's touch. The stresses of the poem are heavy and irregular, with several spondees over the course of only four stanzas, which emphasize the speaker's sense of loss. But the poem is not a traditional elegy: rather than spiritual consolation, the speaker alleviates her grief with the comforts of the flesh. She takes solace in a person's touch, perhaps a lover's—the kind of comfort that the dead, now locked "in their stone boats," can no longer receive. The speaker calls touch a blessing, one that does not offer complete absolution but that might yet help a person to endure. Years later, Sexton would say that this poem was one of two she wrote that carried the most meaning.

The "I" of this poem was unmistakably Sexton, but this was not always the case. "In the Deep Museum," a poem written in the voice of Christ, showed how far the poet could submerge herself in a persona. As she read this poem to the group, she emphasized that no matter how personal the content of a poem, it was never a straight confession. Every poem existed at a remove from the self: the process of composition allowed the poet to gain some purchase on her feelings.

On this February afternoon, the wan winter light coming through the windows, Sexton gave her own kind of writing lesson. If she could show these scholarly women anything, it was that the "I" of a poem was not as simple or straightforward as they might think. Yes, she wrote personal poetry—she drew from her own life—but she often used another character: "someone else that I wasn't, or that I couldn't have been, or that I imagined I was."

Sexton was, in fact, remarkably insightful about poetry, but she lacked her fellow poet's analytical bent. She couldn't always explain why she'd made a given decision: it just looked right on the page, she would explain, or the image just came to her. Perhaps self-conscious about the almost anti-intellectual tone of her presentation, she excused and defended herself throughout the talk. "I'm afraid all my poems are fairly serious that I'm reading today," she said. "I'm sorry my poems are so serious." (At one point, she apologized for apologizing.) She closed her talk with "The Fortress," her poem for Linda; it was her first time reading it in public. She described how she had gotten a "ghastly backache" while writing the poem because she'd spent days at her desk, working straight from eight in the morning until eleven at night. "I was working on it, and my kids were running around, and the cleaning woman ran in and out, dinner wasn't ready and my husband came home, and that's no example of how you're supposed to act as a wife," she said apologetically. (Kayo had stolen a secretary's chair from his office the very next day; he understood her need to concentrate.) It might not be the traditional behavior of a wife, but it was the behavior of an artist or a scholar; it was an experience that many women at the Institute would recognize.

"It's for all of us," Sexton announced, when the poem was over. "Us mothers, the graduate mothers."

"The Fortress" was the final poem that Sexton read that afternoon. Thirty minutes after she'd started reading, she declared that

Anne Sexton with her daughters, Linda and Joy, 1962

the poets were done. The poets had revealed themselves to be two different people after all.

"Turn off the tape!" someone yelled, but the recording continued. Tea was passed; after some time, wine was poured. Sexton helped herself. "I don't really think a wine cellar makes an alcoholic, necessarily," she said, to no one in particular. Like an orchestra starting up, the audience came to life. Some directed questions at the poets; others engaged in side conversation. Someone complained about a local paper's coverage of the Institute: we're not "rusty mothers"! Sexton and Kumin disagreed: they'd both had periods of latency. "We did get rusty," Sexton admitted. Now they were back at their desks. Their children resented them at times, but they also benefited from being exposed to art. Sexton's children, though young, knew what a poem was: "It's what your mummy types all day."

Sometimes Sexton felt like a question was too heady for her, and she would ask Kumin to help her answer. At some point during the discussion, someone asked Sexton about her self-critical process.

How do you know when something is finished? "Oh, that's a most complicated process," Sexton replied, and paused. Then: "I call up Maxine and I ask her."

Her audience hooted and laughed. Sexton went on to describe their work routine: the daily phone sessions, the callbacks. Kumin chimed in: "We've been doing this for years, long before Radcliffe." "We didn't let Radcliffe know when we applied that we knew each other," Kumin said. "We figured they wouldn't want us if they knew." They had applied "very separately," these two women who were each other's superegos, their critical selves. But now the secret was out. They acknowledged publicly for the first time the central role they played in each other's creative lives. If they were worried about how their secret would be received, they needn't have been. The scholars were charmed. After a semester at the Institute, the women all saw the value of a supportive female friend, someone who could give you notes on your work and advice about your youngest child. The two poets performed the kind of mutual support that all the Institute women would recognize. Their confession made, the poets continued to speak, but they were soon drowned out by waves of affectionate laughter.

At one point, Kumin recalled a fight with her middle daughter, Judith, which ended when Judith slipped a note under the door: "Dear Mrs. Kumin, I think your books are bad. The plots are terrible and the rhymes are worse. Yours sincerely, a well-wisher." The other mothers laughed; they understood.

Women are "supposed to destroy each other," as the literary scholar Elaine Showalter once observed. In the scarcity economy that is the heterosexual love market, women have been told they must outdo each other to earn a man's affection and the security he provides. In male-dominated professional environments—a corporate law firm, a tech start-up—women are encouraged to compete with each other, because it seems as though there were only so many spots available for those of their gender. Often, these women, anxious and aggrieved, are more aggressive, more cutthroat, than the men in their circles. Capitalism and patriarchy combine to encourage female competition. Women are trained to be rivals.

At the same time, American culture has long valorized specific forms of female intimacy, the mother-daughter relationship being foremost among them. A mother is charged with teaching her daughter the art of womanhood, with showing her how to navigate a treacherous world. And yet this relationship carries its own danger. So often a mother wants to mold her daughter in her own image, and she reacts with rage if the daughter, skeptical of the mother's decisions, separates and claims her own path. In different ways, Sexton and Kumin had chafed at the prescriptions of their domineering, distant mothers. Each had wanted to carve out a separate identity, although neither stopped wanting her mother's approval. Both had seen how female intimacy could threaten one's very sense of self.

The challenge for Sexton and Kumin, then, was to find a more sustaining way of being close. They began this project in Holmes's seminar, but they perfected it at the Institute, where women supported each other's intellectual and creative work. The poets' intimacy no longer seemed unnatural or dangerous. At Radcliffe, they found an audience for their friendship as well as for their poems; they found, too, the right words to describe their bond. "Maxine and I are very much alike," Sexton said that spring. "First we're good friends, second we both smoke every single minute, we both have a cocktail before dinner, we use the same kind of rhymes, same kind of ambition, same kind of feelings, but we write with a different intent, we're really very different poets." Twelve years after Radcliffe, Showalter asked them if they worried about becoming too similar in their writing:

MAX: No, no, we're different.
ANNE: You can tell we're completely different.
SHOWALTER: Yes, but was there ever a period when it was a
    struggle?
ANNE: No, there was never a struggle. It was natural, it wasn't
    hard.

MAX: It seems to be so normal. It wasn't ever an issue.
ANNE: There was never any struggle.

This dance of sameness and separateness defies easy categorization. One could say they were like sisters, that their relationship anticipated the calls for "sisterhood" that defined the second wave of American feminism; the feminist activist Kathie Sarachild coined the phrase "sisterhood is powerful" in 1968. But this would be to elide their crucial differences, the way that their friendship depended upon their points of contrast. "I would say we never meddled," Kumin once wrote, explaining their habit of collaboration. "I don't know exactly how to explain what that means except to stress that we were different voices, we knew we were different & honored those differences." Neither ever assumed a position of authority relative to the other. Nor did they merge, or become representative of a type, as members of social movements sometimes do. Instead, they alternated speaking and listening, seeking advice and advising—their voices sounding different notes, forming something like a song.

CHAPTER 8

Happily Awarded

I N JANUARY 1962, just a few weeks before she and Kumin came out as intimate collaborators, Sexton sat down to write a long overdue reply to another woman writer. Olsen had written her a letter back in the fall, asking about the Radcliffe Institute. The letter was typed on a sheet of office letterhead; Olsen was working as a secretary again. Sexton knew how her friend loathed this kind of day job; Olsen claimed that typing letters and memos all day ruined her feel for language.

When she wrote to Sexton, Olsen was struggling. She had been struggling for years. In 1959, she had been awarded a two-year grant from the Ford Foundation, which provided her with $3,600 each year (just over $30,000 in today's currency). The list of winners read like a who's who of mid-century American literature: James Baldwin, Saul Bellow, E. E. Cummings, Robert Fitzgerald, Stanley Kunitz, Bernard Malamud, Flannery O'Connor, Katherine Anne Porter, Theodore Roethke, and Niccolo Tucci. But Ford grant or no Ford grant, Olsen was still a mother, with a mother's obligations and commitments. She described her typical grant-time schedule to Sexton in a letter: "Up at six, breakfast in shifts, lunchpacking—then, if no one ill, or it isn't a holiday, or any of the other ORs, the day for work until four, sometimes longer or an evening—depending on housework load, shopping, errands, people, current family or friend crisis." The work came slowly. The interruptions were frequent. "Too much life enters this house," she confided.

Now that her grant had ended, she was back working a day job at San Francisco General Hospital, and she still didn't have the novel manuscript that she'd promised Viking's Malcolm Cowley years earlier. While Cowley had been pleased with the critical reception of *Tell Me a Riddle*, Olsen's story collection, he insisted that his company could offer her an advance only for a novel; story collections didn't sell. "The novel is the book to finish," he'd written to her when she'd started publishing her short fiction. "Only if some accident (pray God there is none) stops you from work'g on the novel should you turn to the stories."

The letter Olsen wrote to Sexton was brief and desperate. She was attempting to plan the next year, she explained, and she needed to find another fellowship that would buy her time to write. Nolan Miller, a mutual friend to Sexton and Olsen, had pointed her in the direction of the Institute. "How interrupting is it?" she asked Sexton. "How free are you for your own work & for what feeds work? What does it involve. Please when you can, write me specifics."

Sexton had meant to respond sooner, but then November had come, and with it her birthday—always a hard time for her—and the anniversaries of her suicide attempts. She had fallen into a depression; she had fought with Kayo; she had again attempted suicide. It wasn't until the New Year that she was in better spirits. She sat down at her typewriter, in her study, and wrote Olsen a generous and enthusiastic reply.

"Write them," she instructed her friend. She provided the address and alerted Olsen to the problem of residence. She supposed that her friend could apply to be a more senior resident fellow, but those positions were usually nominated by an outside observer, and they went to women who were already famous. Sexton concluded her letter with some words of praise for *Tell Me a Riddle* and a description of how she'd spent her time at the Institute. She added a handwritten postscript: "Write if you can—I feel lonely somehow."

Olsen took her friend's advice. In her busy house at 116 Swiss Avenue, in San Francisco's Mission District, she put together an application to the Institute. Though she detested the process of applying for grants and fellowships—she believed that such opportunities should be freely available to all, not meted out to a lucky few—she still worked to make her application stand out.

And it did. Olsen's application was a challenge to the Institute's conception of talent. Under "educational background," she listed her writing grants, making no apologies about the absence of more conventional educational credentials. Elsewhere on her application, she presented her clerical and domestic work as training for her writing: they had made her efficient, competent, and highly observant. She didn't distinguish between paid labor and domestic labor; unlike women of the middle and upper-middle classes, Olsen performed both kinds of work and saw both as equally valuable. After typing out the required information—married, four children, a granddaughter whom she counted as a partial dependent—she listed all of the "unskilled work" she'd taken on since 1928: "Armour's, Mannings, Carpenter Paper Co., Best Foods, Cal Pak, Various warehouses, as Pork trimmer . . . Checker for Baker & Hamilton (warehouse). $1.55 an hour (?) . . . Secretary with Calif. Society of Internal Medicine, one and one-half years; secretary with Graziani & Appleton, att'ys, and temporary office work. $2.00 hourly to $375 monthly." (Her $2.00/hour wage was the equivalent of a $16.00/hour wage today.) Leaving blank the sections on education, languages, and theses, she listed instead her nonacademic talents:

1. A writer's training in observation, perception and steeping.
2. Office work. Fast, accurate typist, transcriber; knowledge various office machines; experience in various offices from legal to industrial.
3. Jugglery of mothering, wifehood, fulltime work on a job, running a household, and somewhere writing or hope of it.

These were Olsen's credentials. She thought that her experiences as a worker and a mother had made her a more sensitive writer of fiction. She was arguably better prepared to write a novel than a woman who had spent all her life within the halls of a university. She had lived in a range of communities, among different kinds of people, and, as an organizer and activist, she had listened to them talk about their hopes, dreams, and fears.

On the last page of the application, Olsen outlined her vision for her future work. She still planned to write the great proletarian novel, a book that would bring to life the struggle of the working class. Her aim was not to instill pity in her readers but to catalyze social change. "It is a social novel, and my intention is to move the reader to that comprehension which alters," she wrote. She wanted to show how "human lives are wasted and barred from full development" and "how most people are denied a society in which they can be valuable." It was a project straight out of the 1930s—something like the work of James Farrell, or Theodore Dreiser, or John Dos Passos—but it was also, she hoped, timeless. The book would "promote reverence for life," she wrote. "Because what is is unendurable otherwise."

She concluded by enumerating the benefits of the Institute for a writer like her:

Economic freedom to work full time on writing for a clear
   space of time
Distance (personal): 3000 miles from happenings and needs
   of those dear to me, which when close can pull from and
   sometimes interrupt writing.
Distance (impersonal, in sense of exile): To live away for a
   while from daily happenings. For balance.
Literary atmosphere. Access to that which is timeless. To be
   able to use a great library, look at mss. of dead writers who
   have been sustenance to me, go sometimes to hear lectures
   and readings, perhaps to talk with someone whose life has
   been literature. Sense of being near a center of evaluation
   and education.

This last benefit—the literary and intellectual atmosphere—was particularly appealing to Olsen. The Olsen household had always been one of books and intellectual inquiry. They were the family that talked politics at dinner, the family that exchanged used books on holidays. "I think it was the first real 'family' I ever saw in action," T. Mike Walker, Julie's friend, once said. "They were talking, laughing, joking, teasing, telling their stories of the day, being listened to with respect, being responded to with love. They discussed literature, music, film, and politics. They wanted to know what I thought, what I believed, what authors I was reading." When a young Julie vocally disagreed with a schoolteacher's depiction of slavery as largely benign, the entire family went out for dinner in celebration. To be in Boston, a culturally elite city, and to study at Harvard, the nation's most prestigious institution of higher learning—these were tantalizing opportunities.

Olsen also made sure to list her publications: her reporting for *Partisan Review*, individual works of short fiction, and the collection *Tell Me a Riddle* (she sent three copies, calling them "an essential portion of this application"). She noted that the collection had been named one of the nine best books of the year by *Time;* she also listed the "response of over a hundred letters" from readers as evidence of her "professional accomplishment."

When she wrote the application to the Institute, the world of higher learning was still a little bit mysterious to Olsen; her classes at Stanford had all been in creative writing, and she wasn't sure what a community of "scholars" would require from its applicants. But she knew there would be at least one person at the Institute she could talk to, whose life had also been saved by literature: Sexton.

Olsen wrote to Sexton, informing her of the submitted application: "Clumsy, ineffectual application, not knowing how to speak for myself, & all those spaces blank, degrees, position, education. TMAR [*Tell Me a Riddle*] all to really plead for me." Full of "desperation," she wrote that she was willing to leave her family and be in residence in Cambridge. As committed as she was to her children, she thought the solitude might be an advantage. Ever since her time at Stanford's creative writing workshop, and even before, Olsen had managed to find people to vouch for her: instructors put her in touch with editors; editors put her in touch with agents. Each reassured the other that Olsen, elusive and unreliable, was nonetheless talented and worth the investment. She was a sympathetic figure, as well as "an attractive woman with a deep warm charm," as one friend described her. At Stanford, she had been beloved by everyone; it was not hard for her to cultivate support. So perhaps when she wrote to Sexton, pleading her case, she anticipated that Sexton would do exactly what Sexton did: advocate for Olsen's acceptance. Sexton too wanted to talk to someone whose life had been literature. And like Olsen, she understood the need for distance from one's family.

After a year at Radcliffe, surrounded by the educated elite, Sexton likely realized that her friend's case would be a litmus test for the Institute. None of the first-year fellows had come from the working class, and none had needed the full financial support that someone like Olsen would require. Olsen was at once a perfect candidate and a problem.

On the one hand, she was a case study in how a woman could be "simultaneously dedicated as a wife and mother, as well as an artist," as one of Olsen's recommenders put it. By this description, she was the kind of creative woman that the Institute wanted to help. On the other hand, Olsen lived out of state, she had produced very little throughout her life, and she lacked a formal education. It's not clear that the Institute would have gone to the lengths it did—sending out an emissary to interview Olsen in San Francisco, entertaining the idea of a full-time fellowship position—without encouragement from one of its more famous fellows. Even after the interview, Olsen wasn't sure that she would merit one of the few fellowships that would be distributed to newcomers. All she knew, in the late winter of 1962, was that she still had a novel in her. She could only hope for time to write it all down.

Just what kind of worker is a writer? Olsen wrestled with that question throughout her career, beginning with her earliest reportage (recall her description of the work of writing in "The Strike") and continuing with her later fiction and nonfiction. It was a question that writers and artists took seriously in the 1930s, when, thanks to President Roosevelt's Works Progress Administration, many of them became federal employees.

A writer at work might look lackadaisical: she jots down words in a notebook; she stares into space. Pressing typewriter keys requires little physical force. But for an artist, the work is physical, laborious. A painter stretches canvases; a lithographer presses stones. The heavy lifting is literal.

And then there is sculpting.

Making sculpture—life-sized sculpture—is a long, draining, physically demanding process. It begins with a block of heavy clay. The sculptor starts by cutting and shaping it, dragging sharp tools through solid mass. Armatures bear some of the weight; human arms bear the rest. Once the image is shaped, the sculptor must smooth the clay surface (errors can be reproduced in the molding process), coat it with several layers of rubber over the course of several days, create a firm outer "jacket" out of a substance like plaster or resin, remove the outer jacket and the rubber to create a "mother mold," and then pour in hot wax. This "wax positive," as it's called, then hardens into a version of the clay original. The wax positive needs work too—imperfections are corrected, rods are inserted (a process called spruing), and a ceramic shell is then made. All this before a sculpture can be cast in bronze. If it's a large sculpture, then the artist must make individual molds, repeating this process multiple times, before piecing the sculpture together later in the process.

This was the work Marianna Pineda, a mother of three with dark hair and a gentle demeanor, did every day in her home studio at 164 Rawson Road in Brookline.

Pineda seemed to live a charmed life; a 1977 oral history finds her describing it as "lucky," "marvelous," "fantastic." But her good humor and grace hid unruly feelings. Sculpture was therapeutic: "Carving is a great way to get rid of all your feelings that you'd like to crash around. You know, hit things!" She lifted clay onto stools and cut and carved and contoured. If she had a particularly heavy lift, she

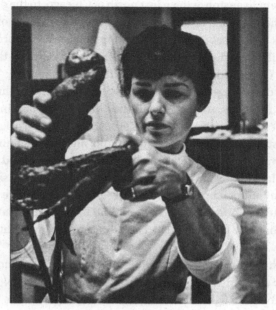

*Marianna Pineda
at the Institute*

called her husband, Harold "Red" Tovish, who was sculpting out in the garage, to come help her. This was a notable event: neither let the other look at unfinished work, though each relied on the other for "critiques" of finished products. When called, Tovish would offer Pineda his physical assistance, then retreat to his garage, the shabbier work space, leaving his wife in the two-story, sun-filled home studio. The arrangement was fitting: though he received more critical attention, Tovish always considered Pineda the better artist. He made art for her eyes alone.

The two sculptors had met in New York City in 1942. Pineda, seventeen at the time, was on leave from Bennington College, where she studied sculpture, and working at the Museum of Modern Art in the children's playroom. Born to a wealthy family in Illinois in 1925, Pineda had come to art at an early age. She spent weekends taking the El from Evanston, a town just north of Chicago, to the downtown, where she marveled at the holdings of the Art Institute of Chicago. She took art classes in Michigan and in Southern California, where her family moved permanently in 1938. It was during these years that she developed her fascination with the human form. Tovish, an orphaned working-class Jewish boy with a wry sense of humor, was already a working sculptor when they met; he'd fallen in love with the craft as a teenager, in an art class run by the Works Progress Administration. Pineda visited his studio, and Tovish, four years her senior, was struck by her beauty: her dark eyes, her broad smile, her gamine look that was somehow also very feminine. He assumed she had many suitors, but when he finally got up the courage to ask her on a date, he found that most would-be beaux, intimidated by her beauty, had left her alone; she spent most Saturday nights washing her hair.

Tovish had already been drafted; the two had only a month to get to know each other before he went overseas. Both left New York in 1943—Tovish to fight the Germans, Pineda to study at the University of California at Berkeley, her second of four formal apprenticeships with master sculptors. It was at Berkeley that she changed her surname from her given name, Packard, in order to avoid confusion with the prominent muralist Emmy Lou Packard. She was inspired by the play *Mariana Pineda,* by Federico García Lorca, which told the life story of Mariana de Pineda y Muñoz, a nineteenth-century Spanish liberalist heroine. At some point during the three years he was away, Tovish broke off the relationship. "I felt we were too different in our background," he later said. "She came from the upper middle-class, Quaker background, and I just thought we would never make it." But not long after the breakup, they started writing to each other again, and Tovish thought, "Oh, the heck with all that." He called up Pineda as soon as he was back in the States and proposed.

Pineda and Tovish spent the early years of their marriage in New York. They lived first in Pineda's apartment near Columbia, then moved to a house in the Gowanus neighborhood in Brooklyn, which they shared with friends. The two sculptors also shared a studio in

Gowanus, where they kept bumping into each other and failed to make much art. This was the last time they ever shared a work space.

Pineda had her first daughter, Margo, in 1946, when she was only twenty-one, and a second child, Aaron, soon after. Her male instructors had warned her that motherhood would end her sculpture career. "Oh, it's very nice what you're doing now," Pineda recalled their saying. "But soon you'll be making babies and you'll forget all about this art." Her pregnancy was unplanned, though not unwanted. "They just happened," she later said of her children. "And we were delighted. And I stopped working, literally, for about a year and a half. And I was miserable! And I realized I wouldn't be a very good . . . anything, if I didn't get back to work."

Risking their financial stability, but determined to advance both their careers, the Tovishes left for France in 1949 to work in the studio of the French-Russian sculptor Ossip Zadkine. Paris proved to be her "great liberation," as Pineda put it, just as it had been for Barbara Swan at roughly the same time. (It does not seem that their paths crossed in France.) Their older child went to nursery school, and they hired child care for Aaron as well as housekeeping. "I didn't have to worry about shopping or cooking," Pineda recalled. Working in Zadkine's studio, Pineda began to turn pregnancy—an experience that her male professors had seen as a problem for an artist—into a source of art. *The Sleepwalker*, produced during that first year in France, is a figure at once apprehensive and adventurous. Obviously pregnant, the sculpted woman stands erect despite her swollen belly; her feet are spread hips width apart to support her uneven shape. Her face is upturned, and her hands clutch at the space above her. She seems as if she were about to rise up into some unknown air. Like Pineda, then a young mother, "she feels her way toward a new mode of being."

Women's bodies—sensuous, mystical, powerful—became Pineda's great subject. Though Tovish was the more vocal of the two (his nickname, Red, referred to his political views), Pineda was in some ways the more political artist. In the 1950s, to portray the female body experiencing sexual pleasure was itself countercultural—but this is what Pineda did in the lead sculpture *Lovers,* then again in the carved wood piece *An Effigy for Young Lovers. Effigy* appeared in 1953, the same year as Alfred C. Kinsey's *Sexual Behavior in the Human Female,* a report that shocked the nation by revealing that women had orgasms and affairs.

By the time the Tovishes landed in Brookline, in 1957—the same year Kumin and Sexton met in Holmes's workshop—they had lived in Paris, Minneapolis, and upstate New York, where Tovish had secured a teaching job. Florence had been their last stop before Boston: when Tovish had needed a break from teaching, the family had moved to Florence for three years, from 1954 to 1957. In 1957, the Boston Museum School had recruited both Tovishes to teaching positions, but Pineda hadn't wanted to teach (she tried to avoid it throughout her career; when she did eventually take a teaching gig, her students criticized her for being a perfectionist and overly harsh). Tovish accepted the job, and the family moved to Tappan Street in Brookline.

After they had lived in the Midwest and Europe, metro Boston felt expensive, but then, thanks to the effort of their gallerist, Hyman "Hy" Swetzoff, their work started to sell. In April 1957, he sold Pineda's *Mother and Child,* one of her many works on this theme, to private collectors for $300 (roughly $2,600 today). A bronze version of *The Sleepwalker,* her breakthrough sculpture, eventually sold in 1960 for $2,000 ($16,600 today). Swetzoff took a third of each payment, a standard commission for the time, and Pineda took home the rest. In the years that followed, she won sculpture prizes from the Art Institute of Chicago, Boston's Institute of Contemporary Art, and the Portland, Maine Museum. She was now a working artist and, as the papers noted, a "Brookline mother of three." Nina, her youngest, was born in 1958.

One of her prizewinning sculptures, *Prelude,* encapsulates what was so elegant and revolutionary about Pineda's work. The piece depicts a woman about to go into labor. The figure lies back on her hips, with her swollen stomach protruding from the cloth wrapped around her hips. Tension is evident: her hands grip the floor behind her, and her body writhes in what must be pain. But her face, turned upward, looks almost rapturous. The piece is expressive, intense, and yet, somehow, dignified. Earthier than a Madonna, *Prelude* makes pregnancy appear human and also cosmically important.

Pineda had managed to do what her instructors had told her was impossible: raise children and make art simultaneously. This was in part because she was a hard worker—she was productive throughout her career—and in part because she benefited from various forms of material and emotional support. Her mother, a wealthy Quaker who was a progressive (she was a civil rights activist long before the movement went mainstream), had encouraged her daughter's artistic endeavors from a young age, and she sent much-needed money when the Tovishes were broke. Tovish, admiring of his wife's talent and aware of what we would now call his male privilege, ensured that Pineda had everything she needed to work. The couple also hired household help. Their neighborhood was safe, and the children ran free, but Pineda took comfort knowing that there was someone looking out for them while she worked.

Still, there was something a bit isolating about Brookline, with its mansions and parks and quiet streets. This wasn't cosmopolitan Paris, nor a midwestern university town. Artistic companionship was important to Pineda and Tovish, even though they relied primarily on each other. Both artists had exacting standards for themselves and distrusted easy praise. They yearned not for the fame of Pollock or Picasso but for recognition from their artistic community.

Pineda felt a specific sense of loneliness. "It was a very lonely business just being a housewife," she later recalled. "I remember feeling totally isolated in my kitchen . . . There wasn't a sense that you'd get together with other women to form a group and you'd take care of the kids together or take turns, you know, none of that. It was—you were really supposed to do it all yourself. And it was rough." She longed for female friends who were also artists. She didn't want to sit in the kitchen and gossip about the neighbors; she wanted to talk about work.

Pineda knew one female artist who also lived in Brookline and had a daughter who was the same age as her youngest child. Her friend was Barbara Swan Fink.

It's not surprising that these two women knew each other: the

Boston art scene was small enough that artists with little in common encountered and reencountered each other at lectures and gallery openings and parties. But it is nonetheless striking that two women with such similar aesthetic preoccupations lived such similar lives. Both had found ways to continue working through the busiest years of child rearing by making that very activity the subject of their art. They were both iconoclastic, though their styles diverged. Swan's paintings and sketches were expressionist, surreal, thick with texture and feeling. Entire personalities emerged in her faces. Pineda favored smooth, clean lines and anonymous figures; her bodies twisted into positions of devotion and repose. Her work was solid, grounded, a bit earthy. While Swan had dispensed with traditional, mystified images of motherhood by channeling the dark and the strange, Pineda had made motherhood look sublimely natural.

One wonders if they talked about their works in progress as they picked up their daughters from nursery school or clinked champagne glasses at a gallery opening. One wonders, too, if Swan mentioned to Pineda that she'd been participating in a little experiment across the river in Cambridge. Swan would have told her about the money, surely, and maybe too about a few of the more colorful characters: the twitchy literary scholars, the shy historians, the dark-haired poets who swept into rooms as if they were riding the air. For so long, Pineda had relied on one fellow artist: the man with whom she traveled and raised children and divided up household funds. She might have been intrigued by the idea of seeing and discussing the work of other artists and equally curious about how other women, much like her, had navigated the competing demands of children and craft.

Pineda decided to apply. She wanted the money and the prestige—she appreciated any recognition of her professional excellence—and she was curious to know other women who were doing interesting work in her community. She also liked the idea of being in a community that comprised both scholars and artists. Both Tovishes were well-read and politically engaged—Pineda thanks to her mother, and Tovish due to his participation in the WPA. Once in Boston, they tapped into Cambridge's intellectual scene; they were friends with both Noam Chomsky and Howard Zinn. Pineda wasn't a firebrand, but she had an appetite for intellectual and political debates. She wanted to mingle with the highly accomplished female scholars who had merited Radcliffe's money and time.

In October 1961, Pineda requested the application blanks and filled out the first page. She listed her age (thirty-six), her children (ages fourteen, twelve, and three), the academies where she'd studied, and the prizes she'd won. When the application asked her to discuss her proposed project, she paused. Self-promotion had never been her strong suit. Both she and her husband believed that good work should be its own advertisement; they balked at chances to sing their own praises, and they looked askance at those who did so easily. They were both reluctant to show work before it was perfect. Once, the Tovishes received an invitation to show their work in a "new-talent show" at the Museum of Modern Art, but they refused, thinking they weren't ready. "Maybe that was a mistake," Pineda later reflected.

But being a working artist means, every so often, transforming oneself into a winning bauble, something that a rich person might buy. When necessary, Pineda would sell herself as best as she could. "It is difficult to describe what I propose to do without becoming needlessly technical," she began. "I hope it will suffice to say that I hope to complete several good-sized sculptures." She described her obstacles in the same opaque way: since she and her family had returned from abroad, where domestic labor was cheap, "my output has lowered considerably." Pineda was far more privileged than someone like Olsen—she was not working a day job, she had household help, she had the occasional gift from her mother—and yet she still needed the Institute's assistance. It was hard to make life-sized sculptures, she explained: few art schools taught the craft, and the decline in "architectural patronage" meant that there was less money available for the necessary materials; Pineda could easily spend $500 (over $4,000 today) on materials alone. (This historical aside was the closest she would come to making—and justifying—her own demand for Radcliffe's funds.) She concluded her project description: "I have hopes some day of doing work which will find its place out of door or in public settings and a modest practical approach to this grandiose goal would appear to be a mastery, first, of life-size scale. I intend to work in clay for bronze casting and to carve wood and stone."

Pineda was a poor salesperson; she would have been a disaster at a Tupperware party or as a representative of Mary Kay. She was better with her fellow sculptors, like her husband, those with whom she could use technical shorthand. And it was her fellow sculptors who ended up speaking for this modest artist: Raymond Puccinelli, her instructor at Berkeley, who in his recommendation called her "one of the most remarkable persons that I have ever encountered" and praised her for keeping up her work through child rearing without "noticeable pause or lessening of vitality"; H. Harvard Arnason, the vice president of art administration at the Guggenheim Foundation, who named her "one of the most accomplished young sculptors working today"; and Hy Swetzoff, her gallerist, who, like Puccinelli, argued that Pineda's sensitive, masterful work spoke for itself.

It was clear to Connie Smith and the rest of the selection committee that Pineda was an accomplished artist, a consummate professional who was respected by her peers. This was both her strength and her weakness as a candidate: the art history department faculty member who reviewed her application called her "a very strong candidate but not a new talent," while a selection committee member noted that she was "well known already." To give her a grant would be to reward a woman who started working from a position of strength: she came from a wealthy family, and her mother had consistently supplemented what money she and her husband earned. She was not desperate; this was not her last chance at a creative life. For her, a grant would not be a second chance, or an on-ramp to an abandoned career. Instead, it would be a reward for her achievements, for succeeding where so many female artists—so many women—had failed. Pineda would have to wait until the spring to learn whether she deserved it.

·   ·   ·

The spring of 1962 found Sexton churning with excitement. Her spirits had risen with the temperatures. *All My Pretty Ones*, her second book, was published by Houghton Mifflin in April. Its title poem—like "The Truth the Dead Know," the poem she'd read in the Institute seminar—represented yet another effort to lay her parents to rest. At the end of "All My Pretty Ones," the speaker, who has been perusing her parents' scrapbooks and diaries, finally closes the books and places them on the shelves. "Whether you are pretty or not, I outlive you," she concludes, "bend down my strange face to yours and forgive you." Sexton had sent a draft of "The Truth the Dead Know" to Olsen in November 1961, when her parents' deaths were still quite present in her mind. Now the poem was bound between the covers of a book, like a body sealed in a coffin.

On May 3, before acceptances for the next academic year were officially announced, Sexton heard from Smith that the writer she was waiting on—the writer whose application she had encouraged, whose face she longed to see—would be among the new class of Institute fellows. Sexton raced to her typewriter to send the good news across the country. "Dear Friend and Happily AWARDED Tillie!" she typed. "You got it! You got it! You got it!" (She'd celebrated her own acceptance in these same words, barely a year earlier.) Sexton was giddy at the prospect of meeting her penpal in person. She trusted that they'd be able to overcome any shyness and have the same literary and intellectual exchanges that they'd been having for years in their letters. And altruistically, she was happy that her friend, a woman who wrote so well and who worked so hard, would experience a time of creative freedom.

Word somehow reached Olsen before Sexton's letter arrived in the Bay Area. The Institute was offering $7,000 (nearly $56,500 today), more than twice as much as it promised its associate scholars. Olsen would be a full-time fellow. It was a professional salary for a professional writer. As the Harvard faculty member who reviewed her application noted, Olsen was a "candidate of unquestionable distinction" and "far beyond the stage of promise and into the realm of achievement."

Here was her chance—maybe her last chance—at redemption.

She would have a room of her own, a library full of books, a proper desk—things she never had when she was living and working in her busy, six-person household. Free from demands and distractions, she could finally write the great proletarian novel. She would not be a novelist manqué; she would not shirk the social responsibility of writing the story of class struggle. She resolved to finish the project she should have finished a long time ago.

Even as she resolved to focus on her writing, Olsen found herself enticed by the idea of studying at the nation's best university. She would audit courses, she resolved; she thought about spending hours prowling the stacks of Widener Library. She decided to take advantage of all the concerts and lectures and readings that Harvard sponsored. A woman of great ambition and greater appetites, Olsen resolved to do it all: study, research, recreate, and write the novel she was born to write.

There were still a few problems to solve, though—mainly, the problem of mothering.

Who would care for her youngest daughter, Laurie? Would her husband, Jack, come with her? How would they find a place to live? Olsen had faced these same challenges a few years earlier, when she was on the Ford grant. Then she had secured a spot at the Huntington Hartford Foundation, a small artist colony in the Pacific Palisades, a coastal neighborhood in Los Angeles just south of the Santa Monica Mountains; she had known that in order to maximize her productivity, she needed to remove herself from the family home. But the commute was long. Jack missed her and called each night. Her children came to visit regularly. On one such occasion, Kathie, her third daughter, recorded her impressions: "I WISH THAT WE ALL COULD LIVE HERE . . . Mama is happy. We are happy, My mother looks really good." Maybe the solution to the problems posed by the Institute was to do as Kathie suggested: move the whole family to the place where "Mama is happy."

The first week of May, Olsen telegrammed her acceptance to the Institute: "JOYFULLY ACCEPT TRUST AND OBLIGATION OF TIME FOR WORK IN SUCH HALLOWED AIR."

The rest of the acceptances went out in the mail, granting seventeen women access to the "hallowed air" that Olsen described. Their number included a printmaker from Cambridge, a musicologist from Newton, a mathematician from Princeton, and a scholar of medieval European literature from West Point. The sculptor Pineda was among the very few artists accepted. She was awarded a stipend of $1,900 (roughly $15,300 today), money that could pay for household help and child care; she was also awarded a separate fund for sculpting materials. She and her cohort would join fifteen women from the inaugural class who stayed on for a second year, including Swan, Sexton, and Kumin. Sexton and Kumin had applied for renewal together in January; they had proposed the compilation of an anthology of living American poets, to be used in secondary schools ("the poets" truly did everything together). Each poet won $2,000 for the coming year.

That summer, the new fellows did their best to prepare for the life changes ahead.

Olsen felt more anxious than most. She lived far from the nation's historical center of higher learning, she had no BA, and she was not a faculty wife, like so many others. She craved the credibility that Radcliffe would offer, but she also feared the move away from the Bay Area, the place where she'd spent nearly all her adult life.

When she was nineteen, Olsen had fled Nebraska with little more than a notebook and a sense of righteous indignation. She'd jumped boxcars and hopped from state to state. Now a silver-haired matriarch, she found herself anxious about living elsewhere; she at once loved to live alone and couldn't imagine such a life. At first, she resolved to leave Jack behind; she wrote to her mentor Dick Scowcroft that she would tell Jack, "I love you (that part no lie) [and will] come back, I'll never leave you again—and try like hell to believe my lies." After several weeks of negotiating with Jack, she agreed to let him come to Cambridge. Now, even as she readied herself for a spell of radical intellectual independence, she had to consider the needs of her family.

She peppered Smith with questions in a series of letters: Could she get a work space in the library? Would she need any special accommodations to audit classes? Would the Graduate Center provide housing appropriate for a family? Where might her youngest go to school? Smith, generous as always with her time and knowledge, pulled strings to make the move easier: she helped the Olsens find a place to live that was within walking distance of Institute headquarters; she also arranged for Laurie, then fourteen, to attend the Putney School, a boarding school in Vermont. Kathie, eighteen and a recent high school graduate, worried for her younger sister; boarding school seemed so unnatural, and wouldn't Laurie feel alienated, surrounded by so much wealth? She decided to quit her job as a stenographer and, sometime in the winter, follow her parents to Cambridge. Julie and Karla, Tillie's oldest daughters, were mothers themselves at this point; they would not travel to Cambridge. Julie, who was used to knowing Olsen was in the same city, would feel her mother's absence acutely. "I was furious. I was like, 'How could you go off to the other side of the country when I have a new baby?'" Julie remembered years later. "On the other hand, I was incredibly proud of her. I used to carry . . . the best American short story book she was in around with me and hand it to people, and I was thrilled she was writing." Later, as she faced her own challenges as a mother and a scholar, she realized how important her mother's work had been.

That summer, as Ivy League men across the Northeast walked through wrought-iron gates and out into the postcollege world, the members of the Olsen family readied themselves for a cross-country move. It was a big decision, one they had not made lightly. They sold the house on Swiss Avenue, paid off their debts, and spent $500—a donation from Cowley—on a U-Haul trailer, which they crammed with their belongings. Jack, a true egalitarian, would follow his wife wherever her career took her—something few men did in an era of male breadwinners and masculine dominance. (Sympathetic husbands were a fixture in the lives of the fellows: "Marianna's generation . . . was still, 'whither though goest, so will I,'" Tovish reflected in 1974. "Very convenient for the male . . . Not so hot for the woman.")

Olsen was about to take a leap of faith, and Jack decided he would jump along with her.

Olsen, Jack, and Laurie set off for Boston, stopping along the way to see Olsen's siblings in Nebraska and Pennsylvania. The plan was for the three of them to live in an apartment close to the Institute; Jack would find a printer job, and when the school year started, the two parents would drive their youngest daughter up to Vermont.

All of the Olsens felt a bit nervous: their lives were about to change dramatically. Olsen, who often tried to alleviate anxiety with bouts of activity, injected joy and play into this trip: the family camped outdoors as they traveled cross-country, and Laurie and Olsen performed impromptu concerts for the family members they visited. Laurie played the fiddle, and Olsen sang folk songs in a high voice that sounded younger than her fifty years.

Such jubilance simultaneously spoke to Olsen's excitement and masked her anxiety. As the Olsen family barreled east, U-Haul trailer bumping along behind them, Olsen, a California dreamer, wondered what, and whom, she would find waiting for her on the nation's other coast.

CHAPTER 9

The Equivalents

O N FRIDAY, SEPTEMBER 21, 1962, Olsen sat at the Institute's first formal tea and waited, nervously, to introduce herself. She didn't feel as though she fit in. For one thing, all these women seemed to be from the Boston area, or at least from the East Coast, whereas she was a transplant. She and Jack had only just settled in their third-floor apartment at 187 Mount Auburn Street in Cambridge. For another, these women had such impressive credentials! They had PhDs, publications, famous husbands. Some of them, the ones returning for a second year, just seemed so comfortable in this space, as if they'd always been there.

When it was her turn to introduce herself, Olsen stuttered, as she often did when nervous. She shared what felt to her like meager credentials: four daughters, many jobs, four short stories. No impressive degree; no famous husband. She wondered if she would ever feel at home at the Institute.

Later, she moved into her office at 78 Mount Auburn. Sexton stopped by as Olsen was setting up. Glancing around the room, she noticed the portraits Olsen had pasted on the wall: these were the same portraits the latter had put up in her prior work spaces, and they included that photo of Sexton from the book jacket. Sexton was pleased to see herself in such impressive company. The two women took a walk along the Charles River—Sexton barefoot, Olsen shod—and talked about poetry.

That same evening, Sexton sat down to write Olsen a letter, just as she had done so many months earlier. It was raining, and Sexton, enclosed in her study, imagined she was living in a solitary cabin, maybe somewhere in the woods. She must have felt a little foolish, writing to a woman who now lived near the Institute's yellow house and whom she could call, just as she did with Kumin, because long-distance charges wouldn't be applied. Even though she was a performer, Sexton was often shy with strangers, and especially shy in groups. (Both Sexton and Olsen expressed themselves more fluidly on the page.) She chided herself for muffing a few quotations in conversation earlier. Her letter gave her a chance to introduce herself again, in better form, and to recall to her friend the bond that they already shared.

"Meeting you and being with you!" she wrote excitedly. Olsen had given Sexton a work by Kafka, and Sexton reported that she'd already read the entire thing and had loved it. She then corrected a quotation that she'd shared earlier. It was from Saul Bellow's *Herzog*, a novel about a twice-married and twice-divorced Jewish intellectual who has taken to writing angry letters—to the president, to his psychiatrist, to *The New York Times*—as a way of venting his spleen. The novel wouldn't be published until the fall of 1964, but somehow Sexton already had a copy of the manuscript, or at least the section she quoted from, in which Herzog prepares to leave his New York City apartment for a week of rest at a country house. "With one long breath, caught and held in his chest, he fought his sadness over his solitary life. 'Don't cry, you idiot!' Live or die, but don't poison everything!'" Sexton shared very little with Bellow's aging, misanthropic protagonist, but she nonetheless found this little bit of stern self-talk inspiring; she'd posted the quotation above her desk at home (for her, Herzog made for a sterner judge than Olsen's Tolstoy). She now copied out the quotation verbatim for her friend. "Live or die"—the phrase reverberated through Sexton's mind: it reminded her that she always had a choice.

Sexton had chosen life—for now. After being with Olsen, she felt newly inspired. "Having been with you today, I feel like a writer again," she wrote. "A creator, a solitary but never poisoner, maker of something." The older writer, a woman who was at once childishly optimistic and worldly wise, recognized something in the younger writer; she confirmed its existence simply by speaking of literature past and present, of writers living and dead. Like the self-admonishing Herzog, Olsen reminded Sexton who she was and what she could choose to be. Validated, and newly hopeful, Sexton signed her letter with love.

Like all of the scholars and writers associated with the Radcliffe Institute for Independent Study, Olsen had come seeking solitude. She thrilled to the idea of a quiet, book-lined carrel; she eagerly imagined occupying a room of her own. And yet what she found in Cambridge was not quiet but community. She'd come hoping to be Virginia Woolf—she'd recently read *A Room of One's Own*—and wound up in a Bloomsbury group.

The first time Kathie visited her mother's office in the old, creaky house at 78 Mount Auburn Street, the young woman could swear she felt electricity rippling between rooms. Moving into the main seminar room, she caught snatches of conversation. "What are you working on?" the fellows asked one another. "Where are you stumbling?" They were versions of the question, What can I do to help? She heard women recommending resources: pick up this book at Widener; send the proposal to this editor at that press. She watched fellows pour cups of tea and sit down to talk about the economics of publishing. As a young woman just starting out in the working world, Kathie couldn't believe how invested these women were in each other's work, how seriously they took each other's intellectual ambitions, no matter how idiosyncratic or unfamiliar. Their intensity and focus coexisted with, and amplified, the general sense of delight.

The Bunting fellows in conversation; Olsen is fourth from left
Photograph by Olive Pierce

"The atmosphere there was one of absolute joy," Kathie said later. "Absolute seriousness and joy both."

It might have felt like something of a miracle. It was a world in which women's society tended to take few and limited forms: in the short-lived community of the Seven Sisters or the solidarity developed between shifts on some factory floors. Women of the fellows' age might have been asked—at cocktail parties, or at their husbands' company Christmas gatherings—to keep it light or to stay quiet.

The Institute was different. Among the testimonies about this early period at the Institute, there are next to no memories of ennui or resentment—the kind of private feelings that might have roiled college campuses or neighborhood networks. In the beginning, face to face, these women worked well together. They traded tips on child rearing and gossiped about men. They developed real affection for each other because they respected each other as serious academics and serious artists. To Kathie, the difference between the social lives of suburban women and the intellectual love that formed among women at Radcliffe was clear: "People were not there to join a country club. They were there to work."

Kathie was in Cambridge for a few reasons: to be closer to her sister, to see more of the country, to find interesting work, and, in part, to support her mother. Kathie was not yet twenty when she arrived in Cambridge, in the spring of 1963. She had known nothing but the Bay Area. She was unprepared for the historic buildings, the maple trees, the antique bookshops tucked away on side streets off Harvard Square. When it first snowed, she was surprised and delighted, as was her mother. Olsen hadn't seen snow since her Nebraska girlhood, and she romped through the transformed landscape with the enthusiasm of a woman half her age. She built snowmen, pegged her family members with snowballs, and dragged the whole gang around wintry New England. "She loved seeing nature wear that garb," Kathie remembered. She knew that there was some energy in her mother yet to be unleashed.

From the fall of 1962 through the spring of 1963, Olsen formed special ties to four creative women—Sexton, Kumin, Swan, and the sculptor Pineda—who would become some of her closest friends. Pineda and Olsen spent many evenings laughing with their husbands. Kumin and Olsen traded ideas about gender and literary history, their debates reviving the sparring of Kumin's undergraduate days, when she stayed up late into the night smoking with her classmates and talking politics. Most significantly, Olsen spent plenty of time with her longtime correspondent Sexton.

Sometime during that first year, Swan produced a portrait of Olsen: a lithograph, not a sketch. She did Olsen's portrait at the same time she was working on one of Emily Dickinson—a hero of Olsen's and a writer whom Swan loved as well. Swan chose to focus on Olsen's face; Olsen's body, a mess of faint lines, barely registers in the engraving. The face, though, comes through clearly: her soft eyes, her gentle, closed-mouth smile. Swan used shade and shadow, rather than line, to create contour; the result is a face free from wrinkles, a face that looks like a young girl's. Swan had captured something of Olsen's youthful exuberance—the spirit of a woman who would still camp in the wilderness at a moment's notice, or dance around an apartment even as the hour grew late. She added the fifty-year-old writer's face to her pantheon of Institute portraits. They were something like Olsen's desk pinups—the faces of women who "sustained and judged" each other.

Over the course of that first year, these five women knit themselves together into a friend group, a sort of institute within the Institute. They collaborated and debated and celebrated each other's work. They saw each other as artists first and foremost and in this way differentiated themselves from the more bookish associate scholars. They did not have PhDs, but as the application had requested, they had "the equivalent" training in artistic craft. Joking about the way the Institute compared artists to scholars, they called themselves "the Equivalents." It was a loose association: there were no regular meetings, no clubhouse rules. The five women and their families occasionally socialized together on weekends, and the women saw each other regularly in the yellow house on Mount Auburn Street. But "the Equivalents" was less a formal title for a tight group of five than a term of affinity, a way of calling each other kindred spirits.

When she first came to the Institute, Olsen felt the most kinship with Sexton. One afternoon, late in the fall of 1962, Olsen persuaded her friend to accompany her on a walk along the Charles River. It was a warm fall for New England—staying in the sixties and seventies throughout October—and Olsen loved being out of doors. She walked out from Harvard Square along Mount Auburn and Brattle Streets, admiring the eighteenth-century houses and copying inscriptions from the tombstones in Mount Auburn Cemetery. A transplant, not a native like Sexton, she delighted in the region's deep history.

An observer might have been struck by their different kinds of beauty: one was lean and dark-haired, her face made up like a catalog model's; the other had silvered curls framing a surprisingly youthful face. Both looked sharp: Sexton favored fitted blouses and she still loved to wear jewelry, while Olsen had taken to wearing clothes from the Finnish company Marimekko, which could be purchased at the Design Research store in Harvard Square. (The company paid women to walk around Harvard Square modeling the latest styles.) Sometimes, she bought bright, patterned cloth from the company and then paid someone to sew blouses and dresses to her measurements: she was stunned that you could pay someone to *make clothes for you*. Moved by the beauty around her, Olsen spoke aloud a few lines of Sara Teasdale's poetry. Teasdale had written short, musical lyrics about beauty, love, and death; though she won prizes in her lifetime, including the 1918 Columbia Poetry Prize (later renamed the Pulitzer), male critics found her unsophisticated. She died by suicide in 1933—a fate that calls to mind the final couplet of her poem "The Answer": "I found more joy in sorrow / Than you could find in joy."

Sexton knew this poem, and others, for when Olsen quoted Teasdale, she became strangely agitated. "Oh, so you love her poems too!" she exclaimed. "But you must never, never admit it to anyone," she cautioned.

Olsen, unfamiliar with the taste making and gatekeeping that preoccupied men of letters on the East Coast, looked bewildered. "What do you mean?" she asked.

Sexton confessed that she'd once shared her preference for Teasdale at the Holmes workshop, where Holmes replied that Teasdale was a poor poet, technically unimpressive and overly sentimental. Sexton had accepted, blindly, Holmes's hierarchy of poets; according to him, Teasdale was "the lowest of the low." But Olsen didn't think in terms of canons and critics; she thought about a writer's relationship to the truth, her vivacity, her intelligence. She evaluated writers by determining how and if they made her want to live. Later, when she gained a public platform, she praised the wide range of writers—men and women, white and black, working-class and aristocratic—who, in her estimation, were engaged in the hard, necessary work of "the maintenance of life." That afternoon with Sexton, she insisted that they talk without shame about the writers who moved and sustained them. Teasdale was one; Edna St. Vincent Millay was another. Sexton admitted to her love of both.

Sexton had once been afraid of becoming a lesser Millay; she had written to male poets for reassurance that she would be something other than a lady poet, a minor writer. This fear waned at Radcliffe, where women echoed and affirmed her tastes—not to mention her loves, her experiences, and her fears. As Olsen put it, "Our love of Sara Teasdale or Edna St. Vincent Millay didn't shame us, with each other."

For the Equivalents, to be "with each other" meant more than simply being in each other's presence; it meant supporting each other as artists and intellectuals, emotionally and practically. Swan's husband, Alan, connected Kathie Olsen with a secretarial job with a science education organization. (Jack, having posted his union card, ended up with a job at the print shop for the *Cambridge Chronicle*, where he worked from 4:00 p.m. to midnight.) Several of them lent Olsen money; Kumin lent her at least $1,100. Kumin and Sexton watched each other's children and tutored each other's daughters. Each of the Equivalents hosted the others and their families for dinner; as Kathie explained, these were easy gatherings to justify because "everybody had to have dinner." The socializing happened around meals because the women wanted to reserve the rest of the time for work. Meals were convivial but informal, such as the picnic that was held on the Fourth of July. Each time an Equivalent took responsibility for feeding the others and their children, she eased the domestic burden on her friends.

During this time, Olsen and Pineda became close friends. It was hard to know what it was about the gifted, cosmopolitan sculptor that attracted Olsen; perhaps it was her seriousness, perhaps her generosity, perhaps her interest in the earthly feminine. (Julie, Olsen's second daughter, believed that it was impossible to pin down the reasons the friendship between Olsen and Pineda bloomed: she asked, why does anyone ever fall in love?) Within weeks of their first meeting, the two women began socializing with their husbands. Evenings, the Olsens hosted the Tovishes in their third-floor apartment for dinner, or they traveled out to the Tovish house in Brookline. They listened to music—a love shared among all four—and ate well. The couples discussed the politics of the day; the Olsens leaned further left than the Tovishes, but all four opposed U.S. military imperialism and believed in civil rights for African Americans. And they shared their work with each other. Olsen lent the Tovishes a copy of *Tell Me a Riddle*. One evening, back in their house in Brookline, the Tovishes stayed up late reading the title story aloud and weeping. They agreed that their new friend was a true talent.

Such book swapping was common. Passing books among each other, the Equivalents created their own canon. It included Olsen's copy of Kafka, collections by the lady poets—including Teasdale and Dickinson—and Virginia Woolf's *A Room of One's Own*. One might argue that Woolf's text, with its emphasis on solitude and resources for the writer, was the theory, and the Institute, the messy practice.

One day, Sexton went to dig up a copy of Woolf's book in the Newton Public Library. She found a copy, gifted to the library in 1929. She took it to the circulation desk, where she learned that the book had never been checked out. It had been sitting on the shelf for more than thirty years, while the women of Newton went to college, quit jobs, contributed to the war effort, and marched back to the kitchen.

"It makes me so mad," she said later. "There are women sitting out there and they don't know this exists . . . there's something wrong with a town, you know, with a marvelous school system and everything else and this book had never been taken out . . . and it's about being a woman! It's about all of it!" Woolf's argument about the need for one's own space resonated strongly with Sexton. She reflected that her study had not only helped her write but also made for a happier home. With a room of her own, she felt as if she had come into herself. She called Woolf's book "health."

Sexton rejoiced in her own room, but she also delighted in the women who occupied the rooms around her. At the Institute, she and Kumin continued to collaborate on individual poems and on their joint projects. Their children's book *Eggs of Things* came out with Putnam's in 1963. Charmingly illustrated by Leonard Shortall, the book follows the adventures of a foursome: Skippy, Buzz, Skippy's younger sister (nicknamed Pest), and their dog, Cowboy. Their mission? To save the neighborhood vegetable garden from cutworms.

The children decide to hatch some toads ("Did you know that two toads can eat a hundred cutworms for breakfast?"), but first they have to harvest the eggs from the nearby pond; these are the "eggs of things" of the book's title. The toads save the garden, but not before tormenting poor Cowboy, who ends up in the bathtub where the tadpoles matured into toads. The book bears the imprint of Kumin's naturalism: her love of seasons and soil, her attention to the invisible riches all around us. A second book, *More Eggs of Things*, followed in 1964. The volumes represent a happy time for both the Sexton and the Kumin families, a time when the children and their mothers remained open to discovery.

Nothing represents this spirit of discovery—the spirit of the Institute—better than *Aspects of the Oracle*, the sculpture series Pineda produced while on fellowship there. Inspired by the Oracle of Delphi—the most renowned oracle in ancient Greece—Pineda crafted a series of oracle sculptures, each of which expressed a different mood: ecstatic, rapturous, jubilant, accusative, portentous, and exhausted.

Her sculptures spoke with their limbs and torsos; they saw visions behind their closed, sunken eyes. In their agonies and ecstasies, they communicated mysteries that only women could understand. The "ecstatic" oracle turns her face up to the sky, as if awaiting benediction. The "rapturous" oracle looks upward too, though unlike her kinswoman she's curled up, her knees tucked, her arms wrapped around her torso in a self-protective gesture. The "jubilant" oracle raises her arms skyward in either celebration or praise; the "accusative" oracle points ahead of her, in a pose not dissimilar to her "portentous" cousin. The "exhausted" oracle sits with her head bowed forward, her feet dangling, her head downcast. More than the others, this last one captures the affect of the historical Pythia, the prophetesses who spoke for the oracle, who forced themselves into trances, and who served visitors all day.

The sculptures are recognizably human and even historically accurate (the bronze tripod, the shapeless dress); they are also, simultaneously, representations of emotions and ideas. The artist once said

Marianna Pineda, Aspects of the Oracle: Portentous

of the series, it "had something to do with the creative process, and struggle of getting something out, speaking something, or delivering it to somebody else."

A woman is at once a figure and an idea, a symbol and a person. Pineda once said that she was interested in how women occupied positions of power in myth and in history, "as we think they may have been in pre-patriarchal societies." She saw in the female figure a range of earthly forces. With this new series, Pineda suggested that the female body, and the emotions it conjured and contained, could be a vessel for knowledge—the kind of wisdom that not even the most learned men could understand. Her oracle was a supernatural woman, but she wasn't a witch—a persona Sexton used in her poetry and occasionally adopted onstage. The oracle was powerful but not menacing. She didn't haunt. Instead, she offered what help she could to those who wished to know more about the mysteries of the world.

CHAPTER 10

Me, Me Too

THERE ARE MANY SITES OF COMMUNION. Churches are one; libraries are another. Some people arrange séances and conjure spirits. Others turn the pages of old books, hoping to touch the dead. The connections they establish might elude language: a person senses the presence of another, even if the latter doesn't speak aloud.

Pineda believed that women were particularly attuned to spirits. She made sculptures of priestesses and prophetesses—and later, in 1980, a bronze statue called *The Spirit of Lili'uokalani*, a representation of Hawai'i's last sovereign monarch—because she thought these works captured women's spiritual powers. But there are other ways that female artists can conjure. In 1962, Swan and Sexton took a journey into the underworld together. Their collaboration happened in the spaces beyond speech.

Swan had spent her first year at the Institute studying with George Lockwood, a master lithographer who had founded the Impressions Workshop in Boston, a school of printmaking. Swan was excited by the chance to learn a new medium, to make it "say what I want it to say," and she joked to her friend about how grateful she was to Lockwood for employing a bunch of strapping, mustachioed young men to do the hard labor involved in printmaking. She laughed whenever these young men referred to women as "chicks."

On May 1, 1962, Swan gave a seminar talk on her lithographs—a "small visual essay," she called it. Her pieces were strewn about the seminar room at 78 Mount Auburn, where they caught the afternoon light. The size of the pieces made it clear that lithography was indeed "backbreaking *labah*," as Swan said, pronouncing the last word like a New Englander. She introduced the audience to the components and techniques of her chosen medium: you draw on the stone, she explained, then etch it with acid so the white parts will be covered and the black released by the pressing. Lithography was remarkable because an artist could revise the piece in between prints: unlike painters, who simply covered up prior versions with more paint, lithographers revealed their artistic process—their errors, revisions, redirections. She paused over a lithograph called *The Musicians*, inspired by a line of Keats: "Heard melodies are sweet, / but those unheard / Are sweeter." This had been one of her first efforts in the medium. Two figures, playing wind instruments, are set against a murky background—a fitting way to figure music, an art form that defies representation. The women in the audience gazed upon the work admiringly; Sexton in particular was captivated.

The Musicians haunted Sexton. She purchased one of the early versions from Swan and hung it first in the living room, then moved it to her study, where she would glance at it in between writing letters and typing out a poem. To her, it had a sense of magic, maybe a twinge of evil. So much of Swan's early work had been expressionist but nonetheless figurative; this lithograph, however, conjured figures only in the loosest sense. Sexton hadn't seen anything like this in Swan's other work, though she liked that work, too, and would have bought more lithographs if she could have afforded them. Occasionally, she would stand up from her desk and sidle up to the lithograph, getting close to it, far closer than one is supposed to get to a work of art. (Think of how an impressionist painting loses its coherence when viewed up close.) She was looking for something, though she didn't know what—something that was *inside* the lithograph, she thought to herself, something that maybe wasn't even there.

She started to write. As always, she started with the images: "old palaces"; a piper, who is also a midwife, with an "unforgettable woman's face"; a flute that "grows out of the wall like something human," that is "driven into the wall like a pipe." She wasn't sure what she was describing; it wasn't music so much as magic, perhaps? The images piled up until she felt herself lost among them. She picked up the phone, as she always did when she felt lost, but instead of calling Kumin, her most frequently phoned friend, she called Swan. Sexton began to read out loud what she'd written. Swan, interested and perhaps bemused, responded that she didn't quite know what Sexton was after, but she felt inspired herself; perhaps she would draw something in response to Sexton's lines.

Sexton kept working her images; she called Swan throughout the process to ask her to reckon with the new writing. A poem began to take shape. A voyager, to whom the poem is addressed in the second person, travels through time and space to arrive at an underground grotto, "a great hole in the earth." A flutist of ambiguous gender plays a magical tune called "Being Inside." "This is the music that you waited for / in the great concert halls, / season after season / and never found," the speaker reports. Other travelers arrive for the concert, drawn by the piper, who, like the flutist, is somehow both woman and man. The dead arrive as well, their "protruding fingernails" having scratched out pathways from their coffins, down into the bowels of the earth. The concert turns sinister; you—the traveler addressed throughout the poem—learn that you will never leave this cave. Other voices clamor to be let in; perhaps they, too, will be granted entrance one day. The speaker promises, "There will be no pain."

Weeks later, on a May morning, Sexton sat in Kumin's breakfast nook, pleading with her more learned friend to provide her poem with an organizing myth. Wasn't there something . . . about the great search for . . . something? In the middle of the earth? Kumin was the kind of poet who would start with a myth and write a poem, while Sexton would write a poem and then look for a myth to match.

Kumin couldn't come up with anything. Sexton acknowledged that she didn't really know what she was looking for—or, really, what she was writing about. The poem itself was an incomplete quest.

Sexton didn't publish the poem until 1966, when it appeared in her collection *Live or Die*, the title taken from that line in Bellow. By then, it had a new title: "To Lose the Earth." But before she changed the title from "The Musicians," she read it aloud, in May 1963, at an Institute seminar. Before the seminar began, she hung Swan's *Musicians* on the wall behind her; the audience could look at it as the poet read her work. Sexton made her typical apologies—in this case, for the poem's length as well as for the fact that "it isn't a good reading poem." The Institute women listened patiently, reading along with their mimeographed copies of the poem and noting that Sexton must have made changes as recently as the night before.

The women in the audience felt themselves addressed by the "you" of the poem. They were along for the ride into the bowels of the earth. The poem moves from "the wreckage of Europe" and the "Common Market" to a cave "that a pharaoh built by the sea," where a musician plays his flute. There, belowground, the dead protrude from the walls. Those who have found themselves in this underworld must try to decide if they want to leave, or even if they can. After all, the music is so enticing, and the figure playing it so mysterious. There might be enough in this cave to entertain a visitor for a long time.

When she finished reading, Sexton addressed Swan, who was listening from the front row. "How about it, Barbara?" she asked. "Can we keep going forever?"

As if Sexton's question had been about their collaborative relationship, rather than a particular poem, Swan responded by revealing both a painting and a drawing she had done based on the fragments she'd heard over the phone. One was called *The Sorcerers*. It was as if the figures from *The Musicians* had shape-shifted in response to the music of Sexton's piper.

"My painting and drawing are extensions," Swan explained. "There are images in your poem that I have yet to conjure with." She sounded like a sorcerer herself.

Swan propped up her new work alongside the old. Her drawing

seemed to be a continuation of Sexton's poem, a further evolution of the murky musician figure that had inspired the writing. It was as if the shape-shifter Sexton described in her poem—her musician, both a woman and a man—had transformed once again. Swan and Sexton were engaged in a strange artistic back-and-forth, passing the musician figure between them and altering him as they did so.

"It's like incest," someone whispered.

Murmurs of agreement and skepticism traveled through the audience. Swan and Sexton paid no attention. As if they were alone in Swan's home studio, the two artists began debating between themselves the "truth" of their respective representations. "It's a false image!" Sexton cried, disgusted with her poem. "It's a poetic lie." Swan tried to convince her friend otherwise, insisting that Sexton had gotten something right about the underground setting and about the enchanting nature of the music. "They're both completely true to themselves," she explained. Sexton, distracted, and at this point probably drunk, began riffing on the idea of a heavenly setting, something undiscovered. "Of course we all want to fly," she said, almost to herself. She didn't sound rational. But that, in a way, didn't matter for Swan; their collaboration was based more on sound than sense.

"The greatest art of all, to me, is music," Sexton continued. "It says . . . it hits people directly, it's so inside of you . . . writing can't do it." Nor could painting. Both writing and painting projected outward an individual's consciousness and unconsciousness. Music, however, most often emerged from collaboration. Consider the composer who writes a score: musicians, and perhaps a conductor, are required to bring the composition to life. There was a reason that Swan's painting features not one musician but two. Even as Sexton marveled at how both the writer and the painter failed to capture music, she engaged in an act of collaboration much like the musicians themselves.

It wasn't like incest, in the end. Sexton and Swan came from two different traditions; theirs was an exogamous love. They always remained a bit strange to each other—through their time at the Institute and throughout their future collaborations, of which there were many. Their friendship endured through—and even depended on—mutual misunderstanding. "Barbara and Anne had one of the most beautiful relationships between women that I've ever seen," Olsen once said. "With Barbara, Anne was her most natural, the way she must have been with her children."

What Sexton and Swan shared was not a medium but a sensibility. They understood how to inspire each other. "Anne moved into my world like a tornado," Swan wrote years later. "She shook it up, rattled it, possessed it like a demon." Swan knew that if she opened up a book about Edvard Munch and showed Sexton *The Scream*, Sexton would be fascinated. She appreciated the way Sexton wrought meaning from the "murky textures" of her painting. "The creative mind deals with a world of the imagination," Swan once explained.

> The artist and the poet carry this world around in their heads. They inhabit it. The scholar with a Ph.D. can study this world, analyze it, criticize it, even try to recreate it in biography, but the scholar can never really know the crazy, intuitive nonsense that whirls around in the mind of an artist.

This is the world in which Sexton and Swan lived with each other.

For the Equivalents, being "with each other" could mean talking on the phone, or writing intimate letters, or sitting together in a seminar, or walking along the river in the late afternoon. Sometimes a friendship existed in multiple forms: Kumin and Sexton's phone calls complemented their in-person bonding. Similarly, at the Institute, Sexton transformed the correspondence between her and Olsen into an in-person friendship.

Meanwhile, a friendship that had once taken place in person—that between Sexton and Sylvia Plath—had become a transatlantic correspondence.

After their time at Yaddo, Plath and Hughes had left the United States and moved to London, where they had a daughter, Frieda. In a letter to Sexton from February 1961, Plath described her daughter as a "marvelous blue-eyed comic" who had convinced the couple that they wanted "to found a dynasty." (Plath and Hughes had a second child, Nicholas, in 1962.) "We thrive in London," Plath declared in her letter. She praised Sexton's *Bedlam*, which she was rereading, and told Sexton to pass along compliments on Kumin's "Fräulein poem," in *The New Yorker*. At the time of writing, Plath had published a poetry collection, *The Colossus, and Other Poems*, in Britain and was hoping to find an American publisher. She was still determined to be a great poetess, even as she strove to be "an Earth Mother in the deepest richest sense," as she had once put it in her journals.

In an effort to accomplish this, Plath, Hughes, and their two children moved to Devon, in the southwest of England. In the winter of 1959, Plath had dreamed about "a house of our children, little animals, flowers, vegetables, fruits." In Devon in 1962, she fulfilled this dream. "I am bedded in the country," she wrote to Sexton in August, "keeping bees and raising potatoes and doing broadcasts on and off for the BBC." She was also working on an autobiographical novel, *The Bell Jar*, which she would publish in 1963 under the pseudonym Victoria Lucas. Her letters to Sexton were happy and chatty, though they also indicated Plath's isolation. "How was the Radcliffe grant, did it really free you from the drudgery of housework?" she asked. "Tell me how things are with you, and Maxine and George. Who do you see, now? . . . I would love one of your newsy letters to stick on the wall."

Plath's beautiful life shattered when Hughes left her for another woman. The couple separated, and Plath contemplated vengeance. She wrote fervently, frantically; the last months of her life were her most sustained and productive as a poet. It was during this time that she produced the work that Hughes, and many others, would come to see as true genius. "Daddy," a controversial poem published in 1965 in the posthumous collection *Ariel*, repurposes fascist imagery to suggest that female suffering can be its own form of vengeance. The speaker, who loves "the boot in the face, the brute," also sees herself killing her torturer. "If I've killed one man, I've killed two," she warns. "Lady Lazarus," a poem from this same period, alludes to suicide. "I have done it again," it begins; later, the speaker refers to "the second time," when she meant "to last it out and not come back at all." The last two stanzas of the poem constitute a warning to male readers as the speaker imagines a ghostly vengeance, wrought upon those who have wronged her. "Out of the ash / I rise with my red hair," she says. "And I eat men like air."

Lady Lazarus's prediction came true: the ghost of Plath had its vengeance. On February 11, 1963, she died by suicide in her home. When the news of her death first broke in February, the Boston poetry community refused to believe that the poet had died from pneumonia, as was initially reported. They knew her death would be revealed to be a suicide, and they were unsurprised when their suspicions were confirmed. Plath had stuck her head in the oven—the site of feminized, domestic labor—and died of asphyxiation. According to the biographer and critic Diane Middlebrook, many Boston poets "saw the suicide as a particularly female revenge wrought on the model of a Greek tragedy, pathetic and terrifying." Two years later, Hughes published the work his wife had written during the furious months before she died. *Ariel*, the posthumous collection, expressed all the rage and betrayal that Plath felt and that she'd hidden, even from her friends overseas.

Plath's death shook Sexton. It awakened her own suicide fantasies, and it concluded a long season of loss: Kumin's father had died the prior fall, reminding Sexton of her own parents' deaths. Plath's crisp, cheerful letters to Sexton hadn't indicated that anything was amiss. She had written "from Devonshire / about raising potatoes / and keeping bees," as Sexton recorded in "Sylvia's Death," the elegy she wrote in the months after learning the news. In the poem, Sexton turned quickly to her own brushes with suicide and articulated something akin to envy. "Thief!" the speaker accuses: "How did you crawl into, / crawl down alone / into the death I wanted so badly and for so long." Plath had usurped Sexton's place as the era's suicidal female poet; the poem was Sexton's effort both to connect to her former friend and to reclaim her cultural position. "And me, / me too," the poem's speaker insists. She knows what suicide means.

Sexton was pleased with the poem. She thought it expressed something about the secret knowledge that she and Sylvia shared. As she would put it in another poem, "Wanting to Die," written a year later, those who contemplate suicide are akin to "carpenters": "they want to know *which tools.* / They never ask *why build.*" The language of craftsmanship is notable. In some strange sense, for a woman constrained to a particularly deadening form of life, suicide itself could become a site of almost professional expertise and achievement. Though she usually took notes well, Sexton, in this case, cared little for the opinions of her readers: though the poem was rejected by *The New Yorker* and criticized, in letters, both by Robert Lowell and by the poet Galway Kinnell, Sexton continued to think it quite good. "You may paste it on your wall," she told George Starbuck, her former lover, who had spent many nights drinking at the Ritz and listening to Plath and Sexton talk about suicide attempts. It was a fitting directive: he is mentioned in the elegy as the "boy," the one who sits in the cab between two women whose knowledge of mortality far surpasses his own.

Sexton and Plath shared a death wish, one that stemmed from their own particular, troubled pasts. Whatever their respective chemical imbalances, it is likely no coincidence that both poets grew up in adjacent, straitlaced suburbs, places where women conformed to traditional domesticity. Their "fascination with death," as Sexton called it, was surely augmented by the constraining, claustrophobic culture of mid-century America. This was a world that told them, again and again, that marrying and raising children were a woman's best and only callings. At every turn, they were faced with the message that unhappy wives must be crazy. Sexton and Plath accepted that diagnosis and behaved according to script.

"It is not *when* I have a baby, but *that* I have one, and more, which is of supreme importance to me," Sylvia wrote in her journal, in June 1959. "And for a woman to be deprived of the Great Experience her body is formed to partake of, to nourish, is a great and wasting Death." Some women, like Pineda, found the generative power of the female body inspiring. Others found it burdensome or terrifying. They longed to be defined otherwise.

CHAPTER 11

Mad for the Message

O N FEBRUARY 19, 1963, just eight days after Plath's death, Betty Friedan's *The Feminine Mystique* was published by Norton. In the book, Friedan argued that women needed to work. They needed to work outside the home, and they needed to be paid. If they didn't, they would sink into the depths of depression. Their sanity, the happiness of their families, and the health of the nation depended on their making "a serious professional commitment."

Friedan's book was an analysis of the "happy housewife" ideology that had set in during the postwar years. College graduation rates for women were down; marriage rates were up. More and more census takers wrote down "occupation: housewife." The women who responded to the census taker in this way—many of whom were white, middle-class, and college educated—were, according to the reigning ideology, supposed to be among the happiest women in the world. Yet many claimed to suffer from a vague malaise that neither money, nor medicine, nor psychoanalysis could fix. One called it "the problem that has no name."

Friedan named the problem—"a vague undefined wish for 'something more' than washing dishes, ironing, punishing and praising the children"—and described the dangers it posed. Women suffered under the spell of the "feminine mystique," a belief that "the highest value and the only commitment for women is the fulfillment of their own femininity." Proponents of the "mystique" argued that Western culture has devalued femininity. Women should stop trying to be like men and should instead accept their distinctly feminine characteristics, which included "sexual passivity, male domination, and nurturing maternal love." This wasn't the same as historical sexism, according to which women were inferior, inhuman—so much property to be protected and exchanged. The feminine mystique even allowed for female sexual pleasure: a vaginal orgasm (as opposed to a clitoral orgasm) from penetrative sex with one's husband was not only appropriate but also a sign of one's femininity. But, as Friedan noted, this newfound attitude toward the feminine aligned perfectly with old prejudices and gender conventions. It wasn't enough for women to give up education and career, to shrink their world down to "the cozy walls of home." According to the feminine mystique, women were supposed to lobotomize themselves and to *like* it.

How did the mystique take hold? Friedan argued that ladies' magazines, their advertisers, and some influential theorists, such as Sigmund Freud and Margaret Mead, had spread the "feminine mystique" throughout the country. Magazine columnists and short fiction writers idolized the "happy housewife heroine," who had supplanted the "spirited career girls of the thirties and forties," a time before the mystique took hold. Meanwhile, advertisers, on television and in print, appealed to the housewife's creativity, suggesting that she could "express herself" by buying products for the home. Advertisers pitched the housewife products that required her to contribute something of herself (she could be "creative"!) while saving her labor. These products granted the housewife more time to spend with her children (though not enough time to pursue a career outside the home). A cake mix, to which she could add eggs and milk and butter, was the prototypical example: a homemade cake generated no profit for the company, while a store-bought cake would leave the woman free for other pursuits. Friedan, who called this tactic the "sexual sell," made the incisive observation that "the really important role that women serve as housewives is to *buy more things for the house.*" In other words, capitalism itself was to blame for women's suffering. Friedan had spent years working as a labor journalist, and her radical roots could be perceived in this critique.

A few other theories and thinkers came under fire. The anthropologist Margaret Mead promoted sex difference. Freud and his popularizers mistook women's longing for economic and political freedom as "penis envy." What Friedan called "sex-directed educators," the high school and college instructors who tailored their pedagogy according to a student's sex, trained women to be mothers and wives, not scholars or professionals. Friedan didn't hesitate to be hyperbolic: she invoked the Nazis several times, suggesting that when it came to the suburban home, the concentration camp made for a useful point of comparison.

Friedan wasn't the first to argue that middle-class American women faced a strange psychological problem; after all, this was the premise of her argument, not the payoff. As she noted in her opening chapter, the problem she wanted to study had burst onto the American scene, "like a boil," in 1960—the same year that the Radcliffe Institute for Independent Study was founded. Magazines published articles titled "The Trapped Housewife." In the month's leading up to the book's publication, women wrote to Friedan to say that they had imagined writing a book on the same topic. A vice president at Norton, attempting to get a blurb from the writer Pearl S. Buck before publication, acknowledged, "Much is being written these days about the plight (or whatever it is) of the educated American woman; therefore this one will have to fight its way out of a thicket."

Friedan's book succeeded because it was synthetic and forceful. She brought together scholarly research, cultural criticism, and personal anecdotes to describe a dangerous epidemic that needed to be neutralized. Additionally, she offered a provocative answer to the eternal revolutionary question: What is to be done? At a time when few could imagine a husband shouldering any child care or house-

work responsibilities, Friedan encouraged women to flee their suburban homes and take up stimulating, paid work that took advantage
of their intelligence and skills. (Friedan did not make any suggestions about who would take up the domestic work; this was a glaring
omission for a former labor journalist.) The education reporter for
The New York Times, the same man who had written the front-page
story on Bunting's Institute, summarized the value of the book: "The
indictment is uncompromising and occasionally extreme. But while
the case may be somewhat overstated, the symptoms of a dangerous trend have in no way been misstated. In fact, the book confirms
and drives home with editorial passion many dangers that educators
themselves often warn against privately."

Many readers loved Friedan's fierceness—that she took "some
hard whacks at some very sacred cows"—but others pushed back on
her thesis. A reviewer in the *Los Angeles Times* called the book "one
of the largest bundles of nonsense ever put between covers" and cited
the increasing number of women awarded bachelor and graduate
degrees—180,650 in 1962, a record high—as proof that women were
not "trapped." (To be sure, women's college graduation rates had by
this point rebounded from their low point in the 1950s, but they had
not yet reached their high points of the 1920s and 1940s.) Angry
letters poured into the *Chicago Tribune*. "I find it a lot of rubbish,"
wrote Mrs. Kenneth Carpenter. "I am sick to death of reading about
oversexed, unhappy suburban wives," complained Mrs. Harold A.
Neuman. "For every one of these there are hundreds of happy, well-
adjusted wives and mothers whose perfectly normal lives include not
even one teensy, bitty extra-marital affair." "What is this woman trying to do," asked another, "plant the seeds of doubt and discontent in
the minds of happy, well-adjusted wives and mothers?"

The problem was that for many women, the seeds of discontent
had been planted long ago. As the historian Stephanie Coontz has
written, *The Feminine Mystique* was a success not because it was
novel, or prescient, but because it said the thing everyone else was
thinking and said it well. Because its arguments echoed and amplified ideas that were already in circulation, the book found an eager

Betty Friedan, 1960

readership. During the year 1964, *The Feminine Mystique* sold over one million copies, becoming one of the the best-selling nonfiction books in history.

By the time Kumin got her hands on *The Feminine Mystique*, it was several months after the book first appeared. She found herself "mad for the message." "Yes yes yes to it all," she wrote to Sexton. "It seemed all too true to me looking back over 3 yrs of college freshmen I taught, the apathy, the disinterest in any kind of abstract idea, the single-minded female goal, to snag a man & make babies." (Lily Macrakis, the historian who befriended the poets during that first year at the Institute, had encountered the same problem among her students—hence her decision to scoff at their engagement rings.) Kumin, who had once embraced psychoanalytic theory, now found herself pushing back against some of psychoanalysis's central, sexist ideas.

In rejecting old doctrines, in revolting against mandatory femininity, Kumin was in good company. All over the country, women were left "breathless" by Friedan's book. "I felt as though Betty Friedan had looked into my heart, mind, and psyche and . . . put the unexplainable distress I was suffering into words," said one reader. Another reported that after reading the book, "I finally realized I wasn't crazy." And yet another understood that the problem wasn't with her; it was with the world. "I can't express how freeing it was for me to realize that my predicament was not all my own fault," she said.

It's not clear who among the Institute fellows obtained that first copy, but whoever did soon lent the book to a fellow associate scholar. It passed from one woman to the next like samizdat. In a memoir, Linda Sexton recalls receiving a copy of *The Feminine Mystique* that her mother had annotated; the notes "showed her identification with the problems Friedan described." Its message resonated with this group of women, now working in an institution that had been designed, in part, based on Friedan's beliefs. In "A New Life Plan for Women," the book's final chapter, Friedan explained how women could get out from under the thumb of "happy housewife" ideology. "Ironically," she wrote,

the only kind of work which permits an able woman to realize her abilities fully, to achieve identity in society in a life plan that can encompass marriage and motherhood, is the kind that was forbidden by the feminine mystique; the lifelong commitment to an art or science, to politics or profession. Such a commitment is not tied to a specific job or locality. It permits year-to-year variation—a full-time paid job in one community, part-time in another, exercise of the professional skill in serious volunteer work or a period of study during pregnancy or early motherhood when a full-time job is not feasible. It is a continuous thread, kept alive by work and study and contacts in the field, in any part of the country.

She might as well have been writing fund-raising copy for the Institute, so close were her prescriptions to the Institute's credo. (One wonders if some of Polly Bunting's notes from the late 1950s might have made their way into Friedan's final draft.)

The Feminine Mystique contained advice for artists, too, that might have spoken to the Equivalents. Drawing on the work of Simone de Beauvoir, who, in her 1949 book, *The Second Sex*, had argued that female artists were often dilettantes, Friedan insisted that women must take up the arts professionally. "The amateur or dilettante whose own work is not good enough for anyone to want to pay to hear or see or read does not gain real status by it in society, or real personal identity," she warned. Amateurism was a particular risk in the arts, more than it would be in politics or science. "The 'arts' seem, at first glance, to be the ideal answer for a woman," Friedan explained. "They can, after all, be practiced in the home. They do not necessarily imply that dreaded professionalism, they are suitably feminine, and seem to offer endless room for personal growth and identity, with no need to compete in society for pay." This might be the description of Sexton at her dining room table, playing with rhymes in order to contain her troubled mind, or of Kumin reading her "how to write poetry" manual, convinced that she would never earn back the investment. Friedan continued, "But I have noticed that when women do not take up painting or ceramics seriously enough to become professionals—to be paid for their work, or for teaching it to others, and to be recognized as a peer by other professionals— sooner or later, they cease dabbling." Sexton had said much the same thing once, about the "lady poets" to whom she loathed being compared: "Women don't strive to make anything real out of [poetry]. They just dabble in it."

This was another place where Bunting and Friedan seemed to be of one mind. The Institute insisted on paying its fellows, even though the stipend couldn't support a family or even a single woman, unless she found subsidized room and board. To some observers, the money seemed superfluous, but to the fellows it was the difference between being dismissed and being taken seriously. When Alice Ryerson, conducting those first-year interviews, asked Sexton what the difference was between a dabbler and a professional, Sexton replied, "Money helps: it's the only thing—in the society I live in."

In an important sense, the Equivalents had already walked some way down the path that Friedan hoped to lay. They had written about female disappointment and domestic drudgery. The creative writers, in particular, produced influential work on this topic before Friedan's book arrived on the scene. In 1962, Sexton published a poem called "Housewife," a brief poem that comprises ten unrhymed lines. The house in the poem is personified; it's identified in the first line as a woman's spouse. In the next two lines, the house is described as having skin, a mouth, and internal organs. The housewife of the poem's title kneels within this living, breathing prison, "washing herself down" and waiting for men to "enter by force." The poem fuses houses and husbands, suggesting that both keep women on their knees.

"Housewife" is unlike many of Sexton's lyrics: there is no "I," no personal detail. The housewife of the poem is a nameless, universal figure, a shell that any female reader could project herself into. She's like any number of the anonymous women quoted by Friedan in *The Feminine Mystique*, except this housewife seems permanently trapped.

Kumin, too, represented the more disappointing aspects of marriage in her work. One poem, "Purgatory," emerged from frustrations with her own family. During her second year at the Institute, the Kumins went to see a performance of *Romeo and Juliet*. Kumin found herself weeping at the play's end—both at the pathos of the final act and at the perfection of the ending. Vic and the children looked askance at Kumin and edged away from her. Almost as an act of vengeance, Kumin wrote a poem that imagined a so-called happy ending for the star-crossed lovers.

"And suppose the darlings get to Mantua," the poem begins. Romeo is "unshaven," with "egg yolk on his chin." He's sick, half-dressed, far from the beautiful romancer he was once. Juliet has fared no better: "the cooking lard has smoked her eye," and there's "another Montague . . . in the womb / although the first babe's bottom's not yet dry." The romance of the play's first four acts has soured: "The fifth act runs unconscionably long." Domestic life, as Kumin presents it here, is dirty, boring, and unending. The poison drunk by Juliet pales in comparison to the frustrations of perpetual pregnancy. Better, perhaps, to end up in the crypt.

By the fall of 1962, then, the Institute poets had already rendered gross, or tragic, the lives of housewives—the women whom Friedan would survey, speak for, and attempt to save. In October of that year, Kumin wrote to *Ladies' Home Journal* to complain about a piece by the poet and writer Phyllis McGinley in which McGinley had negatively portrayed the Radcliffe Institute as implying that "being a housewife is not a noble, useful and rewarding career." Kumin noted that "articles advising American women how to find fulfillment by minding the hearth are written by those . . . who are doing the exact opposite," and said that such articles are "deservedly suspect." (McGinley herself had two daughters and a Pulitzer.) She went on to elucidate the need for other forms of stimulation: "The fact is, that after the youngest child enters kindergarten, keeping house and raising a family do not constitute a full time job for the capable modern woman . . . It is one thing to escort children to the orthodontist, put up jelly and cosset a husband. It is quite another to sweep the hearth compulsively." Such writing would not have been out of place in Friedan's book.

Kumin, Sexton, and the others found that the Institute—a program that offered time and space away from the home, along with a stipend that communicated the seriousness of their endeavors—helped them find that longed-for "something more," without abandoning the parts of domestic life that they loved. They were Friedan's proof of concept.

But there were women who didn't thrill to Friedan's message, including the working-class writer Olsen. At first, Olsen found herself persuaded by parts of *The Feminine Mystique*. During the weeks that the Institute buzzed with news about Friedan's polemic, Olsen, preparing her seminar presentation, thought she would talk on "women" specifically. She had been reflecting on the division of labor in her own home. The Olsen household might have been radical, but it was also very much of its time. In so many ways, Jack was an incredibly supportive husband; he helped out around the house, and he deeply respected his wife. He thought of her as a comrade. But nonetheless Olsen found herself responsible for the bulk of the domestic labor. "If the kids were sick, that was Mom's problem," Julie, Olsen's second daughter, remembered. "Meals were Mom's problem, laundry was Mom's problem, and there were four of us." And like Friedan, Olsen believed in the value of creativity. She abhorred all obstacles— social, political, economic—that got in the way of creative expression. Maybe there was something in all this chatter about women's lives and losses that she could use.

In the end, though, Olsen couldn't sign on to Friedan's project. For her, as for her husband, the true struggle was the class struggle. Looking again at *The Feminine Mystique*, she decided she didn't see herself in Friedan's pages. Who were these women who stayed at home all day, listlessly vacuuming? In the Olsen family, "women worked, period, or you couldn't pay the rent," Julie explained. Like the narrator in "I Stand Here Ironing," her award-winning story from 1957, Olsen longed for more time at home with her daughters—and for the energy to enjoy that time. "I was a young mother, I was a distracted mother," the narrator of the story says at one point, thinking about the early years, when her eldest daughter was small. "We were poor and could not afford for her the soil of easy growth." At once a confession and a defense, "I Stand Here Ironing" communicated powerfully the plight of the working-class mother: a woman trapped not by the "feminine mystique" but by the wage labor that writers like Friedan thoughtlessly portrayed as always emancipatory.

Olsen typified and anticipated critiques of Friedan later levied by working-class women and women of color (and those who belonged to both communities). These women criticized Friedan for failing to recognize how onerous wage labor can be. For many women, work was the problem, not the solution. Women of color, who made up the bulk of domestic workers in the 1960s, spent their time raising other people's children rather than their own. They longed to return to their own homes, to make dinner for their own children. To them, Friedan's complaints were unrecognizable.

At the same time, however, some working-class women *did* identify with the claims Friedan made about the relationship between work and fulfillment. The sociologist Myra Marx Ferree, while researching her dissertation in the 1960s, conducted a comparative study of working-class women who worked outside the home and working-class women who did not. She found that those who worked outside the home were overall happier and more satisfied than those who did not. Later, she recalled interviewing a factory worker in Somerville, Massachusetts, who surprised the sociologist with her desire to work. "I sure would like to quit THIS job," the woman said, "but I can't imagine not working."

But voices like these did not usually reach the public. Because Friedan had the time, resources, and education to write a book, hers was the feminist message that gained mainstream attention in the 1960s. Domestic workers and factory workers might have had insights of their own, but they didn't have time to write them down nor the access to get them published. Olsen was the rare working-class woman with access to the literary and intellectual elite. The Institute had given her a library card, an office, collaborators, and free time. But having come from the working class to her present perch in Cambridge, she saw beyond the intellectual vogue currently sweeping up her friends and colleagues—women who were, after all, better off. She knew about the drudgery that most jobs entailed; she knew how it was a rare job that helped a woman self-actualize. Indeed, the Institute was unusual in its combining paid work and free, creative expression; the vast majority of people would never experience the convergence of these two things.

Olsen had both privilege and responsibility. She could try to speak for those who could not.

CHAPTER 12

Genius of a Sort

Throughout the 1962–1963 academic year, the Olsen family faced a problem every day around dinnertime: they couldn't get Tillie to come home. Olsen put in long hours during her first year at the Institute. She kept her books, notes, and typewriter in her Mount Auburn Street office; she wanted distance between her work and her family life. When she wasn't in her office, she was scouring the stacks in Widener Library conducting research, or she was in the Grolier Poetry Book Shop in Harvard Square, browsing and buying books. She read widely and avidly. The work of great writers was at her fingertips: the Brontës, Melville, Rilke. She read enthusiastically and copied out powerful passages. (She would continue this practice throughout her life, often mailing favorite quotations to her friends.) "It was like giving her the key to the candy store," Kathie said, referring to her mother's library privileges. "She couldn't believe it. We couldn't get her out of there."

Olsen was making up for lost time. She had never had access to such a rich library, nor had she ever had so much free time to read and think. She spent hours browsing the library stacks, making serendipitous discoveries. She was also keen to spend time with the creative women around her; she often dropped into their offices and studios to admire their works in progress.

Jack—who thought his wife was brilliant and who supported her art—seemed disappointed that she wasn't doing her "own work" while on this valuable Institute stipend. He was right: Olsen wasn't really writing her long-overdue novel. She was researching historical context; she was making notes; she was reading for inspiration. But she wasn't making the kind of progress that she'd promised to Cowley and to the Institute. At the end of the fall semester, she had more notes than she had polished pages of prose.

But there was a logic to Olsen's browsing. Sometime that fall or winter, while avoiding her messy notes for a novel, Olsen came across "old volumes, not taken out for years," by Rebecca Harding Davis, a writer she'd long admired. Born in 1831, Davis had once been a celebrated pioneer of realism. Her novella, *Life in the Iron Mills*, first published anonymously in *The Atlantic Monthly* in segments throughout 1861, offered one of the first accounts of life among workers in industrial America. (In 1861, readers, struck by the sternness of the work, assumed the author was a man.) It became a sensation; years later, some compared Davis's work to that of Zola, who was born nine years after her. But Davis never ascended to literary fame. After completing a novel, *Margret Howth*, she married, bore children, and wrote short fiction about her new life. Though she continued to write, Davis was all but forgotten by the time she died in 1910.

Olsen had first stumbled upon *Life in the Iron Mills* when she was fifteen, in an Omaha junk shop. She'd spent a grand total of thirty cents on three old, stained volumes of *The Atlantic Monthly*. She read, amazed, the descriptions of people much like her. She felt that this tattered old story was giving her permission to strive, to *want*, perhaps even to write. "Literature can be made out of the lives of despised people," Olsen wrote later, articulating the message she felt she received. "You, too, must write." Olsen didn't discover the identity of the author until 1958, when she was in the middle of writing the story that would become "Tell Me a Riddle." A stray footnote in the letters of Emily Dickinson pointed her in the direction of Davis. Searching through the card catalog at the San Francisco Public Library, she could find no listing for the author. Davis had disappeared, like so many women writers in history.

Now, in Cambridge, thirty-five years after her first encounter with Davis, Olsen brought the volumes down off the shelves and read again the novella's opening pages. The narrator casts her eyes on the "stream of human life" making its way toward the mills:

> Masses of men, with dull, besotted faces bent to the ground, sharpened here and there by pain or cunning; skin and muscle and flesh begrimed with smoke and ashes; stooping all night over boiling caldrons of metal, laired by day in dens of drunkenness and infamy; breathing from infancy to death an air saturated with fog and grease and soot, vileness for soul and body.

Davis's language rushed forward like the mass of teeming bodies, all moving in the same direction. And yet, Olsen noticed, Davis never denied the individuality of the workers; this is what made her so remarkable. Her achievement, Olsen thought, had been to make the working-class world real: to show the lives of industrial workers in all their complex humanity. Olsen wanted to do the same in what she imagined would be a work of world-altering fiction.

Energized by what she'd read, Olsen felt herself pulled in two directions. Part of her wanted to dive into her novel and write as Davis had. But another part of her, the research-oriented part, wondered why Davis—an author of such talent—had disappeared from literary history. What granted some writers fame, and others not? What kind of writer left a legacy, and what writer never managed to get started? Were there other Rebecca Harding Davises buried in the annals of literary history? For Olsen, these questions were not merely intellectual but personal: as a mother of four who had long struggled to find the time to write, Olsen could not help noticing the way motherhood had interrupted Davis's ascendant career. Just how many mothers were writers, she wondered, and how many writers were mothers? What had happened to other brilliant women like her?

For weeks, Olsen spent her days in Widener, researching literary production—what enabled it, and what got in the way. Finding the time to write wasn't just a problem for women, she realized. Many famous writers struggled to write. They were censored or self-censored; they lapsed into silence when life became too hard or turbulent to sustain creative work. Theodore Dreiser had taken eleven years to write *Jennie Gerhardt*, the novel he published after *Sister Carrie*. Isaac Babel and Oscar Wilde couldn't write while in prison. Thomas Hardy gave up fiction, writing poetry alone during his final years. Melville burned his work. Rimbaud stopped writing entirely. She started to think of these gaps and omissions as "silences"—not the natural kind, the fallow period most writers need, but unnatural, brought on, metaphorically, by something like bad soil or a premature frost. Such "thwarting," as Olsen called it, was both heartbreaking and, strangely, reassuring; Olsen saw that in her struggles to write, she was in esteemed company.

There were, of course, the preternaturally productive writers: Balzac, who wrote with remarkable self-discipline and who described writing as "constant toil"; Rilke, who refused to get a day job to support his family and who preached the value of "unconfined solitude." As she read their writing about writing, she tracked their prescriptions for creativity: no extra duties, no external communication, time, space, predictable schedules—what Conrad called "the even flow of daily life." It must have struck Olsen that the conditions these writers lauded looked a lot like the structure of the Institute.

Looking at who wrote consistently and who did not, Olsen began to notice some patterns. The productive writers were, for the most part, men. What's more, the majority of them had wives: women who soothed them and kept away noisy children, who prepared the meals that the hardworking male writers ingested unthinkingly. To be sure, there were a handful of prolific women writers, but Olsen was struck by how few of these authors had had children of their own. The great nineteenth-century novelist George Eliot did not, and neither did

Olsen's contemporary Katherine Anne Porter. Instead, many of them had servants who took care of the daily domestic tasks. She marveled over a quotation from Katherine Mansfield, who, along with her husband, longed to become a great writer: "The house seems to take up so much time . . . I mean when I have to clean up twice over or wash up extra unnecessary things, I get frightfully impatient and want to be working"—that is, writing. And this from a woman who had no children!

The spring semester started up, as did the weekly seminars. Pineda had delivered her seminar talk during the fall semester, in December 1962. She spoke about monumental art, which she argued was nearly impossible to produce in mid-century America, and asserted that figurative sculpture could only be appreciated fully when contrasted with the monument. It was a forceful, if idiosyncratic, discussion of art history, and though some of the scholars had pushed back on a few of Pineda's claims, the talk had gone smoothly overall. Thus, by the spring, Olsen was the only one of the Equivalents who had yet to present her work to the group.

As Olsen's presentation date drew near, she began to panic. Back in the fall, when asked for a title for her seminar talk, she had promised a seminar "on writing," just as the poets had spoken "on poetry." (They would do so again in the spring.) This was common practice among the Equivalents and their fellow artists: use the seminar to introduce the scholars to the practice of their craft by discussing a work in progress. Swan, in January, had titled her second Institute talk "Some Aspects of Painting by a Practicing Painter." Pineda, similarly, had spoken in February on "some aspects of sculpture." Olsen had planned to do the same.

At this point, however, she'd almost totally forsaken her fiction writing for a research plan that combined literary history and self-help. She spent her days like an industrious magpie, compiling a heap of quotations and observations from Anglo-American authors from the last several centuries. Perhaps she could present this research in lieu of her fiction writing? Even as she entertained this idea, she wondered how her research, informal and associative, would appear to an audience of trained scholars—women who compiled literature reviews, and generated abstracts, and cited the appropriate authorities. Olsen had been accepted to the Institute as a creative, an "equivalent," not a scholar or an intellectual. She felt herself at sea.

The title for her talk changed weekly. She contemplated writing on Friedan's "woman problem," but as she kept thinking, she changed her mind. Her research suggested to her that the problem of creative inequality stemmed from more than just sexism. While combing through lists of successful authors, Olsen had noted the dearth of working-class writers in the canon, as well as the decade—the 1950s—when black writers seemed to emerge. She could not talk only of women, she decided, for that would be to ignore poor writers, and black writers, and, of course, the women who were themselves poor or black. Never one to narrow her parameters, Olsen decided she would talk about all of it: political censorship, illiteracy, poverty, absent mothers, Rebecca Harding Davis, her own missing novel, her near failure of a career. She gave Smith her final title.

The Institute advertised her seminar as "Death of the Creative Process."

On March 15, just before 1:00 p.m., the Institute fellows gathered on the first floor of the yellow house for Olsen's seminar presentation. By this time, many of the fellows had already presented, and the more shy among them were grateful to ride out the rest of the semester in the audience. It was a sunny, cold day in the mid-thirties; the women wore warm tweed or wool jackets over their blouses. Sexton found a spot where she would have a good view of Olsen; she wanted to offer her friend, who would surely be nervous, some visible support. It was going to be Olsen's first public talk since her organizing days.

Smith made her usual announcements and introductions, but she struggled to explain what Olsen would speak about that afternoon. "The reason Connie isn't sure just what the topic is, is because it kept changing," Olsen interjected. "When there was all the to-do about feminine mystiques, it was going to be *Women*."

Women in the room might have noticed the slight dismissiveness of that word "to-do" and wondered what was coming their way. On its face, her talk was about creativity: its ideal conditions, what enabled it, what thwarted it, and what kills it off. It was the start of an intellectual project that would consume the rest of Olsen's working life. It was an entirely new take on the problem of the creative woman. And it was a working woman's subtle, critical engagement with her institutional host.

In Olsen's view, Bunting had underplayed the conflict between child rearing and performing intellectual work, arguing that they interlocked perfectly, like puzzle pieces. Friedan, by contrast, had overplayed conflict and simplified the equation. She presented professional work as every woman's raison d'être, and she encouraged former housewives to sally forth from their suburban homes and walk straight into offices—never looking back, with a pang of regret, at the children they were leaving behind.

The fellows, used to friendly seminar talks about specific works in progress, were not prepared for the wide-ranging, impassioned, and overtly political two-hour talk that Olsen delivered—in associative fashion, entirely from notes. Her silver head bowed over her many papers, she spoke softly and hesitantly, stuttering at times, losing her place, circling back to points she'd made many minutes earlier. She read out long quotations, then spoke extemporaneously, ad-libbing and repeating key phrases. Listeners got the sense that she was articulating some of these thoughts for the first time.

The impromptu nature of the talk didn't hide the force of Olsen's beliefs. Olsen was a Marxist and an organizer; she was comfortable talking class politics with the bourgeois. She started dramatically. "Because I so nearly remained mute, may yet never acquire that which is in me to be, because my whole writing history has been one of interruption, death and the beginning all over again, what it is that happens in others has a special fascination."

This was a crucial but under-studied problem: if we recognize that all children are creative but few adults are, then we must wonder what happens to adults, what strips them of their creative potential. Olsen implied that not many addressed this "revolutionary question" because it was, indeed, revolutionary: that is, it would require "reordering our whole society." Olsen, a longtime revolutionary, was up to the task.

Just as she pinned nineteenth-century authors over her desk, Olsen turned to the writers of the past in order to understand how to solve a problem in the present. She had copied out long quotations from writers' memoirs and diaries, and she proceeded to try her audience's patience by reading out these quotations in full. She wanted to describe the death of the creative process in the words of those who knew it best and intimately. Thomas Hardy, Herman Melville, Arthur Rimbaud, Gerard Manley Hopkins: all were great writers, and all had something to say about how and why creativity atrophies. Hemingway believed he had "destroyed his talent himself," while F. Scott Fitzgerald accused himself of being "but a mediocre caretaker of my own talent." Others, like Isaac Babel, had been censored, made into an emblem of "political silences." Still others were anonymous—quoting the eighteenth-century poet Thomas Gray, Olsen wondered about the "mute inglorious Miltons" who never found established positions from which they might write, or speak.

She contrasted the words of silenced writers with reflections by artists who had found ways to sustain their creative work. Drawing on their self-reflections, she demonstrated that true mastery requires the kind of total focus impossible for most people. Henry James, Balzac, Rilke: all preached the value of immersion in work. Rodin spoke of "living in his work as in a wood" and warned the aspiring artist, "You should work and have patience. You must sacrifice all else." These were the conditions demanded by the creative process—conditions that proved to be elusive for so many: the working class, the uneducated, people of color, women. "What feeds creativity only implies what kills it," she explained.

Listeners must have noticed that most of the writers Olsen quoted were men. There was a reason for this: few women had benefited from the conditions necessary to complete creative work. Those few were most likely from the upper class; they were the historical analogues for the Radcliffe Institute women, who could rely on financial security and household help ("servants" was the word she used throughout the talk). "Yet genius of a sort must have existed among women as it must have existed among the working classes," Olsen speculated—thinking, to be sure, of her own dulled brilliance.

Now and again an Emily Bronte or a Robert Burns blazes out and proves its presence. But certainly it never got itself on to paper. When however one reads of a woman possessed by devils, of a wise woman selling herbs and doctoring, or even of a very remarkable man who had a mother, then I think we are on the track of a lost novelist, a suppressed poet, or some mute & inglorious Jane Austen, some Emily Bronte who dashed her brains out on the moor . . . crazed with the torture that her unused gift had put her to.

Dashing out brains, walking into the water, putting one's head in an oven—the number of women who had destroyed themselves rivaled the number of established female geniuses. Even those who had succeeded had suffered in ways that men could not understand. Perhaps this is why Olsen had initially thought to call the talk "Women."

Even among this short list of female creatives, one rarely found a woman who had written well and who had also borne children. If creative work demands solitude and immersion, then, Olsen argued, it is no wonder that "no mother of children has written greatly." Perhaps some balked at the stringency of her claim; Olsen, her gaze buried in her notes, would have missed the raised eyebrows and skeptical looks. She continued, presenting evidence for her point. Of the famous women writers in the last century, she suggested, most were spinsters, a few were married, and only a few of these had children; almost all of these women had household help. She claimed that little had changed in the twentieth century: most female writers were still unmarried, or were married and childless. Quoting

Virginia Woolf, Olsen argued that a woman desperately committed to her craft would forsake having children for fear that they would distract her from her true calling. The Institute women, nearly all of whom were married with children, must have squirmed in their chairs.

Of course, Olsen too was a mother: once young and distracted, like the anonymous narrator in her short fiction, she was now a silver-haired matriarch, worried that her second chance at a writer's life had come too late. She pulled excerpts from her own diaries and read them aloud to show how motherhood threatened her creative life, how everything became stolen time. She described writing in "minutes on the bus" and spending nights "ironing and jotting down after children were in bed." She spoke of a "brutal impulse" to push her daughter away from her typewriter. She recounted how she felt "divided" between her maternal self and her artistic self: "I who want to run in one river bed and become great." Significantly, she acknowledged her love for her children, and the joy she took in caring for them, without modulating her frustrations and her sense of loss.

Olsen suggested that caring for children might be incompatible with creative life. "The very conditions of motherhood: those that are the same as creative work," she noted. "The intensity, absorption, immersion, the trying and using and demanding and calling upon infinite variety of resources." And yet "children need one now, and often husband distractibility." She reflected that during the early years of motherhood it is nearly impossible to carve out the large chunks of time needed to immerse oneself in a creative project. But she also admitted that she enjoyed taking care of her children, that she loved those who had "claims and needs of me." Hers wasn't an easy binary: Olsen had felt torn—"I keep on dividing myself"—because mothering and writing both fulfilled her. She longed for an impossible life, one in which she could devote adequate time to each.

Olsen's account of navigating among life's competing pressures gave the lie to the era's easy solutions to the problems facing women: how to educate them to their satisfaction, how to encourage their femininity without trapping them in it, how to get them "back on track" after their children have grown. She feared that there was no getting back on track; you might have missed the one moment in which you could've composed that particular short story, just as you might have missed a child's first steps. The right moment would never come again. Memories fade. Material slackens. Work you started years ago seems strange, or bad, or no longer worth completing. Inspiration is as fleeting as infancy; close your eyes, and you miss it altogether.

Olsen, however, was no pessimist. Her Marxist humanism, which came through in her talk, demanded she produce a vision of a better world. She suggested an end to the "strange breadline system" of grants and foundation funding, which interrupt work with other work and which benefit only a lucky few. (These words surely landed awkwardly among the Institute crowd.) She recognized that women were socialized to be self-sacrificing: they were taught to put others' needs before their own. They could be taught differently. She preached "reverence for life," for the capable humans of all races, genders, and classes who, under the right circumstances, could produce miraculous art. Olsen wanted a world in which she wouldn't have to choose between earning a wage, playing with her daughters, and writing her fiction. She wanted to bring into being a world in which all people could explore their creative capacities and fulfill their ambitions without fear of going broke. In her dreams, one heard echoes of that famous line from Marx, about how a communist society "makes it possible for me to do one thing today and another tomorrow, to hunt in the morning, fish in the afternoon, rear cattle in the evening, criticise after dinner." Olsen added child rearing to the mix.

She ended her presentation forcefully, with a series of pledges. "My conflict . . . to reconcile work with life," she said, quoting from an old journal entry. "Where I create I am true . . . I seek no other realizations than those of my work . . . I will take every path back to the beginning . . . I will collect myself from everything that distracts me and out of my too facile proficiency I will win back and husband the things that are mine." She would sequester herself in a solitary room—"my prison cell my fortress"—and listen for the voices from the past. She still feared it was too late for her to recover her writing, but she would try; as she'd said earlier in the talk, she did not detest failure so much as a lack of effort. She would shield the work from the rest of life.

It was an unmistakable rebuke to one part of Bunting's planned program, the idea that "studying . . . mixes wonderfully with home-making," as she'd written in her *New York Times Magazine* piece. Bunting had spent years arguing that motherhood and creative, or intellectual, work sustained each other and that a woman could divide up her day hour by hour and make progress on all fronts. Bunting, for one, could do this: with her daily to-do lists and hourly schedules, she kept up with her research and her homemaking. Most people could not. Bunting came from wealth, and in the early years of her career she had relied on her husband's professional class income. Financial worries didn't impinge on her intellectual life until her husband died. More than that, Bunting was a scientist, not an artist. She prized organization and reason; she didn't while away days imagining fictional worlds. Olsen countered Bunting's "common sense" perspective with her own lived experience. She suggested that there were fundamental incompatibilities between mothering and artistic creation—especially for those with fewer resources than Bunting had possessed throughout her life. Olsen argued that life was not like a calendar: it could not be divvied up and parceled out. Mothering and all its rewards took away from artistic inspiration and execution; you could not live in the world of your novel in progress and live with your children simultaneously. Even as she expressed gratitude for her time at Radcliffe, Olsen pushed back against the premise of the Institute.

Olsen read out her last few half sentences. She had been talking for nearly two hours, twice her allotted time. The women in the audience were restless and annoyed. Some found the talk self-indulgent and self-exculpating—so many empty words to explain why this woman hadn't produced any work, nearly six months into her fellowship time. They hadn't been about to follow Olsen's rambling way of speaking. As women largely from the professional class, they presumably weren't compelled by Olsen's struggle to work.

But Sexton was captivated.

She had listened intently for the entire two hours, her eyes fixated on her older, wiser friend. "If anyone had stopped her, I would have chopped their head off," she later said. She had been worried about failure for the past few months, ever since *The Cure*, her play about religion and psychiatry, had failed to make the impact she'd imagined for it. The play—centered on a suicidal woman, Daisy, who is tormented by childhood trauma (she ran away from home on the night that her family's house burned down, killing her family members) and who seeks help from a psychiatrist and from Christ himself— had been drawn from Sexton's notes on her therapy sessions from 1961. Sexton had staged a reading of the play at the Charles Playhouse during her first year at the Institute, but it had gone poorly, and at that point she threw her copy in the glove compartment of her VW Bug. She later claimed that she left it there for three full years.

Now Olsen was offering her a theory of failure, a way of understanding how and why creativity stalls and sickens. The talk shed light on the failed play, the bad times around her birthday, the stymied poems. Sexton was used to talking about her creative powers as something beyond her control—"Genius flew the coop," she once reported to George Starbuck, her former classmate and lover, during a lull in 1962. But Olsen suggested that it was all less mysterious than Sexton had once imagined. Sexton was particularly moved by Olsen's descriptions of artistic self-sabotage. Hemingway's line about his own failures resonated: he had destroyed his talent, Olsen said, "by not using it, by betrayals of himself and what he believed in, by drinking so much he blunted the edge of perceptions, by laziness, by sloth, by snobbery, by hook and by crook, by selling vitality all his life, trading it for security, for comfort." Sexton, too, felt torn between comfort—respite from her internal demons—and creative success, which she knew depended on her ability not to silence but to *master* those feelings that tortured her. "What kills the creative instinct—what blunts the axe?" she wondered later, thinking back on Olsen's talk. She contemplated trying to do without alcohol and pills: "Maybe I'll have to do without my crutches." She might gamble her life's assistants for her work.

After the talk, as the women dispersed, Sexton shyly approached Olsen and asked to borrow her notes. That summer, Sexton hired a secretary, with whom she spent hours transcribing "Death of the Creative Process." The strange, stuttering document they produced more closely resembled a diary than a formal presentation; it was all notes and abbreviations and quotations. It is fitting, then, that Sexton tucked the copy away among her more private papers— her letters, notebooks, and drafts of poems. There it would remain for decades—a testament to Olsen's influence and to the intimacy between the two artists.

"Tillie rededicates you," Sexton once said. In times of struggle, perhaps Sexton turned to the transcript, read a few lines, and gathered her strength to write once again.

The summer of 1963 was the last time the five Equivalents were all together in the same place. Two of them—Olsen and Pineda—had one more year at the Institute. For the rest of them—Swan, Sexton, and Kumin—their time was up. They would be going on to other things; they had plans to travel and to go back to teaching positions. They were going to revive old routines or maybe explore new opportunities. In any event, these three would not be returning to the yellow house on Mount Auburn Street come fall.

And so they made the most of their remaining time together. At least once that summer, they all went swimming in Rockport, a town on Massachusetts's North Shore about an hour-and-a-half drive from Cambridge. In the nineteenth century, Swan's ancestors had landed in Rockport after emigrating from Sweden. They had stayed there for a generation and had worked in the stone quarries. When she was studying at the Boston Museum School, Swan used to picnic up in Pigeon Cove quarry with her fellow painters. Black-and-white photos in her personal papers show the twentysomething Swan in a printed skirt and a sweater over a collared shirt. Her hair is short and curly. She sits between two men—the painters Ralph Coburn and Ellsworth Kelly—and next to the remains of a picnic: paper packaging and food scraps and drinks in glass bottles. She looks as if she has been caught mid-laugh by the camera. She looks very young.

Now, almost twenty years later, she returned with a new group of friends. There are no photos from this gathering—or at least none in the archives of any of the Equivalents. In fact, there are no photos in the archives that show all five of the Equivalents together. Whatever picnics they enjoyed or laughs they shared that summer are lost to history. Perhaps they thought they would reunite again soon, and so they didn't think to preserve their memories. Or perhaps they knew on some level that they couldn't stop time—that their year together was perfect and ephemeral and impossible to replicate.

On July 4, 1963, the Equivalents held a picnic. It's not clear who hosted or how long they spent together. Still, it's possible to imagine what such a day might have been like: children playing, strawberry shortcake, fireworks. Maybe the men talked about Willie Mays's game-winning home run for the Giants a couple days before. Maybe the women talked about cake recipes, or maybe about their works in progress. It was one of their few purely social occasions, a time when family and fun took priority over work and writing. It must have been a lovely day.

The joy of that summer picnic cannot be retrieved. The traces these women left on paper are necessarily limited, as was their time together: a fleeting window of women's camaraderie and autonomy in a society not designed for such things. In another sense, though, the record of what it meant for the Equivalents to be together is almost limitless, for it is preserved in the essays, poems, sculptures, and paintings that they made. Even after their shared time at the Institute was over, the Equivalents continued to make art and to collaborate with each other. They celebrated each other's publications and went to each other's art openings. They listened to each other give public readings; sometimes they sat in the audience of a lecture hall, and other times they tuned in via radio.

But it wasn't always as easy among them as it had been when they were all in Cambridge. Conflict erupted more easily and was harder to patch up. Someone became jealous; someone else delivered an insult that she couldn't retract. The discord too is part of their story— just as it is part of the story of the women's liberation movement, which swelled and fractured and dissipated in the decade after the Equivalents disbanded. There is no friendship without complexity, and no social movement without internal disagreement.

As the five women turned toward the future, they wondered what they might achieve and what it might cost them in the process.

PART THREE

1964–1974

CHAPTER 13

Do It or Die Trying

O N AN EARLY SUMMER EVENING IN 1963, just over six years since she had made that nervous walk down Commonwealth Avenue toward John Holmes's seminar, Sexton found herself walking down a different city's streets, toward a different group of poets.

She was in the upper Sixties on the West Side of Manhattan, a quiet part of the city close to Central Park. The iconic restaurant Tavern on the Green was in one direction, the new Lincoln Center in the other. As she walked, she could admire beautiful, historic buildings in a range of architectural styles: neo-Renaissance, art deco, beaux arts, an occasional Queen Anne. Sexton was again walking with a companion: her husband, Kayo, who had accommodated himself to his wife's literary success and had decided to go with her on this particular journey. They were together, on their way to a gathering of literary elites.

Eventually, they reached their destination: 15 West Sixty-Seventh Street, the home of Robert Lowell and Elizabeth Hardwick. With a confidence that she hadn't possessed six years earlier, Sexton led her husband up to the one-bedroom apartment. What she found there was very different from the adult education classroom where she'd made her first public appearance as a poet. The apartment—compact but still elegant—was self-evidently the home of writers. Books filled the built-in shelves, and ladders leaned against the walls to facilitate the retrieval of the works that lived near the ceiling. Great windows looked out onto the city streets. Famous writers moved through the sitting room.

Stanley Kunitz, whose *Selected Poems* had won the Pulitzer in 1959—the same year Sexton had enrolled in Lowell's workshop—was in attendance. So was Marianne Moore, the "great lady poet" whom Sexton and Kumin had heard read not so long ago. Then Sexton had been just another anonymous audience member; now she was fit to sit at Moore's table. When the group sat down to dinner, Kayo found himself right next to the intimidating playwright Lillian Hellman, who had been indirectly responsible for Sexton's two delightful years at the Institute when she'd sat on the executive committee. Kayo, the lone salesman among a group of artists, had no idea who his tablemate was.

But Sexton knew Hellman, just as she knew Kunitz and Moore, Lowell and Hardwick: prizewinners and poet laureates, former mentors and current members of the New York intelligentsia. And here she was among them, no longer a student or an amateur but a published, celebrated poet. If she had any moments of feeling intimidated, of feeling less-than, she needed only to recall her newfound credentials: a well-reviewed second collection (*All My Pretty Ones*), a two-year stint at the Radcliffe Institute, and, most recently, an award from the American Academy of Arts and Letters, the very first of its kind.

Sexton had received the award in May, during her last month at the Institute. On the strength of her two collections, the academy had granted her a traveling fellowship of $6,500 (more than $50,000 today); she had not even had to apply. "The Am. Academy offered me the dough and I just couldn't turn it down," she wrote to her old mentor Snodgrass. The award was to support a year of travel in Europe, from the summer of 1963 through the summer of 1964.

With the fellowship funding, Sexton could travel all over Europe—France, Italy, Switzerland, Greece, Egypt, Beirut, Spain, Portugal—visiting all the places her beloved grandmother had once visited. She would write poetry inspired by long-dead European writers. This was a dream, though a daunting one for a woman who preferred intimate companionship and the comforts of home to solitary adventures in unknown lands. But Kayo insisted she grab the opportunity. "It is your chance at life," he told her. "Take it!"

Sexton's triumph was also a victory for the Institute itself. An established institution had recognized the brilliance of one of its first fellows, thus legitimating the selection committee's choice and validating Bunting's hypothesis. The Radcliffe president had argued that a program like hers could serve as an on-ramp to prestigious and important professional opportunities, and for Sexton it had. She was the Institute's first success story. *The New York Times* covered Sexton's fellowship award, and *The Boston Globe* profiled her after the academy announced its prizes. At the year's final seminar talk in May 1963, a joint presentation on poetry by Sexton and Kumin, Connie Smith announced Sexton's award. The entire group of fellows applauded.

Sexton was not the only Equivalent to use the Institute as a launchpad for a new adventure.

Kumin had set two goals for herself when she'd entered the Institute in the fall of 1961: find an escape from the suffocating social life of the suburbs, and make a go at writing fiction. By the summer of 1963, she had made progress toward both. That summer, the Kumins spent their weekends going "up-country," to a farm they'd purchased for $11,500 in the early fall of 1962, after a yearlong search. Kumin had been longing for a country escape since at least 1961. She had wanted to get away from suburban life with what she called its "day-to-day hazards": "The lost socks, the white blouse that has turned pink from proximity to a never-before-washed red sweatshirt. The missing dog leash, followed by the errant dog. And the endless Saturday dinner parties where wives outdid one another with inventive hors d'oeuvres and cocktails of grenadine and pineapple juice." She was determined to get away from all these petty obligations and find time and space to become a "serious female poet." Vic didn't have a particular desire for country living, but he was happy enough to follow his wife, and he could imagine getting back into skiing, a sport he'd learned while stationed in New Mexico. When the Kumin couple inherited roughly $5,000 each—Kumin from her grandmother, Vic from his mother—they began their search for a place far away from the Boston suburbs.

In the spring of 1963, they had found it: a farmhouse, built in 1800, half a mile up a dirt road, and barricaded by blackberry brambles. There was also a large barn and plenty of land that looked as if it had once been used for livestock. Kumin was struck by the isolation: when she first saw the property, she "realized there were no other houses on this nameless road. No sound of vehicles in the distance. No voices. The silence filled with bird calls." This house, known locally as "the Old Harriman Place," was what the Kumins called their "Hope Diamond." Kumin's parents had not approved: her father had instructed her not to buy a place on a hill, presumably because it would be hard to drive to the house in the winter, and her mother, so confused by all of her daughter's dreams, couldn't understand why Kumin wanted to deprive herself of all that Boston had to offer. But Kumin had been certain. Once they'd cleaned out the dead field mice and patched up the roof, the Kumins had begun taking their three children—now ages nine, eleven, and fourteen—up for the weekend, starting in the winter of 1962–1963 and continuing into the following summer. Danny, their youngest, felt that the New Hampshire house was really his mother's project, but at that age he had no objections to running around the countryside.

Each Friday evening, they packed the car and drove up north as the light faded. They would arrive late; Kumin found it "very spooky going up dark rutted hill at 9:30, big barn looming on left, big dark house on right," but soon enough they would turn on the lights and the TV and "all was cheery." They spent the days strawberry picking—

Maxine Kumin outdoors, 1960s

looking for "hidden tiny tits of red all under the pasture grasses"—and exploring the pine groves. "Going in," Kumin wrote, was "like inching into a thicket; once in, its an underground, upsidedown world, only sunlight miles above at tops of pines & nothing growing underfoot except a century of brown needles, all slippery smooth." The place fed her poetic sensibilities; even the cursed blackberry brambles served as inspiration for a poem. She spent much of her day outdoors, clearing the brambles, and was perhaps the happiest she had been since her teenage days at summer camp.

She was also hard at work on her first novel. For Kumin, returning to prose meant returning to that Radcliffe classroom where Wallace Stegner had steered her seventeen-year-old self away from fiction. Now, with a master's degree, a book of poems, and the imprimatur of the Radcliffe Institute for Independent Study, Kumin set out to prove Stegner wrong. "I WILL DO IT OR DIE TRYING," she wrote to Sexton.

She began working on a semiautobiographical novel about a New Jersey pawnbroker and his "Radcliffe Bolshevik" daughter. She spent hours sketching out the plot, continually compressing it until it was narrow and "gemlike." When, in September, Sexton went overseas, Kumin sent her long plot outlines and chapter breakdowns, trusting that her friend would give her honest feedback. Sexton took her role as her friend's first reader quite seriously; as she once put it to Kumin, "Our good critical instincts are the marriage vows that bind us."

When she read the first part of Kumin's novel, Sexton cried. "It was with the words choked in my throat, she did it!" Sexton wrote from Florence. She felt a kind of maternal pride—"it was like I had done it, but not quite an other I, an extension who come out good." In this letter and the ones that followed, Sexton encouraged Kumin to focus on the emotional lives of her characters. In one scene in the draft, the father hits the daughter, and Sexton took issue with the daughter's rational response: her mood, Sexton thought, would be "of self hate, not taking this assessments of good points into mind." The fictional daughter was based on Kumin—cerebral and controlled, a person inclined to think her way into and out of problems. Sexton, so often the beneficiary of her friend's rational reassurances, offered advice about how to grasp unruly emotional reality.

Kumin's novel was published in 1965, under the title *Through Dooms of Love*. It received mixed reviews. *The Boston Globe* called it a "moving story," while the *Los Angeles Times* declared that this "first novel falls short." The *Times* reviewer noted that the novel's "wordy prose . . . cries out for contraction . . . and belies Mrs. Kumin's past record as poet and denies her entry as of now to the ranks of the [Jean] Staffords and the [Eudora] Weltys." She still had work to do as a fiction writer, honing her prose, developing her characters. Kumin was never one to shy away from hard work, whether it entailed wielding a hoe or a pen. She decided to write a second novel. She had accomplished what she had set out to: she had made her escape, she had done everything she planned to do, and she had not died.

Kumin's achievements were long planned; they were the products of foresight, hard work, and persistence. By contrast, Olsen's successes were unexpected. The first surprise came just a few weeks after her March seminar talk, when she received an inquiry from a publisher named Seymour Lawrence. "Sam" to his friends, Lawrence was based in Boston and looking to start a publishing firm. He had heard that Olsen was at the Institute, and he asked her to join him for lunch. A publisher after the fashion of Bennett Cerf (Olsen's would-be publisher at Random House), Lawrence could identify writers of talent who had commercial potential. (He would go on to publish Kurt Vonnegut's *Slaughterhouse-Five* in 1969.) At the time he reached out to Olsen, Lawrence had just published Katherine Anne Porter's *Ship of Fools*, a book more than twenty years in the making. Olsen admired Porter's work, in part because Porter agonized over her writing in a way that reminded Olsen of herself. From working with Porter, Lawrence understood that some writers worked in stops and starts, taking years to produce great work. Olsen was flattered by Lawrence's attention, but she was still bound to Cowley at Viking, to whom she had promised a book by the end of her fellowship time. She declined Lawrence's lunch invitation, but a connection had been forged.

Cowley, for his part, was growing frustrated. He had supported Olsen for years—intellectually, emotionally, even financially—and he was starting to worry that his investment would never be returned. He sent Olsen gently probing letters asking after her long-promised novel. "I think about you fondly & am delighted to hear that you're getting some work done there in the chastely colonial reaches of Brattle Street," he wrote in January 1963. Several months later, in April, he sent a follow-up note inquiring about Olsen's husband, her health, and of course the book. "I have to ask about your novel," he wrote, reminding her that he was her editor, "not that I don't want to hear about it anyway, as friend, not editor." And in September 1963, he insisted, "You should do what I'm trying to do: get it all down on paper & get it printed. I hear your work praised often; what we need is more & more of it."

Olsen had heard these words—or similar ones—from Cowley before, as well as from Cerf. But despite these professions of faith and confidence, she felt pressed by the idea of completing the book to deadline. In March, she sent him an update, saying that she was making progress on the novel. She enclosed some pussy willows, a sign of spring's arrival, and, possibly, her own rejuvenation. But at other moments, she suggested that the book was dead.

Her agent's junior associate, Harriet Wasserman, suggested that Olsen publish *something:* an essay, a short story, anything that would break through the drafting and revising cycle in which she was caught. Olsen volunteered her seminar talk, "Death of the Creative Process." Wasserman sent a transcript to the prestigious New York magazine *Harper's*. In August, *Harper's* agreed to publish the talk, but only if Olsen made some major revisions.

When Olsen received the announcement, she was still in Boston: Connie Smith, miracle worker that she was, had found $2,500 to fund a summer of work. The Olsens had moved to Arlington, a working-class town that borders Cambridge, at the end of Olsen's first Institute year; they'd wanted to be closer to ponds and parks, and they had wanted a cheaper apartment. Even with the Institute money and Jack's income, the Olsens still borrowed money from friends. Olsen had still been making notes toward her novel, but she now shifted her attention to the *Harper's* piece, which needed to be transformed from notes into full sentences. Not long after she heard from *Harper's*, near the end of September, Olsen and Jack flew back to San Francisco, where they moved into a new place on Alpine Terrace. Pineda, who had also lent money to Olsen throughout the Cambridge years, offered to pay an outstanding book bill at the Grolier Poetry Book Shop in Harvard Square, with "no worry about paying back."

Olsen missed the East Coast, though, and just a few months after leaving it, in April 1965, she flew back. On a friend's recommendation, she had applied for and won a two-month stay at the famed MacDowell artist colony in Peterborough, New Hampshire. The colony had been founded in the early twentieth century by Marian MacDowell in honor of her husband, a composer whose muse required silence, solitude, and a lunch left silently in a basket on the porch of his cabin studio. By the 1960s, the colony was a robust cultural institution, led by the American composer Aaron Copland. Thornton Wilder, Willa Cather, James Baldwin, and Alice Walker were just a few of the writers who had walked its woods and worked (or stewed) in the silent cabins. Lunch baskets appeared on porches each day.

At MacDowell, Olsen had not just a room of her own but an entire cabin; instead of seminar talks, she attended daily breakfasts and dinners. The colony was coed, but in most other ways it resembled the Institute, with its mix of solitude and community. The Institute had not only prepared Olsen for this working environment but also helped her gain access to it; honors have a way of snowballing. The literary world has always relied on markers of prestige to determine whom to publish and whom to prize, and Olsen, now the recipient of multiple fellowships, found herself with more grant-funded writing time.

That spring, Olsen had a surprise visitor: Sam Lawrence. Lawrence, who since their first meeting had moved to New York and established a relationship between his own imprint and Delacorte Press, had driven all the way to Peterborough to persuade Olsen to break her contract with Viking and sign with him. He offered her a $3,500 advance for her great social novel (with a check in the same amount upon manuscript delivery), as well as financial help with her daughter Laurie's college tuition. Olsen acquiesced, broke her contract with Viking, and, newly flush, promised she would deliver her novel. It was something like a fresh start, or a third life.

In October 1965, *Harper's* published the first part of a two-part supplement titled "The Writer's Life," which included Olsen's piece on the creative process. The supplement in which it appeared featured an essay in defense of editing by Norman Podhoretz, the editor in chief of *Commentary* magazine; reflections from the novelist Isaac Bashevis Singer; and musings from Gore Vidal, who, with characteristic self-regard, interviewed himself. Olsen was the lone woman contributor. Her essay, now titled "Silences: When Writers Don't Write," was a touched-up version of her Radcliffe seminar talk: there were fewer extended quotations, and all the sentences were now complete and grammatically correct. Olsen had resisted the magazine's edits—she couldn't bear to see relevant material excised—but she eventually gave in. (An obsessive rewriter, she still made changes to the proofs.) Even with cuts, the article still covered seven magazine pages. It concluded with Olsen's poignant personal reflections on her recovered writing life, on how she went from being the "emaciated survivor trembling on the beach" to the author of one published book. "This most harmful of all my silences has ended," she wrote, referring to the period just before her time at Radcliffe, "but I am not yet recovered, may still be a one-book instead of a hidden and foreground silence."

Like "Tell Me a Riddle," "Silences" was a lovely, mournful piece of writing, more art than polemic. It seemed a bit out of place among dutiful, prosaic accounts of the literary life. But publishing in *Harper's* was a coup for a writer published in campus magazines and literary journals more frequently than in high-circulation periodicals.

Sexton, who had loved the talk before anyone else, wrote Olsen a note of congratulations.

The Institute had served its purpose: it had empowered its fellows, granted them access to present and future opportunities, given each woman a boost that she needed and deserved. And the fellows returned their part of the bargain: they published, they prospered, they showed that the Institute's investments had been wise. Swan, who had a successful solo show in 1963, described this kind of symbiosis in a letter to Connie Smith: "My show has already earned the equivalent of another Radcliffe grant. I truly wish that all the Institute alumnae could publish their books, articles, poems and thereby gain a self-endowed grant."

But the Institute couldn't fix every problem. Olsen remained a painfully slow, meticulous writer. She ended her time at the Institute without a finished novel. Kumin, for her part, was still seeking balance—splitting herself between states and responsibilities. Rather than immerse herself fully in farm life, she was driving back and forth to Boston, alternating home renovations with writing prose, trying to keep her needy friend Sexton afloat while tending to her growing children. She determinedly finished every writing project, but she had yet to produce a truly excellent work.

And Sexton, successful and accomplished, arguably at the height of her powers, showed signs of another breakdown. When she'd won her traveling fellowship, she almost immediately began worrying about whether she could survive a year away from her family, her therapist, and Kumin. In the end, she enlisted Sandy Robart—the same neighbor who had accompanied her to the Boston Center for Adult Education in 1957—as her traveling companion in Europe. "I can barely cross a street in Boston alone . . . much less an Alp!" she wrote to Nolan Miller in early August. She was open with Miller and many others about her fears. "I'm terrified," she told *The Boston Globe*, which profiled her on the occasion of her award. "The regularity of my home life, my husband, my daughters mean so much to me, to my sense of security that I am not at all easy about leaving them."

In May, as she contemplated her impending life change, she reached out to her old mentor W. D. Snodgrass. Their correspondence, so constant and necessary for Sexton early in her career, had tapered off, and Sexton picked up other correspondents to take his place. Sexton was often in closest touch with the correspondent who was most attentive and replied most frequently; she sent off letters much as a child, lost in a public space, might reach out to any number of passing adults, hoping that one of them might stop and hear her fears. That summer, in her state of trepidation, she wrote more letters than usual, to friends both old and new. "I wish I were back to the old days when I sat hunched over the typewriter, doing the desperate and lonely and even heart breaking work of trying to write, and rewrite and rewrite 'The Double Image,'" she wrote to Snodgrass. "I was 'true' then." She suggested the poems should be published anonymously; in this way, poets like her could avoid the pressures of fame.

By "true," Sexton meant that she had not yet, back then, developed the persona that she now exhibited at her readings, but she also meant something about professionalism more generally: the way it transforms therapeutic, introspective, self-preserving activities into obligations, a kind of wage labor. While Sexton, during that interview at the Institute, had told the researcher Alice Ryerson how important it was for her to be paid, to be recognized as a professional poet, she also resented some of the pressure that professionalization placed upon her. Poetry, for Sexton, was no longer just about self-inquiry or catharsis, though it was about these things still. It was how she supported her family (for much of her life, she made more money than Kayo). It was a public performance, one that would be admired and judged.

The time for anonymity was over. Sexton was a somebody, and she had to perform. She had to attend dinner parties at the apartments of famous poets, fraternize with important writers, and decide where she ranked among them.

This is what Sexton was doing right before she left for Europe. That night at the Lowells, halfway through the meal, the dinner table supporting the elbows of writers suddenly and inexplicably cracked. Kayo, habituated to cleaning up messes, leaped into action. Sexton was struck by the image of her husband sitting on the floor and trying, futilely, to hold the broken pieces together.

"I shall never forget the table in the midst of its earthquake with Kayo trying to hold it up and undoubtedly making things worse," she wrote, rather uncharitably, to Lowell in early June. "I hope that it was fixable and that you are back in one piece." She herself was patched together, as solid as she would ever be. She readied herself for a reward, one that would feel like a test.

CHAPTER 14

We Are All Going to Make It

FREEDOM, EVEN WHEN IT IS FOUGHT FOR, is a thing to be feared; doubt and disruption often follow its arrival. Sexton, perhaps more than anyone, feared the opportunities that rose in front of her. She relied on the limitations placed on her life—her needy and noisy children, her difficult but dependable husband—to keep her emotionally steady and safe. Wearing a straitjacket is not so different from being swaddled; there is comfort in being constricted and constrained. If the decade of the 1950s didn't offer women equality, or opportunity, or autonomy, it did offer them a set of rules and a clear life course. It promised them certainty—moral, social, existential—if not intellectual or creative fulfillment. In the beginning of the 1960s, the Equivalents and their peers were forced to reckon with problems that they had long felt to be beyond solving.

On August 22, 1963, what she sometimes called her "execution date," Sexton put an ocean's worth of distance between herself and her support system. She and Robart stood on the deck of an ocean liner. They blew bubbles in the direction of the shoreline, where Sexton's children were watching. Sexton had approached her departure date with a good deal of trepidation—at one point, she was so nervous that she passed out in Dr. Orne's office—but she'd fortified herself with a load of reassuring objects: her typewriter, more than fifty pounds of books (and sixty-five pounds of clothes), and a bound volume of letters from her grandmother, to whom she had been very close. She'd also asked Kumin to check in regularly with Kayo and the girls. Sexton wouldn't be able to call Kumin daily—transatlantic phone rates were too expensive—but they promised to write to each other. The day before she departed, Sexton had a final phone call with her best friend, then, perhaps dissatisfied with the farewell, sat down at her typewriter.

The note was brief. "All I have to say is that I love you, and will write, and will not die, and will come home the same," Sexton wrote. She signed the letter "Anne (me)," as if to remind Kumin—and herself—who she was. Kumin, receiving the letter, was "touched all the way down to the callouses on the balls of my feet."

Sexton left for her year abroad with the expectation that she would produce a book's worth of new poems. What better place to write poetry than the land of Rilke and Rimbaud? She and Robart traipsed through the narrow streets of Paris—Sexton with a kerchief wrapped around her undone hair—stopping in cafés when their legs gave out. They particularly loved visiting flea markets. In Belgium, their second stop, their luggage was stolen, and they replenished their wardrobes with European-style blouses. With her new clothes and newfound love of café culture, Sexton was starting to assimilate to Europe.

But she found it nearly impossible to write. She couldn't find adequate solitude; someone, usually Robart, was always in the room with her. "I'm lonely as hell, but I'm crowded too," she wrote to Kumin from Italy in October. Every poem she produced felt flat. She wrote a poem about the Atlantic crossing, which she later found disappointing. She drafted a poem about Venice, which she soon came to feel had a "false note." She was haunted by Europe's history: its many literary representations all pressed upon her, suffocating her creativity and her confidence. "You know whats wrong with poem I wrote in Venice," she reflected to a Kumin, "it's too much like Mary McCarthy who I had just read on Venice." (McCarthy had published *Venice Observed* in 1956; it was a book full of idiosyncratic ideas about what McCarthy called "the world's loveliest city.") Too many American writers had offered their takes on the Continent. What could she say about it that would be new?

The thirty-four-year-old Sexton, never one for vigorous exercise, was also physically and mentally exhausted. During the first few weeks of the trip, she and Sandy walked miles on foot, visiting the sights and searching out restaurants and cafés. She even started to style her own hair, though she was displeased with the results. Sexton was unused to such activity—"can you imagine *me* walking to Boston?" she wrote to Kumin—but she found it calmed her whirling thoughts and eased her anxiety about the trip.

The real problem for the itinerant poet, though, was the absence of her best friend. "God, how awful it is to write and not call you up," Sexton wrote to Kumin in October from Venice. "I mean, it really brings it home to me how much fun we add to our writing lives with our close friendship." Without a creative community—the Institute, a workshop, or even just the collaborative dyad formed by two poets—Sexton found writing nearly impossible. Instead of composing poems, she spent much of her European trip meditating on the conditions necessary for writing poetry—a topic similar to Olsen's seminar talk, which she'd just finished transcribing that past summer. In a letter from Amsterdam in early September, she reflected that the "true nature of the poet" is to be "shut out, to be always the observer of his (her) own life." This was all well and good, but she wondered, "What good is being shut out if you don't have someone to discuss it with." Discussion happened too slowly via airmail; Sexton longed for the instant gratification that a phone call or a face-to-face encounter could provide.

Being separated from Kumin had profound effects on Sexton. First, it destroyed her routine. "Oh Max, how I miss our good morning talk," Sexton mused late in August, not long after her arrival in France. "I feel as sorry as tho I had lost an arm and were still trying to use it." Picking up the phone had become second nature, a reflex that she now had to suppress. Too, Sexton could be honest with Kumin in a way she could be with no one else. (Dr. Orne inspired a different kind of honesty, more childlike and less coherent.) Though she kept up a loving and affectionate correspondence with Kayo, Sexton reserved her truthful, troubled letters for Kumin. Kayo's letters "beg me . . . to be his princess," she explained to her friend in October. "Kayo will always embrace . . . but understand? seldom? know me? never." To Kumin, though, she could talk about her anxiety, her inefficiency, and her fear that she was really, truly mentally ill—that she needed constant care from medical professionals. Sexton thought that Kayo had pushed her to travel in part to demonstrate that she was "cured," and she feared she was not and never would be.

Most important, Sexton had long relied on Kumin for stability and for a sense of self. "Oh Maxine, all this chat is just to say, hello, I'm here," Sexton said in a letter from Florence. It was through listening and talking to Kumin that Sexton affirmed that she really existed and would continue to exist the next day, and the next. Now, without her friend, Sexton began to feel manic and unstable; she had a "strong . . . feeling that I am just barely surviving." She peppered her letters to Kumin with first-person pronouns, each "I" a visible sign of her endurance. Kumin attempted to calm Sexton with reminders that "nothing changes except the ribbon in the typewriter." With her characteristic certitude, Kumin told her friend, "We are all going to make it." The phrase became something of a mantra for Sexton, who insisted in all her letters that she would survive, that she would come home, that she would "make it."

One quiet night in Venice in late September, Sexton found herself thinking back to the year she and Kumin first met. John Holmes had brought them together in that strange little workshop in the Back Bay, but he had also nearly torn apart their incipient friendship. Sexton marveled at how close she and Kumin had come to being separated by him. There had been other tests since then—including the seventy-two hours when Sexton thought that Kumin alone had received the Radcliffe grant—but Sexton felt that these early years had been the real testing ground. In a letter to Kumin, she reflected on these trials: "If John could not separate us ... who could," she wrote. "We, Maxine, have been tried, and found never wanting ... See. Our friendship has survived."

In an era when men dominated households, classrooms, and psychoanalytic studies, Sexton and Kumin nurtured an exclusive female bond. Despite the pressures imposed by the men in their lives, they had generated a love of their own.

If Kumin was at all resentful of doing this caretaking at a distance, if she had perhaps hoped for a respite during Sexton's year abroad, she didn't show it in her letters. She did, however, admit to some jealousy. "I had not realized that I envy you," she wrote to Sexton in August, "but find that I do." While Sexton was jaunting from Brussels to Amsterdam to Zurich, Kumin was cooking, hosting several difficult family members, and treating back pain. "Some people have adventures with parapluies on the Metro," she wrote to Sexton, a bit huffily, in early September, "and some people stay home & make the frigging jelly." Sexton was drinking Negronis and going on gondola rides; Kumin was "downing crème de cacao" and rereading Sexton's letters and "wishing I were there."

Though she ably performed her duties as touchstone and confidante, Kumin wondered at times how she could be someone's friend and nurse, her critic and her caretaker. That fall while Sexton was abroad, Kumin read through Katherine Mansfield's journals. Mansfield was a favorite of Olsen's; perhaps Kumin picked her up at the older writer's recommendation. Mansfield, who'd died at thirty-four in 1923, had been ill with tuberculosis for much of her life. Her husband, the critic and writer John Middleton Murry, had never been good at caring for her, and Mansfield had relied instead on a female friend, Ida Baker, whom Mansfield called "L.M." (she had renamed her friend "Lesley Morris"). Baker was an extraordinarily devoted friend: as Katie Roiphe has written, she would "periodically drop everything and devote herself to Katherine in whatever capacity she was needed—as housekeeper, seamstress, confidante, companion, cook, or nurse." Although Mansfield was often grateful and affectionate toward her friend—"friendship is every bit as sacred and eternal as marriage," she once wrote—she later dismissed Baker's help and abruptly ended the friendship.

Kumin was dismayed by the way that this "touching deep friendship . . . deteriorates into common waspishness or worse over the years of companionship, nursing, gen'l homely looking afters, so that KM eventually despise her, & everything about her is exaggerated to rasp, grate, pick." Though Kumin used the Mansfield anecdote as an occasion to think about the difficulty of taking forward old friendships into a new phase of life ("There ought to be an Exchange open for swopping [*sic*] off used up friendship & trying on other ones," she wrote), it's hard not to see the warning in the story. A person who is too constant, too dependable, can be taken for granted. Someone who assumes completely the mantle of caretaker cannot also be a true friend.

Kumin wanted to be more than a caretaker. She was a friend, not a nurse, and she too had needs. She needed Sexton's intellectual companionship and understanding. She needed Sexton to shake her up and pull her out of her proper, reserved self—her persona of a dutiful daughter of a "beautiful lady." Sexton was the stormy, wind-tossed counterpart to Kumin's stable, grounded self.

Sexton once joked that she was Kumin's first real female friend; in these letters, Kumin admitted as much. "I let you in, bag, baggage, gifts and impediments," she wrote to Sexton, one cold and wet day in late September. She had "dared to have these precious feelings and dare still to hold onto them." She turned some of these "precious feelings" into a poem, a valediction that forbade one friend to mourn the other. "We have our own constants," one line began:

There is a world of water between us
and the humpbacks of these
mink hills between us
and months before we will speak
except in the clipped words of cables
or the mechanical click

that our portables make
talking on onion skin
across the Atlantic.

The "onion skin" might have reminded Sexton of Lowell's seminar, where the sound of onionskins rustling filled the silent classroom. That's where Sexton had met and befriended Plath, who was now dead. Now Sexton was struggling to survive.

In October, Sexton wrote Kumin a desperate letter from Rome in which she alluded to a crisis, one that she would have to explain in person. (It was a brief affair that Sexton had engaged in while in Italy, which she would keep secret from Kayo.) She asked Kumin to drop some hints to Kayo that an imminent return was possible and that it might be all for the best. To her friend, Sexton confessed that she was incurably sick and that she needed therapy, no matter what Kayo said. "Max, the thread is bare," she wrote. "If I don't come home I will die. Some wine does not travel well. I am such a wine."

On Sunday, October 27, Sexton and Robart returned to Boston; Sexton had made it through only about two months of what was supposed to have been a twelve-month trip. Nine days later, she returned to Westwood Lodge, the mental health facility where she'd first stayed in 1956. She'd become suicidal in the days since her ship docked in Boston, and Dr. Orne decided that she needed rest and stabilization more than probing therapy.

When she'd concluded her time at Radcliffe, Sexton had thought she had won her freedom—from therapy, from her family, from a conservative part of the country—but it turned out to be more than she could handle. Now she was nearly a prisoner, kept in an institution she did not much like (she would have preferred McLean Hospital, which housed Lowell during his breakdowns), against her will, and to her husband's disappointment.

Still, she was glad she had traveled, even if only for those two months. She'd glimpsed new sites and gathered material for a poem or two. (She wrote one upon her return, "Menstruation at Forty," that alluded to her European fling.) More important, she'd seen anew the value of her friendship with Kumin. Their letters had forced them to articulate what they meant to each other in new ways. Sexton perhaps put it best in a letter from Rome, written right before she fell apart. "Oh Maxine," she wrote, "to have a friend that loves you as you are . . . that is precious, that, in itself, is an embrace."

Such friendship was exactly what Olsen had found at the Institute and what she couldn't bear to lose when she returned to the Bay Area in September 1964. In the months leading up to her departure, she'd been unfocused and unproductive. On May 8, 1964, she'd given her second Institute seminar, titled simply "Two Years." The weather that day was sweltering; as the fellows assembled in the stale first-floor room, Smith apologized for the heat. The talk Olsen delivered was circular, stuttering, and digressive. Her speech was filled with "ums" and "uhs"; her tone was apologetic, as if she knew she should be talking about her writing, not about why she could not write. She alluded obliquely to class and race, and she suggested that her shifting class position was one reason she, and myriad unnamed others, found writing difficult. Even as she reveled in the fact that she could now "dwell in possibility," as her idol Emily Dickinson once put it, she was distressed that so few people would have a chance like hers, and though she didn't say so, her nervousness suggested that she was ashamed she had done so little with her chance. In some ways, she might have felt that she had betrayed those who were not as lucky as she had been, those whom she wanted to serve.

She left Boston at the end of the summer, with notes toward a book and debts that she had to pay. Back in San Francisco, loneliness assaulted her immediately. Jack was back at work, while Laurie returned to boarding school in Vermont. Olsen had loved the solitary weeks of the past summer after Jack and Laurie had returned to California—"the first time in my life alone," she'd told a friend—and she disliked being back on the West Coast, away from the Boston bookstores, which had amazing stock and let her browse for hours. Her friends were all socializing without her; she heard of their escapades only in retrospect. One fall evening, the Equivalents gathered with their husbands for a dinner party. The only one missing was Olsen, who was back in California, back in her old life. Sexton wrote to Olsen later that they had meant to call her while at dinner, but they had all forgotten. "We thought anyhow and of you very much."

Wounded, isolated, Olsen called and wrote frequently. She sent her East Coast friends colorful vintage postcards and longer typewritten letters, a habit she would keep up for years. "I sometimes get so longing lonesome to talk its only the bonds of my undone work keeps me from flying out for a week," she wrote to Kumin. On another occasion, she wrote, "Sometimes perhaps you [Max] + Anne—poets—come to see me. Or I will—an other day—come to Cambridge. (Perhaps.)" Often she enclosed some small token: rose petals, rhododendron blossoms, sprigs of spring growth. Most of her recipients were grateful, but some, like Sexton, were simply "bemused," both by the curious gifts and by the strange tone of Olsen's letters. Olsen could be at once dramatic and evasive; if received at the wrong moment, her gilded cards and dried flowers could seem excessive or twee.

Desperate for the twinned goods of solitude and community, Olsen turned elsewhere. She had made close friends among some of the writers she had met at the MacDowell Colony. Still, she failed to make progress on the novel. As she had done at the Institute, she wrangled extra time at the colony, but the fiction still didn't come. Age, anxiety, and travel fatigue conspired to prevent her work. For years, she had claimed that her obligations—to a boss, to her children—had held her back from writing. Now those obligations were eradicated, at least for a time, and she still couldn't seem to write. Her grant time was again running out. Olsen feared she was "done for."

When Olsen wrote about being "done for," she was imagining the end of a writing career. Sexton, meanwhile, was envisioning the end of her life. In late 1964, one month after Olsen left Boston, Sexton and Kayo purchased a house at 14 Black Oak Road in Weston, the town in which Sexton had grown up. They wanted a bigger house, a better school system, and, ideally, a full-time housekeeper. "What I need is a mother," Sexton wrote to a friend. "WANTED . . . A RENTED MOTHER!! U.S.A. . . . . That is how the ad ought to read." The colonial they settled on didn't please the poet. The house was too big, and the room that she worked in wasn't private enough. And worst of all, there was no pool. The Sextons later built a pool on the property.

Her mental health deteriorated as her marriage crumbled. Dr. Orne, the therapist she had worked with rather successfully for years, moved to Philadelphia in 1964. Sexton was hospitalized after a suicide attempt in the summer of 1965, then prescribed Thorazine, a powerful antipsychotic with intense side effects, including weight gain. It inhibited her writing and forced her to stay out of the sun. Lethargic, uninspired, and gaining weight, Sexton worried that she had traded her facility with language for so-called sanity. "The g.d. tranquilizers I started to take at M.G.H. this summer have completely stoppered any original idea," she wrote to Olsen. She lived like a shut-in. Everything the Institute had given her—her first home office, her work space in the house on Mount Auburn Street—had been lost.

She would remain in this work slump through the beginning of 1966. Her marriage was "as fragile as a cracked egg," and she feared stepping out of her role as the sick one, lest the egg crack open entirely. Writing to Olsen in October 1965, after her suicide attempt, she enclosed the poem "Self in 1958," acknowledging that that poem was as relevant to her life now as it had been when she'd written it. "I am a plaster doll; I pose," the speaker declares at the poem's outset. She was hollow, lifeless, back in her old dark place.

Even as Sexton regressed emotionally, her critical reputation continued to grow. After Oxford University Press published her *Selected Poems*, which comprised poems culled from her first two collections, Sexton faced criticism from British reviewers who thought her poetry overly personal. Their criticisms echoed some of the worst reviews she'd received in the past. In 1963, the poet James Dickey had used the publication of Sexton's *All My Pretty Ones* as an occasion to attack "the confessional quality" in much recent verse, which to him was a "new kind of orthodoxy." Though he had also faulted Lowell and Snodgrass, he had singled out Sexton as the worst of the lot. "It would be hard to find a writer who dwells more insistently on the pathetic and disgusting aspects of bodily experience, as though this made the writing more real," he had written in *The New York Times Book Review*. It would be many years before Sexton forgave her fellow poet. Until then, she carried a copy of the review in her pocketbook, a spur that she could dig into her side whenever she craved punishment.

The relationship between Sexton's depression and her poetry was a complicated one. Usually, Sexton couldn't write at all during the acute phases of her mental illness. These were the times that she couldn't get out of bed, or that she would go to the hospital. Her writing happened in the aftermath of these episodes. It is also true, though, that she got much of her poetic material from the feelings and experiences she associated with these bad spells, and that the writing had an ameliorative, if not a curative, function. Her disease did, in some sense, inspire her; she approached poetry because of her illness, even if illness and creative practice could never easily coexist.

And so, as Sexton stabilized from this last bout of suicidality, she turned once again to poetry. Just as she had in 1957, she mined her depression and suffering for material. During the brief respites from the lethargy her drugs produced, she wrote what she would later call her "death" poems. "Flee on Your Donkey," the best of this set, describes the experience of returning to a mental institution. The speaker is jaded and weary; "it's the same old crowd, / the same ruined scene," she observes. The "permanent guests" haven't made any changes to the place; meanwhile, doctors offer shock treatments to the "uninitiated." The speaker is more experienced than these neophytes, less shocked. "I have come back," she observes,

recommitted,
fastened to the wall like a bathroom plunger,
held like a prisoner
who was so poor
he fell in love with jail.

Gone is the lyricism of early poems about madness, like "Music Swims Back to Me," Sexton's first real work of art. It's been replaced by sordid similes—the patient is like a "bathroom plunger," a permanent fixture in a dirty space—and a kind of flat tone. The tragedy that the poem describes is not madness itself, but rather the speaker's failure to leave madness behind, either through death or through cure. The command to "flee on your donkey, / flee this sad hotel," near the end of the poem, to "for once make a deliberate decision," might easily be read as a call for suicide—to exit the institution "any old way you please!" The speaker is agnostic about her exit strategy, for her fate feels foretold: everyone in her family has found a different way to die from "the fool's disease."

Writing both signaled and fed Sexton's happiness. By the spring of 1965, she had turned a corner. "For the very first time I WANT TO LIVE and do live," she wrote to Olsen. She began writing poems on the theme of living. Some were for her growing daughters: "Little Girl, My String Bean, My Lovely Woman," written for Linda, and "A Little Uncomplicated Hymn" for Joy. Others were love poems. "Your Face on the Dog's Neck" was written for Olsen's friend Annie Wilder, a San Francisco–based psychiatrist, "short and funny and smart as a whip," who had visited Cambridge right before Sexton sailed for France. The connection between the two Annes was intense and immediate, a kind of *coup de foudre*. "I'm in love with you already," whispered Sexton to Wilder on the day they met. Wilder reciprocated: she referred to Sexton as Icarus, and to herself as Icarus's "catcher." The two began a furious correspondence. They later traveled together and, according to Sexton's biographer Middlebrook, engaged in a sexual relationship. Sexton had found another source of adoration and emotional support.

Sexton published these poems in *Live or Die*, released by Houghton Mifflin in 1966. "Live," the poem that closes the collection, takes its epigraph from Bellow's *Herzog:* "Live or die, but don't poison everything," the line she'd quoted in a letter to Olsen after the two first met at the Institute. It is an unlovely poem, with ugly images and base language: the speaker describes "the baby on the platter, / cooked but still human, / cooked also with little maggots, / sewn onto it maybe by somebody's mother, / the damn bitch!" But its message is one of endurance. "Even so, / I kept right on going on, / a sort of human statement," the second stanza begins. Later, she describes a life that "opened inside me like an egg," an allusion, presumably, to one of her children. The poem ends triumphantly: "I say *Live, Live* because of the sun / the dream, the excitable gift."

The ending, with its repetition and its heavy stresses (*"Live, Live"*) makes the message clear. It's an unambiguous ending, and the poem is weaker because of it. The Holocaust imagery, perhaps inspired by Plath, seems unoriginal, if not in poor taste. But Sexton herself was feeling strong, and the certitude of her final stanza reflects this newfound strength. The hospital of "Flee on Your Donkey" has been replaced by the natural world; the patient's shift has been exchanged for the sun.

Sexton was quite pleased with the collection and its affirmations. "I have a feeling the poems are splendid," she wrote to her agent Cindy Degener. "But then, one has to have some sort of feeling like that about their own work no matter who prints it or likes it." She arranged the poems chronologically—"with all due apologies for the fact that they read like a fever chart for a bad case of melancholy"—in the hopes that the arc of the collection would make apparent, and secure, her own journey from despair to joy.

She was less pleased with the planned cover design. Houghton Mifflin proposed a book cover with pink and blue flowers and green frogs. Sexton thought it looked like the cover of a children's book.

Frustrated, she called Swan—her friend, fellow artist, and former collaborator. "They've sent me a terrible book cover," she explained. "Have you anything I can use?" By this time, Swan had turned away from portraiture—and particularly from the parent-child portraiture—that had fascinated her in the 1950s. She had become interested in painting other things: bottles, glass, still life. She was annoyed by those fans who wanted her to keep doing mother-child portraits: "I've outgrown that, you know, but sometimes your audience doesn't."

She was also grappling with a health challenge: lupus. Swan had faced health problems before. She had been born with a clubfoot, though it didn't impact her life too much. She had received a surgical correction when she was very young, and other than needing to buy different-sized shoes for each foot, she didn't find herself impeded. Lupus presented a much more significant obstacle. She was diagnosed shortly after she finished her term at the Institute. An autoimmune disease, lupus produces inflammation throughout the body and often manifests as joint pain, fatigue, and rashes or lesions. It landed Swan in the hospital for weeks at a time, where Olsen, who was in her second academic year at the Institute, visited her regularly. By March 1965, she was out of the hospital and had moved to a different house in Brookline. She continued to see doctors, rest, and take pills.

Yet Swan remained a dedicated artist and a good friend. She rummaged through her drawings and came up with one she called *Gothic Heads*. It is a delicate drawing, quite different from Swan's bold, expressionist early portraits. The image features two faces turned toward each other, possibly a man and a woman, but it's hard to tell. One has its eyes closed; the other's eyes are open wide, in fear or awe. The eyes, nose, mouth, and chin on each face are all rendered precisely, but the jaw and hairline fade into white. It's as if the models have poked through some invisible plane and left half of their heads on the other side. The image reflected the collection's duality—the twinned, opposing desires that it aims to express.

Sexton persuaded Houghton Mifflin to use this image for the book cover. According to Swan, the design team managed to ruin

Anne Sexton's Live or Die, *published by Houghton Mifflin in 1966*
Jacket art by Barbara Swan

the image by orienting the figures vertically and arranging large type over it, but it was nonetheless far better than the colorful, cutesy image the publisher had first proposed. Swan would go on to draw the cover images for nearly all of Sexton's remaining books: *Transformations* (1971), *The Book of Folly* (1972), *The Death Notebooks* (1973), and *The Awful Rowing Toward God* (1975), which was published posthumously.

Transformations, a book of poems inspired by the Grimms' fairy tales, was their most involved collaboration. The collection had actually been inspired by Linda, who, when she was an adolescent, often read and reread the Grimms' tales at the kitchen table. *Transformations,* published in 1971, was one of Sexton's most popular works. In the estimation of the critic Helen Vendler, the collection was Sexton's most formally successful work. Her "most realized tone is precisely a malevolently flippant one," Vendler wrote in a piece for *The New Republic* in 1981. The "grim tit-for-tat of fairy tales" and the "clean trajectory" they offered appealed to Sexton and allowed her to play the satirist. "No matter what life you lead / the virgin is a lovely number," begins "Snow White and the Seven Dwarfs":

cheeks as fragile as cigarette paper,
arms and legs made of Limoges,
lips like Vin Du Rhône,
rolling her china-blue doll eyes
open and shut.

Here, the beautiful virgin is but a cobbled-together commodity, a patchwork of pleasing products: wine, porcelain, china. She is a thing to be bought or sold, ruined or preserved.

Elsewhere, Sexton mocked the optimism of certain fairy tales, such as "Cinderella." The poem about that tale's princess begins, "You always read about it: / the plumber with twelve children / who wins the Irish Sweepstakes. / From toilets to riches. / That story." Other versions of "that story" follow: "from diapers to Dior," "from homogenized to martinis at lunch," "from mops to Bonwit Teller." There's something deflationary about this litany of success stories; they seem not romantic, or miraculous, but rather banal, even a bit crude. Sexton anticipated the work of the British writer Angela Carter, who published a book of feminist fairy tales in 1979; both writers used the genre to explode myths about virtuous women and the conduct that is required of them.

Swan illustrated each of these witchy poems. A poem would arrive from Sexton in the mail, Swan would suggest an image, and then the two would go back and forth tweaking the design. Though Swan disclaimed any knowledge of poetry, she inevitably saw things in Sexton's poems that the poet herself did not see—just as with the collaboration around *The Musicians*, when she and Sexton saw new things in each other's work. A poem based on the fairy tale "Iron Hans" seemed, to Sexton, to be a warning about the danger and chaos of the world, whereas to Swan it was a story about caretaking and protection. She illustrated the poem with an image of a boy riding safely on the back of a gentle giant.

Sexton trusted Swan "more than I trust myself," she confessed in a letter in 1973. Swan, according to Sexton, was "very sensitive to the poet's word." Swan later also collaborated with Kumin: she provided the cover image and seventeen illustrations for *Up Country*, Kumin's 1972 book of poetry. She did all this even in the midst of her and her family's own challenges: her health, her husband's decision to open his own gallery, her children's complicated teenage lives. Her life was full and fast-paced; Swan only slowed down in her early sixties, when she fell on a step and injured her foot, limiting her mobility. She kept painting throughout everything, even in her later years. Her last show was a posthumous one, a retrospective held at the Danforth Art Museum in Framingham, Massachusetts, in 2013, ten years after Swan died. The show included some of her early portraits, including one of her dear friend Sexton.

"I did it because of friendship . . . with the two poets," she said years later, speaking about her cover designs. "It's not as if I had an agent and I was out there hounding the publishers to please, please let me do a book you know . . . That's not my—I just did it out of friendship."

Live or Die won the Pulitzer Prize in the spring of 1967. The prize, which came with $1,000 and the approval of the literary establishment, elevated Sexton's entire oeuvre, including all those poems about "the pathetic and disgusting aspects of bodily experience," as Dickey described them. (Today the prize comes with $15,000.) Kumin rushed over to the house in Weston to celebrate. Kayo bought flowers. Even Sexton's estranged sister sent a telegram: "Generous greeting from us both it is great to be related to a celebrity."

Sexton accepted the "celebrity" status her sister conferred upon her, and she raised her speaking fees to $700. For the rest of her life, she would measure her fees against those of Dickey, one of the highest-paid readers of poetry, and challenge her agency to match them.

She had also triumphed over her death wish, at least for the moment. Her poetry both gave voice to it and silenced it. "Language"—her favored term for poetic composition, always capitalized—was her life force. It was what she offered her readers, many of whom were similar to how she had been in the late 1950s: young, female, mentally struggling. Unlike many writers of her stature, Sexton read and responded to poems and letters from readers, offering thoughtful yet honest critiques of their work. To one woman, whose work she had criticized fairly harshly in a prior letter, she wrote with significant words of encouragement: "Your poems are sensitive. They show a great inner strength, a deep knowing of things. Keep it up."

This was Sexton's way of nurturing—the task with which she had so struggled as a young mother. She might not be able to bake cookies or a potato, but she could evaluate a line, share her own drafts, be honest about her own difficulties. This is what she offered her elder daughter as Linda became a writer herself. "Mother was generous in teaching me everything she knew about writing," Linda recalls in her memoir. "She also began to ask me for my opinion of her poems as they emerged from her typewriter and thoughtfully considered whatever reaction I could muster. . . . Never once did she laugh at my naïveté, my clichés, the melodrama of my adolescent yearnings." She gave her interlocutors the gift of taking them seriously. Through collaboration and critique, she attempted to "make not so alone the lonely art."

CHAPTER 15

Hurt Wild Baffled Angry

IN NOVEMBER 1966, two months after the release of *Live or Die*, Betty Friedan held a press conference from her apartment on Central Park West. Friedan—once Polly Bunting's co-conspirator, now a best-selling author and a staple on the lecture circuit—held forth from a lilac velvet chair. She wore a tailored black suit with a fur collar; neat and feminine, she seemed to observers "more like a chic-career woman . . . than a Susan B. Anthony–type crusader." Her voice was gravelly and deep; it was a surprise coming from such a small person.

Poised and confident, she began to speak. Women did not have true equality, she explained to the members of the press. They faced sex discrimination in the workplace; they couldn't find affordable child care. They were consistently underpaid. President Johnson had promised that his Great Society would bring citizens on the margins into the mainstream of American life, but as Friedan saw it, there was no concentrated effort to involve women as a distinct class, nor to validate their rights. Such apathy was no longer acceptable; women demanded governmental action now. Punching the air with each point, like a boxer warming up for battle, Friedan declared, "We will take strong steps in the next election to see that candidates who do not take seriously the question of equal rights for women are defeated."

Three weeks earlier, Friedan and hundreds of other women had come together in Washington, D.C., to participate in the National Organization for Women—known by its acronym, NOW. The acronym was Friedan's idea. She had scrawled "NOW" on a cocktail napkin the prior June while attending the third national conference of commissions on the status of women, also held in D.C. Frustrated by governmental inaction and by her own lack of influence, Friedan had turned to activist Pauli Murray, who held a JD from Yale Law School, who was also present at the conference, and asked for her thoughts on how to provoke government action. (Murray was the first African American student to earn a JD from Yale Law.)

This wasn't the first time she had sought Murray's aid. Friedan first made a call to New Haven in 1965, after she read Murray quoted in *The New York Times* saying that women needed to march on Washington as civil rights activists had just done. They began corresponding. The two activists shared similar goals: both wanted the Equal Employment Opportunity Commission, a federal agency established in July 1965, to take further action against sex discrimination and to enforce Title VII, a part of the Civil Rights Act of 1964 that prevented all forms of discrimination in the workplace.

It was Murray—a black queer woman who, as Friedan once put it, "had faced both kinds of discrimination [racism and sexism] and was strong for an organization"—who first suggested something like a women's civil rights march. Friedan was intrigued, and she gathered more than a dozen women in her hotel room to strategize. By the end of the conference, the group had decided to form a new organization, a "kind of NAACP for women."

NOW started with thirty members. By the time Friedan hosted this November press conference in her parlor, the group had grown to five hundred (including a handful of men). Chapters sprang up in cities across America. The group's rhetoric was militant and their goals concrete: they wanted paid maternity leave, income tax deductions for child care, the enforcement of Title VII, and the repeal of anti-abortion laws. The group also advocated against sex discrimination in the government's education, poverty, and welfare programs. These causes were personal to Friedan, who claimed that she had been let go from a news agency when she became pregnant. They announced that they would use sit-ins, pickets, and "ingenious new methods of protest" to win what they called "true equality" for women.

The women of NOW were in good company. By 1966, acts of protest and resistance were features of American public life. The March on Washington for Jobs and Freedom in 1963 brought between 200,000 and 300,000 people to the national capital. In December 1964, Mario Savio, a leader of the Free Speech Movement, encouraged a crowd of students at the University of California at Berkeley to "put your bodies upon the gears and upon the wheels, upon the levers, upon all the apparatus—and you've got to make it stop!" And in 1965, there were at least three acts of self-immolation in protest of America's military actions in Vietnam; the antiwar protests would continue for years. People from different parts of society came together to demand—to force—change.

And now women, long silenced, were starting to speak—loudly. A new social movement was officially under way.

As women across the country came together, the Equivalents found their friend group falling apart. It began slowly and innocently: schedules failed to line up, visits were missed, there were more weeks between letters. The phone rang less often than one would like. Then small disagreements began to arise: Olsen queried her friends' silences, Sexton resented Olsen's self-indulgences, Sexton and Kumin strained to maintain a tight friendship as Kumin spent more and more time away from the suburbs. The visual artists didn't seem to get embroiled in these little spats—throughout the 1960s, Swan remained close with the two poets, while Pineda continued to stay in close touch with Olsen and her daughters—but the three writers started to strain against each other.

The Equivalents also now found themselves out of step with other American women. Though Olsen and Pineda both identified as feminists, the other members of the group didn't necessarily think of themselves or their work as "feminist," though some who read and viewed them would disagree. According to Kumin's son, Daniel (Danny when he was younger), Kumin didn't start using the language of feminism until the women's movement was in full swing. Swan considered herself "self-liberated and pre-liberated," according to her daughter, Joanna. She had "kind of done her own thing," and that thing, as she understood it, was artistically significant and formally radical, though not necessarily, in her eyes, political. Sexton was similar. Sexton "never applied the word 'feminist' to herself," writes Linda in her memoir, though she also recalls Sexton's curiosity about local feminist meetings. Sexton continued to view herself this way through the late 1960s and into the 1970s. In 1974, she confessed, "I hate the way I'm anthologized in women's lib anthologies . . . They cull out the 'hate men' poems, and leave nothing else . . . The feminists are doing themselves a disservice to show just this."

Their readers felt differently. In the late 1960s and early 1970s, women students, critics, and teachers used poems by Plath and Sexton to celebrate women's experience. "Woman with Girdle," a poem from Sexton's *All My Pretty Ones*, is the realistic portrait of a woman's body that so many activists wanted. The poem ends with the woman coming "into your redeeming skin," a statement of celebration. It was of a piece with Sexton's unflattering self-portraits, such as "Menstruation at Forty" and "The Ballad of the Lonely Masturbator." In these poems, she wrote about female experiences that couldn't yet be spoken about in public: this was before the abortion speak-outs of the late 1960s, before *Our Bodies, Ourselves* and woman-centered gynecology. Sexton's great poetic intervention—the presentation of messy female experience as art—was also a political one. In writing about these topics before they entered public discourse, she was an inspiration and ahead of her time.

The sad irony of the Equivalents is that the movement they helped give birth to was not one in which they could participate fully. The Institute was the harbinger of a much more radical reordering of American society. As an institution, it was the beginning of something big, but for the first classes of fellows it was a mid-career move, a last pass at academia, a stopgap measure until more commissions came in. The Equivalents were women born too early; by the time the women's movement gained full steam, each of them was well established in her life and ways.

Olsen was the only one of the five to identify as a feminist consistently and to see her creative career primarily in political terms. But even she raised an eyebrow at some of the ways that "women's lib" infiltrated the world of arts and letters. One evening in 1965, Olsen tuned in to a radio program about "a new dev't [development] in poetry: 'domestic lady poets,'" which the critic, whom Olsen identified as Rella Lossy, defined as those poets "intensely involved in being women in children in domestic subjects they are satisfying what Yeats called the poets unsatisfied hunger for the commonplace," as she later wrote to Sexton. Louise Bogan, Carolyn Kizer, and Sylvia Plath all apparently belonged to this category. So too did Sexton: the critic claimed she was, as Olsen wrote, "our most promising & prominent domestic lady poet"—"wish could see your expression," Olsen wrote cheekily to her friend. The critic on the radio pointed to "Unknown Girl in the Maternity Ward," a persona poem from *Bedlam*, as Sexton's masterpiece. The poem is not Sexton's best, a bit melodramatic and imagined rather than lived: Sexton had never been in the situation of the speaker, an unwed mother lying in a hospital where doctors "guess about the man who left me, / some pendulum soul, going the way men go / and leave you full of child." Olsen claimed that if asked for Sexton's best poem, she would have guessed at seventeen other poems before arriving at that one. In the letter she wrote to Sexton, she described the radio program with sarcasm.

It's a bit surprising that Olsen objected to this celebration of female poetry, especially because it took place while she was revising "Silences"—an essay that is, among other things, about how women writers have historically been oppressed. But then Olsen never cared much for critics or for the academic study of literature; she objected to any teaching of literature that didn't proceed from a reader's immediate, emotional response. She also saw many commonalities among writers of different races and genders; this is why her first seminar talk at the Institute had cited Kafka and Hemingway as well as Woolf and Mansfield. She thus wasn't inclined to discuss women writers in isolation from their contemporaries. She herself loved so many writers—Rilke and Teasdale, Melville and Woolf—and her only criterion was how well they captured human experience.

It is in fact because of her deep commitment to artistic excellence that Olsen sometimes failed to support Kumin and Sexton, her friends and fellow writers, in the ways they would have liked. She praised her friends for their excellence and pushed them to achieve it. Once, writing to Kumin, she exhorted her to keep chasing prizes and public praise: "You need what you merit but have not had—recognition, yes, honor." When Olsen applied for a Guggenheim grant some time after the Institute, she described the process as "last minute, of course, a literal holding my nose & getting the nasty stuff over with as fast as possible (have been retching ever since)." The whole economy felt sordid to her. She made it clear to all of her friends—Kumin and Sexton included—that she would never want to be asked for a blurb.

The trouble began, then, in February 1968, when the publisher of Kumin's second novel, Harper & Row, reached out to Olsen for a blurb. Kumin's novel, *The Passions of Uxport*, was slated to be published in April 1968. In writing it, Kumin had wanted to portray the "great passions that trouble all" through a close study of two women and their families in Uxport, a suburb eighteen miles from Boston and a clear fictionalization of Newton: "The suburb of Uxport was full of friends and cocktail parties, sit-ins, fund-raising hootenannies, political causes." The novel follows Hallie Peakes, a thoughtful, intense, repressed teacher and writer undergoing psychoanalysis, and Sukey Davis, volatile and passionate, a painter with a sick child and a devoted husband. The major event of the novel is the death of Sukey's daughter; she dies of leukemia. Minor characters include Ernie, a mentally ill man obsessed with burying roadkill; Dr. Osip Zemstvov, an old-school Freudian psychoanalyst who treats Hallie; and Teejoe, an untrustworthy colleague with whom Hallie has a brief affair. The early years of the Vietnam War (the novel begins in 1965) provide the backdrop for what is, ultimately, a kind of suburban melodrama; one reviewer, referring to a popular television soap opera, called it the "Boston version of Peyton Place." *Uxport* is occasionally entertaining, but not especially insightful about either manners or mores.

A woman of principle, Olsen declined to write a blurb—not for a friend, not even for a friend whose first novel had sold poorly and who, according to Olsen, merited "recognition" and "honor." "I wish the practice of bookjacket & ad quotes didn't continue debased," she wrote to Harper & Row, "for the few to whom my judgment might have meaning, I would want to help them to the joy of knowing these 2 so different books," referring to *Downstairs at Ramsey's*, a James Leigh novel that the publisher had sent her separately. She believed Kumin's novel would "make its way to its earned literary place of honor regardless," but she would not help it along in a public way. Instead, she claimed she would spread the word about the book to her friends, in the hopes that "some recognition of its achievement . . . might be nurturing for the author." Grassroots promotion, in other words, though one wonders if Olsen, who didn't love *Uxport*, ever followed up on these plans.

It was a gracious refusal, but when Kumin saw it weeks later, she feared that her friend was angry. Kumin wrote Olsen an apologetic and—for her—emotional letter. She explained that she had been in the hospital dealing with complications from a bladder infection, and she claimed that she had purposefully omitted Olsen's name from the list of those to whom galleys would be sent because she knew Olsen was averse to providing blurbs to publishers. Though Kumin was remorseful about her publisher's mistake, she was also hurt: Olsen had seen the product of years of work and said nothing. "I guess I feel pretty sad," she wrote, coming as close as she would to emotional disclosure. "I don't know how you felt about the book . . . In this instance the silence has begun to take on a menacing quality." She closed with "fond greetings, even I, in spite of my acute but momentary paranoia."

Olsen telegrammed immediately upon receiving Kumin's letter. The message was dramatic and self-lacerating, as she often was when caught up in interpersonal conflict: "JUST HOME YOUR LETTER DEAREST MAX UNFORGIVABLE SILENCE AGONIZING AND SHAMEFUL TO ME NOT YOUR FINE BOOK BUT MY VORTEX INCAPACITY WILL TRY AGAIN AS HAVE FOR WEEKS TO RIGHT YOU BE WELL AND PROUD OF YOUR ACHIEVEMENT LOVINGLY EVEN IF THE RIGHT IS GONE FOR IT FAILED TO BE DEED." She followed with a hasty letter in which she apologized again and empathized "when I think of how mysterious hurt wild baffled angry I would be had I sent you my galleys of a book intwo [sic] which I had put so much and then not to hear weeks months . . . it is a good book Max." Olsen tended to shower her friends with love and affection while reserving any negative impressions of them or their work for third parties. She preferred evasion to open conflict.

Kumin wrote an even-tempered letter back, and for a moment the wound seemed to be sewn shut. But then Olsen, anxious and wanting to redeem herself in Kumin's eyes, overcorrected for her silence and wrote a second letter. "Third hand I hear 'Tillie didn't like Max's book; thats why she doesnt write her.' NO Max. If that had been it— (remember me Max as you know me)—I would have written as a matter of course to tell you & to say *why*." She praised the book, in a somewhat backhanded way: "Even that Passions came to be written at all is a miracle of achievement. All those months the pain & disability of your back . . . and you, *you managed to work* regardless." But Olsen admired Kumin's powers of description and made sure to quote some of the book's most beautiful moments, in which the natural world comes alive: "the snow bees that flew into the headlight beams."

But then she shifted into mentor mode, as if her maturity and relative success as a fiction writer made her into Kumin's teacher.

"I think I know what happened. (Not only your weakness that always you must fight: too trembling too modest too respectful too unsure, unrealizing of what you have." Olsen thought that Kumin, in her fiction, consistently "turn[ed] away from what is deepest" and instead settled for what was easy: rather than represent a death, she spent all her time constructing minor characters. In *Uxport*, Kumin had avoided engaging more deeply with "marriage friend-ship humancloseness."

An astute reader of fiction, Olsen wasn't wrong. *The Passions of Uxport* often feels like light reading, despite Kumin's increasing interest in politics. "I have never before had for so long a period so grossly an apocalyptic vision of the future," Kumin had written to Olsen right around the time of the book's publication. "It is very hard not to get completely caught up with my students, angry, articulate, passionately involved in militancy and pacifism." She tried to do justice to the political moment in *Uxport* by having her characters reflect on the turmoil of the times. "Meanwhile, Black Power has now alienated liberal white support," thinks Hallie at one point.

> The U.S. is now bombing the supply depots of Haiphong. Not in the city, in the suburbs. Civilian casualties are light and unavoid-able. The child of her best friend is dying of cancer. Except for, and yet because of this fact, she thinks she would gladly go to bed with Martin Davis. Fifty GI's are encircled in the Vietnam jungle and their captain calls for air strikes. He knows full well that most of them will die.

Politics rarely impinge upon the characters' behavior, however; the Peakes and Davis families remain cordoned off from danger. The problems in the novel are primarily domestic: an unplanned preg-nancy, an ill-conceived affair. These are fine topics for the literary novel—Tolstoy, one of Olsen's idols, did justice to them in *Anna Karenina*—but Kumin didn't demonstrate the psychological acuity that characterizes the great novelist.

What she did get right, or close to right, was the friendship between the two protagonists—avatars of herself and Sexton. Hallie "was a nail biter and an outsider and was built . . . sparingly," while Sukey "was a wild one, the lady artist; buxom, red-mouthed and noisy enough to be a Jew." While Hallie dutifully commutes from her "up-country" farm to teach her courses at Rufus College (a stand-in for Tufts), Sukey destroys her failed paintings "in cold red paint blood" and spends time at Braceland, a mental institution. "Nervous breakdown. Artists had lots of them," Ernie, a kind of choral figure, explains. Hallie can't help but pity Sukey's husband, Martin, who does most of the child care and can't even persuade his wife to stay in bed with him on a Sunday morning. Hallie helps Sukey through her rough patches, visiting her at Braceland and comforting her and Martin after their daughter's death. Hallie has a one-night stand with her colleague Teejoe, but then quickly realizes that an affair is not going to be fulfilling. It becomes clear that Hallie is a reflexive caretaker: she arranges an illegal abortion for a niece (an event averted at the last minute by miscarriage) and sublimates her anger at her cheating husband by performing various domestic tasks. "Hallie, rise, wash out your eyes!" she remonstrates herself at one point. "Go now and baste the chicken; go now and whip the cream; take comfort from the unsorrowing Linda"—her daughter—"ankle deep in wood chips and manure: frosted with horsefly bites, each knee a molehill of saddle sores." As in Kumin's poetry, the natural world, and the sensory delights it offers, comes to the rescue.

Hallie's self-respect depends on differentiating herself from her volatile friend by remaining responsible and in control, though she also envies Sukey's emotional freedom and the ease that accompanies it. (Hallie has a stress stomachache throughout most of the novel, a manifestation of her inner, psychic conflict.) But Hallie can never be the freewheeling Sukey: Hallie regrets her affair, and she works through her marital problems. She is, to her occasional chagrin, the kind of woman who will fix a farmhouse rather than burn it down.

Though many of the book's major plot points have no basis in the poets' real lives (and though Kumin made some alterations to their shared history), the quality of the friendship rings true. Throughout the novel, Kumin tries to hone her description of their bond. At first, describing the constant phone calls, she calls them "snugger than sisters. If one had a headache, the other took the aspirin." Later, she refines this description. "Whatever they undertook jointly became an affair of just proportions," Hallie reflects, while recalling the two of them listening to one of Dr. King's public speeches. "They reinforced each other, their sympathies meshed, a long journey became a light-hearted visit . . . They were nothing like sisters, except in the ideality of sisters. They slandered, praised, fed, robbed. They depended." It's a lovely portrait and possibly an idealized one: an astute reader of the novel might wonder who, ultimately, depended on whom.

It was this friendship that Olsen, unforgivably, criticized. In the same letter in which she pointed out the novel's lack of depth, she offered a strange and damning critique of the friendship it depicted. Assuming Sexton would read the letter she sent to Kumin, Olsen spoke directly to the poet. "I love you," she wrote, "and your friendship for Maxine but you also messed it up (you let her, Max) instead of helping Maxine to her best her great best respecting, insisting on her comprehending, working to what she most nakedly, singularly had to say you had to mix in what you wanted said, thought should be there, shallowized diffused yes putting the attention to surface pattern clutter technique."

It was an odd complaint—that somehow Sexton was responsible for a fictional alter ego constructed by Kumin—but it was not altogether incorrect: indeed Sexton had exercised a strong hand in Sukey's construction. In 1967, while recovering from a broken hip, Sexton called Kumin daily to get updates on the novel in progress and to offer dialogue for Sukey. A visiting nurse, overhearing these phone calls about marital affairs and unintended pregnancies, would mistake them for gossip. For her part, Sexton loved the fictionalized friendship. A woman who knew a thing or two about portraits (recall "The Double Image"), she thought *The Passions of Uxport* was a fine one.

In the end, Olsen's discussion of Hallie and Sukey's friendship amounted to more than a critique of the product: it was also a critique of the process, of the way Sexton sometimes dominated Kumin, and the way Kumin sometimes let her. It was also a critique of a close friendship that Olsen had seen as closed off to her. Reading *Uxport*, she had longed to "get into that Hallie-Sukey talk." She had told Kumin she was "lonesome." Sexton and Kumin always had each other, while at times Olsen felt as if she had no one.

Kumin, not given to quick reaction, fell silent. Sexton, shocked, did as well. It was years before Sexton confronted Olsen about that neologism, "shallowized." When she did, she expressed her hurt plainly, in a way that Kumin never did.

"I was so shocked those many years ago when you said that I shallowized Maxine's book," Sexton wrote in July 1970. "No, Tillie, I never understood what you meant . . . It wouldn't matter to me if I didn't love and respect you, but I do, and it still matters." She wondered if John Cheever, a favorite of Kumin's, was to blame for whatever shallowness Olsen detected. She suggested that Olsen might like Kumin's next novel better. (The novel was *The Abduction*, published in 1971 to reviews that called it "the weakest of Mrs. Kumin's novels.") She closed her letter by wishing Olsen all the best and said she would remain a "devoted reader." Compared with prior letters to Olsen, in which she called Olsen "a genius and a good woman," Sexton's well wishes sounded cold. She was merely a devoted "reader," no longer a devoted friend.

Just as she had with Kumin, Olsen tried to write a letter that would make things right. "Anne—cherished and estranged," she began. She thanked Sexton for her unlisted phone number "in the oddly formal, unsigned message" that Sexton sent her, either before or after the confrontational letter. She felt that she did not have the words to express her feelings, and so borrowed a few from Thoreau. In the end, though, she offered Sexton her own good wishes, more heartfelt than the ones Sexton had offered her: "Estranged or not always I cherish your hopes, feel kind to your dreams, see you nature groping garden like mine, do not like apart (your books, your picture, memories, part of me)—Be and work well—Fare well (not farewell), dearest Anne."

The Passions of Uxport had arrived at a bad time for everyone. Sexton, recovered from her broken hip, was facing negative reviews from overseas. Her British editor, Jon Stallworthy of Oxford University Press, wanted revisions made to her new book, *Love Poems;* he found these new poems too loose and missed the neat, formal poetry that had marked her early collections. Kumin continued to grapple with pain from her bladder infection. "This has been a ghastly year here," she wrote in April, just after *Uxport's* publication. "Almost no days without pain—but a dreadful reluctance to go back in to another hospital for more tests and more poking about." Pain had become so central to her life that it's no wonder that the central drama of Hallie Peakes's life in *Uxport* is her mysterious stomach pain. Olsen, meanwhile, was grotesquely ill and despondent. In February 1968, right around when she received the blurb request from Harper & Row, she wrote a dark letter to Sexton, detailing her suffering:

My pants are pulled down
after a bloody bowel movement that hurt
I am an old woman
the pain in my back nags
thats how they say it on the aspirin ads nags
I use ad language more and more

I come back to my work room
where I do no work
The sick Tolstoy (1904) glares at me
hands wringing the afghan
Emily Hardy Chekhov Anne look away.

But she did not want her friend to look away: she wanted Sexton to see how broken she was. Her sentences snapped in half like dried twigs. Reading this winter note, with its stanzas and enjambment, Sexton might have thought that the fiction writer Olsen had written a poem.

Surely these circumstances shaped the way each woman responded to the disagreement over *Uxport*. Perhaps had everyone been healthier, Olsen's criticisms could have been discussed more calmly. But there is also something predictable about this falling-out—and not just because Olsen on more than one occasion fell out with writer friends. The bond among these three writers had been surprising at the start: Sexton, a woman who came from money, knew so little about how a working-class mother like Olsen lived. For a moment, their common goals had brought them together; now their political and artistic commitments were pushing them apart.

Olsen and Sexton never recovered their formerly affectionate and intimate friendship. Sexton, who depended on her friends for care and support, couldn't understand how Olsen could so casually insult her and Kumin. Olsen, who believed in high standards for all artists, including herself, refused to sacrifice her critical honesty in the service of friendship. Though the three friends had one last lunch together in Boston, during one of Olsen's visits east, they never again felt the ease they'd had at the Institute, where they shared their great literary loves and finished each other's sentences. The closest they came to healing was, fittingly, in their letters; they were writers before they were anything else.

When words failed them, the natural world came to their aid. Olsen often turned to nature for solace. Kumin did as well; she always described the countryside sensuously in her poetry and her prose. Sometimes, a pressed flower or a leaf said what words could not. Once, sometime after the disagreement over *Uxport*, Olsen, traveling somewhere to give a talk or teach a class, found herself carrying three leaves, each pressed between pages of poems by Hardy and Dickinson. Kumin had sent the leaves to her as signs of autumn's arrival in the East. "I take them as your forgiveness of my hurt of you," Olsen wrote. "Thank you, Max. It steadies."

CHAPTER 16

There's Nothing Wrong with Privilege, Except That Everybody Doesn't Have It

"THE CENTER WAS NOT HOLDING," begins Joan Didion's 1967 essay "Slouching Towards Bethlehem," first published in *The Saturday Evening Post*. She's describing "the United States of America in the cold late spring of 1967," a country in distress.

It was a country of bankruptcy notices and public-auction announcements and commonplace reports of casual killings and misplaced children and abandoned homes and vandals who misspelled even the four-letter words they scrawled. It was a country in which families routinely disappeared, trailing bad checks and repossession papers. Adolescents drifted from city to torn city, sloughing off both the past and the future as snakes shed their skins, children who were never taught and would never now learn the games that had held the society together. People were missing. Children were missing. Parents were missing. Those who were left behind filed desultory missing-persons reports, then moved on themselves.

Things were falling apart, as the Yeats poem goes, and Didion had gone to San Francisco—"where the social hemorrhaging was showing up"—to interview hippies and runaways and to describe the broken lives they lived. She recounts her conversations with hippies and her observations of the counterculture. The essay ends with a small fire in a house, started by a three-year-old, and a couple of hippies desperately trying to retrieve "some very good Moroccan hash which had dropped down through a floorboard that had been damaged in the fire." The structure is clearly unsound.

The world Didion described seemed nothing like the world of the 1950s, the one in which the Equivalents came of age. (Didion was born roughly a decade after Sexton and Kumin, but in attitude and manner she was closer to their generation than to the younger one.) In the ten years between 1957 and 1967, a nation defined by consensus and containment—or at least by the illusion of such things—had become one marked by division and disruption. Baby boomers born to members of the "silent generation"—those proud World War II veterans and proper homemakers in pearls—rejected the styles, habits, and mores of their parents. They clamored for civil rights and sexual freedom. The year 1967 saw the "Summer of Love" and a youth exodus to San Francisco. Skirts got shorter. Hair got longer and straighter if you were white, bigger and bolder if you were black. Music got louder and weirder: the Monterey International Pop Festival, the first rock festival in America, took place in June; it featured Jefferson Airplane, the Grateful Dead, and the Jimi Hendrix Experience. Following the advice of Timothy Leary, a researcher and advocate for the use of psychedelics, young people turned on, tuned in, and dropped out. Not even ten years after Sexton and Plath sipped martinis at the Ritz-Carlton, acid had replaced alcohol as some young people's drug of choice.

By this time, the women's movement, like the country itself, had fractured. You could say the break happened in May 1968. One year prior, in 1967, a feminist named Valerie Solanas—a playwright and professed lesbian—had self-published the *SCUM Manifesto;* the acronym seems to have stood for "Society for Cutting Up Men." Solanas identified as a radical feminist—a group that differed from liberal feminists like Friedan in that they rejected the belief that formal equality, at work or under the law, meant anything in a world that was ruled by men. They wanted revolution. In the *SCUM Manifesto*, Solanas advocated the complete destruction of men—as well as the overthrow of the government and the elimination of the money system. A year after publishing this document, and just two months after Dr. Martin Luther King Jr.'s assassination, Solanas shot the artist Andy Warhol, who survived the attempt on his life. (She had wanted his help producing one of her plays.) A prominent member of Friedan's NOW—the blond, ex-Republican Ti-Grace Atkinson—visited Solanas in prison. Atkinson hired the witty black lawyer Florynce Kennedy to help with Solanas's case, which prompted Friedan to send a frantic telegram: "DESIST IMMEDIATELY FROM LINKING NOW IN ANY WAY WITH SOLANAS." Atkinson and Kennedy soon broke from NOW and founded their own radical feminist group, the Feminists.

But this rupture reflected long-standing disagreement around strategy and tactics. Should "women's libbers" pursue legal recourse and policy reform, or should they take to the streets? Should NOW announce official stances on marriage, abortion, and the nuclear family, or should it stay silent on these cultural issues and thus avoid alienating potential allies? Are lesbians part of the women's liberation movement? Just how should feminists relate to men? NOW didn't answer these questions to the satisfaction of women like Atkinson and Kennedy. The organization was particularly problematic on the question of lesbianism: Friedan once called lesbians a "lavender menace" and barred them from the First Congress to Unite Women, a NOW-sponsored gathering held in New York City in 1969. Radical feminists—Shulamith Firestone, Ellen Willis, Kathie Sarachild, Robin Morgan, Patricia Mainardi, and others—had far-reaching goals; they planned to work against the government and the legal system rather than working in collaboration with them. Soon, in New York, an eager, newly liberated woman could choose among rival radical feminist cells: Redstockings, the Feminists, New

York Radical Feminists, and Cell 16. Many of these groups practiced "consciousness-raising," a term coined by Sarachild in 1968. The historian Ruth Rosen defines it as "the process by which women in small groups could explore the political aspects of personal life" and notes that it was a technique borrowed from the civil rights movement, where it was called "speaking truth to power." (Sarachild had worked as a civil rights organizer in Mississippi, where she encountered this organizing tactic.) The idea was that by talking about their daily lives—"speak from your own experience, sister"—women would come to realize how they had been oppressed. They would experience what came to be called the "click" of recognition.

In addition to differentiating themselves from liberal feminists, radical feminists diverged from orthodox socialist feminists, like Olsen, who believed that a working-class revolution and the redistribution of resources would eliminate sexism. Radical feminists saw gender oppression as prior to and separate from capitalism, though it could work in concert with capitalism. But while radical feminists all agreed on the primacy of gender and on the need for a women's movement, they were divided on a number of other important questions. Some believed in the value of consciousness-raising; others thought it hindered the movement. Some believed that the institution of marriage should endure—at least until after the revolution. Others called for its immediate elimination. Still others believed that lesbianism was the only politically coherent sexual practice for feminists. These disagreements—about leadership structures, the value of direct action, and whether a vanguard group was more effective than a group that welcomed many members from all walks of life— split organizing cells and resulted in the proliferation of different groups. Between 1970 and 1973, as the historian Alice Echols writes, "the movement was ravaged by intense factionalism over the issues of elitism, class, and lesbianism."

The conflict over the last of these proved to be particularly heated. On May 1, 1970, a group of protesters, hoping to raise the issue of lesbian rights, interrupted the proceedings of the Second Congress to Unite Women, a gathering organized by Friedan's NOW in New York

City. Some of them wore shirts emblazoned with the slur Friedan had once launched at lesbians in the movement: "Lavender Menace." While a small cadre of women planned the action, many more joined the protesters once they'd taken the stage. That December, a group of prominent feminists, including Gloria Steinem, held a press conference to declare that both women's liberation and gay liberation were "struggling towards a common goal," but for many this statement was both inadequate and too late. Many lesbians had left the movement by this point, and Friedan, who was still homophobic, continued to purge the New York chapter of NOW of lesbian members. The historian Echols calls her chapter about the schism "The Eruption of Difference."

An eruption of difference can be destabilizing, and that can be a good thing. Sometimes an explosion can rock old buildings off their foundations. It can destroy old structures and clear a path for something new.

Despite its reputation for political liberalism, academia is in many ways a conservative realm. Professional dress is formal; hierarchy is the law of the land. Curriculum changes slowly, while canons shift and expand only when pressure is applied. This conservatism is, in part, a function of a professional structure that empowers the old and makes vulnerable the young. Graduate students must please older advisers who can discourage untraditional or radical work. All these factors make the academic world slow to change its ways.

But in the late 1960s, universities were under intense pressure to change. Black students mobilized for African American studies; a group of them staged a sit-in at Cornell University in April 1969. Students and faculty also agitated for increased representation of women, both in university department hires and on college syllabi. (A 1971 report by a university English instructor noted that women represented between 10 and 11 percent of faculty in modern languages and literatures.) In 1968, at what was remembered as a "politically volatile" annual convention, the Modern Language Association

Women's rights demonstration, August 26, 1970, New York City

(MLA), the professional association for graduate students, teachers, and scholars of literatures and languages (including but not limited to English), passed a resolution to create the Commission on the Place of Women in the Profession. (That this commission appeared eight years after Kennedy's nationwide commission on women's status gives one a sense of the lag time in academia.) One year later, the commission began its work. The MLA's president, Henry Nash Smith, appointed seven women to the commission—now called the Commission on the Status of Women in the Profession—including Florence Howe, a woman sometimes described as the "Elizabeth Cady Stanton of women's studies." A graduate of Smith College, Howe had been politically awakened by her students at Goucher College, where she had worked as an assistant professor in the early 1960s. She had dropped out of a PhD program to accommodate her then husband (at the time, assistant professorships, which were teaching positions, did not always require a complete dissertation). She participated in the civil rights movement and, later, the women's movement. Her experience in these social movements radicalized her: she "finally freed herself from marriage and even began to write the dissertation."

Howe believed that women were underrepresented in the academic humanities for two reasons: first, because literary syllabi consistently presented literature as a man's calling, and, second, because the presence of women steadily decreased as one proceeded to the upper levels of academe. By Howe's count, at the end of the 1960s, women made up 80 percent of college students studying English and modern languages but only 20 percent of those applying to doctoral programs. Those who did pursue doctoral study found a hard and uneven path before them. Though most women with PhDs intended to produce scholarship—in one study of women scholars eight or nine years beyond their doctorate, 75 percent had published one article, and most had published three or four—there was still a perception that women PhD students didn't intend to participate in the profession. As a result, many were shunted off to teaching jobs rather than tenure-track positions: women with PhDs were far more likely to teach at two- or four-year colleges, or community colleges, than at research universities. The result was that female doctoral students had only a one-in-nine, or one-in-ten, chance that their professor would be a woman. It was clear, from the numbers, that women were interested in studying literature and languages, perhaps even in professing the subjects, but along the way they were discouraged, rerouted, and dismissed. The future generation of female scholars had few role models before them, not in literature nor in life.

Though she never finished her doctorate, Howe continued to advance in the profession—thanks in part to her prescience (she was teaching "women's studies" before there even was such a category). Radicalized early, she resolved to increase the proportion of women writers, scholars, and editors in the academy. She wanted to change the way women graduate students were regarded and women authors read. And Tillie Olsen—ever vocal, newly visible—would be a part of this change.

.   .   .

It was an unseasonably warm day in late December 1971 when Olsen, holding fiercely to her second chance at a literary life, arrived in Chicago for the annual meeting of the Modern Language Association. The professional association had been gathering since the late nineteenth century for several days of panels, forums, and job interviews. (The MLA annual convention continues to this day.) The conference took place over the course of three days between the Christmas holiday and the first day of the New Year—a time when most universities were on break, leaving faculty free to travel.

How did Olsen, a writer averse to the kind of critical analysis of literature that preoccupied most scholars, end up at an academic convention?

In 1968, as the political concerns of the New Left (civil rights, feminism, anticapitalism) began to penetrate academia, Olsen received an offer to teach at Amherst College, a small, all-male, all-white liberal arts college in western Massachusetts (Amherst went co-ed in 1975). The chair of the English department, Leo Marx, was a left-leaning Harvard graduate—he received both his BA and his PhD from the university—who was concerned by the homogeneity of the faculty at Amherst (Marx himself was one of only a few Jewish faculty). He thought Olsen, a fellow leftist and a woman, could bring the college up to date and prepare its undergraduates for the shifting world they were about to enter.

At the time she received the invitation from Amherst, Olsen was at MacDowell—her second spell at the colony. She took several buses down from New Hampshire to interview at the college. During the interview, she was her unapologetic, provocative self: she shamed the faculty for their reliance on the typical canon and insisted that students could—must—learn about American inequality through the study of American literature. Her diatribe alienated some of the faculty, but it endeared her to Marx, who advocated for a handsome salary—equal to that of male faculty—and found a chauffeur to take Olsen back to New Hampshire. (In the academic year 1975–1976, the average male college professor earned $17,414 for nine months of work, while the average female college professor earned $14,308 for the same amount of time.) She received an invitation to start teaching in the fall of 1969 as a lecturer on a one-year contract. This was the start of her second, unexpected career.

That summer, Olsen and Jack settled into a big house on Snell Street, two blocks from the Amherst English department. The roomy house cost them $220 a month in rent (about $1,535 today), more than they were used to paying in San Francisco. Instead of gabbing with the sex workers in San Francisco's St. Francis Square, Jack took to jogging down the streets of Amherst, lined with beautiful trees and obscenely lovely houses. He also picked up a job at *The Wall Street Journal*, which had an office in Chicopee, a town about ten miles from South Hadley, where Mount Holyoke College is located. Olsen, meanwhile, tacked up her usual portraits—Tolstoy, Woolf, Sexton—and hung the lithograph portrait of Emily Dickinson, completed by Swan during her years at the Institute. She made another room hers.

In a photograph from the time, Olsen—dressed all in black—stands in front of the Dickinson portrait, her elbows on the bookshelf and her hands in front of her. The poet makes the same gesture in the image. Olsen smiles, almost mischievously, as if she were getting away with something. She felt charged with some kind of magic living in the same town where her heroine, Dickinson, had spent her shut-away life. Later that year, she took her class on a field trip to Dickinson's home, preserved as a museum, and cried in the ghostly presence of the poet. But even before she crossed Dickinson's threshold, she felt moved by the town and by its history. Maybe in Amherst she could achieve something new.

At Amherst College, Olsen taught two literature classes: one on what she thought of as the literature of poverty (writers who wrote about poverty, either as something they'd witnessed or as something they'd lived through), and one that she called "The Struggle to Write," a course based on her *Harper's* piece, "Silences." (Authors included several of those quoted in the article: James, Hardy, Conrad.) Students were especially intrigued by her poverty course, though Olsen found it odd to teach the literature of inequality to some of the coun-

Olsen in front of Swan's Dickinson

try's most economically privileged students. As her daughter Julie remembered it, Olsen's first experience with academia brought out her radicalism: teaching at Amherst "really heightened her understanding of class distinctions. I remember her just being horrified at the differences between the adjuncts and the full-time faculty, and the male faculty and the few females that were anywhere around." It wasn't that she begrudged the Amherst students and faculty their good jackets or their nice houses. Indeed, she formed warm relationships with her students, who forgave her scatterbrained nature because she was so fervent in her belief that reading and writing matter. "There's nothing wrong with privilege," she used to say, "except that everybody doesn't have it."

Olsen's courses were revolutionary for their eclecticism and for their representation of women, working-class writers, and writers of color. These were the defining features of her teaching: in one course, titled "Literature of Poverty, Oppression, Revolution, and the Struggle for Freedom," the syllabus included W. E. B. Du Bois's *Souls of Black Folk*, Richard Wright's *Black Boy*, James Agee's *Let Us Now Praise Famous Men*, and Agnes Smedley's *Daughter of Earth*. Students loved the course in part because it spoke to the turbulent times—students cited the Kent State shooting in May 1970 and the war protests as their reasons for taking the course—and in part because it introduced them to new writers, those outside the mainstream. It diversified their reading.

Faculty and scholars admired Olsen's work as well. Paul Lauter, an activist scholar, recalled how teachers passed Olsen's "influential" poverty course syllabus among themselves, as if it were a secret blueprint for a better university. Lauter and his wife, none other than Florence Howe, were new admirers of Olsen's: they had met her in the lobby of an apartment building in New York City, just before Olsen started teaching at Amherst. Olsen was in New York to take care of some health troubles, and a mutual acquaintance had arranged the meeting. Olsen handed the couple a photocopy of Rebecca Harding Davis's *Life in the Iron Mills*. She suggested that they read the novella during the day so they would be able to sleep at night. Both found Davis's work quite moving and couldn't believe it was out of print. *Life in the Iron Mills* proved that Olsen's suspicions were correct: the literary past contained plenty of impressive, important works by women.

Olsen's syllabus, with its women and writers of color, would go some way to changing the canon and, as a result, the composition of the English classroom. Howe believed that one reason few women pursued doctoral study compared with the number of women who majored in English as undergraduates was that they didn't see themselves represented in their readings: the female characters they encountered were either scorned or sexualized. The scholar and critic Elaine Showalter, then a professor at Douglass College (where Bunting had been dean), agreed. At the 1970 Modern Language Association conference, held in New York City, Showalter delivered a talk titled "Women and the Literary Curriculum" (later published in *College English*). Reflecting on her time at Bryn Mawr, Showalter observed that in the twenty-one English courses for sophomores through seniors, students encountered no fewer than 313 men and only 17 women. Writers like Edith Wharton and Christina Rossetti were nowhere to be found. The effect on would-be female scholars, she argued, is devastating. "Women students will therefore perceive that literature . . . confirms what everything in society tells them: that the masculine viewpoint is considered normative, and the feminine viewpoint divergent." Women are minor, men major. The classroom is a male space, full of male writers and a male professor. Women students are asked, therefore, to identify with men, to distrust their own life experiences and perceptions. "Can we wonder," she asked, "that women students are so often timid, cautious, and insecure when we exhort them to 'think for themselves'?"

Showalter's solution was simple: teach literature by women. At Douglass, she taught a freshman course called "The Educated Woman in Literature." Not only did her Douglass students read women, but they also related what they read to their own psychological and social development. Showalter referred to her class as a kind of consciousness-raising. At Goucher College, Howe did the same thing: she asked her female students to identify with women in novels and respond to literary dilemmas as if they themselves were faced with an unintended pregnancy or a diffident husband. Howe's course was featured on the front page of *The Chronicle of Higher Education*, which claimed that she was teaching not literature but "consciousness."

This form of teaching was indeed radical—not only because it was expressly political, but also because it trampled over some of the central principles of the New Criticism, the practice of reading and teaching that had dominated university English departments since the 1950s and that had been pioneered by I. A. Richards, the professor who hosted the educational television show that taught Sexton about the sonnet. New Critics held that the text was a coherent work of art, cordoned off from the world. The student, or scholar, should analyze the text without recourse to history or to the author's biography. New Critics argued strenuously against allowing one's emotional response to a text to override one's rational assessment of the text's value. The method was scientific, a perfect fit for the Cold War university. But Howe and Showalter were encouraging students to respond emotionally, to take these responses seriously, and to break down the barrier between the work of art and the world at large. They believed that lived experience was as good a basis for assessing literary value as a keen understanding of metaphor and metonymy. They believed, in other words, that literature affected lives.

Olsen agreed.

On that warm day in December, Olsen gave her MLA conference talk, titled "Women Who Are Writers in Our Century: One out of Twelve." The talk was later published in *College English*. In "One out of Twelve," Olsen connected the central themes of her 1963 Radcliffe seminar talk—inequality of circumstances, lost writing, her own personal and professional struggles—to contemporary politics. "It is the women's movement," she began that December morning, "that has brought this forum into being; kindling a renewed . . . interest in the writings and writers of our sex." Like Howe and Showalter, Olsen had done her own (admittedly unscientific) count of women on syllabi for college English courses and found that there was roughly one woman writer for every twelve men.

What could account for this difference in achievement and recognition? True to form, Olsen argued that women's historical disadvantages, particularly the burden of child rearing, had either prevented them from producing literature or ensured that their literary reputations never took off. Challenging some prominent contemporary women writers, like the critic Diana Trilling—who believed that the achievement gap between men and women reflected biological difference—and Elizabeth Hardwick—who discounted the idea that female artists struggled more, or differently, than male ones—Olsen spoke of injustice and oppression, of the ways that the circumstances into which one is born determined one's fate. Alluding to Woolf, she discussed how the "angel in the house"—the nurturing feminine ideal—thwarted creative ambition in women. Not everyone could kill that angel. Some women ended up killing themselves.

Oppression, in other words, was everywhere: in the world and in the mind. Even the women born into the privileged class, she noted, struggled against sexism: "Isolated. Cabin'd, cribb'd, confin'd; the private sphere. Bound feet: corseted, cosseted, bedecked; denied one's body. Powerlessness. Fear of rape, male strength . . . Shut up, you're only a girl . . . Roles, discontinuities, part self, part time." "Only in the context of this punitive difference in circumstance, in history," she argued, could we understand why only "one out of twelve" women have achieved literary recognition. She repeated that statistic—one out of twelve—throughout the talk, as if these were the incantatory words of mourning and her talk a dirge.

The solutions Olsen proposed were at once simple and revolutionary. "You who teach, read writers who are women," she challenged her audience. She encouraged biographical criticism: "Teach women's lives through the lives of women who wrote the books, as well as through their books; and through autobiography, biography, journals, letters." And she encouraged them to read and listen to "living women writers"—including herself.

Listen they did. The talk made Olsen's academic reputation—not quite because it was unprecedented (Showalter had made similar points in her 1970 conference talk), but because it was timely, impassioned, and powerful. More than that, Olsen herself was a living example of the underrepresented woman writer and working-class writer. The personal was still political, and unlike some other scholars Olsen could speak of a struggle she had lived. That evening, after the panel was concluded, attendees crowded into Olsen's conference hotel room, where they discussed how to diversify syllabi and faculty. They were drawn to Olsen like parched travelers to water; tireless, passionate, she gave them the courage and energy they needed to continue on their independent journeys as college educators around the country.

Over the next few years, Olsen began to travel, too. A few months after her teaching appointment ended, in August 1970, she and Jack went to Vermont and climbed to the top of Putney Mountain. Laurie, now studying education, held a wedding ceremony in the same mountains. Olsen loved love but hated the cultural practice of spending a lot of money on an overly formal wedding ceremony; she was happy to send a newspaper clipping about Laurie's cheap, bohemian wedding to the Institute. In the months and years that followed, Olsen accepted speaking engagements, fellowships at the MacDowell Colony, and short-term teaching positions at the University of Massachusetts at Amherst and at MIT. She lectured widely and gave readings: in New York, Nebraska, New Hampshire, and Maryland. In later years, she made her way overseas, to China, to England, to Italy, among other places. No matter where she was or what specific text she read, she presented a version of the message she'd so memorably delivered at the MLA conference in 1971: "The greatness of literature is not only in the great writers, the good writers, it is also in that which explains much and tells much; the soil from which greater writers burgeon." She would plant the seeds for women's studies in soil across the country. Admirers started calling her "Tillie Appleseed."

In 1978, Olsen published a book titled *Silences*. It comprised "One out of Twelve," an adaptation of her 1971 MLA talk, her *Harper's* article "Silences," her reading lists from college courses she'd taught, and other writings and "jottings." It is a messy scrapbook of sorts; essays are linked by theme and voice, but there's no real structure or overarching argument. This was in some sense the point: Olsen wanted to show what a writing life looks like when it's happened in fits and starts, on buses and before doing the ironing. Much of the work in *Silences* had been published before, but once again Olsen needed to publish something, and so she turned to past work to provide her with a new publication.

Silences was a surprise success. In the late 1970s, with Marxist and feminist criticism already making inroads in the academy, the time was right for an argument like Olsen's, one that showed how inequality shaped the literary canon. The writer Margaret Atwood praised the book in *The New York Times Book Review*. "It may be comforting to believe that garrets are good for geniuses, that artists are made in Heaven and God will take care of them," she wrote. "But if you believe, as Tillie Olsen does, that writers are nurtured on Earth and nobody necessarily takes care of them, society cannot be absolved from the responsibility for what it produces or fails to produce in the way of literature." The young writer Sandra Cisneros called *Silences* "the Bible." The text was added to syllabi and continued to be used in college classrooms for decades (it's less frequently assigned now). As the scholar Shelley Fisher Fishkin put it in the introduction to the twenty-fifth anniversary edition, "*Silences* changed what we read in the academy, what we write, and what we count; it also gave us some important tools to understand and address many of the literary, social, economic and political silencings of the present and the potential silencings of the future."

This was not the life, or the career, that Olsen had envisioned—not when she was an eager young writer covering the San Francisco strikes, nor when she first set out for Radcliffe, a middle-aged woman with one book under her belt. She had wanted to write novels; indeed, throughout her teaching years, she continued to apply for writing grants. She also revised some old fiction, including a manuscript from the 1930s about the struggles of working-class people in a Wyoming mining town. That manuscript was published as *Yonnondio: From the Thirties* in 1974. She then published a novella, *Requa*, later republished as *Requa I*, to indicate that the narrative remained incomplete. But for the most part, she spent her time talking and teaching, not writing. She became a revered feminist scholar and critic at a time when feminist criticism was sweeping through the academy. This wasn't always easy on her family, and it wasn't always easy on Olsen, who did not travel well. "She was gone a lot," Julie remembered. "She was not around for my kids . . . She was just gone." Jack missed his wife during her absences, too. But like Julie, he was "damn proud" of Olsen, who was making a name for herself as an intellectual and who was finally getting the recognition that she deserved.

CHAPTER 17

Springs of Creativity

O LSEN WAS THE MOST POLITICALLY CONSCIOUS—and politically active—of the five Equivalents. She was not in her lifetime the most successful, nor the kindest, nor necessarily the most talented. But she saw the world differently from the other four women: she saw how creativity arises from material circumstances, how power is wielded against the vulnerable, and—crucially—how class, gender, and race intersect. Each of the others had her political insights—Pineda especially, who, along with her husband, helped plan the Moratorium to End the War in Vietnam from her Brookline living room—but none rivaled Olsen's.

Olsen was clearly unnerved by the whiteness of the Radcliffe Institute. It's possible that some of the other Equivalents noticed the racial problem as well: Pineda cared about the civil rights movement, and Kumin went on to champion writers of color, both publicly and privately, in years to come. But Olsen left the clearest record of her observations. There was not a single woman of color in the Institute's first class of scholars. Race—like material circumstance—was not something the selection committee had considered, and none of the celebratory media coverage of the Institute mentioned its racial composition. Nor did anyone remark on the way that the Institute stipends—a crucial part of its plan to facilitate female creativity—often passed from the white women receiving Radcliffe's largesse to women of color, who provided child care and household help so the scholars could work.

Olsen had tried to address racism in her second Radcliffe Institute seminar talk in 1964, but she ended up talking around the issue. She noted that in contradistinction to her years in San Francisco, she was living in an "all-white community, a community where almost everyone I knew worked in professions that had some respect attached to it." She called the Institute a "ghetto" and suggested that it would do the fellows well to get "outside of themselves." But her critique wasn't especially clear or forceful. Perhaps she was worried about seeming churlish and ungrateful; the Institute had given her so much, more than most of the other fellows received, and she might have hesitated before offering criticism. She might also have simply been characteristically shy and underprepared.

Luckily, others spoke more loudly. On December 10, 1968, two dozen black female Radcliffe undergraduates occupied Fay House, where Bunting had her office and where, eight years before, Sexton, Kumin, and Swan had interviewed for admission to the Institute for Independent Study. The undergraduates were protesting for improvements in admissions. From 1955 to 1964, the college had only one black student, if that, per graduating class of roughly three hundred. The Radcliffe students wanted increased racial representation, black admissions officers, and the coordinated admission of black students. They had made a sign: "Radcliffe Commit Yourself NOW." The college responded: the next year's freshman class had thirty black students—a record high.

By 1971, when the class of 1975 was admitted, the percentage of black students at the university had increased to 8.68 percent (in 1968, black students made up 4.24 percent of the undergraduate student body). Though activists past and present celebrated the victory, current student activists kept pushing for change. In April

1969, Harvard and Radcliffe students took over University Hall and demanded that the university, with the aid of students, recruit faculty for an African American studies department. Ultimately, they sought proportional representation of black students in both Radcliffe and Harvard Colleges.

Keeping in step with the university, the Institute diversified its group of associate scholars. Though black women were never formally barred from admission, the Institute had not made any concerted effort to recruit or to admit them. This changed in the second half of the 1960s. In 1966, Alice Childress, a black playwright and novelist who had previously adapted Langston Hughes for the stage, won a fellowship at the Institute. During her two years there, she wrote *Wedding Band: A Love/Hate Story in Black and White*, a play that described a forbidden interracial love affair in Charleston, South Carolina, at the end of World War I. In 1970, the Institute admitted at least one black woman, Florence Ladd, an environmental psychologist. The following year, it awarded a fellowship to a twenty-seven-year-old writer and teacher named Alice Walker. She would be at the Institute from the fall of 1971 through the spring of 1973.

Walker came to the Institute for a few different reasons, but a big one was to get away from Jackson, Mississippi, where she had been living with her husband, the civil rights lawyer Mel Leventhal, and their young daughter. Walker had found it difficult to write there. Her writing career had taken off in 1967, when an essay she wrote on the civil rights movement was published in the fall issue of *The American Scholar*. That same year, she received the first of two fellowships at the MacDowell Colony. Her first book followed soon after, in 1968. Many of the poems in *Once*, her debut poetry collection, were written while Walker was still at Sarah Lawrence College; she had transferred there from Spelman College, where she had studied with Howard Zinn. *The Third Life of Grange Copeland*—a novel begun in New York City, where Walker lived after college, and finished in Mississippi—described how white oppression produces domestic violence within the black community. It was published in 1970 to mixed reviews, some of which Walker found racist.

Alice Walker, 1970s

Her career stalled in Mississippi. Walker was black, Leventhal was white, and though both were committed to the civil rights struggle, Walker suffered more from the intimidations and threats of violence that that they encountered in Mississippi. Interviewed on the occasion of the publication of her first novel, *The Third Life of Grange Copeland*, Walker explained, "It's very intimidating in Jackson. Living in a hostile community can dry up your creativity."

She applied to the Radcliffe Institute shortly after the novel's publication, in the fall of 1970. In her application, she sketched out a plan for a novel about a young black woman at a black college much like Spelman who travels to East Africa (Walker visited Kenya during her undergraduate years) and falls in love with a man. She described the novel as "a love story in which the beloved is both a man and a continent." The following March she learned that she had received a $5,000 fellowship, much of which would go to rent—she and her daughter, Rebecca, who was not yet two, moved into an apartment on Linnaean Street, near the Radcliffe Quadrangle—and child care. Though she would not be entirely free from mothering duties, the Radcliffe grant offered Walker a more peaceful atmosphere for her writing. In Cambridge, she wouldn't have to monitor the windows for fear that a brick would come flying through one of them. She would instead struggle with language and literary history.

But when she came to Radcliffe, she also found it hard to write in Cambridge. Her first year was marked by sickness—both she and Rebecca suffered from the flu—and writing frustrations. She requested a second year to finish her second novel, explaining that a "renewed fellowship would give me a much needed sense of freedom and possibility." Meanwhile, she taught a course at Wellesley College on black women writers. She told an interviewer, "Though it's often lonely without my family, I can do a lot of work with intensive time."

Walker's presence at the Institute heralded the enduring strength and the new visibility of black feminists. Black feminism did not begin in the 1970s; to the contrary, black women's organizing has a long history, with points of heightened visibility during abolitionism and the long civil rights movement. The fact that black women gained mainstream attention in the 1970s should not suggest that this was an initial or inaugural moment of black feminism.

But questions of race and representation were attracting the attention of governmental and educational institutions, as well as feminist organizations. Around the time that Walker entered the Institute, rifts were forming in the women's movement along racial lines. "As far as many Blacks were concerned, the emergence of the women's movement couldn't have been more untimely or irrelevant," writes the historian Paula Giddings, whose book *When and Where I Enter* traces the history of black women's activism in America. In the early 1960s, when sex discrimination and unequal wages first became national issues, black women—who, in contrast to the women portrayed in *The Feminine Mystique*, had long worked outside the home—were earning just over half of what their white counterparts did (at least when it came to full-time employment). When Friedan published her polemic against suburban domesticity, many black women were unmoved: they couldn't recognize the problem (Friedan's work "seemed to come from another planet," Giddings writes), nor could they bring themselves to care much about a lack of personal fulfillment when their material problems were much more pressing. This isn't to say women of color were entirely absent from the nascent women's movement—Friedan's friend Pauli Murray, the union organizer Aileen Hernandez, and the politician Shirley Chisholm were all among the founding members of NOW—but many of them regarded their white "sisters" with skepticism, even suspicion. "What do black women feel about Women's Lib? Distrust," concluded the novelist Toni Morrison in 1971. "Black women are not convinced that Women's Lib serves their best interest or that it can cope with the uniqueness of their experience." When asked in May 1971 by the poet Nikki Giovanni what she thought of women's liberation, Ida Lewis, the former editor in chief of *Essence*, characterized it as "a family quarrel between white women and white men. And on general principles, it's not good to get involved in family disputes."

Nonetheless, black women mobilized alongside and adjacent to white women throughout the 1960s and 1970s. Conflict was inevitable. One emblematic moment of strife occurred on August 26, 1970, when the Third World Women's Alliance (TWWA)—a socialist feminist organization for women of color—arrived at a Women's Liberation Day March in New York City, held in honor of the fiftieth anniversary of women's suffrage. The group wanted to use the occasion of the march to protest the prosecution of the radical black activist Angela Davis, who had gone underground to avoid arrest for her alleged assistance in a prison uprising; the TWWA members held a banner that read "Hands Off Angela Davis." According to Frances Beal, a leader of TWWA, an angry leader of Friedan's NOW told them, "Angela Davis has nothing to do with the women's liberation." Beal responded, "It has nothing to do with the kind of liberation you're talking about but it has everything to do with the kind of liberation we're talking about."

In addition to being active in the women's movement, black women continued to work for civil rights and, in the late 1960s and the 1970s, for black liberation, a movement led by the Black Panthers that advocated for black self-determination. Their organizing during this period—most significantly for the right to benefit from state welfare programs, without being subjected to burdensome stipulations—represents but one chapter in the long history of black women's activism, stretching back to the antilynching activist Ida B. Wells, who documented lynchings in the 1890s, and including such women as the civil rights organizer Ella Baker and Mary McLeod Bethune, head of the National Association of Colored Women, both of whom were active in the 1940s and 1950s. As an activist, Walker was part of a long tradition of black female organizers.

At the turn of the 1970s, however, black women found themselves in something of a bind when it came to gender politics. While white women fled the civil rights movement to start working for women's liberation, black women were torn between their commitment to black liberation and their desire for gender equality, both in the movement and in the world at large. Unlike some of their white peers, who demonized white men as the oppressors, black women did not resent black men but rather hoped for their empowerment. They also didn't feel the same way about abortion as many white women did, given that the movement for birth control had overlapped historically with eugenics; Margaret Sanger, who founded the first birth control clinic, held some eugenicist views. Both as enslaved people and as free citizens, black women had been forced to undergo sterilizations and abortions. At the same time, black women bristled at some of the edicts coming from prominent black men, such as Imamu Amiri Baraka, who instructed black women to be submissive, feminine, and fertile; as Giddings puts it, if certain Black Power leaders had gotten their way, black women would have been "politically barefoot and literally pregnant." Black women needed their own institutions and manifestos that could speak to their position.

In 1970, the black writer Toni Cade (later Toni Cade Bambara) published an anthology titled *The Black Woman*. A collection of poems, stories, and essays by black women, the anthology both illustrated and articulated the roles black women could play in the liberation movements of the era. In "On the Issue of Roles," Cade argued that the usual "sexual differentiation in roles is an obstacle to political consciousness" and that the revolutionary individual must have "total self-autonomy." In her essay for the collection, Frances Beal articulated the unique and interlocking kind of oppression facing black women, calling it "double jeopardy." (Hers was a theory of intersectionality *avant la lettre*.) Walker contributed a short story, "The Diary of an African Nun," that critiqued religion and the oppression it encouraged. "If you really examine that book, you have to wonder why the black nationalists didn't drop an atomic bomb on Toni," reflected the poet Hattie Gossett, a friend of Bambara's. The book demonstrated that black women would no longer play secondary roles in revolutionary movements. They had served others for long enough. Their moment was now.

The anthology was the first in a series of revolutionary publications for black feminists. In the 1970s and 1980s, theorists such as Audre Lorde (who contributed to *The Black Woman*), bell hooks, and Barbara Smith emerged as leading voices in the black feminist movement. In 1974, Toni Morrison collaborated with editors and collectors on *The Black Book*, a collection of photographs, articles, sketches, and other forms of African American material culture. These decades also saw the publication of more radical anthologies, such as *All the Women Are White, All the Blacks Are Men, but Some of Us Are Brave* (1982), and the founding of the Kitchen Table: Women of Color Press, a publishing organization by and for women of color. In the early 1980s, the Kitchen Table would publish two significant anthologies: Cherríe Moraga and Gloria Anzaldúa's *Bridge Called My Back: Writings by Radical Women of Color;* and Barbara Smith's *Home Girls: A Black Feminist Anthology*. For many black women activists, print culture *was* politics: to write about the lives of black women, to represent these experiences, to create space for these stories, was itself a form of political work.

Walker exemplified this ethic as much as anyone. During her years at the Institute, she committed herself to advancing black feminist politics in three different ways. The first was her literary writing. In addition to a handful of short stories and poems, later collected in *In Love and Trouble* and *Revolutionary Petunias*, respectively, Walker used her time at the Institute to work on her novel. She wrote much of the novel—published as *Meridian* in 1976—during her second year at the Institute. *Meridian*, set within the civil rights movement, turns on a love triangle between a black woman, a white woman, and a white man. Meridian is a "black woman who cannot lie and for whom ideas are simply real and to be acted upon with her life." Like Walker, she commits herself to the civil rights movement, and—also like the author—she gets unexpectedly pregnant and struggles to balance her commitment to family with her commitment to the cause (she later voluntarily has her tubes tied). The novel ultimately sides with politics over motherhood and womanhood, though it warns that martyring oneself in the name of activism is a foolish and costly act. *Meridian* was well received; it merited a positive review from the novelist Marge Piercy, who, writing in *The New York Times*, called it a "fine, taut novel that accomplishes a remarkable amount." With this novel, Walker had gained a firmer foothold in the American literary scene, transforming it as she did so.

Walker's second venue of literary activism was her course at Wellesley College on black women writers—the first of its kind. Wellesley, like Radcliffe, was diversifying; it was no longer the staid, all-white school where Swan had done her undergraduate degree in the early 1940s. But, as Olsen could have pointed out, a more diverse student body didn't necessarily translate into a more diverse English department or course syllabus. Walker's course was thus significant in its insistence that literature by black women deserved the same attention as *Beowulf* or the Romantic poets. Her syllabus, a mixture of poetry and prose, featured the works of Phillis Wheatley, Gwendolyn Brooks, and Nella Larsen, as well as Walker's friends and contemporaries June Jordan and Toni Morrison. Like Howe and Olsen, Walker developed assignments that encouraged her students to write personally about their own lived experience with racism. Reading texts by women like them, about lives like their own, students felt that Walker had "unearthed a part of our history that we had been denied."

The comment is surprisingly apt, for Walker herself was, at that very moment, searching for another part of that hidden history—this would be her third form of activism. While at the Institute, she'd become interested in the African American novelist and anthropologist Zora Neale Hurston. A graduate of Howard and Barnard and a student of the acclaimed anthropologist Franz Boaz, Hurston had been a key figure in Harlem Renaissance circles, stunning men with her beauty and angering them with her refusal to conform to their literary and social expectations. She published seven books before her death at age sixty-nine; the two most prominent were *Mules and Men*, a collection of folktales published in 1935, and *Their Eyes Were Watching God*, a novel written swiftly during a research trip to Jamaica and published in 1937. Written in a black vernacular, *Their Eyes Were Watching God* tells the story of Janie Crawford, a black woman who comes into her own only after surviving two marriages, domestic abuse, a hurricane, and the gossip and vendettas of her friends and acquaintances. The novel is one long flashback, its formal innovations—linguistic and temporal—evidence of Hurston's modernist sensibilities, as well as her studies in ethnography. Though white critics generally admired the novel, it was controversial among black readers and critics because of how it represented the black community. By the time of her death in 1960, all of her books were out of print. With the help of donations, she was buried in an unmarked grave.

Walker didn't discover Hurston until she entered the Institute. Inspired by one of her mother's stories, Walker was at work on a piece of short fiction that incorporated vodou (the story would become "The Revenge of Hannah Kemhuff" and be published in 1973). In the process of researching for the story, she came upon a footnote, in a work by a white author, that pointed her in the direction of Hurston's anthropological work. "Zora, who had collected all the black folklore I could ever use," she wrote later about that discovery. "Having found *that Zora* . . . I was hooked." Hurston was an inspiration, a role model, and, to Walker, a criminally under-recognized writer. *Their Eyes Were Watching God* was a masterpiece; Walker later claimed that there was no book more important to her. Just as Olsen had been inspired by Rebecca Harding Davis and decided to recover *Life in the Iron Mills,* so too did Walker commit herself to resurrecting Zora Neale Hurston.

On August 15, 1973, just weeks after finishing her two-year term at the Institute, Walker took a flight from Boston to central Florida. From the air, the state looked flat and unchanging, the varieties of its terrain flattened by distance. The air on the ground was hot and humid, but Walker, born to sharecroppers in Georgia, was used to the summers of the American South. She picked up Charlotte Hunt, a white graduate student and her traveling companion, and the two women—scholars, detectives, adventurers—drove to Eatonville, Florida, Hurston's hometown (she was born in Alabama, but the family moved to the historically black town of Eatonville when Hurston was quite young). There, they queried city hall bureaucrats and old friends of Hurston's hoping to find information about how the writer had lived and where she might be buried. Throughout the trip, Walker pretended to be Hurston's illegitimate niece. This was a lie, of course, though an unthreatening one, but it also reflected Walker's understanding of artistic lineage, of how black women writers of the past enabled—indeed, gave birth to—those of the present.

Their search took them to Seventeenth Street, in Fort Pierce, Florida, where a cemetery called the Garden of Heavenly Rest can still be found. Walker—her skirt hitched to her waist, insects and sandspurs stinging her bare limbs—weaved her way through the overgrown weeds, clutching a hand-drawn map and looking for Hurston's unmarked grave. In one retelling, she claimed that some kind of ancestral spirit led her to a sunken spot of earth; in another, she credited Rosalee, a local woman, with helping her affirm the spot. Satisfied, Walker drove to a local tombstone maker, determined to mark Hurston's resting spot so future visitors could find it. The tombstone she wanted was too expensive, so she settled for a cheaper stone. She asked for the following words to be etched on it:

ZORA NEALE HURSTON
"A Genius of the South"
Novelist Folklorist
Anthropologist
1901–1960

Even though she got Hurston's birth year wrong (Hurston was born in 1891), Walker ensured that history would not forget Hurston. The tombstone still stands today.

During her second year at the Institute, while researching Hurston's life and teaching under-studied black writers like Wheatley, Walker began to think about what other black women writers might be missing from the literary canon. She thought of her own mother, who ran away at seventeen to marry and who raised eight children. If she had any creative impulse, any suppressed artistic spirit, it came through in the rhythm of her storytelling and in the way she arranged flowers. This is what she had passed on to her daughter Alice, who would be recognized as an artist in a way her mother never was.

That May, just weeks before the end of her fellowship at the Institute, Walker spoke at a Radcliffe symposium called "The Black Woman: Myths and Realities." She'd been invited by Doris Mitchell, a Radcliffe dean and the first black administrator hired at Harvard University. Though officially in charge of recruiting black students, Mitchell had many other responsibilities: mentoring black students, counseling them when they were in distress, acting as a role model and—along with the newly appointed director of financial aid, Sylvia Simmons, also a black woman—as an "all purpose dea ex machina." Black students were better represented now than they had been at the end of the 1960s—the class of 1976 had 45 black students out of 150 total—but black students still felt alienated at Harvard. They felt that their culture wasn't appreciated, nor were their intellectual proclivities and interests. There were complaints about loud soul music, for instance, but not about loud country or classical music. Black students wanted to live together and dine together, but white students resented this seeming "separatist" behavior. And then there was the problem of the university's majority-white faculty. In 1973, there were 13 black professors out of 760 total at the university—an increase from only 3 black professors in the spring of 1969. Working with white faculty members sometimes had negative consequences for black students: Mitchell told a reporter for *The Radcliffe Quarterly* a story about a faculty member writing a negative letter of recommendation for a black student who wanted to go to medical school. "Judging by white standards, perhaps she was less aggressive and self-confident," Mitchell explained. "But if the advisor had taken into consideration the kind of academic, social, economic, and emotional struggle this girl had to make to be here at all and to be graduated with a pre-med concentration, she would have realized that this girl was much more mature than most of the white students." Many black students described their Harvard experience of the early 1970s as "unreal."

"The Black Woman" would expose these black undergraduates to important, inspiring black women, who, in a series of conference talks, would help them reflect on their experiences and encourage them to pursue their dreams. Over the weekend of May 4 and 5, 1973, two hundred people crowded into Agassiz House, in Radcliffe Yard, where Fay House is, to hear fifty-two presenters undermine myths and present role models.

Walker was the keynote speaker. She began by quoting Jean Toomer's *Cane*, a lyrical, nearly uncategorizable book from 1923. Walker admired Toomer both for his language and for his love of the southern landscape; it was in his work that she would find her epitaph for Hurston, "a genius of the South." But she was also troubled by what seemed, to her, like his failure to reckon with black women's full humanity. In this epigraph, the speaker of *Cane* describes to a drowsy prostitute "her own nature and temperament" and instructs her on how to understand her emotions and fashion an inner life. The prostitute falls asleep while he's speaking, a sign both of his pomposity and of her disinterest in anything having to do with Art.

But Walker wanted to trouble the idea that women like this—black, southern, uneducated, sexualized—were not, in their own ways, artists. "For these grandmothers and mothers of ours were not Saints, but Artists," she insisted, "driven to a numb and bleeding madness by the springs of creativity in them for which there was no release. They were Creators, who lived lives of spiritual waste, because they were so rich in spirituality—which is the basis of Art—that the strain of enduring their unused and unwanted talent drove them insane." She cited their quilts, their spirituals, her mother's bouquets. She cited too the writing of black women such as Phillis Wheatley, who, for much of her life, in addition to lacking money and a room of her own had not even legal ownership of herself. "It is not so much what you sang," she said, addressing Wheatley directly, "as that you kept alive, in so many of our ancestors, *the notion of song*." Walker was creating a literary tradition, a genealogy of authorship and influence, where none had been before.

Near the end of her talk, Walker returned to Woolf's *Room of One's Own*, the urtext for feminist critics. She wondered how the genius that Woolf imagined had existed among working-class women must, too, have existed among enslaved people and among the wives and daughters of sharecroppers. Walker's point was that black women's historical oppression both resembled and was fundamentally different from the oppression suffered by the poor at the hands of the wealthy. Black women didn't simply lack resources: they lacked autonomy, the recognition of their humanity. Their struggle was the worker's struggle, and the woman's struggle, but it was also something else.

Walker's talk, first delivered to a couple hundred people—mostly women, mostly black—soon reached a wider audience. It was published in the relatively new *Ms.* magazine, founded by Gloria Steinem and Dorothy Pitman Hughes, in 1974, under the title "In Search of Our Mothers' Gardens: The Creativity of Black Women in the South."

(Walker would begin at *Ms.* as a contributing editor in December 1974.) It then served as the title essay for her first collection of non-fiction, published in 1983. In some important ways, then, "In Search of Our Mothers' Gardens" resembled Olsen's "Silences": it was the work that best articulated her relationship to the literary canon and, crucially, sought to remake that canon so she and her literary predecessors could be included in it. Walker and Olsen sought to recuperate the voices of the silenced as well as explain their silencing. Both essays were influential and shaped reading and teaching practices in the years to come.

Walker and Olsen met in 1974, when Walker happened to be visiting San Francisco and Olsen invited her to a party. The two writers hit it off. Their views on literature and life were similar: both prized equality and justice; both fused activism and art. Walker's "womanism"—her term for a black woman–centered feminism that emphasized capability and strength—resembled, in some ways, Olsen's communist humanism. (Walker once said that "womanist is to feminist as purple to lavender.") The two struck up a correspondence: as she did with most correspondents, Olsen alternated between sending sweet gifts and sharing alarming anecdotes about a "sort of breakdown" and other kinds of distress. Walker responded soothingly, demonstrating a patience with Olsen's ups and downs that not everyone possessed. "I cherish the ins and outs of our friendship," she once wrote. "It is *such* a *living* thing. It is *just like* life."

In addition to the letters they sent and the inspiration they offered each other, the two writers participated in a publishing project that would bring back lost literature by women. In 1972, the Feminist Press—founded in 1970 and managed by Florence Howe and Paul Lauter, fans of Olsen's since her Amherst days—republished Davis's *Life in the Iron Mills*, with a long "biographical interpretation" by Olsen. The book was the press's second published title; *The New York Times* urged readers to "read this book and let your heart be broken."

The press would go on to publish many more such important books—Agnes Smedley's *Daughter of Earth*, Charlotte Perkins Gilman's *Yellow Wallpaper*—including a collection edited by Walker. *I Love Myself When I Am Laughing . . . and Then Again When I Am Looking Mean and Impressive*, a collection of Zora Neale Hurston's writings, was published in 1979. Walker had fought tirelessly to insert Hurston into literary history. Finally, in collaboration with other politically conscious women, she had succeeded.

CHAPTER 18

The New Exotics

B ELATED LITERARY RECOGNITION was not uncommon in the 1970s. Dead women were earning long-overdue accolades. Rebecca Harding Davis. Zora Neale Hurston. Charlotte Perkins Gilman. There was even a second posthumous volume of Sylvia Plath's poetry, called *Winter Trees*, published in 1971. Thanks to the agitation of feminists, both inside and outside the academy, women's writing was newly popular. This proved to be a boon for female writers, young and old, who sought either initial recognition or long-awaited success. "Women have become the new exotics lately," Kumin said to a group of college students in 1973. "They have it lots easier now because the white middle-class male has started feeling guilty for the way women have been treated. Women are in a position of enormous potential when it comes to the arts."

On May 7, 1973—ten years after she and Sexton sat side by side in a sun-filled seminar room, reading to their fellow Institute scholars—Kumin received a belated prize for her poetry: the Pulitzer, awarded to her fourth poetry collection, *Up Country*, published in 1972. Sexton was on the Pulitzer Prize committee in 1973, and she

Portrait of Maxine Kumin by Barbara Swan,
sometime after the Institute

argued vehemently for *Up Country,* persuading her fellow judges, William Alfred and Louis Simpson, to award Kumin the prestigious, life-changing prize. Six years before, Kumin had rushed over to Sexton's house in Weston to celebrate her friend's winning the prize. Now, at forty-eight, Kumin herself was the winner. "I'm just absolutely knocked out," she told a reporter, just after she'd heard the good news. "I just can't believe it."

Her life changed. "Suddenly I was in business," she later wrote, "the poetry business." At the time she won the prize, Kumin was on leave from her job as a lecturer at nearby Newton College of the Sacred Heart. Since finishing at the Institute, she'd gone back to teaching: she'd taught at Tufts, as well as at the University of Massachusetts at Amherst. She was still writing prolifically, but she didn't get reviewed as widely as some other poets. Now, anointed a Pulitzer Prize–winning poet, she was wanted everywhere. She was invited to speak at Stephens College in Missouri, at the University of

Texas at Austin, at Trinity College in Hartford, Connecticut. She was asked to teach a seminar at Columbia University—a big step up from Sacred Heart—and so she commuted every Tuesday from Newton to New York City. She was profiled in magazines, quoted in roundups ("Women of Letters," "Poets and Wine"), and interviewed at length. She stopped enterprising reporters from photographing her domestic space, with its stacks of old *New Yorker* magazines in the corners and sketches by Swan on the walls. "I really dislike all the fuss that comes with being 'the poet,'" she explained.

Unlike Sexton, Kumin had never sought fame—opportunity and respect, yes, but never the media spotlight. She had not set out to become a "lasting poet," as Sexton had put it in her Institute application. She had been relatively happy with her life before the Pulitzer and would have been content to continue living and working in that way for another twenty or thirty years. But she soon learned that was impossible: she now belonged to the world of professional poets— Kumin jokingly referred to the industry as "PoBiz"—and would make her living through residencies and readings and lectures, all paid handsomely. She could be pickier about her teaching appointments and spend more time on the farm. She rechristened the place "PoBiz Farm" and posted a sign with this new name on the dirt road that led to the homestead. It was an ironic homage to the glamorous work that allowed Kumin to retreat from the literary world—leaving Sexton behind her.

"Winning the Pulitzer Prize for my fourth book was wonderful, but it filled me with anxiety," Kumin reflected later.

Being in the limelight terrified me. It was well known that fame often led to writer's block. At that moment I dreaded the paralysis I was certain awaited me. Would I ever write again? As soon as I could, I fled to the farm. There I took Candide's advice to cultivate my garden and started the season's first crop of frost-hardy chard, lettuce, and spinach. I dug compost into the soil, raked, gathered bucketsful of stones, raked again. Once I had dirt packed under my fingernails I recovered my equilibrium.

The experiences Kumin describes here in prose—tuning herself to the rhythms of the seasons, immersing herself in the natural world— are the same as those she renders in verse in *Up Country*. The book, published by Harper & Row, included illustrations by Swan, who sketched, quite realistically, the sights common to the woods of New Hampshire: pine trees, paw tracks, long-beaked birds. A few early poems made their way in: "Morning Swim," one of the poems she had read at her first Institute seminar, and "A Hundred Nights," a poem about her father from her very first collection, *Halfway*. But much of the writing was new, inspired jointly by Kumin's country life and by Henry David Thoreau, whose *Walden* haunts the collection and provides epigraphs for a poem or two. Like Thoreau, Kumin believed that much could be learned about oneself, and one's human companions, through close, uninterrupted study of the natural world.

The collection's greatest strength is its surprising images, a testament to Kumin's powers of observation. In one poem, a group of stones is compared to oysters, mushrooms, and a herd of mammals; they are "as cumbrous as bears." In another, a mare's belly is a "church of folded hands." In yet another, owl talk is "burned babies screaming," a truly horrifying metaphor that somehow fits the mood of the final poem. Not every description works—a comparison between a horse's neck and Victorian furniture is as ungainly as it sounds—but on the whole the natural world is sensitively, surprisingly rendered, in all its beauty and cruelty. Like many a writer, Kumin wanted to defamiliarize her subject, making it seem alien, even shocking, through metaphor and simile. She was particularly invested in portraying the unlovely parts of rural life: the decay and violence of the natural world were her way into the ugliness of human existence. "When people hear about nature poems, they immediately think of God and butterflies," she once said. "But not all is pretty in nature and I am not deceived. The loveliness does not vitiate a raccoon killing a gander, abscesses on a horse's mouth, worms in the excrement."

Divided into four parts, *Up Country* begins with a suite of hermit poems—"The Hermit Wakes to Bird Sounds," "The Hermit Prays," "The Hermit Has a Visitor"—then segues into a series of lyric poems about various features of farm and country life. There is a poem about mud, another about beans, and an exquisite elegy for a dead broodmare. The collection concludes with "Joppa Diary," a series of poems with dates for titles ("June 5th," "August 9th"). The Kumins' farm was located in the Joppa district of Warner, New Hampshire, and the diary is clearly a record of the poet's activities there, but the last poem also alludes to the biblical Joppa, a city in Israel. The allusion is one of several ways that Kumin elevated her worldly experiences— picking berries, birthing foals, shooting woodchucks—to an emotional or spiritual register.

The human soul creeps in at the corners of these poems, even poems in which the focus is fixed on plant or animal life. "Beans," an homage to Thoreau, is a poem about sexual desire: in the last stanza, the speaker stirs like "the shoots / of growing things" at the touch of a lover, a "gardener" like the assiduous Thoreau, who planted a "seven-mile plot" of beans. "Woodchucks" ends with a shock: the speaker, who picks off troublesome critters with a .22 rifle, wishes that the vermin had "all consented to die unseen / gassed underground the quiet Nazi way." Even with this overt reference to World War II, it's hard not to read the violence of the poem in the context of the war in Vietnam, where napalm was deployed frequently and deaths were far from quiet or unseen. The end of "Whippoorwill" is likewise tragic; the speaker, listening to this "indecent bird," realizes that she too is a "discard / and you," an old lover, "you stick in his throat." The poems are subtle, probing at the experiences of love and loss and renewal only indirectly. As one critic put it, the collection "is a concentrate of controlled passion, compassion, and precise diction, seeking no profundities by grasp, but achieving them by indirection, luring the reader into them, happily so." Profundity by indirection:

a pretty good gloss for a reserved, middle-aged poet who, unlike her closest friend, preferred to stay out of the limelight.

The poetry was too good for the critics to keep quiet. The novelist Joyce Carol Oates praised the book in *The New York Times*, alongside Plath's *Winter Trees*, which had been published in 1971. (For the first time, Kumin and Plath were being read together, not Sexton and Plath.) Praising Kumin for her boldness, her variety of viewpoints, and her authenticity, Oates argued that Kumin, though inspired by Thoreau, had done the transcendentalist one better; her work had a "sharp-edged, unflinching and occasionally nightmarish subjectivity exasperatingly absent in Thoreau." She also compared Kumin to Sexton, suggesting commonality where most critics saw difference; both poets, she argued, dramatized the voice of the "universal woman," though they did so in different ways. The comparison preserved the distinctiveness of each poet, but it also equated the two women in a way few critics had done before. Oates concluded, "'Up Country' demonstrates beautifully how the transcendental vision is really the vision of imaginative existential life, available to anyone who seeks it." Kumin, touched by the review, wrote Oates a brief note, expressing "how good it feels to be so closely read."

One imagines that Kumin hung onto that good feeling even in the midst of the Pulitzer furor. For a woman who was so often tending and attending, it must have been a nice change to receive close, critical attention, even if—or perhaps because—that attention changed her life.

By 1972, the year *Up Country* was published, Kumin was spending more and more time at the farm and was contemplating a permanent move. She took her family up in all seasons: in the winter they skied cross-country, and in the summer they swam and rode horses through the pine woods. The Kumins had also accrued quite the collection of farm animals, all of which needed tending: there were Gertrude Stein and Alice B. Toklas, the sheep; a Dalmatian named Caesar; two horses, named Juniper and Tasha; and an arrogant goat named Oliver. Kumin loved the quiet and beauty the farm offered her. In New Hampshire, she found respite from the neuroticism common to writers and intellectuals (herself included) and an easy way of socializing that was entirely different from the "polished silver candlesticks, the ironed tablecloths, the fancy desserts" of Newton. When a neighbor casually offered to host the Kumins for dinner without any of the formality and fanfare that characterized dinner parties in the Boston suburbs, Kumin was light-headed with relief. She marveled at "how seamlessly and graciously Liz's invitation had been extended." This was the way she wanted to live: casually, naturally, without the social protocol that her mother had tried so hard to teach her.

Had Vic not had a job, and had she not also been teaching, Kumin would have moved the family right then. But their lives remained anchored in Newton, and Kumin remained near to Sexton, who, after a period of stability from 1971 to 1972, was once again battling her demons. Her marriage to Kayo was fraying. She drank too much and took too many pills, and she had yet to find a therapist who stabilized her as Dr. Orne had. She began to lean too much on teenage Linda, demanding to be parented as if she were the child. Worst of all, her creative powers seem to have atrophied: while she was still an excellent performer of her earlier poetry, Sexton couldn't generate new work that rivaled the old. Poetry had kept her sane: as she suggested in the poem "With Mercy for the Greedy," poetry was her substitute for religious faith. Without poetry to wrangle the tongue and soothe the mind, death began to look appealing once again. The old death wish had returned. Sexton was starting to ask the old question that she had asked in "Wanting to Die": *"which tools."*

On some level, Kumin knew that she couldn't move up-country as long as Sexton still needed her. Sexton didn't care much for the outdoors. She visited Kumin's farm infrequently, timing her visits so that they corresponded to her daugthers' stays at a nearby overnight camp. There's one photograph from a summer weekend, showing Sexton on one of Kumin's horses. She looks far less comfortable in this one than in the many photos taken of her at her desk, in her indoor sanctuary.

Back in Newton, Kumin was in constant contact with her mercurial friend; she was likely to be the first to notice a sudden shift in mood or an allusion to self-harm. It was as if Kumin had signed a contract way back in 1957: she would be there for Sexton as long as Sexton needed her, and Sexton needed her still. "Anne was really our mother's favorite child," Jane, Kumin's eldest, once quipped. Kumin worried that if she were to leave Sexton for too long, she would miss the last moment of crisis—the ringing phone unanswered, the harried knock on the door unheard—and it would be too late. "It was a terrible responsibility," she later reflected. "And I felt the awesomeness of that responsibility, but I had taken it on."

Up Country closes with a poem about this terrible responsibility—about the impossibility of knowing, let alone controlling, another's mind. It is an old poem, from 1963; Kumin had written it on the occasion of Sexton's sailing to France and sent her a draft, calling it a poem "for my friend on the high seas." It is the poem with the affirmation "We have our own constants," the one that mentions the onionskins of the old poetry classroom. Sexton had liked the poem, then called "September 1"; "all good" she had written in the margins. She had particularly liked the lines in which Kumin described "the humpbacks of these / mink hills between us," referring to the hills near the Kumin farm in New Hampshire.

The published version, "September 22nd," is a revised version of this valediction from 1963. It reads as if written for a lover: "darling" has replaced "dear friend" as a term of address, and the poem is now for some mysterious "Q. on the high seas." The speaker is still "in the country of the no-see-ums," still listening to the owl talk and imagining the sights and sounds of a ship at sea. "Darling what are your noises?" she asks. "Do you dance, play shuffleboard / bet on the ship's pool?" The speaker wonders if her friend has selected a lifeboat—an appropriate worry for Kumin in 1963, when Sexton wondered openly if she would return from Europe alive. Looked at ten years later, the question seems idle, a bit detached; the speaker worries about her

friend's (or lover's) fate from such a great distance. She is too far away
to steer anyone into a lifeboat herself.

By the end of the poem, the speaker is exasperated: with her
addressee, and with herself. "I am tired of this history of loss!" she
declares.

> What drum can I beat to reach you?
> To be reasonable
> is to put out the light.
> To be reasonable is to let go.
> The eye of the moon is as bland
> as new butter. There is no other light
> to wink at or salute
> Now let the loudest sound I send you
> be the fuzzheads of ripe butternuts
> dropping tonight in Joppa like
> the yellow oval tears of some rare dinosaur,
> dropping to build up
> the late September ground.

Read as a lover's lamentation, these lines are bittersweet. The
speaker knows it is only "reasonable" to go to sleep, to accept the
distance between her and her desired, but she can't help reporting
the sounds around her—as if her absent lover, attuned to her drum-
beat, could hear. But when we consider this was first a poem for Sexton, the lines read differently. "What drum can I beat to reach you?"
is both mournful and self-incriminating, as if the speaker has tried
many ways to comfort her friend but not yet landed on the right
strategy. The repetition of "reasonable" calls to mind all of Sexton's
unreasonableness. It also charts a possible course for Kumin, one
that she continually turned away from. "To be reasonable is to let
go" of Sexton, whom Kumin once called a "very demanding friend,"
and to bask in the soft sounds of the Joppa district. But Kumin, like
her speaker, refused to be reasonable—or refused in at least this
one way.

When Sexton first read the poem in draft form, she had suggested reversing the last two stanzas—although based on her marginalia, it seems rather as if she were suggesting a rearrangement of lines. She said something in the margins about wanting the poem to end on the loss, on the sound of loss, rather than "the wet September ground," as it did in the first draft. Kumin stuck with her original arrangement, though the ground became that of "late September," no longer "wet." She ended not with tiredness, or loss, but with an effort at connection: a sound sent across the sea, from up-country on down to Boston, where, for the moment, Sexton lived still.

CHAPTER 19

Which Way Is Home

O N OCTOBER 11, 1973, former members of the Institute for Independent Study returned to the Radcliffe Quadrangle. It was half past twelve on a bright fall day, the grass still green, the leaves just starting to turn. Some of the women present lived just a few blocks from the Quadrangle; others had to come by train or plane or car. For a few, it was their first time back at Radcliffe in a decade.

The women of the Institute were gathered together to celebrate the life of their beloved director, Connie Smith, who had died of cancer in November 1970. She was only forty-eight. The loss shook her friends and colleagues, who had cared deeply for her. There had been a service at Memorial Church in Harvard Yard, where Kumin had delivered a eulogy. Decades after her death, former Institute fellows recalled her warmth and her extraordinary ability to get things done. They insisted that anyone interested in the Institute—how it was, why it worked—attend to the life of dear Connie.

Pineda, as generous with her work as she was with her money, wanted to honor Smith's life by dedicating one of her *Oracle* sculptures to her former director. (Her fellow visual artist Swan had also donated some work to the Institute in 1967: two lithographs and one drawing.) She wanted the work to live in Radcliffe Yard, near Fay House, where Smith had made her first selections for admission to the Institute. The current Institute director, Alice Kimball Smith, rejoiced in the offer from Pineda, but she noted that the organization could not afford to purchase such a large sculpture from such a successful artist, nor could it pay for the installation. Pineda's mother came to the rescue, as she had many times before: she offered to cover the costs of the sculpture.

The day of the dedication arrived. Pineda had chosen *Aspects of the Oracle: Portentous,* an elegant, seated figure with her left hand raised in the air. The statue was placed in a corner of Radcliffe Yard, between the Schlesinger Library (so named in 1965) and a small gate that opened onto Brattle Street. Those attending the dedication ringed themselves round the statue. A photo of the event captures at least two dozen of them, their backs toward the camera, their bodies turned toward the oracle. Light descends from above, bathing the statue and those surrounding it. The dedication ceremony included a flute performance by a young-looking, curly-haired woman in a patterned dress; her presence next to the statue showed off the size of the sculpture. It was a substantial memorial.

There is a photo of Pineda from the dedication ceremony. In it her hair is short, shorter than it was when she was at the Institute, and she is wearing a shirt with a big collar and smiling broadly. The light falls on her face as she turns toward the gesticulating flute player. She seems extraordinarily happy.

Pineda went on to make more sculptures. Her most important achievement was arguably her statute of Queen Lili'uokalani—a commissioned work completed in 1980—that is installed on the south side of the Hawai'i State Capitol. Pineda was especially proud of this work, and she produced a documentary, *Search for the Queen,* about the research and making of the artwork. She and Tovish found studio space—separate studios, of course—in Cambridge's Porter Square. They continued to work there until the end of their careers.

She died, like Smith, of cancer, in 1996. She was seventy-one. Her husband was devastated. In a letter he wrote to her after her death, he reflected on their shared craft: "I tremble to think what it would be like for me if I had no work to do. In the studio, mixing plaster, repairing casts—all the kitchen chores of our trade allows me, for a moment, to let you escape from my mind. But you return soon enough, and you are always welcome." Tovish lived until 2008.

The sculpture that Pineda dedicated to Smith still stands in Radcliffe Yard today. The oracle sits on a small, elevated bench; her feet dangle over a small rock garden. She stabilizes herself with one arm, one hand grasping the corner of the bench, while the other arm arches over her bowed head, as if to pluck something from the air. Her face is nearly featureless, but she is nonetheless recognizably female: her breasts swell under the cloth that drapes her body. She has weathered rain and snow; her surface, oxidized from exposure, is now a green color that blends with the surrounding shrubs. Her pose is at once contemplative and full of tension as her torso twists and her arm strains skyward. She is poised, waiting, preparing for whatever comes next.

One March day in 1974, Kumin's phone rang. It was around five in the evening, not quite dark in not-quite-spring New England. There was an emergency on Black Oak Road. Sexton was sitting in her kitchen, she told Kumin, with a glass of milk and a pile of pills. She was taking the pills one by one until they and she were both gone.

Kumin rushed over to Weston, put Sexton in her car, and drove them both straight to the hospital; this was Sexton's fourth hospitalization in the past twelve months. Rather than feeling relieved, Sexton was furious at being thwarted. "You won't get another chance to save me," she told a friend. Kumin, upon learning of Sexton's threat, responded, "Well, Annie, if you're going to telegraph your intentions, you don't give me any choice: I have to rescue you." Even in her frantic state, Sexton absorbed the message: if she truly wanted to kill herself, she would have to dissemble and conceal. She would have to act like a healthy and resilient person. In other words, she would have to adopt a persona.

Sexton had always been a good performer. In fact, the same month she attempted suicide, she sold out a reading in Harvard's Sanders Theatre, which seats one thousand people. Clad in a black-and-white skirt with a knee-high slit, Sexton read from what she liked to call her "posthumous work": the just-published collection *The Death Notebooks* and poems that would later be published in *The Awful Rowing Toward God*. (The latter would indeed be published posthumously.) Swan, who designed the cover for *The Death Notebooks*, loved "the SPIRIT" of the collection, as she put it in a letter. "I felt you deal with the UNDERBELLY of our lives. You aren't afraid to describe the areas we never mention, our SHIT, our garbage," she wrote to Sexton. That evening at Sanders, Sexton read these new poems and some old ones, including "Music Swims Back to Me," the very first poem she had shown Kumin on that winter afternoon sixteen years earlier. When she was done, she received a standing ovation.

Offstage, though, Sexton was flailing. Kumin, so steadfast and reliable, began to feel overwhelmed. As she wrote to a concerned friend of Sexton's, "I have been through a lot with her in 17 years but nothing so terrible and distraught as this time."

Sexton, 1974

Sexton's descent had started in 1973, when she and Kayo divorced. The marriage had been charged and violent for decades: Sexton knew how to goad Kayo until he exploded in rage. He hit her on more than one occasion. Linda Gray Sexton's memoir contains a frightening scene in which Kayo bangs Sexton's head against the wall. But in the memoir, both parties are described as being active participants in orchestrating the violence. To complicate matters further, Kayo was also Sexton's primary caretaker: the person who made her dinner and made sure she took the correct number of sleeping pills, which she had relied on for years to sleep. In her marriage, Sexton acted like a needy child; she did so both to prevent Kayo's rages (she worried that he would become angry if she expressed her true feelings) and to get the care she needed. "We get along pretty well . . . with my talking baby talk," Sexton once explained to Kumin. "Can't really talk, damn it. Try. But can't." The marriage was premised on Sexton's infantile weakness and Kayo's competence, patience, and endurance. Only with her lovers did Sexton feel that she could be a full adult.

Kayo and Sexton engaged in this dance of codependency until, in February 1973, Sexton decided that she wanted a divorce. Her work was going well; she was teaching at Boston University, writing poems, and earning enough from her readings to support her and her children. She felt flush and independent, ready to take on life as a single woman. And she wasn't alone: inspired by the women's movement and the ways it punctured the dream of the perfect nuclear family, women all over the country were walking out of their marriages and into new, exhilarating, terrifying lives. No-fault divorce, first instituted in California in 1969, made it easier to dissolve a marriage without ruining the reputation of one of the parties. Other states picked up the practice. (Massachusetts adopted no-fault divorce in 1976.) The divorce rate rose rapidly, doubling between 1962 (the year Sexton's *All My Pretty Ones* was published) and 1973. In the year 1975, the number of divorces exceeded one million for the first time in U.S. history.

When she and Kayo first separated, Sexton hopped from one friend's house to another's, staying with Kumin during the early days of the separation. But Sexton couldn't live a vagabond life forever; by

March, she was back on Black Oak Road in Weston, alone in a grand house with no pool. (Kayo had found a separate apartment, while Linda was at college and Joy at boarding school in Maine.) Sexton found a couple to live with her; they helped with yard duties and cooking. To her friends and neighbors, Sexton seemed strong and independent, as if she were setting out on a fresh start.

But her good spirits eventually disappeared. By summer, Sexton was sleeping until ten, drinking three or four vodkas with lunch, napping away the afternoon, and drinking again at dinner, with up to eight sleeping pills to follow. "It is a Christly time for me in the midst of a contested divorce with no one to marry," she wrote in early September to the poet Adrienne Rich, who had left her husband in 1970. (He killed himself soon after their separation.) Sexton had not been alone since age nineteen.

The divorce became final in November, just in time for Sexton to regret the very process she had set in motion. Once again, she had overestimated her inner resources. She had made a similar error a decade earlier, when she had thought herself strong enough to forgo therapy and travel overseas. This time, however, she couldn't simply return home, for such a place no longer existed. Like the lyric speaker in "Music Swims Back to Me," Sexton found herself asking, "Which way is home?"

As she struggled to set up a new life for herself, Sexton began having bad dreams and hearing voices. She self-medicated with alcohol and pills and disappeared into fugue states like the ones she'd first experienced with Dr. Orne in the late 1950s. Sexton's friends had trouble with her when she was drunk and needy, and they began to distance themselves.

Linda, now a junior at Harvard, struggled to carve out a separate identity without abandoning her mother completely. "As the situation grew more and more intense, I grew angrier and angrier with Mother," she wrote in her memoir. "I'd been able to move into an apartment"—in Inman Square, for the summer months—"to escape her antics, but Joy was still in high school." Joy—home for the summer, warier of her mother, and less entwined with her than Linda was—eventually moved out in the middle of the summer and went to stay with Kayo. In July, just before her twenty-first birthday, Linda went over to her mother's house for dinner and received a strange birthday present: a check for $1,000 and a copy of Sexton's will, which named her Sexton's literary executor.

Sexton might have been able to cope with Kayo's absence had she been able to keep her best friend by her side. But 1973 was also the year Kumin won the Pulitzer and began traveling to workshops and residencies. The two friends still talked every day, and neither ever published a poem without first consulting the other, but they talked more by phone than they did in person, and their conversations could be strained. "I had a little fame to deal with in my own life," Kumin later explained. "I had won the Pulitzer; I was doing a lot more readings; I was in a lot more demand; I was traveling a lot more, and I was not just physically as available to her as I had been. And I think although she certainly did not take it as a betrayal on my part, she certainly felt some small alienation."

Kumin harbored her own feelings of betrayal. She bristled at being asked to play nurse. As she had hinted to Sexton years earlier, she didn't want their friendship to slide into "common waspishness" as Katherine Mansfield and Ida Baker's had. But as Sexton deteriorated, Kumin was more and more often thrust into the role of caretaker, just as her own career was taking off. Kumin never felt manipulated by Sexton—the latter's distress was surely genuine—nor did she ever threaten to break with her friend entirely. But neither did she always alter her plans to accommodate her friend. She accepted a weeks-long residency in Danville, Kentucky. (She and Sexton agreed in advance to split the phone bill.) She went up-country nearly every weekend. In 1974, she planned a three-week trip that would take her overseas—to Europe, Israel, and Iran—during Sexton's birthday, a time when Sexton historically had needed care. Kumin was beginning to feel acutely the "dichotomy between the city life and the country life." The only thing now keeping her in Newton, she eventually realized, was Sexton.

Kumin and Sexton experienced different kinds of career arcs:

the one started off unknown and ascended to fame, while the other burst onto the scene and won attention and accolades and then, like a falling star, descended into darkness. And yet, though they followed opposing trajectories, they remained deeply invested in each other's work. For it wasn't as though Kumin had nothing to do with Sexton's incendiary arrival on the poetry scene: it was Kumin who had approved Sexton's first real poem, Kumin who had accompanied Sexton to those early readings by esteemed poets, where the budding poet learned the tricks of the trade.

Likewise, Sexton had continued to support Kumin and vouch for her friend's work. "She made me see that the cerebral really needed a strong admixture of the visceral," Kumin once said of her friend. As Kumin began to write more, and better, Sexton feared that her friend would surpass her and leave her far behind. She once dreamed of visiting Kumin at the Bread Loaf School of English at Middlebury, where both poets taught at various points in their careers. In the dream, Kumin left Sexton to go to a lecture, though Sexton pleaded with her to stay. "Please," she said in the dream, "I've come all this way to see you." But Kumin kept walking, leaving behind her tremulous friend.

Any fear or jealousy never affected Sexton's judgment of her friend's work. When she had the opportunity to award Kumin the Pulitzer, she fought hard to do so. It was an act of self-sacrifice, for Sexton knew that if Kumin won the prize, "I was going to lose her."

Sexton never entirely lost Kumin, but their hidden jealousies and resentments and fears—long buried under the surface of love and mutual regard—eventually surfaced in April 1974. The two poets were giving a reading at Douglass College, barely a month after Sexton's suicide attempt, and though the poet no longer seemed suicidal, she was not her best self. They agreed to give an interview to the scholars Elaine Showalter and Carol Smith, and though the conversation began well, Sexton soon took over and began rambling, as if she were on the couch in an analyst's office. Sexton began talking about her troubled relationship with her mother and her grandmother, hinting at inappropriate contact. "I think I'm dominating this interview," she acknowledged. Kumin replied in annoyance, "You are, Anne." Sexton confessed, "I've been having an upsetting time." Kumin usually tolerated Sexton's self-involvement, but this time she lost her temper. After the interview was over, she upbraided Sexton for being selfish and needy—both during the interview and over the past few months. Those words—"selfish," "needy"—stuck with Sexton. For ten days, she turned them over in her mind, wondering what exactly she had done wrong, fearing that she was in fact the succubus that Kumin had implied. Back in Weston, the reading and the shameful interview behind her, Sexton sat down with her typewriter and attempted to explain herself to her friend.

The letter began like a memo: "Subject: Selfish; needy." She acknowledged that everyone was selfish, and that she was no exception, but she suggested that Kumin's irritation at this quality was a recent development. At first, she'd thought that the divorce might have changed her relationship to Kumin, but in the letter she speculated that it was perhaps Kumin's Pulitzer Prize that had changed the relations between the two friends. Sexton reminded Kumin of all the ways she had helped her and tried to be sensitive to her needs; each example was followed by a parenthetical question—"(Selfish?)"—as if to prompt Kumin to reexamine her ideas. "Yes, I am needy," Sexton acknowledged. "But you too, Max, have been needy, and I have never resented it." Sexton had talked Kumin to sleep after a disk operation. She had listened to Kumin complain about analysis. She had understood when Kumin, rushing to get up-country, had forgotten to call Sexton back to talk about a promising poem. Now, she confessed how upset she'd been at their separation, even though she understood how the New Hampshire farm fed Kumin's creative spirit. "I suppose in a way this left me *more* needy for your presence, but at least I understood," she concluded. "Could you perhaps try to understand me . . . ?"

In truth, Kumin did understand Sexton, better than anyone else. She recognized her friend's talent, calling her a true "original," the likes of which would not be seen again soon. She also understood that in her own way the demanding Sexton was a thoughtful, giving person. "Annie gave as good as she got," Kumin once said. "She was extremely generous and giving, loving." Sexton loved easily (arguably too easily) and volubly. Her letters were covered with hand-drawn flowers and filled with expressions of affection. She answered fan mail from adolescents and the institutionalized. She gave poetry lessons to Kumin's daughter (Kumin did the same for Linda); she let her own daughter host large groups of friends at the Weston house.

These acts of generosity weren't exactly selfless: Sexton needed contact with people constantly. Like a hummingbird buzzing from flower to flower, she went from person to person sucking up affection and care until she could see that her current host—or student, or friend—was worn out. In her own way, Sexton was deeply sensitive to the needs and limitations of others, and though this awareness didn't always stop her from demanding more than people could offer (she certainly asked too much of her children), it did provide a check on some of her behavior. This was why, after her separation from Kayo, she left the Kumin home after only five days; she could tell "how upsetting my presence was" to Kumin and her husband. "Thus I did not stay again," she later explained, "not wanting to cause pain to you and yours."

Such was Sexton's bind: to suffer great pain without causing it in others, to ask for the help she needed without asking too much of anyone. By 1974, as her loneliness and drinking increased in tandem, she could no longer navigate these competing claims. The only way to keep herself together without wearing out friends and family was to return to the mental institution, to the bedlam of her first poetry book—the place that her art had helped her escape. Sexton, who wrote about "the quality of life in mental hospitals" when "mental illness was still a prissy epithet," knew all too well what an institutional life would be like. It would be "antiseptic tunnel[s]" and "the moving dead," handmade moccasins—a common crafting activity in mental hospitals—and dinners without knives. Noon walks on institutional lawns, ringing bells, a "world . . . full of enemies" and "no safe place." Sexton would not be able to abide it, not again.

On Friday, October 4, 1974, Sexton drove from her therapy appointment to Kumin's house in Newton. As they had done for decades, the two poets ate lunch and discussed work in progress. Sexton had a quadruple vodka and a tuna fish sandwich. At 1:30 p.m., they parted ways; Kumin had to pick up a passport for her three-week trip. Sexton reassured her friend, "Don't worry. I'm not a Berryman yet," referring to the poet who had died by suicide in 1972. Kumin was not particularly worried; ever since the March suicide attempt, Sexton had appeared "*healed*—at least cured for the moment of her terrible obsession," as Kumin later put it in a letter. Sexton reminded Kumin to return a borrowed dress, then drove home, where she dug her mother's fur coat out of a closet. Wrapped in the coat, with a glass of vodka in hand, she proceeded to the garage and climbed into her car. Alone, in the closed garage in Weston, she started the car's engine.

To the horror of her friends and family, Sexton's death was an event. The Associated Press published a long article. Memorials were held in classrooms around the country. The nation's poets, both those who knew Sexton and those who didn't, offered their remarks. The poet and critic J. D. McClatchy scrambled to transform his critical work on Sexton into a set of posthumous remembrances.

Poets felt that they had to respond. Denise Levertov vehemently denied any connection between poetry and suicide. "The tendency to confuse the two has claimed too many victims," she mourned. "Anne Sexton herself seems to have suffered deeply from this confusion." Lowell, now divorced from Hardwick and remarried to Caroline Blackwood, offered strange commentary, calling Sexton an "amateur" and lamenting her downward trajectory. "For a book or two, she grew more powerful," he mused. "Then writing was too easy or too hard for her. She became meager and exaggerated. Many of her most embarrassing poems would have been fascinating if someone had put them in quotes, as the presentation of some character, not the author."

One poet who remained strangely reticent about Sexton's legacy was Kumin. After offering some quick remarks to the Associated Press, Kumin clammed up. She was put off by what she called the "necrophiliac cult" that wanted to know the details of Sexton's death. After granting an interview to the Associated Press in the immediate aftermath of Sexton's suicide, Kumin decided to refuse all future requests. For her, Sexton's death was "the open wound I must live with day by day," as she wrote to a friend. Along with Vic, Kumin left the country for three weeks. She toured the sites by day and dreamed of Sexton by night. "I carried Anne's death in my pocket," she wrote to Swan.

Everyone knew the role Kumin had played in Sexton's life. In the months after her death, Kumin was bombarded with messages: from Sexton's fans, friends, and ex-lovers, as well as from her own friends and acquaintances. Kumin dutifully tried to respond to those she felt deserved responses, though she struggled to be compassionate in this moment, and she resented the infringement on her own grieving process. She was particularly annoyed by Olsen's strange, grief-stricken note that, among other things, remonstrated Kumin to be "a more active sworn enemy" of suicidal thoughts. Kumin responded mildly, but she made clear that she wanted "no more reproachful little notes I can't read." Three years later, after receiving several more "reproachful little notes," Kumin wrote a more forthright letter. She was sick of Olsen's playing the victim, and frustrated, too, that Olsen had never repaid her monetary debts, even after winning grants and fellowships. Kumin resented Olsen's performance of pain, her insistence that it was she "alone who bleed[s]." Such a performance was not entirely dissimilar to Sexton's, but Kumin had not signed on as Olsen's helpmate, nor did she feel that Olsen, like Sexton, "gave as good as she got." "A line out of Sexton fits exactly what you do," Kumin wrote in frustration. "'My pain is more valuable.' You may make a profession out of it with others, but please do not rub my nose in it." It does not appear that Kumin ever wrote to Olsen again.

Eventually, Kumin opened up to the public about her friendship with Sexton. She wrote an introduction for *The Awful Rowing Toward God*. Before her death, Sexton had asked for the book jacket to feature a Pineda statue. The statue was one of Pineda's more abstract ones, a curved, life-sized sculpture that had looked, to Sexton, like a woman bent over as if rowing. (There are a couple of Pineda's works that fit this description: *Figure Bending over Another Figure* and *Sculpture of a Woman Bending to Embrace a Reclining Figure.*) This would have been Sexton's first collaboration with Pineda, another instance of the Equivalents inspiring each other across artistic media. But after Sexton's death, the Houghton Mifflin design team refused to abide by her wishes. They pointed out that the sculpture would look like an unidentifiable lump on a book jacket. They proposed a text-only cover design, something quite different from the rest of Sexton's books. Linda—who, as her mother's literary executor, was in charge of making decisions about the publication of posthumous works— persuaded the design team to go with a sketch of Sexton done by Swan. It was Swan's final gift to her friend.

Several years later, Kumin wrote a touching remembrance of Sexton, called "How It Was," a foreword to Sexton's *Complete Poems*, published in 1981. In the essay, she reminisced about their first meeting, discussed the transformations in Sexton's poetry, and touched on Sexton's troubles at the end of her life. She concluded by placing her friend in the canon of groundbreaking female poets—those who had paved the way for the radical writing and organizing of the 1970s. "Before there was a Women's Movement, the underground river was already flowing, carrying such diverse cargoes as the poems of Bogan, Levertov, Rukeyser, Swenson, Plath, Rich, and Sexton."

In early 1976, nearly two years after Sexton's death, Kumin and Vic left the Boston suburbs for good. "We left the comforts of central heating for woodstoves, dependable wattage for frequent power outages due to storms, and shades in every window, as well as downstairs curtains, for a wide-open lifestyle," Kumin wrote in a later memoir. They were now permanent residents of the state of New Hampshire. Kumin felt free. She was done with social niceties, with dinner parties and guest lists and gossip. She was done, too, with a life that had required being on call at all hours, with reading the signs of suicidal desires and responding to Sexton's alarms. In a poem written after Sexton's March 1973 suicide attempt, Kumin described the awful responsibility of keeping her friend alive. "I stopped you a dozen times, I was / the linebacker prying the pills out of your hand / calmly ordering the ambulance / teaching your classes / covering up and angry every time / furious you'd want to leave me behind." She had always known that Sexton would "one more time come unglued."

Kumin missed so much about Sexton—"the instant criticism . . . the kind of ongoing complete encouragement of whatever piece I pick up"—but she also recognized the ways that the loss of her friend had enabled her to start a new phase of life.

"It would be blinking the truth if I didn't say that Annie's death freed me at last to move to the country," Kumin wrote to a friend the fall after she had moved north. "The lifestyle seems to agree with us—we both immediately lost ten lbs & got brown and tough from the outdoor work—our horses are thriving & we are very insular." Kumin would remain on PoBiz Farm, happily picking berries and birthing foals, until her death in 2014.

"We have had enough suicidal women poets, enough suicidal women, enough of self-destructiveness as the sole form of violence permitted to women," wrote Adrienne Rich in 1974, in a eulogy for Sexton. Rich was living in New York City and teaching at City College when she heard the news. Some of her students and friends wanted to hold a memorial for Sexton, and Rich wanted to "try to speak to the question of identification which a suicide always arouses"; in other words, she wanted to speak to women who might identify with Sexton's self-destructive impulses.

Though Sexton and Rich had come up in the same Boston poetry scene, they had not been close. They had met once or twice; they congratulated each other on publications and prizes. Rich once asked Sexton to help her translate some poems by a South African poet (they were written in Afrikaans), and Sexton asked Rich for a Guggenheim recommendation. While Sexton's close friends like Kumin and Swan wrote personal remembrances, Rich wrote a remembrance that treated Sexton as a representative of feminist consciousness—which, sort of despite herself, she had indeed come to be. "She wrote poems alluding to abortion, masturbation, menopause, and the painful love of a powerless mother for her daughters, long before such themes became validated by a collective consciousness of women, and while writing and publishing under the scrutiny of the male literary establishment," she wrote of Sexton. (Rich remembered the old masters well.) "Her head was often patriarchal, but in her blood and her bones, Anne Sexton knew."

Now Sexton, like Plath, was dead. But Rich argued that suicide was not the only way that women destroyed themselves. "Self-trivialization is one. Believing the lie that women are not capable of major creations." "Horizontal hostility" was another, by which Rich meant "the fear and mistrust of other women, because other women *are* ourselves." The list went on: "misplaced compassion," and addiction—to sacrificial love, to sex, to drugs, and to depression, which Rich called "the most acceptable way of living out a female existence." Rich named these self-destructive impulses in order to encourage other women to purge themselves of "this quadruple poison" so that they would have "minds and bodies more poised for the act of survival and rebuilding." What Sexton's poetry offered, Rich wrote, was work that "tells us what we have to fight, in ourselves and in the images patriarchy has held up to us. Her poetry is a guide to the ruins, from which we learn what women have lived and what we must refuse to live any longer."

Rich's remembrance signaled that a kind of militant feminism had infiltrated the literary world, both its theory and its practice. Whereas Sexton had once been maligned for her poems about birth and body parts (recall Dickey's criticism of "the pathetic and disgusting aspects of bodily experience"), she was now celebrated for her prescience and her guidance. As Kumin explained in a private letter, Sexton was writing truths about women's lives long before there was a women's movement. Poems like "Menstruation at Forty" and "Abortion" "came not out of any sense of herself as iconoclast, ground-breaker, exhibitionist, but from a direct need to say them," Kumin explained to a friend. "She was the most honest person I ever knew." By 1974, it was not only acceptable to write poetry out of personal experience but also, as Rich argued, politically necessary. One way women could thwart their self-destructive impulses was by reading work, like Sexton's, that presented "images patriarchy has held up to us," in all their fixed perfection, and then, line by line, undid them. For women, writing was more than self-expression, more than therapy. It was a matter of life or death. As Olsen once said, "Every woman who writes is a survivor."

Rich used Sexton's work to ground her argument about poetry as feminist practice, but she might equally well have used her own. Like many women in America, Rich had spent the 1960s undergoing a personal and political transformation. She had begun as the proper Boston poet, a formalist whose work was praised for its quietness and modesty. In 1963—a year after Sexton published *All My Pretty Ones*, a collection that is in large part about her relationship with her parents—Rich published *Snapshots of a Daughter-in-Law*, a much more personal collection than her earlier work, much of it written in blank verse. "A thinking woman sleeps with monsters," she declared in the title poem, a crusade against chivalry as well as male standards of art and thought. In step with other women of her generation, and arguably a year or so ahead of them, Rich was becoming a feminist.

Rich started to become politically active when she moved to New York with her family, started teaching, got involved in antiracist and antiwar organizing in the city, and soon started spouting the "Women's Lib rap" to close friends. She separated from her husband in 1970. In the years immediately following her separation, 1971–1972, Rich composed the poems that would solidify her reputation as a forceful feminist poet. They were later collected in *Diving into the Wreck: Poems, 1971–1972*. The poems, especially the title poem, cracked something open in many women readers: when the writer Margaret Atwood first heard Rich read the poems aloud, she "felt as though the top of my head was being attacked, sometimes with an ice pick, sometimes with a blunter instrument: a hatchet or a hammer." Rich won the National Book Award for the collection. She insisted that Alice Walker and Audre Lorde accompany her to the ceremony and help her accept the prize on behalf of all women. It was a resonant action that symbolized, among other things, a changing of the guard.

In February 1977, Rich wrote a letter to Olsen about one of their shared favorite writers, Virginia Woolf. Elaine Showalter, the feminist literary scholar who had spoken at the MLA conference and who had interviewed Kumin and Sexton several months before the latter's death, had just published a new work on British women novelists, *A Literature of Their Own*. Rich wondered if Showalter would have written the book slightly differently if she hadn't been haunted by "the academic version of the 'Angel in the House,'" a nineteenth-century ideal of self-sacrificing womanhood. (In *A Room of One's Own*, Woolf suggests that the woman writer must kill off this angel in order to write.) The book's conclusion, as Rich paraphrased it, explained "that the 'room of our own' is not enough: we must find community, collectivity." Rich agreed:

> I believe profoundly that the woman artist, even if she can find the space and support herself in it, must not fall into the trap of working, or trying to work, in isolation. But even Woolf implies . . . that a female community must come into being.

For several years in the 1960s, Olsen had immersed herself in this kind of female community. Though she found other creative communities over the course of her life—at MacDowell, in San Francisco, at academic conferences across the nation—she never found any quite like the community of the Radcliffe Institute. In fact, Olsen returned there for a second fellowship in the mid-1980s, but it produced neither the work nor the friendships that the first one had inspired. Few relationships in Olsen's life ever rivaled those she had with the Equivalents.

For thirty-nine years, from 1960 to 1999, female community

thrived at the Institute. In 1978, the Radcliffe Institute for Independent Study was renamed the Bunting Institute after its founder. Bunting herself had left Radcliffe by that point; she'd served as president until 1972, then had worked for several years as a special assistant to the president of Princeton, William Bowen, who, like Bunting, was interested in enacting coeducation. Bunting had hoped to merge Radcliffe and Harvard during her presidency, and though Harvard's president, Nathan Pusey, was sympathetic to the cause, alumni of both colleges resisted the change. The result was something called the "non-merger merger," enacted in June 1971, that merged many aspects of the two institutions while preserving Radcliffe's control of its property and endowment. Harvard College took control of the undergraduate educations of all Radcliffe students, feeding, housing, and educating the female undergraduates alongside their male classmates, even though these same women applied to and graduated from Radcliffe. It was an imperfect solution, but one that satisfied many current and prospective students at both Radcliffe and Harvard, who wanted a coeducational experience. The non-merger merger, like the Institute, became a part of Bunting's legacy.

Always energetic, Bunting continued to pursue new life experiences. In 1979, she married Dr. Clement A. Smith, a pediatrician who had been a friend of hers for the past eighteen years. Sixty-eight at the time of her second marriage, Bunting found her life with "Clem" to be "quite wonderful." They split time between Cambridge and Vermont, and as they both aged, gardening and bird-watching began to supplant formal dinners and academic events. Bunting died on January 21, 1998. She had witnessed and brought about so much change.

By the time Bunting left academia, at the beginning of the 1980s, American higher education was quite different than it had been when she started her deanship at Douglass. The majority of Ivy League colleges were coed, Title IX had passed, and—partly as a result of the first of these events—the Seven Sisters declined in prestige. Soon enough, there were no longer separate schools or separate spheres for women; they fought their way into the Gothic buildings of Yale and Princeton and into the halls of power.

But the Institute endured as a place where women could think and work together. In Radcliffe Yard, women came out of isolation to collaborate, complain, and exchange work and affection both. Over the course of its existence as a women-only space, the Institute hosted many important scholars and artists, including the playwright Anna Deavere Smith, the activist Kathleen Cleaver, the novelist Jayne Anne Phillips, the philosopher Martha Nussbaum, and the psychologist Carol Gilligan, who wrote her groundbreaking theory of gender difference, *In a Different Voice*, while there. What had started as a "messy experiment" with twenty-four mostly local women had become an established institution of national renown.

In October 1976, two years after Sexton's death, Kumin wrote a letter to Rich, whose groundbreaking book *Of Woman Born*, about the "institution of motherhood," had just been excerpted in *Ms.* magazine. In this radical work, Rich distinguished the patriarchal vision of motherhood—its depiction of motherhood as a kind of "sacred calling"—from the actual caretaking of children. "The institution of motherhood is not identical with bearing and caring for children," Rich explained, "any more than the institution of heterosexuality is identical with intimacy and sexual love. Both create the prescriptions and the conditions in which choices are made or blocked; they are not 'reality' but they have shaped the circumstances of our lives." Rich aimed to deconstruct the ideology of motherhood so that women could love and live more freely.

Of Woman Born was groundbreaking, but its path had been laid by those who wrote about motherhood before Rich did: by Sexton and Olsen, and by Kumin herself. Though Kumin had been the least disclosing of the Equivalents, the least inclined to use her personal experience as material for her poetry, she too had broken taboos, and she had been part of a female community that enabled writers and artists to do the same. Rich's words resonated with Kumin, who wrote one of the relatively few fan letters that can be found in Kumin's archives. "How lucid and exact and fair this is!" she wrote to Rich. She spared Rich her memories of her own thwarted mother, but she said that she understood why Rich had taken up this project, and that she celebrated both the book and the woman who had written it.

Her letter indicated how much had changed in Boston since the days of Lowell and Holmes. Men no longer dominated the poetry scene, and women no longer felt unfeminine competing in it, as Rich had complained decades earlier. More and more, female solidarity was replacing female anxiety. Now there was a community of creative women who came together, broke apart, and then reconnected, through letters and love. Kumin closed her letter with words that captured the gratitude that the Equivalents and the women of the Radcliffe Institute felt for each other, and that we, in turn, might feel for them: "I just wanted to say hooray for what you've written."

Epilogue

ONE MINUTE AFTER MIDNIGHT on October 1, 1999, Harvard and Radcliffe formally merged. *The Harvard Crimson* explained how "a greater acceptance of educated women in society and the unusual circumstances of history required Radcliffe to continuously redefine its role." Since the "non-merger merger," undergraduates at Radcliffe had enjoyed a sort of "dual citizenship" status at the university: they applied to Radcliffe College, but they were educated in Harvard classrooms, by Harvard faculty, and with Harvard students. They lived in coed dormitories; before the "non-merger merger," all Radcliffe undergraduates had lived in the Radcliffe Quadrangle. Upon graduation, Radcliffe seniors received two diplomas, one from each college. But once the merger went into effect, all 3,071 Radcliffe undergraduates became Harvard College students. Radcliffe ceased to exist as an independent college. As *The Washington Post*, which covered the merger, put it, "Because Radcliffe long ago abdicated its role in undergraduate life, the emotional fallout from sentimental 'Cliffies' is likely to be more dramatic than any actual changes on this Ivy League campus."

But there was one major change: Radcliffe College became the Radcliffe Institute for Advanced Study, an institution that was open to men as well as women and that replaced the all-female Bunting Institute. Once Radcliffe merged with Harvard, it could no longer, under Title IX, support a single-sex institution; if it did so, it would forgo federal funding. In an interesting twist, the merger ended up flooding the Institute with money: Radcliffe transferred all of its $200 million assets to Harvard upon merging, but it then received $150 million back—with a matching amount from Harvard's endowment—in order to fund the coed Institute for Advanced Study. Linda S. Wilson, Radcliffe's seventh president, affirmed that all this was "cause for celebration." President of Radcliffe for ten years, Wilson stepped down from her position after the merger took place. She was the last president of Radcliffe; from there on out, the Radcliffe Institute, like Harvard University's professional schools, has been headed by a dean.

Lily Macrakis, the historian who had befriended Sexton and Kumin during the Institute's first year, disagreed with Wilson's statement. She fired off an angry note, lamenting the change to the Institute. Why did they have to bring men into this space? How could men possibly need more help? The doors were already open for them, but women, she argued, still needed to push—even at the turn of the twenty-first century. She joined a chorus of disgruntled former fellows, who had expressed their concerns to the *Crimson* before the decision was finalized. "It would be a completely different environment," said one fellow, referring to the possibility of a coed institute. "You might as well stay at your home institution and feel like you're one of the only women," said another. Even Wilson, who approved of the change, acknowledged what had been lost. "It's almost like magic," she said, referring to the all-female institute. "It's a comfortable community."

Today, the Radcliffe Institute for Advanced Study is dedicated to supporting "creative work in all disciplines—humanities, sciences, social sciences, and the arts," performed by people of all identities.

.   .   .

Seventeen years later, Macrakis was still angry about the end of the women-only institute. "Men have everything," she fumed. It was the spring of 2016; Macrakis and I were sitting in her living room in Cambridge, just a few blocks from Harvard Square. Still an impeccable hostess, Macrakis had purchased Greek pastries from her favorite local bakery and prepared strong coffee. She insisted on refilling my cup nearly every time I took a sip.

Macrakis felt passionately about the Institute because it had propelled her to a life that she loved. After her year as a fellow, she had taken a temporary teaching position at Regis College, a Catholic women's college in Weston. It became a permanent job. She found she loved teaching. She stayed at Regis for forty years. From there, she became the dean of Hellenic College Holy Cross, a small Greek Orthodox college and seminary in Brookline. By the time we met, she was a professor emerita and a grandmother.

Throughout our conversation, she emphasized how important the Institute had been for a woman like her, someone who was demure rather than demanding. She marveled at how timid she had been, at how much she'd been willing to accept. "I cannot say I was a fighter," she confessed. It was the Institute that made her demand more from life, that gave her the confidence to accept challenging jobs and, when she was offered the deanship at Hellenic, to ask for a 40 percent raise. She felt like a changed woman.

But she wasn't sure the world itself had changed as much as we might think. "I think that we have to really talk a lot about men," she said, speaking of the need for further gender equality. "In other words, how do you find good men to accept you?"

"It's a great question," I responded, thinking of my own difficulties in that department.

"Because I'm not sure at all," she continued. "Men are not yet sure if this should happen. I can tell you that."

I'm not so sure, either.

I started researching this book in the spring of 2016, during the final, frenzied months of the presidential campaign. I began writing it in the late fall of the same year, following the election of Donald Trump—a man who has been accused multiple times of sexual assault. I was in Washington, D.C., for the inauguration: I had taken advantage of my university's winter break to visit the Archives of American Art at the Smithsonian, where I delved into the papers of Marianna Pineda and Barbara Swan. As I made the twenty-minute walk to and from the archives, I passed patriotic floats and protest signs. I overheard more than a few arguments between strangers on the street.

The day after the inauguration, my archival research finished, I joined over 200,000 others in Washington, D.C., for the first Women's March. It was both confusing and exhilarating. On the one hand, it seemed clear that the differences of race, class, and sexual orientation made the idea of a coherent "sisterhood" idealistic. On the other hand, I had never seen so many people concerned, at least superficially, with women's equality. I couldn't help but think of all the women's marches I'd read about as I was researching: in New York City, in San Francisco, and right here in Washington, D.C. I had the sense that time was collapsing.

I have had that same sense again and again over the last three years. As I worked, I felt that I had one eye on the sexism of the present and one on the sexism of the past, and yet my vision was remarkably unified. I wrote about how the Equivalents navigated male-dominated poetry workshops and art schools, while I read tweets about workplace sexual harassment, tagged with the hashtag #MeToo. I read about the depression and domestic violence that afflicted 1950s married mothers, while "public intellectuals" like Jordan Peterson argued for "enforced monogamy," and self-styled "incels" (involuntary celibates) violently protested female sexual freedom. I revised my chapters on radical feminism while abortion access diminished across the country and *Roe v. Wade* came under threat.

These similarities—across seventy years—make me wonder how much has changed since the founding of the Institute. To be sure, workplace discrimination and domestic violence are not nearly as prevalent as they were during the 1950s and 1960s—or at least not as prevalent for middle-class and upper-class white women. The formal equality granted by laws like Title VII and Title IX does mean something: for example, a person who loses a job on account of pregnancy can now sue (when this happened to Friedan, she had no legal recourse). But lawsuits are expensive and often lost. Sometimes, the risk of causing a fuss doesn't seem worth it.

As I watched women sharing stories of abuse and harassment in #MeToo posts, I thought about how the legal protections offered by Title VII and Title IX had allowed a lot of other suffering to go unnoticed. Were these industries—Hollywood, academia, the federal government, literary New York—truly open to women? Sure, we didn't need our husbands' approval to publish a piece of writing, as Kumin once did, but perhaps we still needed male benefactors or protectors who could vouch for our seriousness and keep the predators away? I scrolled through Twitter and read the news, thinking as I did of the women who had fought like hell to make our country much better than it currently is.

Not all the resemblances I noticed between my era and the 1960s and 1970s were frightening; some were enlivening. The years during which I wrote this book have also been years of resurgent activism: Black Lives Matter protests, strikes and walkouts at universities and throughout the media industry, and more Women's Marches, in the nation's capital and elsewhere. As someone who grew up during the relative complacency of the Clinton presidency, I marveled at seeing people regularly take to the streets. The vibrant protest culture of the 1960s didn't seem as unimaginable to me as it once had.

More than that, over the course of the past few years, I noticed literature that built upon the work of Sexton, Kumin, and Olsen. Confessional writing was everywhere. I read memoirs, personal essays published on women's websites, and works of "autofiction," writing that deliberately blurred the boundaries between autobiography and fiction. In fact, confessional writing was so pervasive (and profitable for the sites that published it) that by the time I finished this book, the backlash had begun. (In 2017, two different critics declared the personal essay dead.) I also noticed that in the second decade of the twenty-first century, the literature of motherhood took a new turn: female writers described the messiness of motherhood—both physical and emotional—with candor and complexity. Elena Ferrante, Rivka Galchen, Sheila Heti, Meaghan O'Connell, Maggie Nelson— these writers described pregnancy, labor, and child rearing in compelling works of fiction and nonfiction. Their stories were untraditional: Galchen's book was epigrammatic and formally innovative, while Nelson's narrative explored ideas about gender, heterosexuality, and family. These women weren't the first writers to use motherhood as material for their art, but—unlike the Equivalents—they were critically acclaimed, successful, and rarely scolded for being too "personal," as Sexton had once been. It seemed to me that the Equivalents had cleared the way for innovative, intimate writing by women—the kind of writing now in the critical spotlight.

As a historian, I have tried to get as close as I could to the 1960s and 1970s, decades of literary innovation and civil unrest. I read books; I sifted through archives; I watched documentaries. I visited Joanna Fink, Swan's daughter, at Alpha Gallery, the gallery founded by Alan Fink. It used to be on Newbury Street in Boston's Back Bay, close to the building in which Sexton took that first poetry class. I arrived at its new location in Boston's South End on a cold January afternoon, and I sat for hours talking with Joanna about her mother's career while admiring paintings by Swan and her Museum School friends.

In the winter of 2017, a friend and I visited Olsen's daughter Julie and her husband, Robert, in Soquel, California. They live in the same small house where Olsen in her later years had lived and worked. My friend—a labor historian and union organizer—and I fell into an easy conversation with the older couple about labor history and leftist politics. We drank herbal tea and tried to glimpse the ocean from the west-facing window. I felt a kinship with Julie, who also taught undergraduates. I hoped that in my own small way—as a teacher, a writer, and a union organizer myself—I could be part of a long tradition of feminism in this country.

I knew that the women who had gone before me—Polly Bunting, Betty Friedan, Alice Walker, and each of the five Equivalents—had fought hard, and under difficult conditions, to change their lives and the lives of the women they knew and loved. Their most important insight, to my mind, is that women's creative and intellectual lives are shaped by their material conditions and that those conditions must change if women are to be the artists, the writers, the mothers, and the minds that they want to be. Those who dedicated themselves to the feminist cause, Olsen among them, refused to give up even when factionalism and cultural backlash pushed the feminist movement from the mainstream.

This work continues today. It demands new strategies and tactics, befitting a different historical moment. A women-only space like the Institute might not be right for the twenty-first century, a time when the gender binary is being increasingly challenged. And, as the theorist Kimberlé Crenshaw has argued, women who occupy different racial and class positions experience sexism differently; it is thus hard to imagine how a single policy solution could serve all women equally (though state-sponsored child care comes close). But this isn't a reason to repudiate institutions like the Institute; it is instead a reason to understand them and to adapt their ideas and approaches to our own time. How could institutions—educational and otherwise—better support women? How could universities work to eradicate ongoing gender disparities? How can we, as writers and thinkers, be bold, creative—even revolutionary?

When Polly Bunting was later asked why so many women responded to her "messy experiment"—why they called the office nonstop, sent letter after letter, applied year after year—she responded modestly: "We spoke to their condition." Women today live under new conditions. It is time for another messy experiment and for a new group of women to speak.

Acknowledgments

The Radcliffe Institute was founded on an idea: when provided with institutional support and intellectual community, artists, writers, and scholars will produce better work than they would on their own. I can attest to this idea's validity. Over the course of the four years I worked on *The Equivalents*, I benefitted from the support of so many people and institutions. The book that resulted is infinitely better thanks to their help; any errors are my own.

First, thank you to LuAnn Walther, whose insightful editing made this book truer, smarter, and more engaging. Thanks to Catherine Tung for wonderful, thorough editing and patient assistance with book production. Thanks to Anna Kaufman and Ellie Pritchett for stepping in to see this book toward its conclusion. I cannot thank Elias Altman enough for his faith in me and in this project since its earliest days. He has guided me through some challenging times, and I am very grateful.

Rena Cohen has been a wonderful research assistant and has helped with so many different parts of the book. Jeanie Reiss fact-checked the manuscript carefully and saved me from errors. Dan Novak offered invaluable legal counsel.

This book would not exist without the librarians and archivists who catalogue archival sources and help researchers use them. I am grateful to librarians and archivists at the following places: the Harry Ransom Center, the Schlesinger Library, the Beinecke Rare Book & Manuscript Library, Stanford's Special Collections and University

Archives, and the Archives of American Art. Special thanks to Diana Carey, Tim Noakes, and Ellen Shea for their help.

I was honored to speak with people with first-hand and second-hand knowledge of the Institute. I am especially grateful to relatives of the Equivalents who spoke with me. Thank you to Julie Olsen Edwards, Joanna Fink, Daniel Kumin, Lily Macrakis, Kathie Olsen, Linda Gray Sexton, and Nina Tovish. I am especially grateful to Julie for granting me permission to quote at length from Olsen's unpublished writing.

Anastatia Curley, Merve Emre, Andrew Martin, Charles Petersen, Gabriel Winant, and Stephen Squibb all read parts of the manuscript. They are smart and dear friends, and their suggestions made the book much better.

This book builds on the work of many scholars, critics, and historians. They are all credited in the notes, but a few deserve special mention here: Stephanie Coontz, Alice Echols, Paula Giddings, Elaine Tyler May, Panthea Reid, Joanne Meyerowitz, and Ruth Rosen. The work of Diane Middlebrook inspired me to pursue this project. There are also some feminist thinkers and writers who have influenced me greatly, though they are not discussed extensively in the book. They include Kimberlé Crenshaw, Nancy Fraser, Silvia Federici, and Arlie Hochschild.

There are very many people at Harvard University who deserve my gratitude. I have taught in the Harvard Writing Program since 2014; in that time, the Program has supported my work in many ways. Thanks to Karen Heath, Tom Jehn, and Rebecca Skolnik. This project was supported by a Fuerbringer Grant for professional development as well as a grant for manuscript preparation.

Thank you to Harvard's History and Literature, an ideal place for a young scholar to work and teach. Particular thanks to Kevin Birmingham, Jordan Brower, Jenni Brady, Caitlin Casey, Alex Corey, Thomas Dichter, Lauren Kaminsky, Lynne Feeley, Tim McCarthy, Kristen Roupenian, and Duncan White. Thank you to my students and advisees, who made sharp observations about the past and future of feminism. I have learned much from them, especially from

Megan Jones, who introduced me to the Kitchen Table: Women of Color Press in her outstanding senior thesis.

Thanks to the faculty and graduate students of the Harvard University Department of English, where I learned many of the skills needed to research and write this book. Thanks especially to Lawrence Buell, Glenda Carpio, Philip Fisher, and Luke Menand, the last of whom taught me how storytelling could be its own form of scholarly argument. Thanks as well to members of the American Colloquium, especially Nick Donofrio, and to participants in the New England Americanists Workshop, especially David Hollingshead and Jennifer Schnepf. Alison Chapman and Kathryn Roberts have supported me in infinite ways since our earliest days in graduate school together.

I'm lucky to live among many thoughtful, brilliant, passionate people in Cambridge. Tim Barker, James Brandt, Jon Connolly, Katrina Forrester, Laura Kolbe, Jamie Martin, Rachel Nolan, Ben Tarnoff, Kirsten Weld, and Moira Weigel all offered intellectual inspiration. Anya Kaplan-Seem, who was also part of this community, improvised a writing retreat for me on a farm in upstate New York.

Ming-Qi Chu, Jessica Loudis, Rachel Mannheimer, Hannah Rosefield, and Annie Wyman have all provided me with the female community that the women in this book sought and found. I am lucky to know them.

My parents, Diane and Jay, encouraged my love of books and taught me, from a young age, about gender equality. My sister, Ana, and my brother, Jack, have filled my life with humor, affection, and a lot of fun.

Max Larkin, a brilliant thinker and a gifted writer, read every page of this book—many of them multiple times—and told me how each page could be better. His enthusiasm for the project, and for the art of storytelling itself, kept me going when I was flagging. With him, I have thought more deeply, talked more passionately, and laughed more joyfully than I ever thought possible. I am so grateful for him, and for the life we have made together.

Notes

Introduction

ix golf course: Linda Gray Sexton, interview by author, 12 Feb. 2019.

x work at home: Sexton to Brother Dennis Farrell, 16 July 1962, in *Anne Sexton: A Self-Portrait in Letters*, ed. Lois Ames and Linda Gray Sexton (Boston: Mariner Books, 2004), 142.

xi "wooden tower": Ibid.

xi "nature . . . becomes my": Ibid., 143.

xi While working, she sat either: Diane Middlebrook, *Anne Sexton: A Biography* (Boston: Houghton Mifflin, 1992), 128.

xi "I hoard books": Sexton to Farrell, 16 July 1962, in *Self-Portrait in Letters*, 143.

xi edge of the pool: Middlebrook, *Anne Sexton*, 157.

xii "climate of unexpectation": "One Woman, Two Lives," *Time*, 3 Nov. 1961, 68.

xii "intellectually displaced women": Fred M. Hechinger, "Radcliffe Pioneers in Plan for Gifted Women's Study," *New York Times*, 20 Nov. 1960.

xiii "Radcliffe Pioneers": Ibid.

xiii 160 letters: Elaine Yaffe, *Mary Ingraham Bunting: Her Two Lives* (Savannah: Frederic C. Beil, 2005), 176.

xiii "thought there was something wrong": Betty Friedan, "Up from the Kitchen Floor," *New York Times*, 4 March 1973.

xiv "messy experiment": Yaffe, *Mary Ingraham Bunting*, 171.

xiv "salvation": Lily Macrakis, interview by author, May 2016.

xv "the personal is political": Ruth Rosen, *The World Split Open: How the Modern Women's Movement Changed America* (New York: Penguin Books, 2007), 196.

xvi "the Equivalents": Middlebrook. *Anne Sexton*, 197. This is a good moment to give Middlebrook, who wrote the only existing biography of Anne Sexton, credit for planting the seed of this project. To the best of my knowledge, she is the only scholar or writer to note the convergence of these five women at the Institute. Her essay "Circle of Women Artists: Tillie Olsen and Anne Sexton at the Radcliffe Institute," adapted from the Sexton biography and published in *Listening to Silences: New Essays in Feminist Criticism*, ed. Shelley Fisher Fishkin (New York: Oxford University Press, 1994), inspired this book.

xvi   "lasting": Anne Sexton application to the Radcliffe Institute for Independent Study, 7 March 1961, Institute Archives.

xvii   "mythological": Oral history interview with Marianna Pineda, 26 May—14 June 1977, Archives of American Art, Smithsonian Institution.

xvii   "a real turning point": Swan to Constance Smith, 27 Aug. 1963, Institute Archives.

xviii   the first book: A few scholars have discussed the Institute, usually in writing about women who were involved in it. For instance, biographers including Middlebrook, Panthea Reid (author of a biography about Tillie Olsen), Elaine Yaffe (author of a biography about Mary Ingraham Bunting), and Evelyn White (author of a biography of Alice Walker) all describe the Institute and its importance to their subjects. The Institute itself has published a number of histories, such as *Radcliffe Institute, 1960 to 1971* (published by the Institute in 1972), and *Voices and Visions: Arts at the Mary Ingraham Bunting Institute, 1962–1967*, edited by the former fellows Iris Fanger and Marilyn Pappas (and published in 1997). These histories, while helpful to the researcher, are necessarily celebratory and promotional and are far from objective. In writing about the Institute, I have tried to take an objective look at its strengths and its flaws while also attempting to see it through the eyes of the women who gathered there.

xviii   "sold approximately": Stephanie Coontz, *A Strange Stirring: The Feminine Mystique and American Women at the Dawn of the 1960s* (New York: Basic Books, 2012) 148.

xix   groundwork for feminist revolt: Labor historians and feminist historians have productively troubled this understanding of the immediate postwar years. Dorothy Sue Cobble's *Other Women's Movement: Workplace Justice and Social Rights in Modern America* (Princeton, N.J.: Princeton University Press, 2004) shows how women labor organizing continued throughout the mid-century. The essays collected in *Not June Cleaver: Women and Gender in Postwar America, 1945–1960*, ed. Joanne Meyerowitz (Philadelphia: Temple University Press, 1994), likewise demonstrate how nurses, abortionists, beatniks, immigrants, and activists all challenged the gender norms of the time. Stephanie Coontz has engaged in a complementary project in *The Way We Never Were: American Families and the Nostalgia Trap* (New York: BasicBooks, 1992); she pokes holes in many of the myths about mid-century life. This is but a sampling of the important books in this field.

xix   "A woman must have money": Virginia Woolf, *A Room of One's Own* (1929), retrieved from victorianpersistence.files.wordpress.com.

xxii   eighty cents on the dollar: Ariane Hegewisch and Heidi Hartmann, *The Gender Wage Gap: 2018 Earnings Differences by Race and Ethnicity* (Institute for Women's Policy Research, 2019).

CHAPTER 1: Little White Picket Fences

4   She stepped into the room: My sources for this opening section are Middlebrook and the remembrances of Kumin and Sexton in "A Nurturing Relationship: A

Conversation with Anne Sexton and Maxine Kumin, April 15, 1974," conducted by Elaine Showalter and Carol Smith, *Women's Studies* 4, no. 1 (1976): 115–35, as well as Kumin's remembrances in the essay "How It Was," which opens Sexton's *Complete Poems*.

5 "I was trying my damnedest": Sexton, interview by Barbara Kevles, in *No Evil Star: Selected Essays, Interviews, and Prose*, ed. Steven E. Colburn (Ann Arbor: University of Michigan Press, 1985), 84.

5 "terrible nervous wreck": Sexton, interview by Alice Ryerson and Martha White, Jan. 1962, Radcliffe Institute Archives. Details about Harvey household from Middlebrook, *Anne Sexton*, 9, and from the interview.

5 "Oh, your mother is smart": Interview with Sexton, Institute Archives.

6 failed to impress her mother: Sexton tells a less detailed version of the story in ibid. Middlebrook, *Anne Sexton*, 20–21, fills in some of the details.

7 seven bathrooms and five garages: Middlebrook, *Anne Sexton*, 13.

7 "I had to be just awful": Interview with Sexton, Institute Archives.

7 "My heart pounds": Quoted in Middlebrook, *Anne Sexton*, 36.

8 "Her family was not": Ibid., 34.

8 "I walk from room to room" Ibid., 36.

8 "Who would want": Ibid., 37.

8 *Sense of Poetry:* Mark Garrett Cooper and John Marx, "New Critical Television," *Openvault*, WGBH, 2015, openvault.wgbh.org.

9 "I could do that": Interview with Sexton, Institute Archives.

10 Many referred to therapy: Middlebrook, *Anne Sexton*, 52.

10 "unconsciously": Interview with Sexton, Institute Archives, and hereafter

10 "You can't kill yourself": Ibid.

10 "trickery": In 1958, she even composed a poem on the topic, "An Obsessive Combination of Ontological Inscape, Trickery, and Love," in *Selected Poems of Anne Sexton*, ed. Diane Wood Middlebrook and Diana Hume George (Boston: Houghton Mifflin, 1988), 4.

10 "my people": Sexton, interview by Kevles, in *No Evil Star*, 87.

10 "taken": Showalter and Smith, "Nurturing Relationship," 116.

10 "tall, blue-eyed": Maxine Kumin, "How It Was," introduction to *The Complete Poems: Anne Sexton* (Boston: Houghton Mifflin, 1981), xix.

10 "much more closed up": Showalter and Smith, "Nurturing Relationship," 117.

11 "chief frump": Ibid., 116.

11 "Nothing seems worth while": Quoted in Middlebrook, *Anne Sexton*, 36.

11 "I chafed against the domesticity": Maxine Kumin, *The Pawnbroker's Daughter: A Memoir* (New York: W. W. Norton, 2015), 72.

11 "great fear and trembling": Showalter and Smith, "Nurturing Relationship," 121.

11 "My earliest visions": Kumin, *Pawnbroker's Daughter*, 21.

12 "The passage through adolescence": Ibid., 28.

12 "one of the most important": Lewis quoted in James R. Hepworth, "Wallace Stegner, the Art of Fiction," *Paris Review*, no. 115 (Summer 1990).

12 "Some element of the unexpected": Stegner quoted in ibid.

12 "I was just floundering": Kumin, interview by Alice Ryerson and Martha White, Jan. 1962, Institute Archives.

14 "And I made a pact": Showalter and Smith, "Nurturing Relationship," 120.

14 "There never grows": Kumin, *Pawnbroker's Daughter*, 73.

14 "I had found": Ibid.
14 Vic had had to supply: Ibid., 75.
14 "I continued to write": Ibid.
15 "Up sooner than betimes": Ibid., 77–78.
16 She decided to keep her distance: Showalter and Smith, "Nurturing Relationship," 121.
16 "ghastly": Ibid., 118.
17 "eye of the hurricane": Phillip Newton, "Years of Study, Writing Cheers Newton Lady Poets," *Boston Traveler,* 7 June 1961.
17 "Sh! poem! Maxine!": Showalter and Smith, "Nurturing Relationship," 123.
17 She'd had to climb: Ibid., 121.
17 "Is this a poem?": Ibid., 122.
17 "everyone . . . was crazy": Anne Sexton, "Music Swims Back to Me," in *The Complete Poems* (Boston: Houghton Mifflin, 1981), 6.
18 "Unknown Girl": Ibid., 24.
19 "It must have been": Maxine Kumin, "Halfway," *Harper's Magazine,* 1 Jan. 1959, 37.
19 "avenging ghost": Maxine Kumin, "A Hundred Nights," *Harper's Magazine,* 1 June 1960, 73.
19 "Jane at thirteen": Maxine Kumin, "The Journey," *Harper's Magazine,* 1 Feb. 1961, 49.
20 "I, too, dislike it": Marianne Moore, "Poetry," in *Others for 1919: An Anthology of the New Verse,* ed. Alfred Kreymborg (New York: N. L. Brown, 1920).

CHAPTER 2: Who Rivals?

21 by 1956, two-thirds had come to fear: Elaine Tyler May, *Homeward Bound* (New York: Basic Books, 1988), 23.
22 "terribly famous": Alan Riding, "Grandpa Picasso: Terribly Famous, Not Terribly Nice," *New York Times,* 24 Nov. 2001.
23 by 1975, there were fifty-two programs: Mark McGurl, *The Program Era: Postwar Fiction and the Rise of Creative Writing* (Cambridge, Mass.: Harvard University Press, 2009), 24.
24 The latecomer sashayed: This is how Kathleen Spivack, a classmate of Sexton's, remembers her entrances (see next citation, 54–55). Sexton discusses smoking in class in her essay "Classroom at Boston University," in *No Evil Star,* 3–5.
25 "This is the best part": Kathleen Spivack, *With Robert Lowell and His Circle: Sylvia Plath, Anne Sexton, Elizabeth Bishop, Stanley Kunitz, and Others* (Boston: Northeastern University Press, 2012), 48.
25 "Lowell's class yesterday": Sylvia Plath, 25 Feb. 1959, *The Unabridged Journals of Sylvia Plath,* ed. Karen V. Kukil (New York: Random House, 2000), 471. I consulted several sources in order to describe Lowell's seminar. First, there is Sexton's remembrance, "Classroom at Boston University." Plath's journals provided me with various details of the classroom and of Plath's mental and physical state at the time. I also consulted Spivack's memoir, *With Robert Lowell and His Circle.*
25 "publish a bookshelf": Plath, 25 Feb. 1957, *Journals of Sylvia Plath,* 270.

26 "Arrogant, I think I have written": Plath, 29 March, 1958, *Journals of Sylvia Plath*, 360.

26 "She has very good things": Plath, 20 March 1959, *Journals of Sylvia Plath*, 475.

27 *"Negro woman* poet": Hughes quoted in Kumin, *Pawnbroker's Daughter*, 79.

27 "Carolyn Kizer is a beautiful girl": Sexton to Kizer, 1 April 1959, in *Self-Portrait in Letters*, 68. Details about Lowell's classroom from Spivack's memoir.

27 "whole establishment was male!": Spivack, *With Robert Lowell and His Circle*, 57.

27 "Competing in the literary establishment": Quoted in Middlebrook, *Anne Sexton*, 111.

28 "primary task": Adlai E. Stevenson, "A Purpose for Modern Woman," *Women's Home Companion*, Sept. 1955, 30–31.

28 "at the edges": Anne Roiphe, *Art and Madness: A Memoir of Lust Without Reason* (New York: Anchor Books, 2011), 141.

28 "Being a 'poet' in Boston": Sexton to Carolyn Kizer, 5 Feb. 1959, in *Self-Portrait in Letters*, 56.

28 In a letter to the poet: Sexton to Snodgrass, 6 Oct. 1958, *Self-Portrait in Letters*, 40.

29 "Part of me would be free": Quoted in Middlebrook, *Anne Sexton*, 47.

29 "Ugly angels spoke to me": Anne Sexton, "The Double Image," in *Complete Poems*, 35–42.

30 "I *think* this means": Sexton to Snodgrass, 11 March 1959, in *Self-Portrait in Letters*, 65.

30 "A leaf from Ann [*sic*] Sexton's book": Plath, 23 April 1959, *Journals of Sylvia Plath*, 477.

30 "Anne was more herself": Ian Hamilton, "A Conversation with Robert Lowell," in *Robert Lowell: Interviews and Memoirs*, ed. Jeffrey Meyers (Ann Arbor: University of Michigan Press, 1988), 170.

31 "the only public place in Boston": Elizabeth Hardwick, "Boston," in *The Collected Essays of Elizabeth Hardwick* (New York: New York Review Books, 2017), 74.

31 "It's okay": Anne Sexton, "The Bar Fly Ought to Sing," in *No Evil Star*, 7. Additional details of their nights drinking from this essay.

31 "intense, skilled, perceptive": Ibid., 10.

31 "I told Mr. Lowell": Ibid., 9.

31 "smug as a cream-fed cat": Plath, May 20, 1959, *Journals of Sylvia Plath*, 484.

32 "There is an increasing market": Plath, June 13, 1959, *Journals of Sylvia Plath*, 495.

32 "college girl suicide": Ibid.

32 "I am just not sure": Sexton to Kizer, April 1, 1959, in *Self-Portrait in Letters*, 70.

32 "Lowell removes the mask": M. L. Rosenthal, "Poetry as Confession," *Nation*, 19 Sept. 1959, 154.

32 "Jesus, I'm a defensive creature!": Sexton to Snodgrass, 9 June 1959, in *Self-Portrait in Letters*, 79.

33 "I have no life separate": Plath, 7 Nov. 1959, *Journals of Sylvia Plath*, 524.

33 "in such despondency": Quoted in Middlebrook, *Anne Sexton*, 111.

33 "spindly-legged . . . slightly mad": Hardwick, "Boston," 70.

34 "Oh, the poets!": Quoted in Showalter and Smith, "Nurturing Relationship," 127–28.

34 "During this period, all of us": Kumin, "How It Was," xxiv.

34 "it was like they were taking": Quoted in Showalter and Smith, "Nurturing Relationship," 128.

34 "insistent me-me-me": Holmes to Kumin, 6 Aug. 1961, Kumin Papers, Beinecke Library, Yale University, and hereafter.

35 "firm patience and a kind smile": The letter, which is presumably to Holmes, is reprinted in Paula Salvio, *Anne Sexton: Teacher of Weird Abundance* (Albany: State University of New York Press, 2007), 67.

35 "something worth learning": Sexton, "For John, Who Begs Me Not to Enquire Further," in *Complete Poems*, 34.

36 "Mrs. Sexton's craft is quick": Thomas Lask, "Books of the Times," *New York Times*, 18 July 1960.

36 "changed his mind": Quoted in Middlebrook, *Anne Sexton*, 125.

36 "on my mind unpleasantly": Holmes to Kumin, 6 Aug. 1961, Kumin Papers.

37 "Here was my Christian academic daddy": Quoted in Showalter and Smith, "Nurturing Relationship," 122.

37 he wrote another letter: Holmes to Kumin, 13 Aug. 1961, Kumin Papers.

37 "disapproval and anger": This is gleaned from Holmes's response: Holmes to Kumin, 16 Aug. 1961, Kumin Papers.

CHAPTER 3: Writer-Human-Woman

41 "There are no guards": Quoted in Middlebrook, *Anne Sexton*, 146.

41 "Tranquility from having the empty house": Tillie Olsen, "Tell Me a Riddle," in *Tell Me a Riddle, Requa I, and Other Works* (Lincoln: University of Nebraska Press, 2013), 60–61.

41 "help her poor body to die": Ibid., 98.

41 "Because I'm use't": Ibid., 58.

41 "light, like a bird": Ibid., 92.

42 "I read Tillie Olsen's": Sexton to Miller, 14 Nov. 1960, in *Self-Portrait in Letters*, 116.

42 "My eyes are still crying": Sexton to Olsen, 5 April 1960, Sexton Papers, Harry Ransom Center, University of Texas at Austin, and hereafter.

42 Sexton's admiration: Sexton to Olsen, 1 March 1964, Sexton Papers.

42 "many Latin American, Negro, Samoan": Olsen to Sexton, 26 Jan. [n.d., but presumably 1961], Sexton Papers.

43 "most sought-after writer": Quoted in Panthea Reid, *Tillie Olsen: One Woman, Many Riddles* (New Brunswick, N.J.: Rutgers University Press, 2010), 88.

45 talked over every ballot issue: Julie Edwards Olsen, interview by author, 30 Jan. 2016.

45 "nothing but girls": Quoted in Reid, *Tillie Olsen*, 174. The details of Olsen's twenties come from a few different sources: Reid's biography, interviews with Olsen's daughters Julie and Kathie, my impressions from reading collected archival material from the 1930s, and my reading of her reportage from this period.

46 "early genius": Robert Cantwell, "Literary Life in California," *New Republic*, 22 Aug. 1934.

46   "Do not ask me": Tillie Lerner, "The Strike," *Partisan Review* 1, no. 4 (1934): 3–9.

47   "She worked, she had a job": Julie Olsen Edwards, interview by author.

47   surprise visit from FBI agents: Reid, *Tillie Olsen*, 250.

47   "Not a moment to sit": Undated scrap of paper (possibly a journal entry), Olsen archives, Special Collections & University Archives, Stanford University, and hereafter.

47   "I don't even know": Ibid.

48   "Pushed by the most elementary force": Quoted in Reid, *Tillie Olsen*, 190. I quote from Reid here to give her credit for the archival labor in dating these notes and ordering them correctly.

48   "Dr. Raimundi fellowship": Quoted in ibid., 191.

48   "a young mother": Tillie Olsen, "I Stand Here Ironing," in *Tell Me a Riddle*, 5–14. Olsen retitled "Help Her to Believe" for publication in *The Best American Short Stories 1957*, ed. Martha Foley (Boston: Houghton Mifflin, 1957).

49   she had just taken Kathie: Reid, *Tillie Olsen*, 195.

49   she had three new stories: For more on Olsen's years at Stanford, see ibid., 197–203.

50   money for a washing machine: Julie Edward Olsen and Kathie Olsen, interviews by author, 13 June 2016.

50   "Last night": Undated scrap of paper (possibly a journal entry), Olsen archives.

51   "substantial . . . sze. 14 clothes": Olsen to Sexton, 26 Jan. [n.d., but presumably 1961], Sexton Papers.

51   "Jesus God! You're publishing everywhere!": Quoted in Middlebrook, *Anne Sexton*, 94.

51   "I suppose some would say": Nolan Miller, Letter of Recommendation in Olsen application, 10 Jan. 1962, Institute Archives.

52   most productive when her conditions: Dick Scowcroft, Letter of Recommendation in Olsen application, 12 Jan. 1962, Institute Archives.

52   "writers who help": Olsen to Sexton, "November, a late night note," n.d. [presumably 1960], Sexton Papers.

52   "That was your *first* one": Olsen to Sexton, 26 Jan. [n.d., but presumably 1961], Sexton Papers.

52   "As a writer": Sexton to Olsen, n.d. [1961], Sexton Papers.

53   "leave writing": Olsen to Sexton, 20 May [n.d., presumably 1961], Sexton Papers.

53   "It takes such time to build": Sexton to Olsen, n.d. [presumably 1961], Sexton Papers.

54   by 1950, only 1 percent of Americans: May, *Homeward Bound*, 12.

54   Twenty percent of American workers: Ralph Brown, *Loyalty and Security: Employment Tests in the United States* (New Haven, Conn.: Yale University Press, 1958).

54   "We were an uneasy, shifty-eyed generation": Janet Malcolm, *The Silent Woman: Sylvia Plath and Ted Hughes* (New York: Vintage, 1993), 41.

CHAPTER 4: A Messy Experiment

56   "intellectually displaced women": Hechinger, "Radcliffe Pioneers."

56   "difficult, if not impossible": Ibid.

57 "a group of gifted but not necessarily widely recognized": Ibid.

57 "it was she": Linda Gray Sexton, *Searching for Mercy Street: My Journey Back to My Mother, Anne Sexton* (Boston: Little, Brown and Company, 1994), 36.

59 "We were scared stiff": Quoted in Yaffe, *Mary Ingraham Bunting*, Kindle ed.

59 federal R&D spending increased: Laura Micheletti Puaca, *Searching for Scientific Womanpower: Technocratic Feminism and the Politics of National Security, 1940–1980* (Chapel Hill: University of North Carolina Press, 2014), 86.

59 "the security of the Nation": National Defense Education Act of 1958, Title 1: General Provisions, sec. 101.

60 "all of the males": Quoted in Yaffe, *Mary Ingraham Bunting*, Kindle ed.

60 "I was deeply puzzled": Mary Bunting, speech to Annual Women's College Conference at Douglass, 7 March 1981, quoted in ibid.

60 "her awakening": Mary Ingraham Bunting-Smith Oral History, Bunting Personal Papers, Schlesinger Library, Radcliffe College, 87.

60 "never been interested in women": Mary Bunting, "New Patterns in the Education of Women" (speech at Old Guard Summit, 22 Oct. 1956), Bunting Professional Papers, Schlesinger Library, Radcliffe College.

61 "Well this housekeeping game": Quoted in Yaffe, *Mary Ingraham Bunting*, Kindle ed.

61 The same could be said of their careers: I have drawn on several sources to describe Bunting's biography and career trajectory. One is an oral history included in the papers of Mary Ingraham Bunting-Smith, 1959–1972, at the Schlesinger Library. Others are a profile of Bunting in *Time* as well as Yaffe's biography. The former is "Education: One Woman, Two Lives," *Time*, 3 Nov. 1961, 68–73.

62 "I didn't have to worry": Bunting-Smith Oral History, 17.

62 Bunting realized how many factors conspired: "One Woman, Two Lives," 68.

62 "educated womanpower": Mary I. Bunting, "A Huge Waste: Educated Womanpower," *New York Times*, 7 May 1961.

62 number of women enrolled in college: Linda Eisenmann, *Higher Education for Women in Postwar America, 1945–1965* (Baltimore: Johns Hopkins University Press, 2006), 44.

62 "incidental students": Ibid., 5.

63 "climate of unexpectation": According to the oral history in the Bunting-Smith Papers, Bunting first used this phrase at an American Council meeting in 1957. She continued to use this phrase frequently: for instance, in a speech to the AWA on February 17, 1960.

63 "GIs of Douglass": Katheryne McCormick, quoted in Yaffe, *Mary Ingraham Bunting*, Kindle ed.

64 "The research of those years": Esther Raushenbush, *Occasional Papers on Education* (Bronxville, N.Y.: Sarah Lawrence College, 1979), quoted in Eisenmann, *Higher Education for Women in Postwar America*, 1.

64 "boiling very fiercely": Bunting-Smith Oral History, 87.

64 "ways in which women": Ibid.

65 "small book": Ibid.

65 "in terms of men against women": Ibid., 88.

65 "I was thinking much more": Ibid.

66 "Every one of these neat little brick houses": Quoted in Yaffe, *Mary Ingraham Bunting,* Kindle ed.

67 "I wish Harvard had a president": "Down-to-Earth College President: Mary Ingraham Bunting," *New York Times,* 29 April 1969, 28.

68 She secured a five-year, $150,000 grant: Press release, 20 April 1961, Institute Archives.

68 she was officially appointed: Bunting to Smith, 17 Jan. 1961, Bunting Professional Papers.

68 "a sweet kind of whirling dervish": Kathie Olsen, interview by author, 16 June 2016.

68 "terrific": Lily Macrakis, interview by author, May 2016.

68 "deplore[d] the lack of incentive": "Radcliffe Institute for Research or Radcliffe Center for Continuing Scholarship," press release, Nov. 1960, Institute Archives.

68 "This sense of stagnation": "The Radcliffe Institute for Independent Study," brochure, Nov. 1960, Institute Archives.

69 In 1960, the median full-time female worker: U.S. Census Bureau, Current Population Survey, 1961 to 2009 Annual Social and Economic Supplements, census.gov.

69 By the academic year 1952–1953: Paula Giddings, *When and Where I Enter: The Impact of Black Women on Race and Sex in America* (New York: Amistad, 2006), 245–46.

69 upwardly mobile black women: Ibid., 251.

70 "waste of highly talented, educated womanpower": Bunting, "Huge Waste."

70 "a place to work free": Ibid., 112.

71 "Dear Radcliffe, I love you!": Chamberlain to Bunting, 21 Jan. 1961, Bunting Professional Papers.

71 "children are sick": Lucie Hainier to Bunting, 22 Nov. 1960, Institute Archives.

CHAPTER 5: I Got It!

73 "preliminary applicants": Bryant to the Executive Committee of the Institute, memo, 1960, Institute Archives.

73 "caliber of applicant": Bryant to Bunting, memo, 30 Dec. 1960, Bunting Professional Papers.

73 women made up 33 percent of master's: Eisenmann, *Higher Education for Women in Postwar America,* 44.

74 "anemic": Sexton application to the Radcliffe Institute for Independent Study, 7 March 1961, Institute Archives.

75 "Amorality and the Protagonist": Maxine Kumin application to the Radcliffe Institute for Independent Study, 29 Feb. 1961, Institute Archives.

76 "also were you going to become bohemian": Oral history interview with Barbara Swan, 13 June 1973–12 June 1974, Archives of American Art, Smithsonian Institution.

77 "I was running like a business": Ibid.

77 Swan trained with Karl Zerbe: To describe Zerbe, the Museum School, and figu-

rative modernism as a movement, I have relied on Judith Bookbinder's *Boston Modern: Figurative Expressionism as Alternative Modernism* (Durham: University of New Hampshire Press, 2005).

77 "to be dissolved so completely": Clement Greenberg, "Avant-Garde and Kitsch," in *The New York Intellectuals Readers*, ed. Neil Jumonville (New York: Routledge, 2007), 146.

78 "one of the more gifted students": Dorothy Adlow, "Barbara Swan Shows Group Show of Portraits," *Christian Science Monitor*, 6 Nov. 1947, 4.

78 "They didn't trust a woman": Quoted in Bookbinder, *Boston Modern*, 221.

78 "absolutely categorized all women": Quoted in ibid., 219–20.

78 "I was so determined": Quoted in ibid., 221.

78 "somber tonalities": Oral history interview with Swan.

79 "There is a quivering vitality": Dorothy Adlow, "Artist's First Solo Display at the Boris Mirski Gallery," *Christian Science Monitor*, 23 March 1953, 7.

79 "I was involved in the mother-child relationship": Oral history interview with Swan.

80 "humanistic shot in the arm": Edgar J. Driscoll, "This Week in the Art World: Barbara Swan's Exhibit Humanistic Shot in the Arm," *Boston Globe*, 10 Nov. 1957.

80 "bogged down": Barbara Swan, "Premier Cru," *Radcliffe Quarterly*, June 1986, 17.

80 "be all": Swan to Mary Bunting, 22 Nov. 1960, Institute Archives.

81 "I feel that a woman artist": Barbara Swan application to Radcliffe Institute for Independent Study, 24 Feb. 1961, Institute Archives.

82 "permanent quarters": "Fay House Reopens After Renovations," Radcliffe Institute for Advanced Study at Harvard University, 9 May 2012, www.radcliffe .harvard.edu.

83 she expressed enthusiasm: Sexton application, Institute Archives.

83 "WOW! We'll know she's around": Connie Smith, Notes on Sexton interview, 29 April 1961, Institute Archives.

83 "Epithets with which I had been branded": Kumin, *Pawnbroker's Daughter*, 39.

84 "interests and attitudes and values": Kumin, interview by Alice Ryerson and Martha White, Jan. 1962, 30, Institute Archives.

84 "I would say that the unhappiness": Ibid.

84 "supremely and sublimely happy": Ibid., 31.

84 "playing the triple role": Kumin application, Institute Archives.

84 "fine teacher": Frank A. Redinnick, Letter of Recommendation in Kumin Application, Institute Archives.

85 "Has many interests": Smith, Notes on Kumin Application, 29 April 1961, Institute Archives.

86 "of a little known family of spiders": Rosen to Bunting, 18 May 1961, Bunting Professional Papers.

86 "at long last": Pavone to Bunting, 23 July 1961, Bunting Professional Papers.

87 "I hope that the present program": Blanchard to Bunting, 23 Nov. 1960, Bunting Professional Papers.

87 "a simple style": Levertov to Bunting, 5 Dec. 1960, Institute Archives.

87 loft above a ham-canning factory: Donna Krolik Hollenberg, *A Poet's Revo-*

lution: The Life of Denise Levertov (Berkeley: University of California Press, 2013), 173.

87 "was ripe for such a conception": Rene Bryant to Bunting, 30 Dec. 1960, Institute Archives.

87 37 percent of all college students: Eisenmann, *Higher Education for Women in Postwar America,* 44.

87 "Women are going back to work": "The Married Woman Goes Back to Work," *Woman's Home Companion,* Oct. 1956, 42, repr. in *Women's Magazines, 1940–1960: Gender Roles and the Popular Press,* ed. Nancy A. Walker (Boston: Bedford/St. Martin's, 1998), 87.

88 nearly 40 percent of American women: In November 1960, 38.2 percent of women were in the workforce: U.S. Bureau of Labor Statistics, Civilian Labor Force Participation Rate: Women [LNS11300002], retrieved from FRED, Federal Reserve Bank of St. Louis, fred.stlouisfed.org.

88 "It's liberating to read": These alumnae are quoted anonymously in a memo from Rene Bryant to Bunting, 2 Dec. 1960, Institute Archives.

88 "pulling woman-the-homemaker": Bethany M. Hamilton to Bunting, 23 March 1961, Institute Archives.

89 "seeing her child": Lynne Gaines to Bunting, 13 Jan. 1961, Institute Archives.

89 "on those who have done": Bethany M. Hamilton to Bunting, 23 March 1961, Institute Archives.

89 "Dear Mrs. Kumin": Connie Smith to Kumin, 27 May 1961, Institute Archives (the language is the same in all of the acceptance letters).

91 the Sexton family went out for dinner: Anecdote from interview with Sexton, Jan. 1962, Institute Archives.

91 "I think everyone must have thought": Ibid. Sexton was quite candid about her disappointment and her elation in this interview; it thus serves as my source for her feelings about nearly missing, and then receiving, the grant.

91 "Hark Hark the lark": Quoted in Middlebrook, *Anne Sexton,* 145.

91 Her neighbors enjoyed: Interview with Sexton, Jan. 1962, Institute Archives.

91 "flush and important": Quotation is from Showalter and Smith, "Nurturing Relationship"; detail about December telephone line installation from Maxine Kumin and Anne Sexton, "On Poetry," Seminar for Radcliffe Institute, 13 Feb. 1962, Radcliffe College Sound Recordings.

92 "contributing": Interview with Sexton, Jan. 1962, Institute Archives.

92 first twenty-four women: Institute press release, 2 June 1961, Kumin Papers.

92 The vast majority of the women: "Ages of Children of Affiliate and Associate Scholars, 1961–1962," Institute Archives.

92 Nine of them were married: Press release, 2 June 1961, Bunting Professional Papers.

93 It was a rare thing: Wendy Wang and Kim Parker, "Record Share of Americans Have Never Married," Pew Research Center's Social & Demographic Trends Project, 14 Jan. 2015.

93 "six rude answers": Beryl Pfizer, "Six Rude Answers to One Rude Question," in Walker, *Women's Magazines, 1940–1960,* 142.

93 graduate student housing: Wittlin biography from press release, 2 June 1961, Bunting Professional Papers.

CHAPTER 6: The Premier Cru

98 preferred to host intimate dinners: Mary Lawlor, "Do Dishes? No, Rather Paint," *Boston Traveler,* 13 May 1963.

98 each fellow's stipend: Smith to Swan, 26 Sept. 1961, Institute Archives.

99 "pounced on each other": Swan to Smith, 6 Oct. 1961, Institute Archives.

100 "exotic birds": Brita Stendahl, "On the Edge of Women's Liberation," *Radcliffe Quarterly,* June 1986, 16.

100 The two frequently traded clothing: Diane Middlebrook, "Remembering Anne Sexton: Maxine Kumin in Conversation with Diane Middlebrook," ed. Nancy K. Miller, *PMLA* 127, no. 2 (2012): 292–300.

100 They were both poets: Kumin and Sexton, "On Poetry."

100 "rabbit warren": Swan, "Premier Cru," 17.

101 mid-gesture, and probably mid-speech: Portrait accompanied Elizabeth Barker, "Typically Atypical," *Radcliffe Quarterly,* June 1986, 6.

101 Swan was in awe of Niebuhr: Swan, "Premier Cru," 17–18.

103 "Premier Cru": Ibid.

103 Swan took care to pose Smith: Ibid.

104 "Radcliffe's new baby": Ian Forman, "Motherhood End Career? Not with Radcliffe's New Baby," *Boston Morning Globe,* June [2?], 1961, Institute Archives.

104 In one photo: Newton, "Years of Study, Writing Cheers Newton Lady Poets."

104 Kumin sits with her arm around Daniel: Ibid.

104 "Do Dishes?": Lawlor, "Do Dishes? No, Rather Paint."

104 "We were pioneers": Untitled reflection, Kumin Papers.

104 "reasonable, constructive, moderate": "Education: One Woman, Two Lives," *Time,* 3 Nov. 1961, 68.

104 Only 11 percent of families: These statistics come from the following three sources: Wendy Wang, "Breadwinner Moms," Pew Research Center, 29 May 2013, www.pewsocialtrends.org; Sarah Jane Glynn, "Breadwinning Mothers Are Increasingly the US Norm," Center for American Progress, 19 Dec. 2016, www.americanprogress.org; and "Black Women and the Wage Gap," National Partnership for Women and Their Families, April 2019, www.nationalpartnership.org.

105 Even middle-class women: Premilla Nadasen, *Household Workers Unite* (Boston: Beacon, 2016), 65.

105 "which is more of a status symbol": Both quotations from untitled reflection on Institute, Kumin Papers.

105 Two fellows used the money: These and other details from "Women of Talent," *Newsweek,* 23 Oct. 1961.

105 one-third of all employed black women: Nadasen, *Household Workers Unite,* 2.

105 "Black and Hispanic women": *The Gender Wage Gap by Occupation 2017 and by Race and Ethnicity,* report, Institute for Women's Policy Research, April 2018, iwpr.org.

105 "women of talent": "Women of Talent," *Newsweek,* 23 Oct. 1961.

106 "He doesn't like a messy house": Interview with Sexton, Jan. 1962, Institute Archives.

106   She swam her laps: Pool details from Middlebrook, *Anne Sexton*, 150–51.

106   "the frightening world": Quoted in ibid., 151.

107   There is a photo of Sexton: "Women of Talent," *Newsweek*, 23 Oct. 1961.

107   Sexton was unusually happy: Sexton to Olsen, 11 Nov. 1961, Sexton Papers.

107   "It is more work": Sexton to Olsen, 5 Jan. 1962, Olsen Papers.

108   "status symbol": Interview with Sexton, Jan. 1962, Institute Archives. Linda, Anne's eldest, contests Anne's assessment of how Kayo and his mother (Anne's mother-in-law) viewed Anne's poetry. Linda remembers both her father and her grandmother supporting Anne's work, even if they didn't understand it. She doesn't recall the Radcliffe grant changing their views dramatically. See Middlebrook, *Anne Sexton*, 152.

108   "first reading": Middlebrook, *Anne Sexton*, 152, 161.

108   Sexton lay down: Kumin and Sexton, "On Poetry."

108   "The Fortress": Sexton describes the composition in interview with Sexton, Jan. 1962, Institute Archives.

109   "the leaves have been fed": Anne Sexton, "The Fortress," in *Complete Poems*, 66–67.

109   "woman's dying": Anne Sexton, "The Operation," in *Complete Poems*, 57.

110   "You've got to be hard": Interview with Sexton, Jan. 1962, Institute Archives.

110   It wasn't until she received: Linda disputes this; see note above.

110   "being a woman": Interview with Sexton, Jan. 1962, Institute Archives.

111   "Yes. Much better": Ibid.

111   "I don't think that many of us": Macrakis, interview by author, May 2016.

112   "opposed to country clubs": Roiphe, *Art and Madness*, 73.

112   "anti-Smith girl": Ibid.

113   "There were certain things": Macrakis interview.

113   "So what?": Ibid.

114   wanton display of wealth: "Women of Talent," *Newsweek*, 23 Oct. 1961.

114   "doing my duty": Macrakis interview.

114   "I thought that before": Interview with Sexton, Jan. 1962, Institute Archives.

115   "So you felt the same as me?": Macrakis interview.

115   "exact carbon copy": Interview with Kumin, Jan. 1962, Institute Archives.

115   "I would just as soon": Interview with Sexton, Jan. 1962, Institute Archives.

115   "Can we play?": Ibid.

115   "There are times": Ibid.

116   "My writing, Bah": Sexton to Olsen, Nov. 1961, Sexton Papers.

116   "not very different": Foreword to "The American Female: A Special Supplement," *Harper's*, Oct. 1962.

117   "They were horrid": Macrakis interview.

118   It was not a choice: "A Literary Woman 'at Home' in Newton," *Newton Times*, 15 Nov. 1972, 12–14.

118   "There were friends and neighbors": Untitled reflection, Kumin Papers.

119   "charged with evaluating": Elizabeth Singer More, *Report of the President's Commission on the Status of Women: Background, Content, Significance*, report, History and Literature, Harvard University.

119   "How little we knew": Stendahl, "On the Edge of Women's Liberation," 16.

120   "a readiness to listen": Kumin, untitled reflection, Kumin Papers.

CHAPTER 7: We're Just Talking

121 The seminars were not mandatory: Stendahl, "On the Edge of Women's Liberation," 16.

121 Vilma Hunt: Untitled news clipping, Institute Archives.

122 "mother hen": Stendahl, "On the Edge of Women's Liberation," 16.

122 She had also annotated: Maxine Kumin, mimeograph of "Morning Swim," Kumin Papers.

122 "I think we might as well": Kumin and Sexton, "On Poetry."

123 There were several reasons: Sexton and Kumin discuss their wariness in Showalter and Smith, "Nurturing Relationship," 129–31.

123 women made up only: Gail Collins, quoted in Francine Prose, "Women's Progress: Gail Collins's 'When Everything Changed,'" *New York Times*, 20 Oct. 2009.

124 Even later in their careers: A sentiment expressed in Showalter and Smith, "Nurturing Relationship."

124 "You enter into the voice": Ibid., 125.

124 "My books make me happy": Quoted in Middlebrook, *Anne Sexton*, 151.

124 "We're just talking": Showalter and Smith, "Nurturing Relationship," 127.

125 "It is the most stimulating": Ibid.

125 "winked and sulked": Maxine Kumin, "A Hundred Nights" and "Casablanca," in *Selected Poems, 1960–1990* (New York: Norton, 1997), 24.

125 Though *Halfway* sold only three hundred copies: Maxine Kumin, *Always Beginning: Essays on a Life in Poetry* (Port Townsend, Wash.: Copper Canyon Press, 2000), 98.

125 "had unquestionably": Harold Rosenberg, "Six American Poets," *Commentary*, Oct. 1961.

126 "set out, oily and nude": Kumin, "Morning Swim," in *Selected Poems*, 31.

126 "Water and I": Kumin and Sexton, "On Poetry."

126 "Hungry for oysters": Maxine Kumin, "In That Land," in *Bringing Together: Uncollected Early Poems, 1958–1989* (New York: W. W. Norton, 2005).

127 "an apologia for": Kumin and Sexton, "On Poetry."

127 "I'm not awfully well-prepared": Ibid.

128 "morbid sensibilities": Ibid.

128 "stiff procession": Anne Sexton, "The Truth the Dead Know," in *Complete Poems*, 49.

129 "someone else that I wasn't": Kumin and Sexton, "On Poetry."

129 "I'm afraid all my poems": Ibid.

129 "It's for all of us": Ibid.

130 "Turn off the tape!": Ibid.

130 "It's what your mummy": Ibid.

131 "Oh, that's a most complicated": Ibid.

131 "We've been doing this for years": Ibid.

131 "Dear Mrs. Kumin": Ibid.

131 "supposed to destroy each other": Showalter and Smith, "Nurturing Relationship," 129.

132 "No, no, we're different": Ibid., 125.

133 "I would say we never meddled": Kumin to Irving Weinman, 13 Jan. 1975, Kumin Papers.

CHAPTER 8: Happily Awarded

134 $3,600 each year: Tillie Olsen application to the Radcliffe Institute for Independent Study, 13 Jan. 1962, Institute Archives.

135 "Up at six": Olsen to Sexton, 26 Jan. n.d., Sexton Papers.

135 "The novel is the book": Cowley to Olsen, 2 Feb. 1960, Olsen Papers.

135 "How interrupting is it?": Olsen to Sexton, n.d., Sexton Papers.

135 "Write them": Sexton to Olsen, 5 Jan. 1962, Olsen Papers.

136 "unskilled work": Olsen application, Institute Archives.

137 *"Economic freedom"*: Ibid.

138 They were the family: Kathie Olsen and Julie Olsen, interviews by author, June 2016.

138 "I think it was the first": Quoted in Reid, *Tillie Olsen*, 194.

138 "an essential portion": Olsen application, 5, Institute Archives.

138 "Clumsy, ineffectual application": Olsen to Sexton, n.d., Institute Archives.

139 "an attractive woman": Hannah Green, Letter of Recommendation in Olsen Application, 15 Jan. 1962, Institute Archives.

139 "simultaneously dedicated": Anne Wilder, Letter of Recommendation in Olsen Application, 12 Jan. 1962, Institute Archives.

140 "lucky": Oral history interview with Pineda.

142 She was inspired by the play: "Marianna Pineda," *Sartle*, 30 April 2018, www .sartle.com.

142 "I felt we were too different": Oral history interview with Harold Tovish, 24 June 1974 and 17 March 1977, Archives of American Art, Smithsonian Institute.

143 "Oh, it's very nice": Oral history interview with Pineda.

143 "great liberation": Ibid.

143 "she feels her way": Quoted in Patricia Hills, "Marianna Pineda's Sculpture," in *Marianna Pineda: Sculpture, 1949 to 1996* (Boston: Alabaster Press, 1996), 2.

144 he sold Pineda's *Mother and Child:* Marianna Pineda Papers, 1943–1998, Archives of American Art, Smithsonian Institution.

144 Swetzoff took a third: Nina Tovish, interview by author, 23 June 2016.

145 "It was a very lonely business": Oral history interview with Pineda.

146 they were friends: Nina Tovish, interview by author.

147 "Maybe that was a mistake": Oral history interview with Pineda.

148 "I have hopes": Marianna Pineda application to the Radcliffe Institute of Independent Study, 15 Oct. 1961, Institute Archives.

148 "a very strong candidate": Ibid.

149 "Dear Friend": Sexton to Olsen, 3 May 1962, Sexton Papers.

149 "candidate of unquestionable distinction": Anonymous evaluation, 5 April 1962, Institute Archives.

150 "I WISH THAT WE ALL": Quoted in Reid, *Tillie Olsen*, 215.

150 "JOYFULLY ACCEPT TRUST": Telegram from Tillie Olsen, 2 May 1962, Institute Archives.

151 "I love you": Quoted in Reid, *Tillie Olsen*, 224–25.

152 she also arranged for Laurie: FBI file, Olsen Papers.

152 She decided to quit her job: Kathie Olsen, interview by author, 16 June 2016.

152 "I was furious": Julie Olsen Edwards, interview by author, 3 June 2016.

152 "Marianna's generation": Oral history interview with Harold Tovish.

153 As the Olsen family: Reid, *Tillie Olsen*, 225.

CHAPTER 9: The Equivalents

154 She wondered if she: Reid, *Tillie Olsen*, 226.

155 The two women took a walk: Ibid.

155 "Meeting you and being with you!": Sexton to Olsen, n.d., "Monday night," Olsen Papers.

155 "With one long breath": Ibid.

156 "Having been with you": Ibid.

156 she felt electricity: Kathie Olsen, interview by author.

156 "What are you working on?": Ibid.

157 "People were not there": Ibid.

158 "She loved seeing nature": Ibid.

158 Swan produced a portrait of Olsen: The portrait is printed in an insert in Reid, *Tillie Olsen*.

159 It was a warm fall: "Boston, MA Weather History, October 1962," Weather Underground, www.wunderground.com.

159 she delighted: Details from Reid, *Tillie Olsen*, 225, and Kathie Olsen, interview by author.

159 The company paid women: Jane Thompson and Alexandra Lange, *Design Research: The Store That Brought Modern Living to American Homes* (San Francisco: Chronicle Books, 2010), 76.

160 she bought bright, patterned cloth: Kathie Olsen, interview by author.

160 Teasdale had written: "Sara Teasdale," Poetry Foundation, accessed July 14, 2019, poetryfoundation.org.

160 "I found more joy": Sara Teasdale, "Morning," *Poetry Magazine*, Oct. 1915, poetry foundation.org.

160 "the lowest of the low": Quoted in Middlebrook, *Anne Sexton*, 196.

160 "the maintenance of life": Tillie Olsen, *Silences* (New York: Feminist Press at CUNY, 2014), 34.

161 "Our love": Quoted in Middlebrook, *Anne Sexton*, 196. Entire anecdote drawn from Middlebrook.

161 Swan's husband, Alan: Kathie Olsen, interview by author; detail about shift from Reid, *Tillie Olsen*, 227.

161 "everybody had to have dinner": Kathie Olsen, interview by author.

161 why does anyone ever fall in love?: Julie Olsen Edwards, interview by author.

162 the Tovishes stayed up: Reid, *Tillie Olsen*, 227.

162 "It makes me so mad": Kumin and Sexton, "On Poetry."

162 "health": Quoted in Middlebrook, *Anne Sexton*, 197. Anecdote from Sexton's seminar talk in May 1963, Radcliffe Sound Recordings.

163 *More Eggs of Things*: Maria Popova, "Eggs of Things: Anne Sexton and Max-

ine Kumin's Science-Inspired 1963 Children's Book," *Brain Pickings*, 18 Sept. 2015.

164 "had something to do": Oral history interview with Pineda.

164 "as we think they may have": Ibid.

CHAPTER 10: Me, Me Too

165 studying with George Lockwood: "Art of George Lockwood at the Library," *Duxbury Clipper*, 4 March 1971.

166 "chicks": Lois Swirnoff and Barbara Swan, "On the Fine Arts," Institute seminar, 1 May 1962, Radcliffe College Archives Sound Recordings.

166 "small visual essay": Ibid.

167 "old palaces": "The Musicians," mimeograph from Kumin and Sexton, "On Poetry."

167 "a great hole in the earth": Ibid.

168 "it isn't a good reading poem": Ibid.

168 "How about it": Ibid.

168 "My painting and drawing": Ibid.

169 "It's like incest": Ibid.

169 "It's a false image!": Ibid.

169 "The greatest art": Ibid.

169 "Barbara and Anne": Olsen quoted in Middlebrook, *Anne Sexton*, 197.

170 "Anne moved into my world": Barbara Swan, "A Reminiscence," in *Anne Sexton: The Artist and Her Critics*, ed. J. D. McClatchy (Bloomington: Indiana University Press, 1978), 82.

170 "The artist and the poet": Ibid., 81.

170 "marvelous blue-eyed comic": Plath to Sexton, 5 Feb. 1961, Sexton Papers.

171 "an Earth Mother": *Journals of Sylvia Plath*, 500.

171 "a house of our children": Ibid.

171 "I am bedded": Plath to Sexton, 21 Aug. 1962, Sexton Papers.

171 "the boot in the face": Sylvia Plath, "Daddy," in *Ariel: The Restored Edition* (New York: HarperCollins, 2004), 75.

171 "I have done it again": Sylvia Plath, "Lady Lazarus," in *Ariel*, 14.

172 "saw the suicide": Middlebrook, *Anne Sexton*, 198.

172 "Thief!": Anne Sexton, "Sylvia's Death," in "The Bar Fly Ought to Sing," in *No Evil Star*, 11.

173 "those who contemplate suicide": Anne Sexton, "Wanting to Die," in "The Bar Fly Ought to Sing," in *No Evil Star*, 8.

173 "You may paste it": Quoted in Middlebrook, *Anne Sexton*, 200.

173 "fascination with death": "Bar Fly Ought to Sing," 11.

173 "It is not *when* I have a baby": *Journals of Sylvia Plath*, 495.

CHAPTER 11: Mad for the Message

174 "a serious professional commitment": Betty Friedan, *The Feminine Mystique* (New York: W. W. Norton, 2001), 477.

174 "the problem that has no name": Ibid., 66.
174 "a vague undefined wish": Ibid., 114.
175 "the highest value": Ibid., 91.
175 "sexual passivity": Ibid., 92.
175 "happy housewife heroine": Ibid., 93.
176 "sexual sell": Ibid., 299.
176 "sex-directed educators": Ibid., 227.
176 "Much is being written": Quoted in Coontz, *Strange Stirring*, 144.
177 "The indictment is uncompromising": Fred M. Hechinger, "Women 'Educated' Out of Careers," *New York Times*, 6 March 1963, 7.
177 "some hard whacks": Charlotte Armstrong, "The Feminine Mystique Explored," *Los Angeles Times*, 2 June 1963, B17.
177 "trapped": Jean Litman Block, "Who Says American Women Are 'Trapped'?," *Los Angeles Times*, 6 Oct. 1963, C10.
177 Angry letters poured into: Letters from readers, "In Defense of Today's Woman," *Chicago Tribune*, 9 June 1963, H40.
177 said it well: As Coontz puts it, "Books don't become best sellers because they are ahead of their time. They become best sellers when they tap into concerns that people are already mulling over, pull together ideas and data that have not yet spread beyond specialists and experts, and bring these all together in a way that is easy to understand and explain to others."
178 one of the best-selling nonfiction books: Coontz, *Strange Stirring*, 145–49.
178 "mad for the message": Kumin to Sexton, 23 Aug. 1963, Kumin Papers.
179 "I felt as though": Quoted in Coontz, *Strange Stirring*, 81.
179 "I finally realized": Ibid.
179 "I can't express": Ibid., 83.
179 notes "showed her": Linda Gray Sexton, *Searching for Mercy Street*, 98.
179 "the only kind of work": Friedan, *Feminine Mystique*, 476.
180 "The amateur or dilettante": Ibid., 477.
180 "The 'arts' seem": Ibid., 476–77.
180 "But I have noticed": Ibid., 477.
180 "Women don't strive": Interview with Anne Sexton, Jan. 1962, Institute Archives.
180 "Money helps": Ibid.
181 "washing herself down": Anne Sexton, "Housewife," in *Collected Poems*, 77.
181 "And suppose the darlings": Maxine Kumin, "Purgatory," in *Selected Poems*, 43.
182 "The fact is": Letter from Maxine Kumin, *Ladies Home Journal*, 1 Oct. 1962, Kumin Papers.
183 "If the kids were sick": Julie Olsen Edwards, interview by author.
183 "women worked, period": Ibid.
183 "I was a young mother": Olsen, "I Stand Here Ironing," 298.
184 "I sure would like": Quoted in Coontz, *Strange Stirring*, 132.

CHAPTER 12: Genius of a Sort

185 "It was like giving her": Kathie Olsen, interview by author.
186 "own work": Ibid.

186 Olsen had first stumbled: Olsen, *Silences*, 117.
186 "Literature can be made": Olsen, afterword to *Silences*, 117.
186 A stray footnote: Ibid.
187 "Masses of men": Rebecca Harding Davis, "Life in the Iron-Mills; or, The Korl Woman," in *Life in the Iron Mills, and Other Stories*, ed. Tillie Olsen (New York: Feminist Press at the City University of New York, 1985), 12.
188 "thwarting": Olsen, *Silences*, 6.
188 preternaturally productive writers: Ibid., 12.
189 "The house seems to take up": Ibid., 8.
189 "on writing": Seminar Schedule, Kumin Papers.
189 "some aspects of sculpture": Marianna Pineda, "Some Aspects of Sculpture," 1 Feb. 1963, Institute seminar, Radcliffe College Archives Sound Recordings.
190 "The reason Connie isn't sure": "Death of the Creative Process," transcript of a seminar talk given by Tillie Olsen, Radcliffe Institute for Independent Study, 15 March 1963, Sexton Papers.
191 "Because I so nearly": Ibid.
192 "revolutionary question": Ibid., 2.
192 "political silences": Ibid., 3.
192 "mute inglorious Miltons": Ibid., 7.
192 "living in his work": Ibid.
192 "What feeds creativity": Ibid.
193 "Now and again": Ibid.
193 "no mother of children": Ibid.
194 "minutes on the bus": Ibid., 31.
194 "The very conditions": Ibid.
195 "strange breadline system": Ibid., 9.
195 "makes it possible": Karl Marx, "Opposition of the Materialist and Idealist Outlook," *The German Ideology* (1845).
195 "My conflict": Olsen seminar transcript.
197 "If anyone had stopped her": Middlebrook, *Anne Sexton*, 168.
197 "Genius flew the coop": Sexton to Starbuck, 18 Nov. 1962, in *Self-Portrait in Letters*, 149.
197 "by not using it": Olsen seminar transcript.
197 "What kills the creative instinct": Quoted in Middlebrook, *Anne Sexton*, 198.

CHAPTER 13: Do It or Die Trying

204 "The Am. Academy": Sexton to Snodgrass, in *Self-Portrait in Letters*, 163–64.
205 "It is your chance": Ibid.
205 "The lost socks": Kumin, *Pawnbroker's Daughter*, 97.
206 "realized there were no other houses": Ibid., 100.
206 "the Old Harriman Place": Ibid., 91, 101.
206 "very spooky": Kumin to Sexton, 24 June 1963, Kumin Papers.
207 "I WILL DO IT": Kumin to Sexton, 9 Sept. 1963, Sexton Papers.
208 "gemlike": Ibid.
208 "Our good critical instincts": Sexton to Kumin, 29 Sept. 1963, Kumin Papers.
208 "It was with the words": Sexton to Kumin, 4 Oct. 1963, Kumin Papers.

208 "of self hate": Sexton to Kumin, 6 Oct. 1963, Kumin Papers.

208 It received mixed reviews: Millicent Bell, "Newton Poet's Novel Offers Moving Story," *Boston Globe,* 12 April 1965, 12; Irvin Gold, "First Novel Falls Short," *Los Angeles Times,* 4 April 1965, N15.

209 "I think about you fondly": Cowley to Olsen, 22 Jan. 1963, Olsen Papers.

209 "I have to ask": Cowley to Olsen, 15 April 1963, Olsen Papers.

209 "You should do": Cowley to Olsen, 4 Sept. 1963, Olsen Papers.

210 her own rejuvenation: Cowley to Olsen, 21 May 1963, Olsen Papers.

210 $2,500 to fund a summer: Reid, *Tillie Olsen,* 231.

210 "no worry about paying back": Ibid., 233.

211 Sam Lawrence: Ibid., 234–35.

212 "This most harmful": Tillie Olsen, "Silences: When Writers Don't Write," *Harper's,* Oct. 1965, 161.

212 Sexton, who had loved: Sexton to Olsen, 2 Oct. 1963, Sexton Papers.

212 "My show has already earned": Swan to Smith, 4 Nov. 1963, Institute Archives.

213 "I can barely cross": Sexton to Miller, 5 Aug. 1963, in *Self-Portrait in Letters,* 172.

213 "I'm terrified": Herbert A. Kenny, "Commitment Necessary to Be a Poet," 19 May 1963, *Boston Globe,* B16.

213 "I wish I were back": Sexton to Snodgrass, May 1963, in *Self-Portrait in Letters,* 164.

214 "I shall never forget": Sexton to Lowell, 6 June 1963, in *Self-Portrait in Letters,* 170.

CHAPTER 14: We Are All Going to Make It

215 "execution date": Sexton to Brother Dennis Farrell, in *Self-Portrait in Letters,* 170.

216 "All I have to say": Sexton to Kumin, 21 Aug. 1963, Kumin Papers.

216 "touched all the way": Kumin to Sexton, 23 Aug. 1963, Sexton Papers.

216 Sexton left for her year: Sexton to Kumin, "Sunday, 3:00 PM," Kumin Papers.

216 "I'm lonely as hell": Sexton to Kumin, 6 Oct. 1963, Kumin Papers.

216 "You know whats wrong": Anne Sexton to Maxine Kumin, 9 October 1963, Sexton Papers.

217 "the world's loveliest city": Quoted in Charles Poore, "Books of the Times," *New York Times,* 27 Nov. 1956.

217 She even started to style: Sexton to Kumin, 9 Oct. 1963, Kumin Papers.

217 "can you imagine *me*": Sexton to Kumin, 30 Aug. 1963, Kumin Papers.

217 "God, how awful it is": Sexton to Kumin, 3 Oct. 1963, Kumin Papers.

217 "true nature of the poet": Sexton to Kumin, 13 Sept. 1963, Kumin Papers.

217 "Oh Max, how I miss": Sexton to Kumin, 30 Aug. 1963, Kumin Papers.

218 "beg me . . . to be his": Sexton to Kumin, Oct 17 1963, Kumin Papers.

218 "Oh Maxine, all this chat": Sexton to Kumin, 9 Oct. 1963, Kumin Papers.

218 "nothing changes": Kumin to Sexton, 23 Aug. and 4 Sept. 1963, Sexton Papers.

219 "If John could not separate us": Sexton to Kumin, 29 Sept. 1963, Kumin Papers.

219 "I had not realized": Kumin to Sexton, 23 Aug. 1963, Sexton Papers.

219 "Some people have adventures": Kumin to Sexton, 4 Sept. 1963, Sexton Papers.

219 "downing crème de cacao": Kumin to Sexton, 3 Oct. 1963, Sexton Papers.

219 "periodically drop everything": Katie Roiphe, *Uncommon Arrangements: Seven Marriages in Literary London, 1910–1939* (London: Virago, 2009), 75.

220 "friendship is every bit": Ibid.

220 "touching deep friendship": Kumin to Sexton, 9 Sept. 1963, Sexton Papers.

220 She was the stormy: My analysis of their relationship is in part informed by an interview conducted with Linda Gray Sexton, 12 February 2019.

220 "There is a world of water": Maxine Kumin, "September 1," Kumin Papers.

221 "Max, the thread is bare": Sexton to Kumin, "October something" 1963, Kumin Papers.

222 "Oh Maxine": Sexton to Kumin, 12 Oct. 1963, Kumin Papers.

222 "the first time in my life": Quoted in Reid, *Tillie Olsen*, 232.

223 "We thought anyhow": Sexton to Olsen, 2 Oct. 1965, Sexton Papers.

223 "I sometimes get so longing": Olsen to Kumin, birthday note, n.d., Kumin Papers.

223 "Sometimes perhaps you": Olsen to Kumin, 15 May [n.d.], Kumin Papers.

223 "bemused": Sexton to Olsen, 2 Oct. 1965, Sexton Papers.

223 "done for": Quoted in Reid, *Tillie Olsen*, 233.

224 "What I need is a mother": Sexton to Annie Wilder, in *Self-Portrait in Letters*, 255.

224 The house was too big: Sexton to Olsen, n.d. [around Valentine's Day], Sexton Papers.

224 Her mental health deteriorated: Sexton to Olsen, 2 Oct. 1965, Sexton Papers.

224 "The g.d. tranquilizers": Sexton to Olsen, 1965, Sexton Papers.

224 "as fragile as a": Sexton to Olsen, presumably early Jan. 1966, Sexton Papers.

224 as relevant to her life: Sexton to Olsen, 2 Oct. 1965, Sexton Papers.

225 "It would be hard": James Dickey, review of *All My Pretty Ones*, by Anne Sexton, *New York Times Book Review*, 28 April 1963.

225 she carried a copy: Linda Gray Sexton, *Searching for Mercy Street*, 102.

225 These were the times: Linda Gray Sexton, interview by author, 12 Feb. 2019.

225 "it's the same old crowd": Sexton, "Flee on Your Donkey," in *Collected Poems*, 97–105.

226 "For the very first time": Sexton to Olsen, 17 or 18 May 1965, Olsen Papers.

226 "short and funny": Kathie Olsen, email to author, 20 Jan. 2018.

226 "I'm in love with you already": See Middlebrook, *Anne Sexton*, 213.

227 "the baby on the platter": Sexton, "Live," in *Complete Poems*, 167.

227 "Even so": Ibid.

227 "I say *Live*": Ibid., 170.

227 "I have a feeling": Sexton to Degener, in *Self-Portrait in Letters*, 287.

227 "with all due apologies": Sexton, "Author's Note," in *Complete Poems*, 94.

228 "They've sent me": Sexton, "Author's Note," in *Complete Poems*.

228 "I've outgrown that": Oral history interview with Swan.

228 By March 1965: Swan to Connie Smith, 11 March 1965, Institute Archives.

229 The collection had actually been inspired: Linda Gray Sexton, interview by author.

229 "most realized tone": Helen Vendler, "Malevolent Flippancy," *New Republic*, 11 Nov. 1981.

230 "No matter what life": Anne Sexton, *Transformations* (Boston: Houghton Mifflin, 1971), 3.

230 "You always read about it": Ibid., 53–54.

230 A poem based on the fairy tale: Joanna Fink, interview by author, 9 Feb. 2019.

231 "more than I trust myself": Swan, "Reminiscence," 85.

231 "I did it because of friendship": Oral history interview with Swan.

231 "Generous greeting": Quoted in Middlebrook, *Anne Sexton*, 272.

231 For the rest of her life: Ibid.

232 "Your poems are sensitive": Sexton to Dorianne Goetz, in *Self-Portrait in Letters*, 263.

232 "Mother was generous": Linda Gray Sexton, *Searching for Mercy Street*, 96–97.

232 "make not so alone": Sexton to Olsen, 2 Oct. 1965, Sexton Papers.

CHAPTER 15: Hurt Wild Baffled Angry

233 "more like a chic-career woman": Dolores Alexander, "NOW May Use Sit-Ins, Pickets to Get Equality," *Newsday*, 25 Nov. 1966, 2B.

234 "We will take strong steps": Lisa Hammel, "They Meet in Victorian Parlor to Demand 'True Equality' NOW," *New York Times*, 22 Nov. 1966, 44.

234 "had faced both kinds": Alexander, "NOW May Use Sit-Ins, Pickets to Get Equality," 2B.

235 "ingenious new methods": Ibid.

235 "put your bodies": Mario Savio, "Sit-in Address on the Steps of Sproul Hall" (speech, Free Speech Rally, University of California, Berkeley, 2 Dec. 1964).

236 Kumin didn't start: Daniel Kumin, interview by author, 15 Jan. 2019.

236 "self-liberated and pre-liberated": Joanna Fink, interview by author, 9 Feb. 2019.

236 "never applied the word": Linda Gray Sexton, *Searching for Mercy Street*, 98.

236 "I hate the way": Showalter and Smith, "Nurturing Relationship," 129.

236 "into your redeeming": Sexton, *Complete Poems*, 70–71.

237 "intensely involved": Olsen to Sexton, [n.d., presumably 1965], Sexton Papers.

237 "guess about the man": Sexton, "Unknown Girl in the Maternity Ward," in *Complete Poems*, 24.

238 "You need what you merit": Olsen to Kumin, n.d., Kumin Papers.

238 "last minute, of course": Olsen to Sexton, [n.d., presumably 1965], Sexton Papers.

238 "The suburb of Uxport": Maxine Kumin, *The Passions of Uxport: A Novel* (Westport, Conn.: Greenwood Press, 1975), 19.

239 "Boston version": Fortunata Caliri, "Boston Version of Peyton Place," *Boston Globe*, 23 April 1968, 3.3.

239 "make its way": Olsen to M. S. Wyeth, 25 Feb. 1968, Kumin Papers.

239 "I guess I feel pretty sad": Kumin to Olsen, 12 March 1968, Kumin Papers.

240 "JUST HOME YOUR LETTER": Olsen to Kumin, telegram, n.d., Kumin Papers.

240 "when I think of how mysterious": Olsen to Kumin, n.d., Kumin Papers.

240 "Third hand I hear": Olsen to Kumin, second n.d. letter, Kumin Papers.

241 "I think I know what happened": Ibid.

241 "I have never before": Kumin to Olsen, 30 April 1968, Kumin Papers.

241 "Meanwhile, Black Power": Kumin, *Passions of Uxport*, 175.

242 "was a nail biter": Ibid., 8.

242 "Nervous breakdown": Ibid., 9.

242 "Hallie, rise, wash out": Ibid., 60.

243 "snugger than sisters": Ibid., 45.

243 "They reinforced each other": Ibid., 70–71.

243 "I love you": Olsen to Kumin, n.d., Kumin Papers.

243 A visiting nurse: Middlebrook, *Anne Sexton*, 269.

244 "get into that Hallie-Sukey talk": Olsen to Kumin, n.d., Kumin Papers.

244 "I was so shocked": Sexton to Olsen, 21 July 1970, Sexton Papers.

244 "the weakest": "Review of *The Abduction*," *Kirkus Reviews*, 22 Sept. 1971.

244 "devoted reader": Sexton to Olsen, 21 July 1970, Sexton Papers.

244 "a genius": Sexton to Olsen, Nov. 1961, Sexton Papers.

244 "Anne—cherished and estranged": Olsen to Sexton, 7 Oct. [n.d.], Sexton Papers.

245 "This has been a ghastly year": Kumin to Olsen, 30 April 1968, Kumin Papers.

245 "My pants are pulled down": Olsen to Sexton, Feb. 1968, Sexton Papers.

246 "I take them": Olsen to Kumin, n.d., Kumin Papers.

CHAPTER 16: There's Nothing Wrong with Privilege, Except That Everybody Doesn't Have It

247 "The center was not holding": Joan Didion, "Slouching Towards Bethlehem," *Saturday Evening Post*, 23 Sept. 1967.

249 "DESIST IMMEDIATELY": Andrea Long Chu, "On Liking Women," *n+1*, no. 30: *Motherland* (Winter 2018), nplusonemag.com.

250 "the process by which": Rosen, *World Split Open*, 197.

250 "the movement was ravaged": Alice Echols, *Daring to Be Bad: Radical Feminism in America, 1967-1975* (Minneapolis: University of Minnesota Press, 2019), 202.

251 "struggling towards a common goal": Quoted in ibid., 217.

251 "The Eruption of Difference": Ibid., 203.

251 A 1971 report: Florence Howe, "A Report on Women and the Profession," *College English* 32, no. 8 (May 1971): 848.

251 "politically volatile": "CSWP Is Born," cdn.knightlab.com.

252 "Elizabeth Cady Stanton": Florence Howe Biography, www.florencehowe.com.

253 "finally freed herself": Howe, "Report on Women and the Profession," 849.

253 women made up 80 percent: "VFA Honors the Founder of the Feminist Press, Florence Howe," Veteran Feminists of America, archive.constantcontact.com.

253 only a one-in-nine: Howe, "Report on Women and the Profession," 848.

254 In the academic year: National Center for Education Statistics, https://nces.ed.gov/programs/digest/d10/tables/dt10_267.asp.

255 She received an invitation: The description of the Amherst appointment is from Reid, *Tillie Olsen*, 241–42.

255 Instead of gabbing with the sex workers: Sex worker anecdote from Kathie Olsen, interview by author; jogging from Reid, *Tillie Olsen*, 245.

255 At Amherst College, Olsen taught: Reid, *Tillie Olsen*, 246.

256 "really heightened her understanding": "The Tillie Olsen Project," Amherst College, www.amherst.edu.

256 "There's nothing wrong": Ibid.

257 "Literature of Poverty": Tillie Olsen, Syllabus for "Literature of Poverty, Oppression, Revolution, and the Struggle for Freedom," 1969, Olsen Papers.

257 "influential": "Tillie Olsen Project."

258 twenty-one English courses: Elaine Showalter, "Women and the Literary Curriculum," *College English* 32, no. 8 (May 1971): 856.

258 "Can we wonder": Ibid., 857.

258 "consciousness": "VFA Honors the Founder of the Feminist Press, Florence Howe."

259 "It is the women's movement": Tillie Olsen, "Women Who Are Writers in Our Century: One out of Twelve," *College English* 34, no. 1 (Oct. 1971): 6.

260 "Isolated. Cabin'd, cribb'd, confin'd": Ibid., 7–8.

260 "You who teach": Ibid., 16.

261 Olsen loved love: Reid, *Tillie Olsen*, 221, 250.

261 "The greatness of literature": Olsen, "Women Who Are Writers," 17.

261 "Tillie Appleseed": Quoted in Reid, *Tillie Olsen*, 263.

261 "It may be comforting": Margaret Atwood, "Obstacle Course," *New York Times*, 30 July 1978, 27.

262 "*Silences* changed what we read": Shelley Fisher Fishkin, "Reading, Writing, and Arithmetic: The Lessons *Silences* Has Taught Us," introduction to Olsen, *Silences*, xii.

262 "She was gone a lot": Julie Olsen Edwards, interview by author.

262 "damn proud": Ibid.

CHAPTER 17: Springs of Creativity

263 Pineda especially: Nina Tovish, interview by author, 23 June 2016.

264 "all-white community": Tillie Olsen, "Two Years," Institute seminar, 8 May 1964, Radcliffe College Archives Sound Recordings.

264 the percentage of black students: Marcia G. Synnott, "The Changing 'Harvard Student': Ethnicity, Race, and Gender," in *Yards and Gates: Gender in Harvard and Radcliffe History*, ed. Laurel Thatcher Ulrich (New York: Palgrave Macmillan, 2004), 203.

265 Alice Walker: In its early years, the Institute did not record the race of its fellows, though it did record their marital status, number of children, and degrees.

266 "It's very intimidating": Evelyn C. White, *Alice Walker: A Life* (New York: Norton, 2006), 284.

266 "a love story": Quoted in ibid., 208.

266 The following March: Ibid., 217–18.

267 "renewed fellowship": Quoted in ibid., 286.

267 "Though it's often lonely": Sara Sanborn, "A Woman's Place," *Harvard Bulletin*, June 1972, 29, Institute Archives.

267 "As far as many Blacks": Giddings, *When and Where I Enter*, 299.

268 "What do black women feel": Toni Morrison, "What the Black Woman Thinks About Women's Lib," *New York Times*, 22 Aug. 1971.

268 "a family quarrel": Ibid.

268 "Angela Davis has nothing": This exchange is quoted in Peniel E. Joseph, *The Black Power Movement: Rethinking the Civil Rights–Black Power Era* (New York: Routledge, 2006), 141.

269 "politically barefoot": Giddings, *When and Where I Enter*, 318.

270 "sexual differentiation": Toni Cade, "On the Issue of Roles," in *The Black Woman*, ed. Toni Cade (New York: New American Library, 1970), 101.

270 "double jeopardy": Frances Beale, "Double Jeopardy: To Be Black and Female," in Cade, *Black Woman*.

270 "If you really examine": Quoted in White, *Alice Walker*, 217.

271 "black woman who cannot lie": Marge Piercy, review of *Meridian*, by Alice Walker, *New York Times*, 23 May 1976.

271 Walker developed assignments: White, *Alice Walker*, 224.

272 "unearthed a part of our history": Ibid., 222.

272 In the process of researching: Alice Walker, "Saving the Life That Is Your Own," in *In Search of Our Mothers' Gardens: Womanist Prose* (San Diego: Harcourt Brace Jovanovich, 1983), 10.

272 "Zora, who had collected": Ibid., 12.

273 Walker later claimed: White, *Alice Walker*, 249.

273 Throughout the trip: Alice Walker, "Looking for Zora," in *In Search of Our Mothers' Gardens*, 94–95.

273 In one retelling: Ibid., 105.

274 "all purpose": Aida Kabatznick Press, "The Black Experience at Harvard," *Radcliffe Quarterly*, June 1973, 7.

275 "Judging by white": Ibid., 8.

275 "unreal": Ibid., 10.

276 "For these grandmothers": Walker, *In Search of Our Mothers' Gardens*, 233.

276 "It is not so much": Ibid., 237.

277 "womanist is to feminist": Ibid., xii.

277 "sort of breakdown": Walker to Olsen, 3 May 1978, Olsen Papers.

277 "I cherish the ins and outs": Walker to Olsen, 23 Jan. 1979, Olsen Papers.

277 "read this book": Norma Rosen, "The Ordeal of Rebecca Harding," *New York Times*, 15 April 1973, www.nytimes.com.

CHAPTER 18: The New Exotics

279 "Women have become": Pat Murphy, "Poems Bring Instant Fame," *St. Louis Tribune*, Kumin Papers.

280 "I'm just absolutely knocked out": "Newton Poet's Book: A 'Bony Stare,' Lyrical Look," *Boston Globe*, 8 May 1973, 22.

280 "Suddenly I was in business": Kumin, *Pawnbroker's Daughter*, 131.

281 She was profiled in magazines: Helen C. Smith, "Women of Letters: Female Writers Discuss the New Literature," *Atlanta Constitution*, 12 June 1976; Charles A. Brady, "Poets and Wine," Kumin Papers.

281 "I really dislike": Yvonne Chabier, "From the Hermit to Amanda: A Conversation with Maxine Kumin," Kumin Papers.

281 "Being in the limelight": Kumin, *Pawnbroker's Daughter,* 127.

282 "as cumbrous as bears": Maxine Kumin, *Up Country: Poems of New England, New and Selected* (New York: Harper & Row, 1972), 21.

282 "church of folded hands": Ibid., 40.

282 "burned babies screaming": Ibid., 80.

282 "When people hear": Maria Karagianis, "Maxine Kumin: A Poet Awakens," *Boston Globe,* 19 Aug. 1974, 10.

283 "the shoots": Kumin, "Beans," in *Up Country,* 26.

283 "all consented to die unseen": Kumin, "Woodchucks," in *Up Country,* 29.

283 "indecent bird": Kumin, "Whippoorwill," in *Up Country,* 39.

283 "is a concentrate": Herbert A. Kenny, "A Gifted Poet in Top Form," *Boston Globe,* Kumin Papers.

284 "sharp-edged, unflinching": Joyce Carol Oates, "One for Life, One for Death," *New York Times,* 19 Nov. 1972, BR7.

284 "how good it feels": Kumin to Oates, 19 Nov. 1972, Kumin Papers.

284 The Kumins had also accrued: Karagianis, "Maxine Kumin."

285 "polished silver candlesticks": Kumin, *Pawnbroker's Daughter,* 126.

285 *"which tools"*: Sexton, "Wanting to Die," in *Complete Poems,* 142.

285 She visited Kumin's farm: Linda Gray Sexton, interview by author.

286 "Anne was really": Quoted in Middlebrook, *Anne Sexton,* 185.

286 "It was a terrible responsibility": Middlebrook, "Remembering Anne Sexton."

286 "all good': Kumin, "September 1," 1963, Kumin Papers.

CHAPTER 19: Which Way Is Home

291 "I tremble to think": Tovish to Pineda, 5 Jan. 1997, Pineda Papers.

291 "You won't get another chance": Quoted in Middlebrook, *Anne Sexton,* 392; Middlebrook, "Remembering Anne Sexton," 298.

292 "the SPIRIT": Swan to Sexton, July 1973, Sexton Papers.

292 "I have been through": Kumin to Phil Legler, 18 Oct. 1973, Kumin Papers.

293 Linda Gray Sexton's memoir contains: Linda Gray Sexton, *Searching for Mercy Street,* 44-45.

293 "We get along": Sexton to Kumin, 26 May 1964, Kumin Papers.

293 In the year 1975: Alexander A. Plateris, "Divorce and Divorce Rates, United States," United States, National Center for Health Statistics, April 1980, www.cdc.gov.

294 Sexton was sleeping until ten: Middlebrook, "Remembering Anne Sexton," 297.

294 "It is a Christly time": Sexton to Rich, 19 Sept. 1973, Sexton Papers.

294 "As the situation grew": Linda Gray Sexton, *Searching for Mercy Street,* 178.

295 In July: Ibid., 180–81.

295 "I had a little fame": Middlebrook, "Remembering Anne Sexton," 298.

295 "dichotomy between the city life": Ibid., 296.

296 "She made me see": Ibid., 294.

296 "I've come all this way": Sexton to Kumin, 22 Aug. 1969, Kumin Papers.

296 "I was going to lose her": Quoted in Middlebrook, *Anne Sexton,* 368.

297 "You are, Anne": Showalter and Smith, "Nurturing Relationship," 134.

297 "I've been having an upsetting time": Ibid., 126.

297 "Subject: Selfish; needy": Sexton to Kumin, 25 April 1974, Kumin Papers.

297 "original": Middlebrook, "Remembering Anne Sexton," 293.

298 "Annie gave as good": Ibid., 296.

298 "how upsetting my presence": Sexton to Kumin, 25 April 1974, Kumin Papers.

298 "the quality of life": Kumin to Irving Weinman, 13 Jan. 1975, Kumin Papers.

298 "antiseptic tunnel[s]": Anne Sexton, "You, Doctor Martin," in *Complete Poems*, 3.

298 "world . . . full of enemies": Anne Sexton, "Noon Walk on the Asylum Lawn," in *Complete Poems*, 28.

299 "Don't worry": Kumin to Bruce [possibly Bruce Berlind], 16 Oct. 1974, Kumin Papers.

299 "*healed*": Kumin to Barbara Swan, 20 Nov. 1974, Kumin Papers.

299 Wrapped in the coat: Details from Middlebrook, *Anne Sexton*, 396–97; and Kay Bartlett, "Death of a Poet," Associated Press, in Kumin Papers.

299 "The tendency to confuse": McClatchy, *Anne Sexton*, 74.

299 "For a book or two": Lowell in ibid., 71.

300 "necrophiliac cult": Kumin to Irving Weinman, 13 Jan. 1975, Kumin Papers.

300 "I carried Anne's death": Kumin to Barbara Swan, 20 Nov. 1974, Kumin Papers.

300 "a more active sworn enemy": Olsen to Kumin, n.d., Kumin Papers.

300 "no more reproachful little notes": Kumin to Annie Wilder, 16 Jan. 1975, Kumin Papers.

300 "alone who bleed[s]": Kumin to Olsen, 15 Aug. 1978, Kumin Papers.

300 "A line out of Sexton": Middlebrook, "Remembering Anne Sexton," 296.

301 The statue was: Linda Gray Sexton, interview by author, 2 Feb. 2019.

301 "Before there was a Woman's Movement": Kumin, "How It Was," xxxiii.

301 "We left the comforts": Kumin, *Pawnbroker's Daughter*, 133.

302 "I stopped you a dozen times": "The Lifetime Friend," 1973, Kumin Papers.

302 "the instant criticism": Middlebrook, "Remembering Anne Sexton," 293.

302 "It would be blinking": Kumin to Lois Ames, 2 Sept. 1976, Kumin Papers.

302 "We have had enough": Adrienne Rich, *On Lies, Secrets, and Silence: Selected Prose, 1966–1978* (New York: W. W. Norton, 1995), 121.

302 Rich once asked Sexton: Sexton to Rich, 28 June 1967, Sexton Papers.

303 "She wrote poems alluding to": Rich, *On Lies, Secrets, and Silence*, 121.

303 "Self-trivialization is one": Ibid., 122.

303 "tells us what we have": Ibid., 123.

303 "came not out of": Kumin to Irving Weinman, 13 Jan. 1975, Kumin Papers.

304 "Every woman who writes": Quoted in Rich, *On Lies, Secrets, and Silence*, 123.

304 "A thinking woman": Adrienne Rich, "Snapshots of a Daughter-in-Law," in *Collected Poems, 1950–2012* (New York: W. W. Norton, 2016), 118.

304 "Women's Lib rap": Quoted in Michelle Dean, "The Wreck," *New Republic*, 3 April 2016, newrepublic.com.

304 "felt as though the top": Margaret Atwood, "Diving into the Wreck," *New York Times*, 30 Dec. 1973, www.nytimes.com.

304 She insisted that Alice Walker: "Adrienne Rich," Poetry Foundation, 2012, www.poetryfoundation.org.

305 "I believe profoundly": Rich to Olsen, 5 Feb. 1977, Olsen Papers.

306 "non-merger merger": Robin Freedberg, "Merger Yielded to Non-merger Merger," *Harvard Crimson*, 17 Sept. 1973.

306 "quite wonderful": Quoted in Yaffe, *Mary Ingraham Bunting*, Kindle ed.

307 "institution of motherhood": Adrienne Rich, *Of Woman Born: Motherhood as Experience and Institution* (London: Virago, 1979), 32.

307 "How lucid and exact": Kumin to Rich, 20 Oct. 1976, Kumin Papers.

308 "I just wanted to say": Dean, "The Wreak."

Epilogue

309 "a greater acceptance": Adam A. Sofen, "Radcliffe Enters Historic Merger with Harvard," *Harvard Crimson*, 21 April 1999.

309 But once the merger: Pamela Ferdin, "Radcliffe to Merge with Harvard, to Become a Center for Advanced Study," *Washington Post*, 21 April 1999.

310 Radcliffe transferred all: Katherine S. Mangan, "Radcliffe College Will Merge into Harvard," *Chronicle of Higher Education*, 30 April 1999.

310 "It would be a completely different environment": Ibid.

310 "creative work": "About Us," Radcliffe Institute for Advanced Study, Harvard University, www.radcliffe.harvard.edu.

311 "I cannot say": Lily Macrakis, interview by author.

315 "We spoke to their condition": Yaffe, *Mary Ingraham Bunting*, Kindle ed.

Index

ILLUSTRATION CREDITS